The Antietam Campaign

Military Campaigns of the Civil War

The Antietam Campaign

Edited by Gary W. Gallagher

THE UNIVERSITY OF NORTH CAROLINA PRESS

CHAPEL HILL AND LONDON

© 1999 The University of North Carolina Press
All rights reserved
Manufactured in the United States of America

The paper in this book meets the guidelines
for permanence and durability of the Committee on
Production Guidelines for Book Longevity of the
Council on Library Resources.

Library of Congress Cataloging-in-Publication Data

The Antietam campaign / edited by Gary W. Gallagher.
 p.   cm. — (Military campaigns of the Civil War)
 Includes bibliographical references and index.
 ISBN 0-8078-2481-x (alk. paper)
 1. Antietam, Battle of, Md., 1862.   2. Maryland
Campaign, 1862.   I. Gallagher, Gary W.   II. Series.
E474.65.A59   1999
973.7'336—dc21   98-37086
                                                  CIP

03 02 01 00 99   5 4 3 2 1

FOR SUSAN WELCH,
who personifies academic leadership at its best
and whose friendship I value highly

Contents

Introduction ix

The Net Result of the Campaign Was in Our Favor
Confederate Reaction to the Maryland Campaign 3
GARY W. GALLAGHER

General McClellan's Bodyguard
The Army of the Potomac after Antietam 44
BROOKS D. SIMPSON

Maryland, Our Maryland
Or How Lincoln and His Army Helped to
Define the Confederacy 74
WILLIAM A. BLAIR

Dirty, Ragged, and Ill-Provided For
Confederate Logistical Problems in the 1862 Maryland
Campaign and Their Solutions 101
KEITH S. BOHANNON

Who Would Not Be a Soldier
The Volunteers of '62 in the Maryland Campaign 143
D. SCOTT HARTWIG

All Who Went into That Battle Were Heroes
Remembering the 16th Regiment Connecticut
Volunteers at Antietam 169
LESLEY J. GORDON

Defending Lee's Flank
J. E. B. Stuart, John Pelham, and Confederate
Artillery on Nicodemus Heights 192
ROBERT E. L. KRICK

It Appeared As Though Mutual Extermination
Would Put a Stop to the Awful Carnage
Confederates in Sharpsburg's Bloody Lane 223
ROBERT K. KRICK

We Don't Know What on Earth to Do with Him
William Nelson Pendleton and the Affair at Shepherdstown,
September 19, 1862 259
PETER S. CARMICHAEL

From Antietam to the Argonne
The Maryland Campaign's Lessons for Future Leaders
of the American Expeditionary Force 289
CAROL REARDON

Bibliographic Essay 317

Contributors 321

Index 323

Introduction

The Maryland campaign of September 1862 ranks among the most important military operations of the American Civil War. Robert E. Lee moved into Maryland on the heels of his impressive victory over John Pope's Army of Virginia at Second Manassas. George B. McClellan, recently returned to the limelight after a fumbling effort during the Seven Days battles, sought to reorganize Union forces in the vicinity of Washington as Confederates crossed the Potomac. Lee hoped his march northward would enable him to maintain the strategic initiative while reaping a logistical bounty from areas untouched by the war. He and most other Confederates also believed the appearance of the Army of Northern Virginia would embolden Marylanders to embrace the nascent southern republic. Confederate success on Union soil might yield yet another benefit by prompting British and French political leaders to recognize the Confederacy. On the northern side, Abraham Lincoln saw Lee's invasion as both threat and opportunity. Elections loomed in November, which meant that the Republican administration could not tolerate a rebel army north of the Potomac for long. But Lincoln reckoned that as Lee marched away from his sources of supply in Virginia his army must become increasingly vulnerable. The president hoped that McClellan, whose previous record included little evidence of aggressive proclivities, would make Lee pay dearly for his decision to carry the war into United States territory.[1]

Events unfolded rapidly in a sequence well known to students of the Civil War. Lee divided his army while at Frederick, Maryland, sending the bulk of it under "Stonewall" Jackson to capture Harpers Ferry and directing the remainder to march toward Hagerstown. Shortly thereafter, a copy of Lee's strategic blueprint fell into McClellan's hands, and the Federal chief bestirred himself to press the invaders. While Jackson laid siege to Harpers Ferry, McClellan's troops forced Lee's defenders out of the gaps of South Mountain in sharp fighting on September 14. Lee briefly thought about abandoning Maryland, then decided to concentrate his army near Sharpsburg and face McClellan. Two days passed with little action on Lee's and McClellan's front, but Harpers Ferry surrendered on the 15th, freeing Jackson to hasten to Lee's support. The climactic clash came on September 17 at the battle of Antietam, where more than 23,000 men fell in the conflict's single bloodiest day. The armies remained on the battlefield to glower at one another for another tense day, after which McClellan permitted Lee to recross the Potomac unmolested. A Federal thrust across the river at Shepherdstown late on the 19th gained some success, but a counterattack by A. P. Hill's Confederate division the following day drove the northerners back to the left bank of the Potomac.

The Maryland campaign sputtered to a conclusion during the remainder of September and October. The strategic frontier remained along the Potomac, with Lee maneuvering in the lower Shenandoah Valley, gathering food and fodder from the region, and striking at the Baltimore and Ohio Railroad. Despite Lincoln's best efforts to prod him into action, McClellan mounted no major effort to get at the rebels. Not until November, when Lincoln replaced McClellan with Ambrose E. Burnside, did the war in the Eastern Theater take on a more active character.

By then, important results of the Maryland campaign had become evident. Neither side had won a clear-cut military decision. The surrender of 12,000 Union troops at Harpers Ferry galled the North and cheered the South. The vicious tactical stalemate at Antietam took on the nature of a Union victory when Lee retreated. Lincoln determined that Lee's withdrawal justified issuance on September 22 of the preliminary emancipation proclamation—an act with enormous implications for the future direction of the war. Both sides also knew that Marylanders had not rallied to the Confederate cause. Nor had the governments in London and Paris taken steps to intervene in the American war. Northerners and Confederates understood all too well that the war would continue. Those watching events in the Eastern Theater soon would be digesting news about the battle of Fredericksburg.[2]

The essays that follow do not provide a chronological narrative of the Maryland campaign. Anyone seeking such a treatment should consult Stephen W. Sears's well-researched and beautifully written *Landscape Turned Red: The Battle of Antietam*.[3] Nor do the essays touch on all the major military figures who fought in the campaign or on the range of nonmilitary factors that influenced or were influenced by what transpired in Maryland. As with all titles in the Military Campaigns of the Civil War series, the goal is to explore a variety of questions and topics with an eye toward underscoring the potential of Civil War military operations as subjects for research and interpretation. Some of the essays stray far from the battlefield and from the days in September 1862 when the armies marched and fought in Maryland. Others delve more deeply than have previous scholars into specific events on September 17. As a group, the essays expand our understanding of the Maryland campaign, its impact at the time, and the ways in which later Americans chose to remember or learn from it.

The book opens with an essay that explores Confederate reaction to the Maryland campaign. Although historians often portray the battle of Antietam and Lee's retreat to Virginia as a major turning point that dealt a severe blow to Confederate hopes for independence, this essay suggests that it makes as much sense to view the campaign as the last act in a much larger watershed — one that witnessed the dramatic reorientation of the war in the Eastern Theater from the outskirts of Richmond to the Potomac River. During the period from late June through mid-September 1862, Confederate citizens watched as Robert E. Lee won victories at the Seven Days and Second Manassas and then carried the war into United States territory. The capture of Harpers Ferry, together with the sharp repulse of a small part of the Union army at Shepherdstown five days later, helped offset news of Lee's withdrawal from Maryland after what was widely perceived as a bloody tactical standoff at Sharpsburg. Most Confederates maintained a high level of confidence in Lee, who together with his army increasingly served as their nation's principal rallying point.

In the second essay, Brooks D. Simpson focuses on George B. McClellan, his subordinates, and sentiment in the Army of the Potomac during the aftermath of Antietam. Contrary to historians who believe McClellan could have inflicted greater damage on Lee's battered army after the bitter fighting on September 17, Simpson finds that most of the Army of the Potomac probably supported their commander's decision to proceed cautiously. Far from eager to renew the tactical offensive on September 18, many officers and soldiers in the army also complained about insufficient supplies over the next several weeks, bridled at the thought of political interference in military affairs, and opposed the idea of pressing the rebels during a winter campaign. McClellan's attitudes and actions may have influenced the men in his army, but the latter stood ready to be influenced and held fast to McClellanesque tendencies long after "Little Mac's" departure. Perhaps the soldiers loved McClellan, concludes Simpson, because he and they were so much alike.

Maryland had loomed large in the Confederate imagination long before the Army of Northern Virginia crossed the Potomac in early September. William A. Blair argues that the Lincoln administration's sometimes heavy-handed treatment of Marylanders who expressed sympathy for the Confederacy in 1861–62 convinced many white southerners, most notably those who had doubted the logic of secession, that resistance to northern oppression lay at the core of the sectional conflict. Believing Lee's soldiers entered Maryland as liberators, Confederates expressed surprise, and then disappointment, when the state's citizens did not flock to the southern colors. That disappointment eventually turned into widespread indifference or even hostility toward Marylanders perceived as unwilling to sacrifice in a war against northern tyranny. Yet although Maryland's people generally did not support the southern cause overtly, notes Blair, their perceived travail early in the war helped Confederates define themselves as freedom-loving people justified in leaving a Union dominated by an oppressive North.

Many Marylanders looked askance at the bedraggled Confederate army that crossed their border in 1862. Historians frequently have alluded to the wretched physical circumstances under which Lee's men labored, but none has examined Confederate logistics in Maryland as carefully as Keith S. Bohannon. Mining a lode of evidence from Confederate newspapers and records in the National Archives, Bohannon addresses the full range of logistical problems Lee faced in the areas of ordnance, commissary, and quartermaster supply. His conclusions leave little doubt that the Army of Northern Virginia suffered to a degree that calls into question Lee's decision to undertake an active offensive campaign. Moving beyond the specific events of September 1862, Bohannon demonstrates that pervasive revulsion at the pitiful condition of Lee's soldiers helped bring significant change. By the summer of 1863, a series of reforms had improved significantly the Confederacy's ability to feed and supply its premier army.

Most students of the Civil War assume that the Army of the Potomac entered the Maryland campaign in far better condition than its opponent. Mustering more than 80,000 men, it seemed well equipped to overwhelm an Army of Northern Virginia that almost certainly numbered considerably fewer than 40,000 at Antietam. In the fifth essay, D. Scott Hartwig raises questions about the prowess of a Union army that included approximately 20,000 green troops. Raised in the summer of 1862 and rushed to the front, new regiments often had undergone no formal training before being thrown into battle against veteran Confederates who had won a string of victories over the past three months. The untried soldiers often fought bravely, but they and their equally green officers lacked the ability to maneuver effectively in combat. At Harpers Ferry, South Mountain, and Antietam, they often proved a hindrance rather than an asset to McClellan, and their inept attempts to respond to battlefield pressures sometimes caused even seasoned northern units to break. Hartwig considers the Maryland campaign a particularly brutal form of on-the-job training for the green units, most of which would prove themselves on subsequent battlefields.

The 16th Connecticut Infantry stood among the greenest of McClellan's regiments. Mustered into service in late August and ordered to the field with no real training, the 16th found itself in a critical position on the far Union left on September 17. A brief period of furious action late that afternoon witnessed the rout of the 16th, which suffered 25 percent casualties without contributing anything positive to the Union effort. Lesley J. Gordon describes the 16th's role in the campaign, the efforts of its members to explain what happened at Antietam, and the postwar process by which their ignominious debut in combat was recast into a story of heroic striving. By the time survivors of the regiment gathered in 1894 to dedicate a monument at the place where Confederates of A. P. Hill's division had overwhelmed them thirty-two years earlier, gallantry and glorious sacrifice rather than fear and failure formed the dominant theme.

At the opposite end of the battlefield from the 16th Connecticut's arena of painful initiation, Confederate cavalry chief James E. B. Stuart orchestrated a masterful deployment of southern artillery. Robert E. L. Krick brings into sharp relief events on Nicodemus Heights and Hauser's Ridge, where Confederate artillery, usually depicted as hopelessly outclassed at Antietam, stalwartly contested a series of Union infantry assaults against the Miller Cornfield and the West Woods. Krick demonstrates that Stuart, with able assistance from John Pelham and other young southern gunners, used batteries from the Horse Artillery and Stonewall Jackson's wing of the army to back up southern defensive lines repeatedly pushed nearly to the breaking point. Krick maintains that September 17 should not be understood as the day of unfolding disaster for hopelessly outgunned Confederate cannoneers so often depicted in earlier studies; indeed, that day's fighting marked one of the better performances for Lee's "Long Arm."

Unlike the action on Nicodemus Heights and Hauser's Ridge, fighting along the sunken farm road in the Confederate center has been intensively studied. The Bloody Lane, as the little road was christened soon after the battle, ranks with the Dunker Church and Burnside's Bridge as one of the great landmarks on the battlefield. Robert K. Krick's essay on the Confederate defense of Bloody Lane demonstrates that assiduous research can enable historians to shed new light on seemingly exhausted topics. Krick exploited an impressive array of manuscript and published materials to flesh out the men and events associated with this phase of the battle. Perhaps most usefully, he devotes considerable attention to the collapse of Richard H. Anderson's division, which arrived on the field in time to buttress the defense of the Bloody Lane by Robert E. Rodes's Alabama brigade and George Burgwyn Anderson's North Carolina brigade but quickly lost cohesion because of poor leadership and horrific casualties among its officers. Krick shows that anyone hoping to understand what happened to Confederates in the Bloody Lane must also consider the decisions and movements of officers and units well removed from the road itself.

The Army of Northern Virginia suffered a near catastrophe on September 19, 1862, when Federals crossed the Potomac at Shepherdstown and threatened to seize the Confederate reserve artillery. Brig. Gen. William Nelson Pendleton stood at the vortex of events that day. Assigned the task of protecting the army's rear guard, he proved utterly incapable of decisive leadership—yet retained his position as chief of artillery under Lee for the remainder of the conflict. Peter S. Carmichael uses the debacle at Shepherdstown, which he ascribes to a combination of Pendleton's ineptitude and the fact that Lee allocated too few infantry units to cover the fords over the Potomac, as a point of departure to evaluate the artillerist's role during the Maryland campaign and in the broader history of the Army of Northern Virginia. Why did Lee retain in high position a man so obviously lacking key attributes of command? Carmichael finds part of the answer in Pendleton's warm relationship with Jefferson Davis, who supported and protected his friend throughout the war.

Carol Reardon closes the volume with a look at the ways in which United States soldiers in the early twentieth century used Antietam to learn lessons about their profession. The Department of War lobbied for the Congress to build roads and place descriptive markers on the site to enhance its value as an outdoor classroom, and the U.S. Army War College sent promising officers to the battlefield to study the strategic and tactical elements of the Maryland campaign. Drawing on material in the curricular archives of the War College classes that visited Antietam in the decade prior to American entrance into World War I, Reardon reconstructs the framework within which the students and their teachers studied the campaign. She suggests that staff rides to Antietam not only taught practical lessons about such things as leadership in combat, logistical problems, and communication on a battlefield but also infused participants with a sense of pride in the accomplishments of officers and soldiers of an earlier era (their admiration for common soldiers often exceeded that for some of the high-ranking generals).

Anyone familiar with the Military Campaigns of the Civil War series knows that the titles have not attempted to examine the conflict's operations in chronological sequence (although the four volumes on Fredericksburg's major battles did appear in order). True to that tradition, the series will look backward from the 1862 Maryland campaign with volumes on the Seven Days and Second Manassas, which should appear in 2000 and 2001, respectively.

I wish to thank Bill Blair, Keith Bohannon, Peter Carmichael, Lesley Gordon, Scott Hartwig, Bob Krick, R. E. L. Krick, Carol Reardon, and Brooks Simpson for their contributions to this collective enterprise. Both the quality of their scholarship and their cheerful responses when I picked nits about citations or other elements of their work made my task as editor much easier than I probably had any right to expect. I thank George Skoch as well, who has prepared the maps for every title in the Military Campaigns of the Civil War series. Individuals who assisted the contributors are acknowledged at the beginning of the notes in each essay. Finally, I extend my gratitude yet again to Eileen Anne Gallagher, who exhibited admirable patience as editorial work on this manuscript and preparations for a move to Virginia clashed during an exceedingly hectic spring.

NOTES

1. For a summary of the strategic picture in the Eastern Theater in September 1862, see Gary W. Gallagher, "The Autumn of 1862: A Season of Opportunity," in *Antietam: Essays on the 1862 Maryland Campaign,* ed. Gary W. Gallagher (Kent, Ohio: Kent State University Press, 1989), 1–13. On Lincoln's belief that Lee should be punished while north of the Potomac, see his letter to McClellan dated September 12, 1862, in Abraham Lincoln, *The Collected Works of Abraham Lincoln,* ed. Roy P. Basler, 9 vols. (New Brunswick, N.J.: Rutgers University Press, 1953–55), 5:418. Responding to information suggesting that Lee might be recrossing the Potomac into Virginia, Lincoln admonished McClellan: "Please do not let him get off without being hurt."

2. For summaries of the impact of the Maryland campaign, see James M. McPherson, *Battle Cry of Freedom: The Civil War Era* (New York: Oxford University Press, 1988), 544–45, and Gary W. Gallagher, "The Maryland Campaign in Perspective," in Gallagher, *Antietam,* 85–94.

3. New York: Ticknor & Fields, 1983.

The Antietam Campaign

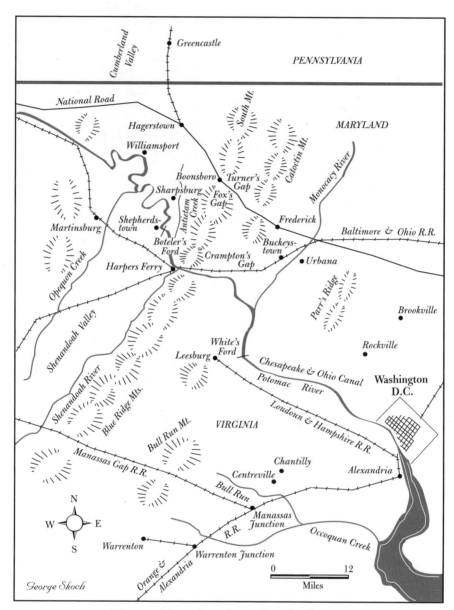

Theater of Operations, September–October 1862

GARY W. GALLAGHER

The Net Result of the Campaign Was in Our Favor

Confederate Reaction to the Maryland Campaign

The roads leading from Sharpsburg to Boteler's Ford choked under the strain of men, vehicles, and animals during the night of September 18, 1862. Trudging through a sheltering fog that helped mask their movement toward the Potomac River, Confederate soldiers hoped that an enemy who had been quiescent all day would remain so for a few hours longer. A North Carolina chaplain, carried along through the predawn Maryland darkness on this martial tide, left a vivid impression in his diary: "Though troops and wagons have been passing all night, still the roads and fields were full. Ram! Jam! Wagons and ambulances turned over! One man was killed by the overturning of an ambulance." An artillerist described a more orderly withdrawal, mentioning especially that Robert E. Lee "stood at the ford in Shepherdstown and gave directions to the teamsters and others, showing a wise attention to details which many men in less elevated positions would think beneath their notice." By eight o'clock on the morning of September 19, all were safely across the Potomac onto Virginia soil.[1]

Thus ended a fifteen-day campaign in Maryland that represented the final act of a drama begun eighty-five days earlier with Confederate assaults at the battle of Mechanicsville outside Richmond. These twelve momentous weeks had witnessed Lee's offensive victory over George B. McClellan in the Seven Days and an equally impressive thrashing of John Pope's Army of Virginia at Second Manassas, which together shifted the strategic focus in the Eastern Theater from Richmond to the Potomac River. Surging across the national frontier into Maryland less than a week after Second Manassas, Lee and his army had hoped to make the reorientation even more striking. Dramatic events in the gaps of South Mountain, at Harpers Ferry, and amid the rolling countryside near Sharpsburg had punctuated Lee's foray north of the Potomac—and would dominate the thinking of most contemporary observers and later critics who sought to judge what the Army of Northern Virginia had won or lost.

Historians typically have assessed the Maryland campaign from the perspective of its long-term impact, looking back with later events in mind to label it a major turning point that foreshadowed Confederate defeat. Writing in the mid-1950s, Clement Eaton touched on the two factors most often mentioned in this connection—Lincoln's preliminary proclamation of emancipation and Europe's decision to back away from recognition of the Confederacy in the autumn of 1862. "The checking of the Confederate invasion at Antietam . . . was disastrous to the cause of Southern independence," wrote Eaton. "The retreat of Lee not only gave Lincoln a favorable opportunity to issue his Emancipation Proclamation but it also chilled the enthusiasm of the British government to recognize the independence of the Confederacy." Nearly two decades earlier, Robert Selph Henry had argued similarly in his widely read history of the Confederacy, pointing to Antietam and suggesting that "[o]n the seventeenth day of September in 1862 the decline of the Confederacy began." Clifford Dowdey, who in the 1950s and 1960s inherited Douglas Southall Freeman's mantle as the leading popular writer about Lee and his army, added his voice to this chorus, stating bluntly, "Politically, the war ended at Sharpsburg for the Confederacy. That was the last chance the Southern states had really to win independence."[2]

More recent historians have continued this interpretive tradition. James M. McPherson's magisterial history of the conflict reminded readers that the battle of Antietam "frustrated Confederate hopes for British recognition and precipitated the Emancipation Proclamation. The slaughter at Sharpsburg therefore proved to have been one of the war's great turning points." In summary comments about Antietam from his overview of the Civil War era, Brooks D. Simpson asserted that "most people, North and South, American and European, interpreted a pitched battle followed by a Confederate withdrawal as a defeat." The result was diminished chances for European recognition and Lincoln's opening for the proclamation—a conclusion Charles P. Roland echoed in his insightful survey of the Civil War.[3]

A decade ago, I summarized the impact of the Maryland campaign on Confederate fortunes in similar terms: "Lee went north and fought, avoided a series of lurking disasters, and found refuge in the end along the southern bank of the Potomac River. But the military events of mid-September 1862 bore bitter political and diplomatic fruit for the Confederacy. The nature of the conflict changed because of Lee's Maryland campaign." No longer a contest to restore the antebellum status quo, "the new war would admit of no easy reconciliation because the stakes had been raised to encompass the entire social fabric of the South. The war after Antietam would demand a decisive resolution on the battlefield, and that the Confederacy could not achieve."[4]

The understandable desire to highlight the broad implications of the Maryland campaign has left another important question relatively neglected, namely, how did Confederates at the time react to Lee's campaign in Maryland? Did the operations of September 1862 engender hope? Did they cause Confederates to lose heart at the thought that their struggle for independence had taken a grim turn downward? Did the campaign provoke a mixed reaction? In short, what impact did Lee's foray across the Potomac have on his men and on their fellow Confederates?

A survey of military and civilian testimony during the period following Lee's retreat from Maryland underscores the challenge of assessing the relationship between military events and popular will during the Civil War. Although any such survey is necessarily impressionistic, searching letters, diaries, and newspaper accounts for patterns of reaction is worthwhile.[5] Examined within the context of what people read and heard at the time, and freed from the powerful influence of historical hindsight, Confederate morale assumes a complex character. Rumors and inaccurate reports buffeted citizens long since grown wary of overblown prose in newspapers. Knowing they often lacked sound information, people nonetheless strove to reach satisfying conclusions about what had transpired.

As the autumn weeks went by, they groped toward a rough consensus that may be summed up briefly. The Maryland campaign did not represent a major setback for the Confederacy. Antietam was at worst a bloody standoff, at best a narrow tactical success for Confederates who beat back heavy Union assaults and then held the field for another day. Stonewall Jackson's capture of 12,000 Union soldiers and immense matériel at Harpers Ferry, as well as A. P. Hill's stinging repulse of Union forces at Shepherdstown on September 20, marked unequivocal high points of the campaign. McClellan's inaction throughout late September and October demonstrated how badly his army had been damaged, and Lincoln's emancipation proclamation betrayed Republican desperation and promised to divide northern society. Reconciled to the fact that the war would not end anytime soon, most Confederates looked to the future with a cautious expectation of success.[6]

In one important respect, the Maryland campaign served as the coda to a different kind of watershed than most historians have described. Lee and his army emerged from Maryland as a major rallying point for the Confederacy. Their operations between July and September began the process that, within another eight months, would make them the focus of Confederate national sentiment. Starting in the autumn of 1862, white southerners increasingly contrasted Lee's and Jackson's successes in the Eastern Theater with repeated failures in the Western Theater, concluding that prospects for victory would rest largely on the shoulders of Lee and his lieutenants and on the bayonets of their soldiers. Better attuned to Confederate sentiment than many later historians would be, Edward A. Pollard of the Richmond *Examiner* touched on this point in his wartime history of the Confederacy. "The army which rested again in Virginia had made a history that will flash down the tide of time a lustre of glory," wrote Pollard in 1863 of the aftermath of the Maryland campaign. "It had done an amount of marching and fighting that appears almost incredible, even to those minds familiar with the records of great military exertions." The "remarkable campaign . . . extending from the banks of the James river to those of the Potomac," concluded Pollard, "impressed the world with wonder and admiration."[7]

Newspapers supplied most Confederates outside Lee's army with their initial impressions about the Maryland campaign. As is always the case, such accounts must be read with the understanding that editors often tried to shape public opinion as well as inform readers about what had transpired. During the initial phase of reporting, editors typically took the stance that Sharpsburg ranked among the bitterest of engagements and, though perhaps not a clear southern victory, reflected well on Confederate prowess. Six days after the battle, for example, Charleston's *Mercury* admitted that accounts of fighting at Sharpsburg were "meagre and somewhat contradictory, but all agree in representing it to have been the most bloody and desperately contested engagement of the war." The outnumbered Confederate army had "again illustrated its valor and invincibility by successfully repelling the repeated onsets of the enemy." The Charleston *Daily Courier* noted that "[a]ll accounts agree in representing that the fight of Wednesday was closely contested," adding that a reliable witness quoted General Lee as saying he "looked upon the struggle of that day as favorable to our arms." Richmond's *Dispatch,* which had the largest circulation among the capital's newspapers, took a bit more optimistic view: "[I]t is evident that we were victorious on Wednesday. We acted on the defensive. The enemy tried a whole day to drive us from our position. He utterly failed. We held our position, and slept on the

Lee's crossing of the Potomac River in early September 1862 opened the final phase of a campaign that had begun outside Richmond three months earlier. *Harper's Weekly*'s depiction of the event featured rebels illuminated by a bright moon.
Harper's Weekly, September 27, 1862

ground, ready to renew the contest the next day." Even less restrained was the Richmond *Enquirer,* which breathlessly announced that "the battle resulted in one of the most complete victories that has yet immortalized Confederate arms."[8]

The capture of Harpers Ferry received wide coverage and almost universal praise,[9] as did the battle of Shepherdstown. Little remembered now, the latter loomed much larger in September 1862 and satisfied Confederate yearnings for offensive victories. In reporting on Shepherdstown, the Richmond *Weekly Dispatch* described how a Union column had crossed at Boteler's Ford in pursuit of the Army of Northern Virginia, only to be driven back by A. P. Hill's outnumbered division: "Our forces poured the grape and canister into them as they crossed the Potomac, and the slaughter was terrible." Fleeing Federals fell in such profusion that the "river was black with them." The Charleston *Daily Courier* termed the fight "a severe engagement . . . in which the Yankees were almost annihilated. They were driven into the river, shot down by hundreds, and those who survived taken prisoner." Peter W. Alexander, among the best of the Confederate military correspondents, reported "additional particulars . . . of the affair at Shepherdstown" for the Savannah *Republican* on September 23. Quoting a

Federal surgeon, Alexander stated that "about 2,000 Federal infantry attempted to cross after us, and out of that number only ninety lived to return. Such as were not killed and drowned, were captured." [10]

Lee's decision to seek shelter south of the Potomac after Sharpsburg provoked far more disagreement among editors than the apparently uncomplicated Confederate successes at Harpers Ferry and Shepherdstown. The Charleston *Mercury* somewhat sarcastically called the crossing at Boteler's Ford a "movement which, to the unmilitary eye, with no more subtle guide than the map, would certainly resemble a retreat." Richmond's *Dispatch* disagreed, emphasizing "the wearied and almost starving condition of our men" and rationalizing the withdrawal as "made necessary not by any reverse in battle, but by the stern exigency of the absence of commissary supplies." The *Enquirer* reported that "McClellan's army was too badly used up on Wednesday . . . to perform any rapid movement for strategic effect." As a consequence, continued this pro–Davis administration paper, the "movement of a portion of our forces to the South side was purely a matter of precaution, to provide against possible contingencies." Seldom has more nebulous language been used to place a positive gloss on an army's retreat (the degree to which the *Enquirer* achieved its goal cannot now be determined). [11]

Newspapers also argued about Lee's goals in entering Maryland. The *Enquirer* claimed that "our distinguished General projected the movement into Maryland as a cover to his march against Harper's Ferry, and for the purpose of drawing McClellan out of Washington." Having established a standard by which to evaluate Lee's operations, the paper added: "He has entirely succeeded. Harper's Ferry has fallen, and McClellan enticed sixty-five miles from Washington, has been defeated." With an eye toward those who questioned the retreat on September 18, the *Enquirer* concluded that "[s]uch glorious triumphs should teach our people the utmost reliance on General Lee, and make them easy even when they do not understand his movements." [12]

In Charleston, the *Mercury* would have none of this, noting dismissively that the *Enquirer* "professes, in a soothing article, to believe that Lee contemplated only the capture of Harper's Ferry in his advance into Maryland." The *Mercury* suspected that more had been intended, and less accomplished. For one prominent Confederate, at least, the *Enquirer*'s position carried the day against that of the *Mercury*. According to the *Southern Confederacy* of Atlanta, Vice President Alexander H. Stephens considered the capture of Harpers Ferry to have been "Lee's principal object in going into Maryland, . . . [and] one of the most brilliant achievements of the war." The battle of Sharpsburg was "only an *incident* to the main object, in which our forces were victorious, though the victory was dearly bought." [13]

Like their southern counterparts, northern newspapers addressed the topic of Confederate
straggling. This sketch shows "Rebel cavalry driving stragglers and skulkers back
to their duty at the battle of Antietam."
Frank Leslie's Illustrated Newspaper, October 25, 1862

All of the newspapers discussed the problem of straggling among Lee's soldiers. "Candor compels me to say," admitted one correspondent from the field,
"that the straggling and desertion from our army far surpasses anything I had ever
supposed possible." Although editors strongly deplored the absence of stragglers
at Sharpsburg, where comrades in their units fought bravely and fell in profusion,
most expressed at least some sentiment similar to that in a piece written for the
Savannah *Republican.* "A fifth of the troops are barefooted; half of them are in
rags, and the whole of them insufficiently supplied with food," wrote this observer on September 19 from near Smithfield. "Men in this condition cannot be
relied on to the same extent as when they are properly clothed and subsisted. The
best soldiers, under such circumstances, will straggle on the march and in battle."
The *Dispatch,* which shared some of this compassion for worn-out soldiers, nevertheless suggested that if "only as many as five thousand of the stragglers who
left their colors and lingered behind had been present, McClellan's rout would
have been irremediable" on September 17.[14]

During the first two weeks of October, newspapers drew on extensive reporting from correspondents in the field, letters from soldiers, and coverage in
the northern press to render generally optimistic final verdicts about the campaign. The Richmond *Whig* touched on themes repeated in many other papers.

Northern sheets such as New York's *Times* and *Tribune,* observed the *Whig,* no longer claimed Antietam as a great victory for McClellan. Indeed, many northern correspondents "deny outright that it was a Federal victory at all; and all of them admit the immense loss sustained by McClellan's army, and its shattered condition after the action." The *Whig* also stressed three other points: Lee's men had occupied the field through the 18th, withdrawn in perfect order to the Potomac, and held their position along the river ever since. The Charleston *Daily Courier* joined numerous papers in stressing the odds against which the Confederates had contended: "Seventy thousand men, weary and weak with labors and marches, and fasting for fifteen hours, struggled with two hundred thousand, and after repulsing the heavy columns hurled upon them, remained masters of the battle ground." McClellan's immobility supported the idea that Lee had bested his opponent in Maryland. If "General McClellan had not been severely beaten and his army demoralized," suggested a piece in the Richmond *Dispatch,* "it is very natural to suppose he would not have hung so closely to the Maryland shore for the past three weeks." [15]

Among the more restrained sets of conclusions appeared in the Charleston *Mercury,* which lamented the "moral and political consequences" of the campaign for the people of Maryland. Other papers also had raised the issue of Lee's failure to liberate Maryland from the yoke of Lincoln's tyranny. Yet even the *Mercury* reckoned that in "prisoners and arms, we got greatly the advantage of the enemy, as we did in the casualties sustained by the respective armies. Considered apart, therefore, from the effect upon Maryland of our retreat across the river, the net result of the campaign was in our favor." [16]

Lincoln's preliminary emancipation proclamation spurred generally optimistic responses from the Confederate press. In light of emancipation's eventual role in weakening the southern war effort, this reaction might strike modern readers as disingenuous. How could Confederates interpret the proclamation as anything but a crushing blow to their hopes of maintaining an effective national military resistance? A number of editors undoubtedly sought to put the best face on the situation; however, they also had at hand encouraging news from the pages of northern newspapers, which provided ample details about Democrats and others unhappy at the prospect of risking white lives for black freedom. Southern papers insisted that weakness arising from indifferent Union performances on the battlefield had pushed Lincoln toward precipitate action. The president had "at last shaken the rod of terror he refrained from raising till the cause he is engaged in should be compassed about with such perils that it became desperate," stated one editor. "The South rejoices in the publication of his emancipation proclamation. It cannot do us any harm; it will do us great good. It breeds divisions in his own borders; it will compose differences and produce a greater unanimity throughout these Confederate States." Another editor saw in the proclamation indication "of a current of distrust" in the North, "a distrust swelling even to desperation," while a piece in the *Enquirer* characterized the proclamation as a measure out of step with most northern civilians and soldiers. Lincoln had surrendered the government "into the hands of the Abolitionists," suppressing "the last lingering hope of a restoration of the Union, even on the part of those who sustained his Administration under the honest belief that he was endeavoring in good faith to accomplish that end."[17]

Newspaper coverage of the Maryland campaign suggests the extent to which popular expectations had risen for Lee and his army. More than one editor chided readers, who remained enthralled by the Seven Days and Second Manassas, for lamenting the absence of an unequivocal victory north of the Potomac. Too many Confederates were "cast down" by Lee's withdrawal from Maryland, remarked the Charleston *Daily Courier,* which asked rhetorically: "Was not Southern prowess as splendidly illustrated at Sharpsburg as it was before Richmond or on the plains of Manassas?" The Richmond *Dispatch* reminded readers that just a few months earlier, "at a time when our city was actually beleaguered by the enemy," citizens had manifested great fortitude. Since then, Lee's generalship had created a situation where "people are disappointed because we did not gain a victory as decisive as those around Richmond and at Manassas." Confederates simply could not "expect such victories always." The Richmond *Daily Enquirer* joined other papers in placing the Maryland campaign within the larger chronology of events since Lee took charge of the Army of Northern Virginia. The Confederate commander had outwitted McClellan on the Chickahominy, made a fool of Pope at Manassas, and bested "Little Mac" again by capturing Harpers Ferry. Viewed against this record, the retreat to the south bank of the Potomac meant little. The difference between that position and one on the north bank amounted to "an hour's march" and no more.[18]

In a widely published dispatch from Winchester dated September 26, Peter W. Alexander elevated Lee's army to a singular position among Confederate forces. "No army on this continent has ever accomplished as much or suffered as much," affirmed the native Georgian, "as the Army of Northern Virginia within the last three months.—At no time during the first Revolutionary war—not even at Valley Forge—did our forefathers in arms encounter greater hardships, or endure them more uncomplainingly." Alexander's invocation of the Revolutionary example anticipated innumerable Confederates who later would compare Lee and the Army of Northern Virginia to George Washington and the Continental army. Lest anyone underestimate how vital Lee and his soldiers had become, Alexander explicitly spelled out their role as the nation's primary defenders: "The army in Virginia stands guard this day, as it will stand guard this winter, over every hearthstone throughout the South. The ragged sentinel who may pace his weary rounds this winter on the bleak spurs of the Blue Ridge, or along the frozen valleys of the Shenandoah and Rappahannock, will also be your sentinel, my friend, at home."[19]

The civilians to whom Alexander addressed his comments watched the autumn's campaigning with great interest. They pored over newspapers, lingered over letters from relatives in the army, and plotted the respective armies' geographic positions. Moods and attitudes on the home front fluctuated as new information became available. By mid-October, most people had reached their ultimate conclusions about the campaign. Some pronounced it a mistake, but the majority seem to have favored the positive side of the scales, taken comfort in the overall record Lee's army forged between June and October, and looked toward the winter with cautious confidence in Confederate prospects for success.

Inconsistent early reports about the fighting on September 17 left many people on edge. "I have waited for time to clear the mists that lie around our recent actions on the Potomac," wrote a North Carolina diarist on September 25, "but even now I cannot tell if what I record is correct." Four days later this woman accused "the authorities in Richmond" of suppressing news about casualties, which she considered "a bad sign for us!" From near Richmond, the old fire-eater Edmund Ruffin complained that "reports from our army in Md. & on the Potomac, & those from the northern papers, are so contradictory that it can scarcely be recognized that they speak of the same actions." A Georgian believed that even bad news was preferable to maddening uncertainty, arguing that Jefferson Davis should bend every effort to make public the results of big battles. "Our nation has by past acts," he averred, "demonstrated the fact that with astonishing composure it can bear alike the joys of success and the disheartening influences of reverses." The Davis administration should not withhold "authentic information in reference to past occurrences and accomplished facts"; to do so left people dependent on "the uncertain reports of letter-writers and the lying statements of Northern presses . . . for a knowledge of the true status of affairs."[20]

Precise casualty figures for Sharpsburg never reached the Confederate home front, leaving citizens certain only that the fighting had been costly. A quartet of diarists from Virginia, Georgia, and Louisiana reflect a consensus that the battle had been bloody and far from decisive. Lucy Rebecca Buck, whose family lived near Front Royal, described "a most terrific battle at Sharpsburg, Maryland in which we had nearly been defeated but had succeeded in driving the enemy from the field and then slowly fell back ourselves." A native of Maine long resident in

Photographer Alexander Gardner preserved graphic images of the Confederate dead at
Antietam. This view shows infantrymen killed just west of the Hagerstown Pike.
National Archives

Georgia, Dolly Lunt Burge wrote with other Confederate families in mind: "This
month, the 17th & 18th has been fought the bloodiest [battle] of the war. My heart
sickens when I think of it & the affliction it has brought upon thousands and thousands of our countrymen."

Youthful Sarah Morgan wondered about the impact on her own circle. "Our
army, having accomplished its object, recrossed the Potomac, after what was
decidedly a drawn battle," she observed from her vantage point in the Trans-
Mississippi. "Both sides suffered severely. Hardly an officer on either side escaped unhurt. . . . I expect the list will contain the names of many friends when
it comes." From Lynchburg on September 22, William M. Blackford claimed "a
victory to our arms" in "one of the bloodiest and best contested" engagements of
the conflict. Two days later, this father of five Confederate soldiers revised his earlier statement, remarking that the "weight of evidence is to the effect that we have
been in the main victorious." The Federals, added Blackford, "as usual, claim a
victory and publish lying bulletins as they did in the fights around Richmond." [21]

Stonewall Jackson's success at Harpers Ferry and A. P. Hill's tidy victory
at Shepherdstown stood out as elements of the Maryland campaign that helped

offset doubts about Sharpsburg. "We have had a glorious victory at Harper's Ferry," cheered the daughter of a merchant in Orange, Virginia, "with but slight loss to ourselves—a number of *prisoners, guns, small arms, horses, servants,* & stores of all sorts." Mary Fielding of Limestone County, Alabama, whose brother served in the 9th Alabama Infantry of Cadmus M. Wilcox's brigade, noted that the "surrender of Harper's Ferry clears the Shenandoah valley of Yankees"; closer to the scene, a diarist near Paris, Virginia, reported "quite a victory at Harper's Ferry yesterday—several thousand taken prisoner and several hundred contrabands." Anne S. Frobel, whose section of Fairfax County had been occupied by Federal troops for much of the war, seemed to take special comfort from Jackson's seizure of large numbers of runaway slaves. "We have just heard of the recapture by the Confederates of Harper's ferry," she wrote on September 17, "with 12000 yankees, and immense quantities of ordnance, ammunition, commissary stores and a large number of Contrabands, which in yankee parlance means negro." The Yankees admitted all of these facts, stated Frobel, who then asked rhetorically: "[I]f they acknowledge such a great loss what must the reality be."[22]

While Harpers Ferry conjured images of prisoners and loot, the action at Shepherdstown conveyed more gory—but probably no less satisfying—images of dead Federal soldiers floating in the Potomac. Two witnesses captured the essence of what most Confederates had to say about Shepherdstown. "On the 19th a division of the enemy crossed over to Shepherdstown," stated a woman in Fredericksburg, Virginia, with typical hyperbole. "Jackson captured or killed the whole of them. The Potomac was damned up with their bodies." Another diarist estimated that "[t]en thousand Yankees crossed at Shepherdstown, but unfortunately for them, they found the glorious Stonewall there." Combat erupted near Boteler's Mill, and Jackson's troops "totally routed" the enemy, "as we succeeded in driving a good many of them into the Potomac. . . . The account of the Yankee slaughter is fearful."[23]

As in these two accounts of Shepherdstown, Stonewall Jackson dominated many of the more enthusiastic descriptions of Confederate successes in Maryland. He was the Confederacy's most famous officer in the summer and autumn of 1862, and his fellow citizens embraced the idea that he smashed Yankee opponents at will. Three soldiers outside the Army of Northern Virginia wrote typical passages about the dour Virginian's exploits. On September 29, a captain in Texas informed his wife of recent news about Harpers Ferry, which he called "another of Stonewall Jackson's victories," before closing with a rousing "Huzzah for Stonewall. he's the man of the times." Enthusiasm trumped accuracy when a sergeant serving in Mississippi described the fight at Shepherdstown: "[N]ews is rattling over the wires of victories again of Stonewall Jackson over Burnside killing and capturing his whole army save 2000. . . . Stonewall was ordered to fall on Burnside while crossing and rumor says he dammed up the River with the slain." A private in the 10th Texas Infantry employed inelegant language to make a similar point. "[M]ore good news from the other side of the river—," wrote Benjamin M. Seaton; "the report says that Stonewall Jackson has gained another battle and McClenan lost 18,000 kild and woned in crossing the river—a considerable loss on their side."[24]

"Jeb" Stuart's slashing cavalry raid into Pennsylvania in mid-October added another bright vignette to many civilians' overall picture of the Maryland campaign. Carried out while Lee's army remained defiantly along the Potomac frontier, it reinforced the idea that McClellan was a timid commander and reassured citizens who favored offensive action. One man compared it to Stuart's first ride around McClellan during the Peninsula campaign, calling it "not less brilliant than the grand round in June" and pointing out that "[t]his was the enemy's country." In Richmond, where he documented reaction to the war in his famous diary, War Department clerk John B. Jones termed the raid "a most brilliant affair" that yielded much "public property" captured or destroyed. "The Abolitionists," wrote Jones with obvious satisfaction, "are much mortified, and were greatly frightened."[25]

In contrast to such hopeful expressions, Maryland's anemic response to Lee's army engendered feelings of disappointment and anger. Many Confederates were torn between an inclination to criticize Maryland for not doing more and a desire to give residents of a sister slave state the benefit of the doubt. Some blamed tepid support among Marylanders for Lee's decision to abandon the state after just two weeks. "Our army returned to Va after this battle [Sharpsburg]," wrote one woman in this vein, "as they were unprepared for an advance into Pennsylvania and could not be sustained in that unfriendly part of Maryland." Conditioned by newspaper accounts to believe that only Federal bayonets held Maryland in the Union, many Confederates had invested considerable hope in the prospect of wooing another state to their slaveholding republic. Reports of a cold reception for Lee's veterans prompted a number of these people, including Ada W. Bacot, a volunteer nurse in Charlottesville, to suggest that Maryland's cause was not worth the expenditure of Confederate blood: "I fear Maryland is not going to come to our relief, a few of her sons may be loyal but not so many that we might risk our army in her borders." After Sharpsburg, a disappointed Bacot looked to providence rather than to Maryland. "God help us," she wrote; "we can do nothing of ourselves." Others put the case with more bitterness, as when a Louisiana woman described "great disappointment over Maryland. . . . There has been but little enthusiasm and few recruits. Well, let the Old Bay State go, if her people had rather be slaves in the Union than masters in the Confederacy. They must abide by their choice." [26]

For Confederates who had doubted the propriety of invading the North, Maryland's behavior confirmed that the South should do no more than defend its own borders. A Georgia clergyman alluded to the popular clamor for invasion that had risen in the wake of Lee's victories in July and August. Attempting to carry the war to the Federals "in the most favorable moment and upon the most favorable soil—at least one upon which the people were, to a good degree, at least, so friendly as not to rise upon us," Lee had marched into Maryland. There he found that he "could advance but a little way" because the "people did not come to his standard." This individual looked upon the whole episode "*as a special providence in our behalf*" and hoped "this taste of invasion will be satisfactory—at least for the present. . . . The Maryland pear certainly is not ripe yet." [27]

Most Confederates seem to have emulated their newspaper editors in viewing Lincoln's emancipation proclamation as a potentially positive development. At a distance of more than a century and a third it is impossible to know whether people believed one thing and wrote another, but considerable testimony suggests that many white southerners expected emancipation to weaken the Union war effort. Some looked to fissures behind the lines in critical northern states, as when a Virginia physician pronounced it "more than probable" that Lincoln's action would "redound to our benefit, in . . . that it will produce dissentions among his own followers, as it has already done in New York." Diarist Catherine Edmondston, scrutinizing the war from her home in eastern North Carolina, discerned that "[e]vidences of division at home appear in the Northern journals— the Emancipation Proclamation meets with some bitter opponents & M Clellan is like to have a fire in his rear." Pennsylvania-born Josiah Gorgas, the Confederacy's resourceful ordnance chief, initially considered the proclamation worthy of notice only "as showing the drift of opinion in the northern gov." A few days later, however, he recorded that Lincoln's action triggered "marked opposition at the north, & is denounced by the democrats generally." [28]

Unhappiness in the Union army relating to emancipation impressed some Confederates as particularly noteworthy. The northern press served as the primary source for information about this topic in late September and early October. "General McClellan has issued a mild general order cautioning the troops against political discussion," observed a man who relied on Union newspaper accounts: "It is a very significant production and goes to corroborate the report that great trouble exists in their camps on account of the war becoming one for the abolition of slavery." Witnesses such as Cornelia Peake McDonald and Anne S. Frobel reached similar conclusions based on firsthand testimony from the enemy.

Thrown together with Federals in Winchester, McDonald observed, "There seems no doubt now that the Yankee army is disgusted with the war, now that the real object of it has been made manifest, and many go so far as to say that they will fight no longer if the fight is for the freedom of the negroes." As if to clinch her point, she added, "Some of their soldiers have said so in my presence." In occupied Fairfax County, Frobel wrote that "Lincoln's recent proclamation has caused great dissatisfaction" among troops loyal to McClellan. They feared Lincoln would replace their hero with John C. Frémont, and "that does not accord at all with the wishes of the army." Northern soldiers said the proclamation would "put a speedy termination to the war"—welcome words to Frobel, yet she knew "they talk a great deal of what they know nothing about."[29]

In late September, John B. Jones prophesied that Lincoln's measure would "intensify the war, and add largely to our numbers in the field." A subsequent passage in his diary highlighted outrage over the proclamation and hope that it might spawn a crisis of command in the Army of the Potomac—sentiments voiced frequently across the Confederacy. "Yesterday in both Houses of Congress," Jones wrote, "resolutions were introduced for the purpose of retaliating upon the North [for] the barbarities contemplated in Lincoln's Emancipation proclamation." Meanwhile, he continued, the "Abolitionists of the North want McClellan removed." Believing that a change of generals would discomfit the most famous Union army, Jones found himself in the odd position of aligning himself with the abolitionists: "I hope they may have their will."[30]

Just before news of Sharpsburg spread across the South, a man from Lynchburg lauded the success Lee's army had achieved since the Seven Days. "[V]ictory after victory has crowned our arms and our gallant and victorious army [is] yet driving the enemy before them," he wrote enthusiastically. "[M]ay we continue to drive them until not a vestige of that invading army tramp on that soil, ever again tread upon southern soil." Following the turbulent middle third of September, the bulk of McClellan's army *did not* mount an effort to tramp across Virginia's Potomac frontier. No major action erupted, and the armies entered a somnolent spell that prompted innumerable comments like John B. Jones's "All quiet in Northern Virginia" on October 7 and Cornelia McDonald's "No news from our army, and no further indication of a falling back" eighteen days later. Confederates relaxed after a protracted season of stirring military operations, content that Lee and his army would meet whatever challenge the Yankees might offer.[31]

Contemporary comparisons of Lee and his army with their counterparts in the Western Theater reveal another outcome of operations in the summer and autumn. Because Lee had won two major offensive victories in Virginia and,

Confederates continued to portray the Emancipation Proclamation as problematical for the North well after the Maryland campaign. The *Southern Illustrated News* printed this cartoon from *Punch* in the spring of 1863. In the caption, Abraham Lincoln seeks to persuade a reluctant freedman to take up arms: "Why I du declare it's my dear old friend Sambo! Course you'll fight for us Sambo. Lend us a hand, Old Hoss, du!"
Southern Illustrated News, March 14, 1863

according to the dominant view, left a crippled Union army cringing in Maryland, relatively few Confederates judged his actions harshly. Braxton Bragg and Earl Van Dorn, architects of the retreat from Kentucky and the defeat at Corinth, respectively, received less forgiving treatment. British traveler W. C. Corsan's journal suggests the extent of the double standard. Corsan described the military situation in the Confederacy upon his arrival in Richmond in November 1862, mentioning Jackson's presence at Winchester, Lee's at Culpeper, and McClellan's at Warrenton—without a word about the impact of the Maryland campaign. Poor Bragg did not fare as well: "Of course," stated Corsan matter-of-factly, "his conduct and plans were criticised severely."[32]

William Blackford typified this willingness to forgive Lee but not Bragg. After the former's return to the Virginia side of the Potomac, Blackford praised his "splendid campaign around Richmond, in the Valley and in Maryland." But the similar withdrawal from Kentucky, against which no solid triumphs on Bragg's part could be juxtaposed, elicited a withering blast. "The evacuation of Kentucky by Bragg is un fait accompli," stated Blackford. "He brought out immense quantities of plunder of all kinds, but the result has been disastrous if not disgraceful to our arms." Lamenting Bragg's inability to deny Don Carlos Buell access to Louisville, Blackford voiced a sentiment that undoubtedly would have been widely seconded: "Oh, that we had another Lee and another Jackson to send out there."[33]

Jefferson Davis almost certainly took a more pessimistic view of the Maryland campaign than did the majority of his people. Robert Garlick Hill Kean, head of the Confederate Bureau of War and nephew-in-law of Secretary of War George Wythe Randolph, recorded a famous description of the president's mood: "He was very low down after the battle of Sharpsburg. . . . I remember the then Secretary of War told me that he said our maximum strength had been laid out, while the enemy was but beginning to put forth his."[34] George Washington Custis Lee, who served as the president's military aid, may have contributed to Davis's doubts. Having joined the army near Martinsburg in late September, Robert E. Lee's oldest son reported that officers told him "our troops were shaky from the day they went into Maryland, . . . that if even the few (comparatively) who were present had fought with their usual spirit at both Boonsboro, and Sharpsburg, the enemy would have been badly whipped. As it was, I believe from what I have heard, that they got the worst of it." Lee predicted that the army would make a better fight when resupplied with food and clothing and reinforced by the return of stragglers; however, "the worst of it" was that the enemy "can refit faster than we can."[35]

Davis unburdened himself to Robert E. Lee about pressures from behind the lines. Members of Congress, newspaper editors, and private citizens—none of whom, in Davis's view, had a proper understanding of the military situation—had clamored for an aggressive strategy. With Lee's troops arrayed along Virginia's northern frontier after Sharpsburg, many of these people called for the army to take up a defensive position closer to Richmond. "The feverish anxiety to invade the North," wrote Davis with scarcely concealed temper, "has been relieved by the counter irritant of apprehension for the safety of the Capital in the absence of the Army, so long criticized for a 'want of dash.'" Davis trusted that Lee would be unmoved by the demands of such amateur strategists, and raised the prospect of reinforcements for the Army of Northern Virginia from Louisiana and elsewhere. Whatever his expectations for the future, Davis knew what Lee had wrought since June, and he sent his heartfelt expression of gratitude: "In the name of the Confederacy I thank you and the brave men of your Army for the deeds which have covered our flag with imperishable fame."[36]

The soldiers of that army knew better than anyone else what they had endured. Their letters and diaries evaluated the various components of the Maryland campaign, shed light on the physical condition and morale of the army, judged the quality of the army's leaders, and speculated about the likely short- and long-term direction of the war.

Men and officers alike described Sharpsburg as a cataclysmic battle that had pushed them to the breaking point, but virtually all their accounts stress that Lee's battered units held the field. The emphasis on maintaining ground might seem like a transparent effort to deflect attention away from the fact that the Army of Northern Virginia eventually retreated; however, for Civil War soldiers the ability to avoid being driven from a battlefield carried great psychological weight. As they would do after Gettysburg ten months hence, Lee's veterans took pride in overcoming disadvantages of ground, numbers, and matériel and in inflicting horrendous casualties on the Federals. Many historians, including myself, have taken Lee to task for remaining on the battlefield at Sharpsburg through the 18th after nearly suffering disaster the previous day. To do so with his back against the river, and with only Boteler's Ford available as a possible route of escape, seemingly placed his army at risk without the potential of any real gain. But testimony from soldiers proud of holding the field in the face of a powerful enemy suggests that Lee might have known better than his critics in this instance.[37]

Five witnesses convey the tenor of innumerable Confederate reactions to the battle. "The fight Raged all day with great fury," wrote a private in the 13th Mississippi Infantry. "It was indeed a frighfull scene and looked as if we would be completely annihilated but we drove them back with great loss." This man admitted a heavy Confederate butcher's bill but insisted it was "not[h]ing to compare with that of the enemy" and proudly stated that "[w]e Slept on the Battle field last nigh[t]." An officer on Stonewall Jackson's staff told his uncle that at Sharpsburg "the greatest battle of this war was fought, at least the longest—We repulsed the enemy with heavy loss & he was too crippled to renew the attack the next day, tho we waited & invited him to do so." Sgt. Daniel Lane of the 2nd North Carolina Infantry survived the maelstrom of the Bloody Lane, confiding to his diary that night, "It was surely a hot day with us. . . . Our loss was heavy in wounded & near half of the company is missing. Our troops held part of the battle field at night & the enemy held a portion of it." On the 18th, Lane recorded that the Confederates "held their position all day"; the nonaggressive Federals, he guessed, "were satisfied with what they got yesterday."

A member of the 56th Virginia—who considered Sharpsburg "the grandest battle of the war, or indeed that was ever fought"—captured the ebb and flow of the fighting: "Sometimes the enemy drove us, and sometimes we drove the enemy. He made a desperate effort to dislodge us from our position, *but failed most signally*. Some of us count it a drawn battle. Others claim it as a great victory." After mentioning that Lee held the field for "a whole day" after the battle, this soldier strove for a literary touch in addressing casualties. "The loss of the enemy is immense," he noted. "His dead are scattered in the Antietam valley about as 'thick as leaves in Vallambrosa.'" A South Carolina enlisted man looked back to the Seven Days for a point of comparison. "We were in the hottest part of the fight under Jackson," wrote Taliaferro N. Simpson, "and for me to give an idea of the fierceness of the conflict, the roar of musketry, and the thunder of artillery is as utterly impossible as to describe a thousand storms in the region of Hades. The Malvern Hill fight was a circumstance." Although Federals "fought better than they ever did before," the Confederates repulsed every attack and pushed the enemy back on both flanks.[38]

Powerful Union artillery dominated several sectors of the battlefield at Sharpsburg, leading southern gunners to term the contest an "artillery hell" and prompting frequent comments in letters and diaries. Two Georgians in infantry regiments dwelled on the fact that the Federal long arm had occupied advantageous ground. "Their artillery was placed where we could not charge it, and it was used with terrible effect," Theodore Fogle of the 2nd Georgia explained to his parents; when Union guns could not sweep the field, however, "we just used up their infantry wherever it met us." The singularly named Lt. Ujanirtus Allen of the 21st Georgia Infantry echoed Fogle's thoughts and language. "The enemy had the best position in the last fight and made an artillery fight of it," he wrote. "He had some heavy batteries which controlled the right of the field. They were on the side of the mountain and we could do nothing with them." An artillerist made essentially the same points in a letter to the Richmond *Weekly Dispatch*.

"But for the disposition of the enemy's artillery," he claimed, "I am satisfied we would have whipped him. . . . It was almost impossible to charge batteries posted upon such high hills." This gunner also fulminated about the "almost worthless" southern artillery ammunition. "The shells and spherical case," he said, "generally don't explode at all." Another gunner suggested that Lee retreated across the river "partly on account of batteries, which the enemy were erecting on the mountain (running perpendicular to our right flank) which would have swept the rear of our army." [39]

Although nearly all of Lee's soldiers took pride in not being driven from the field, they differed in assessing the consequences of the withdrawal to the south bank of the Potomac. Some were openly chastened by the retreat. Brig. Gen. Roswell S. Ripley, who had been wounded leading his brigade on the morning of the 17th, confided to P. G. T. Beauregard that he feared "we have lost in the moral effect on the north by our being obliged by circumstances to evacuate Maryland." A Georgia captain who judged the fighting at Sharpsburg a draw also was pessimistic about its aftermath: "I fear this Md. trip has rather injured us more than good done. Wee lost more than wee gained in it, I think." A gunner in the Fluvanna Artillery listed a number of positive aspects of the campaign, including the capture of Harpers Ferry and heavy Union losses at Sharpsburg, yet seemed thrown off balance by the retreat. Combat on the 17th "resulted unexpectedly to me and inauspiciously for the early ending of the war, in the withdrawing of our army from Maryland and, consequently a triumph for the enemy or rather an apparent triumph." [40]

A larger number of Confederates treated the recrossing of the river as no more than the last phase of a largely successful campaign. Lt. John Hampden Chamberlayne of the Purcell Artillery cataloged the bright spots of the operation—including Harpers Ferry, the slaughter of Yankees at Sharpsburg, and the rearguard action at Shepherdstown—before cautioning his sister: "Don't begin to suppose we were driven out of Maryland: no such thing; our campaign is almost unexampled for quickness & completeness of success. We have done much more than a sane man could expect." In an account published shortly after the end of the campaign, Chaplain Nicholas A. Davis of the Texas Brigade marshaled the same evidence as Chamberlayne to support his conclusion that Lee had carried out a "brilliant campaign of twelve days across the Potomac." A private in the 21st Georgia Infantry wasted no words in making the point that the army's hard work had changed the strategic picture in the Eastern Theater for the better: "Most all the Yankees is whiped out of Virginia," stated Edward J. Jones. "Went over in [Maryland] and had one fight and then we retreated back into Virginia." Another believer in brevity, James E. Keever of the 34th North Carolina Infantry summed up action since the Seven Days in six short sentences: "We have been in ten battles and marched over one thousand miles. The first battle was at Cedar Run. The second at Manassas Junction, also three hard fightings on Bulls Run where the big fight was last year. The sixth battle was at Ox Hill, the seventh at Harpers Ferry and the eight[h] in Marriland. We whip the enemy and drove them back every time with great slotter. Our loss was not half as many as the enemy." His tolerance for campaign narrative exhausted, Keever abruptly announced, "I will now quit the fighting subject and tell you of the crops." [41]

Walter H. Taylor of Lee's staff also considered the campaign an overall success. "I suppose it will be generally concluded that our march through — or rather into — Maryland & back was decidedly meteoric," he wrote while the army was near Martinsburg. "It was however by no means without happy results." The taking of Harpers Ferry alone "was sufficiently important to compensate for all the trouble experienced"; moreover, the fight at Sharpsburg left the enemy too battered to maintain the offensive and "taught us the value of our men, who can even when weary with constant marching & fighting & when on short rations, contend with and resist three times their own number." Taylor did not claim a victory on the 17th, but "if either had the advantage, it certainly was with us." With some badly needed rest and reinforcements, the army would be ready to fight again and "with God's help we will again be victorious." [42]

Doubts about the long-term influence of military events plagued some of the soldiers who proudly tallied an unbroken string of victories since the Seven Days. Elisha Franklin Paxton, Ujanirtus Allen, and Benjamin Franklin Jones expressed opinions typical of this group. Paxton saw operations between June and mid-September as one huge campaign that would go down in history as "the most astonishing expeditions of war, for the severity of the battles fought and the hardships endured by our soldiers." Should McClellan advance against Lee again, Paxton projected "a splendid victory for us." "Our victories, though, seem to settle nothing," he went on, "to bring us no nearer the end of the war. It is only so many killed and wounded, leaving the work of blood to go on with renewed vigor." Shortly after the army reached safety in Virginia, Lieutenant Allen assured his wife that the "anemy had been too roughly handled" to strike again at the Confederates. But he foresaw no early end to fighting: "We defeat them again and again but like the hordes of Goths and Vandals that laid waste to South Europe; still they come. . . . Our regiment has been under fire about twenty times and is not much larger than a company now." Jones had decided by late fall of 1862 that the Confederacy would need assistance to vanquish the North. "I think that some other Nation will have it to settle this winter though we whip them every fight we get into," he observed, "but there is so many of them that it looks like that they are ready for another fight rite off."[43]

Soldiers who held various opinions about the retreat agreed that the army had not been able to bring off all the wounded from Sharpsburg. Just as holding ground carried immense psychological weight, so also did protecting disabled comrades. To their credit, Confederates forthrightly admitted their failure in this regard—though often in tandem with assurances that the army had exhibited valor at Sharpsburg. "[W]ee crost back on the virginia side of the potomac last fridy nite," wrote South Carolinian S. M. Crawford; "our forses faught the yankeys manful but wee had to leave some of our friends in Maryland." Jesse Steed McGee of the 7th South Carolina Infantry mirrored Crawford in substance (if not in facility at spelling): "We remained on the field untill the next night after the fight when we fell back across the River leaving behind several of our dead [and] wounded among the rest." Walter Battle of the 4th North Carolina Infantry, who had helped treat wounded men during the battle, probably found it especially difficult to leave some of them behind. "Many were wounded and left on the battlefield," he informed his mother, "and had to be left in the hands of the Yankees when we fell back this side of the Potomac." Another participant, whose account was published later in the war, described the retreat as "slow, orderly, and unmolested." But it could not be denied "that large numbers of dead and wounded were left behind to the tender mercies of the foe."[44]

Nor did anyone in the army deny that straggling on an immense scale bedeviled Lee in Maryland. From generals down through soldiers in the ranks, Confederates wrote about the extent of the problem, its impact on the battlefield, and the need to correct it. As in the civilian sphere, some veterans expressed empathy for men whose physical condition prevented their keeping up with Lee's fast-moving force. Others considered the stragglers unpatriotic slackers who willfully shirked their duty, calling for harsh penalties that would send a message to anyone who contemplated falling out of the ranks.

The physical condition of the army explained much of the straggling. Because evidence of this phenomenon is abundant and frequently cited, a few examples will suggest the degree to which Lee's men, many of whom were poorly fed and insufficiently clothed and shod, had been driven to the verge of collapse. As the army marched through Maryland, a member of the 15th Georgia Infantry observed "that a great many of our soldiers were barefoot." This man "had on a pair of shoes one No. 5 and the other No. 10," but neither he nor anyone else in the regiment had changed their clothes for the past forty-five days. "The men are very much exhausted and need rest imperatively," wrote a diarist in the 35th North

Carolina Infantry shortly after Sharpsburg. A march the previous day from Martinsburg to Shepherdstown and back had left them "completely exhausted." On September 22, a Mississippian sketched a pathetic picture: "Our army is very much wornout and that is not all, it is almost starved out. Our Rations has been Beef and flour since we left Richmond and not more than half enough of that. Many times we have had Green Corn and apples issued to us and were glad to get that." A man in the 8th Georgia Infantry reported only ten men in his company on September 23. Several of those present lacked shoes, and "8 others are at Winchester with no prospect of getting any." If ordered to march, the men would "suffer terrible." In late September, a pair of soldiers in Georgia regiments provided tellingly terse comments. "The Army is in poor condition, half naked and barefooted," said a private in the 4th Georgia Infantry. "My own clothes and shoes are in pieces and there is no chance of getting them replaced." The second man used only eight words to make his point: "Times is hard hear. Provision is scarce hear."[45]

Some soldiers tried to find something hopeful in their raggedness and hunger. Members of the 47th Alabama Infantry, for example, interpreted the extreme shortage of shoes and clothing as a sign that the war was about to end. "[T]he oficer has made out requicition for close for us," stated James P. Crowder, "tho we hav never got any yet and I dont think that we will ever get any. that is the reason why we think peace will bea made thay are not a fixing for winter." After detailing how dirty and hungry he and his comrades in the 53rd Georgia Infantry had been, William Stillwell sounded a positive note: "[A]fter summing up the whole matter, I think our independence ought to be worth a great deal, for it cost enough. But, thank God, men fighting on corn and baked apples was never subdued and never will be."[46]

Everyone understood that factors other than fatigue and material deprivation had contributed to the straggling. Thousands of men had left the ranks because they chose not to cross the Potomac or simply because they had seen enough campaigning.[47] The absence of such men infuriated many of those who had risked their lives on the seemingly endless day of combat at Sharpsburg. A soldier wounded on the 17th vented feelings certainly shared by many others in calling for stringent measures to end straggling. "It is truly disgraceful to see the number of stragglers after a battle has been fought or even while it is raging furiously, and the day still doubtful," he wrote to the Richmond *Enquirer*, "while hundreds of both officers and privates would be startled and made to blush, could they see the long list of this class." Brig. Gen. William Dorsey Pender attacked stragglers even more stridently, calling them the most "filthy unprincipled set of villains" he had ever seen. "The officers are nearly as bad as the men," Pender insisted. "In one of my Regts. the other day when they thought they were going to get into a fight, six out [of] ten officers skulked out and did not come up until they thought all danger over." Half the brigade left ranks the same day. "Oh dear, oh dear, our army is coming to a pretty pass," concluded the shaken young brigadier. Capt. Alexander Cheves Haskell of Brig. Gen. Maxcy Gregg's staff chose less volatile language to make essentially the same point. "Our Army is small, but fights gloriously. . . . Great numbers of men have straggled off, until none but heroes are left."[48]

Many of Haskell's "heroes" could imagine a different outcome at Sharpsburg had stragglers shouldered their muskets on the firing lines. Sgt. Sanford W. Branch of the 8th Georgia Infantry described the Army of the Potomac as "too badly crippled to renew the contest" on the 18th. The Confederates were equally fought out, but "[i]f we had of had our 30 thousand stragglers engaged we would of been in Baltimore by this time." Two soldiers invoked higher authority on this topic. "General Lee said we would have routed the enemy at Sharpsburg, Maryland, if it had not been that our army straggled so," commented an artillerist. "I think there was about 20,000 of our army that straggled off and were not in the fight." A lieutenant from Georgia expressed the same idea: "Genl Lee says if evrybody else had fought like we did it would have been a great victory. He also says we had them whiped if our reinforcements had come time enough." A North Carolinian probably had stragglers in mind when he claimed, "If we had only been supported by the rest of our troops we would have carried the day before us for we broke their lines completely."[49]

The army remained in the lower Shenandoah Valley through the weeks following Sharpsburg, welcoming back thousands of stragglers and recovering wounded. During that period, a pervasive sentiment favored continued rest and refitting before reengaging the enemy. In early October, a Georgia private confessed ignorance about what lay ahead but avowed that for the present "one thing sure we need rest verry bad we have been going ever since we have been in Va sure and fought as hard as any body." Thomas J. Goree, who served on James Longstreet's staff, commented shortly thereafter that the soldiers were "enjoying the rest and quiet so much needed." With supplies of shoes and clothing arriving daily, Goree thought the army would "soon be in better fighting condition than at any time since the battles around Richmond." By mid-October, a second lieutenant in the 49th Georgia Infantry could enter an optimistic passage in his diary: "We have had a long rest, and the army has greatly increased both in numbers & health." Writing a week later, Reuben A. Pierson of the 9th Louisiana Infantry offered an even more upbeat assessment. "Our troops have been stationed in camp about five weeks resting and recruiting," he stated. "They are now as jovial as a set of college students and are in remarkable good health."[50]

Unlike comrades who welcomed a respite from campaigning, a significant minority of Confederates probably preferred a return to the strategic offensive. At Stonewall Jackson's headquarters, where aggressive thinking almost always held sway, staff officer Sandie Pendleton calculated on October 8 that 25,000 men had returned to the army. He hoped this enlarged force could "fight McClellan's army about Sharpsburg again," projecting not only a result "very different from that of the battle of September 17" but also rejuvenation of the army. "We have been idle now for more than three weeks, and our generals are not given to inaction," he opined with considerable understatement. "Activity and motion have gotten to be a necessity for us, as giving some food to the mind." An officer in the 5th South Carolina Infantry also deplored the army's inactivity in the region around Winchester. He found that a "state of idleness after having been so actively employed is very trying . . . soldiers and all would hail an order to march with tokens of delight."[51]

Virtually no one in the Army of Northern Virginia would have supported another campaign designed to liberate Maryland. Two uncomfortable weeks in that state had soured the soldiers, who, like the four men quoted below, took every opportunity to inveigh against its residents. Walter Taylor remarked about Marylanders who practiced the "disreputable & unmannerly habit of shooting at Confed. soldiers from windows." "Don't let any of your friends sing 'My Maryland,'" Taylor scribbled at the top of a letter to his sister, "not 'my Westn' Md anyhow." In response to a query from his brother about how he liked Maryland, William R. Montgomery of the 2nd South Carolina Infantry responded, "Well it is the prettiest country I ever saw, but as for enjoyment I don't want to go any more & I think we had better let (Md) alone for she seems joined to her Idols ('Union')." Another South Carolinian agreed with Montgomery's view, hoping that whatever movement lay ahead would not be "to Maryland for we are all tired of Maryland there are too many Unionist there for us, . . . the majority I think is against us." A Georgian evinced even less charitable feelings in a letter to the editor of a newspaper in Macon: "We do not like the idea of crossing the Potomac again, unless they allow us to pillage and inflict some retribution for the outrages of Federals in Virginia."[52]

No element of the Maryland campaign exceeded in importance its role in strengthening the bond between Lee and the men in his army. When he stepped into Joseph E. Johnston's place after Seven Pines, Lee had inspired mixed reactions among his soldiers. Some considered him too cautious, and others certainly saw him as a temporary stand-in until Johnston recovered from his wounds.[53] Between June and October 1862, Lee went a long way toward making the army his own, winning the trust and admiration of soldiers who rapidly came to expect dramatic movements and victories from their chief. Although Stonewall Jackson remained the Confederacy's preeminent military idol, Lee stepped firmly onto center stage as the fledgling nation's premier field commander. The troops saw Lee as the grand designer, Jackson as the brilliant lieutenant who executed his superior's plans. This is not to say that everyone in the army cast only rapturous looks toward army headquarters. Testimony about Lee from men who had straggled or deserted is hard to find, but by the end of September thousands of soldiers undoubtedly had cursed him for pressing them unmercifully on the march and in battle. The army's hemorrhaging in Maryland underscored the inability or unwillingness of as many as a third of the army to meet Lee's high standard of performance. By the end of the quiet period following Sharpsburg, however, most of the troops who had reflected on their accomplishments since the previous June looked to Lee as one whose intellect and daring would yield many future triumphs.

Statements from four soldiers underscore how far Lee had gone toward achieving his later stature as the Confederacy's primary national hero. Just after the army crossed the Potomac, one man wrote, "We have confidence in Genl. Lee in directing our operations, confident of the justness of our cause." An officer in the 3rd Georgia Infantry remarked that at Sharpsburg "Gen. Lee, as usual, displayed his splendid military talents in a great degree, and in his retreat across the Potomac completely foiled the Federal commander." "The army almost worship him," stated this Georgian, "and believe that with Lee, Jackson, and Longstreet at the head, nothing is impossible." Theodore Fogle, another Georgian, said roughly the same thing in fewer words: "I have every confidence in our generals and am perfectly willing to trust our cause and safety in their hands." Artillerist Ham Chamberlayne went much further, fixing Lee at the center of the Confederacy's war. "With Lee for our great archer," he wrote metaphorically, "though string after string be frayed and broken, and the bow, the nation itself, be bent & weakened, yet arrow after arrow goes home to the mark and the prize is won at last." Whenever Chamberlayne happened to see Lee, or even to think about him, "there looms up to me some king-of-men, superior by the head, a Gigantic figure, on whom rests the world."[54]

Unlike soldiers such as Chamberlayne, William Dorsey Pender and William Nelson Pendleton resisted lavishing unqualified praise on Lee. Enthusiastic as the Army of Northern Virginia camped at Frederick during the first week in September, Pender gushed that "Gen. Lee has shown great Generalship and the greatest boldness. There never was such a campaign, not even by Napoleon." Yet the wretched physical state of the army alarmed Pender, who argued that "Jackson would kill up any army the way he marches and the bad management in the subsistence Dept.—Gen. Lee is my man." Sharpsburg and the retreat to Shepherdstown dramatically influenced the North Carolina brigadier. He decided that the incursion into Maryland had been a mistake and objected when Lee elected to keep the army close to the Potomac River. "I had supposed we would have left here before this," he wrote from near Bunker Hill, "but strategy or Gen. Lee's great dislike to give up Md. prolongs our stay beyond what looks to us inferiors as useless." Also frustrated because he had no idea where the army would move next, Pender directed another gibe at Lee: "If the keeping of our own counsel goes to constitute a general, Lee possesses that to perfection."

Artillery chief Pendleton, who nearly had lost all of the army's reserve guns at Shepherdstown on September 19, chose to criticize Lee obliquely. He favored falling back from the Potomac, both to shorten the army's "immensely long line of communication" and because he believed the men "did not fight as well in Md as in Va." An implicit sigh of resignation accompanied Pendleton's next pair of sentences, which anticipated that Lee would remain along the Potomac: "Still wiser heads must determine that. I am willing as the old bishop said to 'defend Rome under the walls of Carthage.'"[55]

Closely related to the growing faith in Lee was a sense that the Army of Northern Virginia might carry an increasing share of the burden of winning Confederate nationhood. Bad news from Mississippi, Kentucky, and elsewhere west of the Appalachians engendered low expectations for southern forces in the Western Theater, a fact illustrated by three letters written on October 13, 1862. "I understand that General Brag got whipt in the west," commented James W. Lineberger of the 49th North Carolina Infantry, "but I dont think that we will be whipt on this side soon. . . . [I]f the yanks comes over they will knot find it sharpsberge in mariland for our boys is rested and is ancious for a fite again." Georgian Shepherd G. Pryor, who had called Sharpsburg a drawn battle and believed that if McClellan pursued Lee "wee can whip them back again," rendered a gloomy verdict about Bragg's efforts. "I think the news of our army in the West is rather unfavorable," he stated. "The last fight, weev been whiped pretty badly. I hope the next news from there is more favorable."

Ham Chamberlayne alluded to reports from the West as "grave certainly, but, after all, such as might at any time be possible, such as we must always be ready for." Chamberlayne condescendingly suggested that the western news affected the common soldiers but little, because "they never know the full bearings of such a thing." As for Lee's officers, they "seem to feel the news as they should do, that is it makes them cease idle dreams of furloughs or of peace, but I have yet to see any who are so unreasonable as to despond over it."[56]

As people across the Confederacy sought to understand what had happened

A month after the Army of Northern Virginia marched into Maryland, this
engraving of Lee appeared in the northern press.
Frank Leslie's Illustrated Newspaper, October 4, 1862

in Maryland, Robert E. Lee revealed his own thoughts about the campaign in a series of letters to Jefferson Davis and others. Lee had marched north in an effort to maintain the strategic initiative gained during the period from the Seven Days through Second Manassas, as well as to push the military frontier even farther from the Virginia heartland on which his army relied for food and fodder. He hoped to maneuver in Maryland or southern Pennsylvania through the autumn, provisioning his men and animals and forestalling another Federal offensive against Richmond in 1862. He also joined Jefferson Davis in believing his army's presence might inspire Marylanders to rise in support of the Confederacy. Although Lee understood before leaving Virginia that his army lacked "much of the material of war," was "feeble in transportation," and contained thousands of men "poorly provided with clothing, and . . . destitute of shoes," he thought invasion his best option.[57]

The truncated stay north of the Potomac satisfied some of Lee's goals but left him frustrated about others. On the positive side, he had pulled the Army of the Potomac out of Virginia and, in the fighting at Sharpsburg, rendered it immobile for several weeks. On October 11, Lee informed Secretary of War Randolph that "[w]hatever may be General McClellan's ultimate intentions, I see no evidence as yet of any advance upon Richmond; and, notwithstanding the assertions in the Northern papers, I think this army is not yet sufficiently recuperated from its campaign in Maryland to make a vigorous forward move." While McClellan sat in the vicinity of Sharpsburg, Lee's men consumed provisions in the lower Shenandoah Valley that otherwise would be lost to the Federals. "If the enemy can be detained in our front for some weeks," predicted Lee, "it will give them but little time before winter to operate south of the Potomac." In the meantime, reinforcements were arriving from Richmond and stragglers and the wounded returning to their units. On October 8, Secretary Randolph cheerfully noted "an increase of 20,000 men in eight days" and, citing returns from September 30, remarked that the army's "strength cannot now be much short of its standard when you left Richmond."[58]

Whatever the condition and intentions of the Federal army, Lee knew that the Army of Northern Virginia suffered from serious problems. Lack of supplies remained vexing, and he repeatedly pressed officials in Richmond to forward additional shoes, clothing, and other material as soon as possible.[59] Even more alarming was the continued absence of thousands of stragglers and deserters. The loss of so much manpower had helped convince Lee to retreat to Shepherdstown. During the first few days back in Virginia, he bluntly acknowledged the scope of the problem. He described the army on September 21 as "greatly paralyzed by the loss to its ranks of the numerous stragglers." Although he had "taken every means in my power from the beginning to correct this evil," it had grown worse since the army returned to Virginia. Lee ordered Jackson and Longstreet to see that their officers made "greater efforts . . . to correct this growing evil," and he suggested to Secretary Randolph that Congress give the president or the War Department authority to "degrade . . . from their positions" all officers found guilty of exhibiting "bad conduct in the presence of the enemy, leaving their posts in time of battle, and deserting their command or the army in the march or in camp." An unacceptable level of plundering accompanied the problem of absenteeism, casting into sharper relief the army's uncertain discipline.[60]

Maryland's reaction to the Confederate invasion also disappointed Lee. On September 8, he had issued a proclamation to its people announcing that the Army of Northern Virginia came among them "to assist you with the power of its arms in regaining the rights of which you have been despoiled. . . . This army will respect your choice whatever it may be, and while the Southern people will rejoice to welcome you to your natural position among them, they will only welcome you when you come of your own free will." Maryland's choice soon became all too clear. In terms of both gathering provisions and attracting recruits, the operation had to be reckoned a failure. "I regret that the stay of the army in Maryland was so short as to prevent our receiving the aid I had expected from that state," Lee told the secretary of war in late September. Summoning a measure of forced optimism, he went on to say that "[s]ome few recruits joined us, and others are finding their way across the river to our lines." In a similar vein, Lee speculated that Lincoln's recent actions had suppressed civil liberty in Maryland to the degree that conservative Marylanders, "unless dead to the feelings of liberty, will rise and depose the party now in power."[61]

Lee's greatest disappointment stemmed from having to abandon the strategic initiative to McClellan. He had wished to operate in Maryland for several weeks, forcing the Federals to react to his movements, spreading fear and doubt through the northern government, and choosing the place and time to bring his opponent to battle. He might forage successfully after Sharpsburg from his position south of the Potomac, but he had taken a step backward toward the time when McClellan set the strategic agenda in the weeks leading up to the Seven Days.

No period of the war better illustrates Lee's pronounced preference to be the aggressor than the month following the retreat from Sharpsburg. Outnumbered, plagued by absenteeism, and severely short of supplies, he nevertheless chafed to regain the initiative. In a message to Jefferson Davis written on September 21 from the Confederate encampment on Opequon Creek, he expressed his continuing "desire to threaten a passage into Maryland, to occupy the enemy on this frontier, and, if my purpose cannot be accomplished, to draw them into the Valley, where I can attack them to advantage." Two days later, in language that told how grudgingly he had relinquished the offensive, Lee informed Davis that he retired from Maryland only because losses at Sharpsburg and the absence of deserters and stragglers had left him "unable to cope with advantage with the numerous host of the enemy." On the 25th, Lee wrote again to Davis, revealing that his intention at the time of the retreat had been "to recross the Potomac at Williamsport, and move upon Hagerstown." The army's condition had prevented such a movement, but Lee still believed that in "a military point of view, the best move . . . the army could make would be to advance upon Hagerstown, and endeavor to defeat the enemy at that point." He would do so immediately even with his "diminished numbers, did the army exhibit its former temper and condition." But morale was such that Lee feared the "hazard would be great and a reverse disastrous."[62]

Lee projected that many of the hard-won fruits of the past ten weeks could slip away if his army simply awaited another Federal offensive. Should Richmond be the object of such a Union advance, the Army of Northern Virginia might find itself on the Rappahannock or, perhaps, even near the battlegrounds of the Seven Days. A letter to Maj. Gen. Gustavus W. Smith, who held a command at Richmond, indicated how precarious Lee considered the strategic situation: "I fear, for want of sufficient force to oppose the large army being collected by General McClellan, the benefits derived from the operations of the campaign will be but temporary." Lee knew that Smith's small force at Richmond was vulnerable. "If I felt sure of its safety," he stated, "I could operate more boldly and advantageously."[63]

In the end, Lee settled for a series of maneuvers in the lower valley, during which his soldiers destroyed sections of the Baltimore and Ohio Railroad and other lines. Walter Taylor attested to the difficulty with which Lee reconciled himself to the situation. "I believe my Chief was most anxious to recross the Potomac into Maryland," he observed in late September, "but was persuaded by his principal advisers that the condition of the army did not warrant such a move. This is conjecture on my part. I only know of his opinion & *guess* why he did not follow it." Taylor agreed with those who counseled against another lunge northward, believing that "it would have indeed been hazardous to reenter Maryland."[64]

Disappointments aside, Lee had learned that he led an army capable of astonishing feats. Just as the men had developed a deeper trust in him during the campaign from Richmond to Maryland, so too had he formed a high opinion of their bravery and tenacity. He expected no less than a superior performance. "[T]he army has had hard work to perform, long and laborious marches, and large odds to encounter in every conflict," he conceded, "but not greater than were endured by our revolutionary fathers, or than what any army must encounter to be victorious." The men who steadfastly faced the Federals at Sharpsburg, and whose conduct contrasted so strongly with that of the stragglers, met Lee's unforgiving standard: "There are brilliant examples of endurance and valor on the part of those who have had to bear the brunt in the battle and the labor in the field in consequence of this desertion of their comrades."[65]

As the army lay in camps near Winchester in early October, soldiers who had discharged their duty received formal congratulations from Lee. "In reviewing the achievements of the army during the present campaign," read General Orders No. 116, "the commanding general cannot withhold the expression of his admiration of the indomitable courage it has displayed in battle and its cheerful endurance of privation and hardship on the march." Lee tallied the army's many victories, including the Seven Days, Cedar Mountain, Second Manassas, Harpers Ferry, and Shepherdstown. At Sharpsburg they had fought a foe three times their number, repulsed all of his attacks, and during the "whole of the following day . . . stood prepared to resume the conflict on the same ground" before retiring "without molestation across the Potomac." History offered "few examples of greater fortitude and endurance than this army has exhibited." Having fed his men's egos, Lee gave notice that more hard work beckoned. "Much as you have done, much more remains to be accomplished," he warned. "The enemy again threatens with invasion, and to your tried valor and patriotism the country looks with confidence for deliverance and safety. Your past exploits give assurance that this confidence is not misplaced."[66]

Lee did not exaggerate how important his soldiers' activities would be to future Confederate morale. Between June and September 1862, the Army of Northern Virginia had earned spectacular victories that helped cancel the effects of defeats in other theaters. The retreat from Maryland, itself counterbalanced by the capture of Harpers Ferry and the tidy success at Shepherdstown, did not detract appreciably from laurels won at Richmond and Second Manassas. Similarly, the bitter contest at Sharpsburg, seen by most Confederates as a bloody drawn battle, confirmed the gallantry of Lee's soldiers. In the space of less than three months, the Confederate people had come to expect good news from the Army of Northern Virginia, investing ever more emotional capital in its leaders and soldiers. That investment led to a belief in possible victory that would be as important as any other factor in lengthening the life of the Confederacy.

ACKNOWLEDGMENTS

The author acknowledges the assistance of Keith S. Bohannon, Peter S. Carmichael, Robert E. L. Krick, Robert K. Krick, and Robert Sandow, all of whom provided material or suggested avenues of investigation relating to the topic of this essay.

NOTES

1. Jedediah Hotchkiss, *Make Me a Map of the Valley: The Civil War Journal of Stonewall Jackson's Topographer*, ed. Archie P. McDonald (Dallas, Tex.: Southern Methodist University Press, 1973), 83–84; Alexander D. Betts, *Experiences of a Confederate Chaplain, 1861–1865*, ed. W. A. Betts (190[?]; reprint, [Sanford, N.C.]: n.p., n.d.), 16–17; letter signed "A. B. C.," September 24, 1862, in Richmond *Weekly Dispatch*, September 30, 1862.

2. Clement Eaton, *A History of the Southern Confederacy* (New York: Macmillan, 1954), 193; Robert Selph Henry, *The Story of the Confederacy*, rev. ed. (New York: Bobbs-Merrill, 1936), 191; Clifford Dowdey, *The Land They Fought For: The Story of the South as the Confederacy, 1832–1865* (Garden City, N.Y.: Doubleday, 1955), 218. In *The Confederacy* (Chicago: University of Chicago Press, 1960), 80–81, Charles P. Roland added Earl Van Dorn's defeat at Corinth and Braxton Bragg's retreat from Kentucky, both in October, to Lee's withdrawal from Maryland to make a similar point about Confederate fortunes in the fall of 1862: "These reverses spread demoralization throughout the South and crippled the prestige of the administration. . . . Many Southerners began to doubt the ability of the Confederacy to win the war."

3. James M. McPherson, *Battle Cry of Freedom: The Civil War Era* (New York: Oxford University Press, 1988), 545; Brooks D. Simpson, *America's Civil War* (Wheeling, Ill.: Harlan Davidson, 1996), 86–87; Charles P. Roland, *An American Iliad: The Story of the Civil War* (Lexington: University Press of Kentucky, 1991), 83.

4. Gary W. Gallagher, "The Maryland Campaign in Perspective," in *Antietam: Essays on the 1862 Maryland Campaign*, ed. Gary W. Gallagher (Kent, Ohio: Kent State University Press, 1989), 94.

5. The conclusions in this essay rest on testimony from more than two hundred Confederates, including officers and soldiers within Lee's army, government officials, and men and women behind the lines. All major sections of the Confederacy are represented, and every effort was made to include people of various economic and social classes. As is often the case with Confederate witnesses, however, slaveholders are overrepresented, and the sample would not meet any social scientific standard.

6. In *The Road to Appomattox* (Memphis, Tenn.: Memphis State College Press, 1956), 60–61, Bell I. Wiley argued that a revival of Confederate spirits in the summer and early fall of 1862 "began to lose force with the coming of winter" and continued downward until reaching a crisis in the summer of 1863. The testimony examined for this essay does not sustain Wiley's conclusions.

7. Edward A. Pollard, *Southern History of the War. The Second Year of the War* (1863; reprint, New York: Charles B. Richardson, 1865), 142–43.

8. Charleston *Mercury*, September 23, 1862; Charleston *Daily Courier*, September 24, 1862; Richmond *Dispatch*, September 23, 1862; Richmond *Enquirer*, September 23, 1862.

9. The Charleston *Mercury* departed from the majority of papers in running a column on September 25 that suggested Lee gambled too much in sending most of his army to capture Harpers Ferry: "With the lights before us, the taking of Harper's Ferry looks like a military mistake—risking a pound to gain a penny. Hill's corps, at Boonsboro' was so exhausted by McClellan's attack in force, that it must have been of little use afterwards. Had we kept our army together we might have sent McClellan back to Washington, and that would have been worth many Harper's Ferries."

10. Richmond *Weekly Dispatch,* September 26, 1862; Charleston *Daily Courier,* October 3, 1862; Macon (Ga.) *Journal & Messenger,* October 8, 1862, reprinting Alexander's piece from the Savannah *Republican.*

11. Charleston *Mercury,* September 23, 1862; Richmond *Dispatch,* September 23, 1862; Richmond *Enquirer,* September 23, 1862.

12. Richmond *Daily Enquirer,* September 24, 1862. See also the Richmond *Dispatch,* September 23, 1862, which argued that "the great object of the operations in Maryland was the capture of the Yankee army of the Valley. That object was triumphantly accomplished."

13. Charleston *Mercury,* September 29, 1862; Atlanta *Southern Confederacy,* October 30, 1862.

14. Richmond *Weekly Dispatch,* September 26, 1862 [piece dated September 22 from near Winchester]; Macon (Ga.) *Journal & Messenger,* October 8, 1862, reprinting a piece from the Savannah *Republican;* Richmond *Dispatch,* September 30, 1862.

15. Richmond *Whig,* October 2, 1862; Charleston *Daily Courier,* October 4, 1862; Richmond *Dispatch,* October 13, 1862.

16. Charleston *Mercury,* October 15, 1862. For other expressions of disappointment at the failure to win Maryland to the Confederate cause, see the Macon (Ga.) *Journal & Messenger,* October 8, 1862, and the Charleston *Daily Courier,* October 4, 1862.

17. Charleston *Daily Courier,* October 4, 1862; Richmond *Whig,* October 2, 1862; Richmond *Enquirer,* October 14, 1862.

18. Charleston *Daily Courier,* October 4, 1862; Richmond *Dispatch,* September 23, 1862; Richmond *Daily Enquirer,* September 24, 1862.

19. Macon (Ga.) *Journal & Messenger,* October 8, 1862, reprinting Alexander's piece from the Savannah *Republican.*

20. Catherine Ann Devereux Edmondston, *"Journal of a Secesh Lady": The Diary of Catherine Ann Devereux Edmondston, 1860 –1866,* ed. Beth Gilbert Crabtree and James W. Patton (Raleigh: North Carolina Division of Archives and History, 1979), 261, 267; Edmund Ruffin, *The Diary of Edmund Ruffin,* ed. William Kauffman Scarborough, 3 vols. (Baton Rouge: Louisiana State University Press, 1972–89), 2:449 [entry for September 23, 1862]; Charles C. Jones Jr. to Charles C. Jones, September 27, 1862, in Robert Manson Myers, ed., *The Children of Pride: A True Story of Georgia and the Civil War* (New Haven: Yale University Press, 1972), 966–67.

21. Lucy Rebecca Buck, *Shadows on My Heart: The Civil War Diary of Lucy*

Rebecca Buck of Virginia, ed. Elizabeth R. Baer (1940; revised reprint, Athens: University of Georgia Press, 1997), 151 [entry for September 19, 1862]; Dolly Lunt Burge, *The Diary of Dolly Lunt Burge,* ed. James I. Robertson Jr. (Athens: University of Georgia Press, 1962), 82 [entry for September 29, 1862]; Sarah Morgan, *The Civil War Diary of Sarah Morgan,* ed. Charles East (1913; revised reprint, Athens: University of Georgia Press, 1991), 293 [entry for October 4, 1862]; Susan Leigh Blackford and Charles Minor Blackford, eds., *Memoirs of Life in and out of the Army in Virginia during the War between the States,* 2 vols. (1894; reprint, Lynchburg, Va.: Warwick House, 1996), 1:217.

22. Fanny Hume, *The Fanny Hume Diary of 1862: A Year in Wartime Orange, Virginia,* ed. J. Randolph Grymes Jr. (Orange: Orange County Historical Society, 1994), 151 [entry for September 20, 1862]; Faye Acton Axford, ed., *"To Lochaber Na Mair":* *Southerners View the Civil War* (Athens, Ala.: Athens Publishing Company, 1986) [Fielding diary entry for September 28, 1862]; Amanda Virginia Edmonds, *Journals of Amanda Virginia Edmonds: Lass of the Mosby Confederacy, 1859–1867,* ed. Nancy Chappelear Baird (Stephens City, Va.: by the editor, 1984), 116 [entry for September 16, 1862]; Anne S. Frobel, *The Civil War Diary of Anne S. Frobel of Winton Hill in Virginia,* ed. Mary H. Lancaster and Dallas M. Lancaster (Birmingham, Ala.: by the editors, 1986), 70.

23. Betty Herndon Maury, *The Civil War Diary of Betty Herndon Maury (June 3, 1861–February 18, 1863),* ed. Robert A. Hodge (Fredericksburg, Va.: by the editor, 1985), 69–70; [Judith W. McGuire], *Diary of a Southern Refugee during the War* (1867; reprint, Lincoln: University of Nebraska Press, 1995), 157 [entry for September 25].

24. Elijah P. Petty, *Journey to Pleasant Hill: The Civil War Letters of Captain Elijah P. Petty, Walker's Texas Division, C.S.A.,* ed. Norman D. Brown (San Antonio: Institute of Texas Cultures, 1982), 87; Edwin H. Fay to his wife, September 26, 1862, in Edwin H. Fay, *This Infernal War: The Confederate Letters of Sgt. Edwin H. Fay,* ed. Bell Irvin Wiley (Austin: University of Texas Press, 1958), 162; Benjamin M. Seaton, *The Bugle Softly Blows: The Confederate Diary of Benjamin M. Seaton,* ed. Harold B. Simpson (Waco, Tex.: Texian Press, 1965), 23–24 [entry for September 29, 1862].

25. Blackford and Blackford, *Memoirs of Life in and out of the Army,* 1:218 [William M. Blackford diary, October 14, 1862]; John B. Jones, *A Rebel War Clerk's Diary, at the Confederate States Capital,* 2 vols. (1866; reprint, Alexandria, Va.: Time-Life, 1982), 1:172 [entry for October 17, 1862].

26. Jane Howison Beale, *The Journal of Jane Howison Beale of Fredericksburg, Virginia, 1850–1862,* ed. Barbara P. Willis (Fredericksburg, Va.: Historic Fredericksburg, 1979), 64 [entry for October 4, 1862]; Ada W. Bacot, *A Confederate Nurse: The Diary of Ada W. Bacot, 1860–1863,* ed. Jean V. Berlin (Columbia: University of South Carolina Press, 1994), 149–50 [entry for September 21, 1862]; Kate Stone, *Brokenburn: The Journal of Kate Stone, 1861–1868,* ed. John Q. Anderson (Baton Rouge:

Louisiana State University Press, 1955), 146 [entry for October 2, 1862]. For another example of anti-Maryland sentiment, see Susan Middleton to Harriett Middleton, September 20, 1862, in Isabella Middleton Leland, ed., "Middleton Correspondence, 1861–1865," *South Carolina Historical Magazine* 63 (July 1962): 172.

27. Charles C. Jones to Charles C. Jones Jr., October 2, 1862, in Myers, *Children of Pride,* 972.

28. Benjamin Fleet to Alexander F. Fleet, October 12, 1862, in Betsy Fleet and John D. P. Fuller, eds., *Green Mount: A Virginia Plantation Family during the Civil War, Being the Journal of Benjamin Robert Fleet and Letters to His Family* (Lexington: University of Kentucky Press, 1962), 174; Edmondston, *Journal,* 277 [entry for October 18, 1862]; Josiah Gorgas, *The Journals of Josiah Gorgas, 1857–1878,* ed. Sarah Woolfolk Wiggins (Tuscaloosa: University of Alabama Press, 1995), 53–54 [entries for October 4, 17, 1862].

29. Blackford and Blackford, *Memoirs of Life in and out of the Army,* 1:225 [William M. Blackford diary entry for October 13, 1862]; Cornelia Peake McDonald, *A Woman's Civil War: A Diary, with Reminiscences of the War, from March 1862,* ed. Minrose C. Gwin (Madison: University of Wisconsin Press, 1992), 83 [entry for October 14, 1862]; Frobel, *Diary,* 73 [entry for September 27, 1862].

30. Jones, *Diary,* 1:157, 161–62 [entries for September 27, October 2, 1862].

31. John W. Stone to Julia A. Wood, September 22, 1862, in Margaret Williams Bayne, ed., *The Wood Family of Fluvanna County, Virginia, 1795–1969* (Norfolk, Va.: privately printed, 1984), 187–88; Jones, *Diary,* 1:164; McDonald, *Woman's Civil War,* 85.

32. W. C. Corsan, *Two Months in the Confederate States: An Englishman's Travels through the South,* ed. Benjamin H. Trask (Baton Rouge: Louisiana State University Press, 1996), 76–77.

33. Blackford and Blackford, *Memoirs of Life in and out of the Army,* 1:218, 225, 219 [entries for September 26, October 23, September 30]. For a representative comment about Van Dorn's defeat at Corinth, see Susan Emeline Jeffords Caldwell to Lycurgus Washington Caldwell, October 10, 1862, in John K. Gott and John E. Divine, eds., *"My Heart Is So Rebellious": The Caldwell Letters, 1861–1865* (Warrenton, Va.: Fauquier National Bank, n.d. [ca. 1992]), 157. "[O]f course you read of our defeat at Corinth—I was grieved to hear of it. Oh! that we could have peace to reign once again in our dear land and prosperity abound—the cloud seems to darken again over and around us—."

34. Robert Garlick Hill Kean, *Inside the Confederate Government: The Diary of Robert Garlick Hill Kean,* ed. Edward Younger (New York: Oxford University Press, 1957), 86 [entry for June 27, 1863]. Kean commented on Davis's post-Sharpsburg state of mind in the context of the president's pessimistic attitude in the early summer of 1863: "Judge [John A.] Campbell told me this morning that a member of the Cabinet

and an intimate friend of the President told him that Mr. Davis *despairs* of success in our struggle. . . . He is liable to exultation and depression."

35. G. W. C. Lee to Jefferson Davis, September 25, 1862, in Jefferson Davis, *The Papers of Jefferson Davis,* ed. Lynda Lasswell Crist and others, 9 vols. (Baton Rouge: Louisiana State University Press, 1971–), 8:405–6.

36. Jefferson Davis to Robert E. Lee, September 28, 1862, in Davis, *Papers,* 8: 408–9. On September 30, 1862, the Charleston *Mercury* leveled the latest in a series of blasts at what it perceived to be the president's overly defensive strategy: "Our readers are aware that, from the commencement of the existing war, we have condemned the inactive defensive policy of the Administration, and have advocated an active aggressive policy in carrying it on. . . . We are rejoiced now to find that the overwhelming majority of the popular branch of Congress approve of the policy we so early advocated, and which exposed us to some unmerited obloquy."

37. On the Confederate reaction to Gettysburg, see Gary W. Gallagher, "Lee's Army Has Not Lost Any of Its Prestige: The Impact of Gettysburg on the Army of Northern Virginia and the Confederate Home Front," in *The Third Day at Gettysburg and Beyond,* ed. Gary W. Gallagher (Chapel Hill: University of North Carolina Press, 1994). For criticism of Lee's decision to hold the field on the 18th, see Gallagher, "Maryland Campaign in Perspective," 89.

38. John E. Fisher, ed., "The Travels of the 13th Mississippi Regiment: Excerpts from the Diary of Mike M. Hubert of Attala County (1861–1862)," *Journal of Mississippi History* 45 (November 1983): 309 [entries for September 17, 18, 1862]; Edward Willis to uncle, October 4, 1862, drawer 71, box 76 (microfilm), Georgia Department of Archives and History, Atlanta; Daniel Lane, Diary, typescript provided by Robert E. L. Krick; letter from "Valley" [probably a member of the 56th Virginia Infantry], September 20, 1862, printed in Richmond *Daily Enquirer,* September 25, 1862; Taliaferro N. Simpson to Anna Talullah Simpson, September 24, 1862, in Guy R. Everson and Edward H. Simpson Jr., eds., *Far, Far from Home: The Wartime Letters of Dick and Tally Simpson, 3rd South Carolina Volunteers* (New York: Oxford University Press, 1994), 150. For other similar testimony, see Charles E. Denoon to his father, September 25, 1862, in Charles E. Denoon, *Charlie's Letters: The Civil War Letters of Charles E. Denoon,* ed. Richard T. Couture (Collingswood, N.J.: Civil War Historicals, 1989), 28, and James A. Graham to his father, September 29, 1862, in James A. Graham, *The James A. Graham Papers, 1861–1864,* ed. H. M. Wagstaff (Chapel Hill: University of North Carolina Press, 1928), 132.

39. Mills Lane, ed., *"Dear Mother: Don't grieve about me. If I get killed, I'll only be dead." Letters from Georgia Soldiers in the Civil War* (Savannah, Ga.: Beehive Press, 1977), 190; Ujanirtus Allen to his wife, September 23, 1862, in Ujanirtus Allen, *Campaigning with "Old Stonewall": Confederate Captain Ujanirtus Allen's Letters to His Wife,* ed. Randall Allen and Keith S. Bohannon (Baton Rouge: Louisiana State Uni-

versity Press, 1998), 165; letter from "A. B. C.," September 24, 1862, printed in Richmond *Weekly Dispatch,* September 30, 1862; Greenlee Davidson to his mother, September 19, 1862, in Greenlee Davidson, *Captain Greenlee Davidson, C.S.A.: Diary and Letters, 1851–1863,* ed. Charles W. Turner (Verona, Va.: McClure Press, 1975), 54.

40. Roswell S. Ripley to P. G. T. Beauregard, September 29, 1862, in Ripley's General and Staff Compiled Service Record, M331, roll 212, National Archives, Washington; Shepherd G. Pryor to his wife, September 23, 1862, in Shepherd G. Pryor, *A Post of Honor: The Pryor Letters, 1861– 63; Letters from Capt. S. G. Pryor, Twelfth Georgia Regiment and His Wife, Penelope Tyson Pryor,* ed. Charles R. Adams Jr. (Fort Valley, Ga.: Garret Publications, 1989), 262; William B. Pettit to his wife, September 20, 1862, in Charles W. Turner, ed., *Civil War Letters of Arabella Speairs and William Beverly Pettit of Fluvanna County, Virginia, March 1862 –March 1865,* 2 vols. (Roanoke: Virginia Lithography and Graphics, 1988), 1: 54–55.

41. John Hampden Chamberlayne to Lucy Parke Chamberlayne, September 22, 1862, in John Hampden Chamberlayne, *Ham Chamberlayne—Virginian: Letters and Papers of an Artillery Officer in the War for Southern Independence, 1861–1865,* ed. C. G. Chamberlayne (Richmond, Va.: Dietz, 1932), 110–12; Nicholas A. Davis, *The Campaign from Texas to Maryland, with the Battle of Fredericksburg* (1863; reprint, Austin, Tex.: Steck Co., 1961), 93; Edward J. Jones to his brother, October 6, 1862, in Georgia Division of the United Daughters of the Confederacy, *Confederate Reminiscences and Letters, 1861–1865,* 8 vols. to date (Atlanta: Georgia Division of the UDC, 1995 –), 5: 203; James E. Keever to Alexander Keever, October 2, 1862, in Elsie Keever, ed., *Keever Civil War Letters* (Lincolnton, N.C.: by the editor, 1989), 9.

42. Walter H. Taylor to Mary Louisa Taylor, September 21, 1862, in Walter H. Taylor, *Lee's Adjutant: The Wartime Letters of Colonel Walter H. Taylor, 1862–1865,* ed. R. Lockwood Tower (Columbia: University of South Carolina Press, 1995), 44 – 45.

43. Elisha F. Paxton to Elizabeth Paxton, October 12, 1862, in Elisha Franklin Paxton, *The Civil War Letters of General Frank "Bull" Paxton, CSA. A Lieutenant of Lee & Jackson,* ed. John Gallatin Paxton (Hillsboro, Tex.: Hill Jr. College Press, 1978), 58; Ujanirtus Allen to Susan Fuller Allen, September 21, 1862, in Allen, *Campaigning with "Old Stonewall,"* 164 – 65; Benjamin Franklin Jones to W. Sanford Jones, November 1, 1862, in Georgia Division UDC, *Confederate Reminiscences and Letters,* 5: 204.

44. S. M. Crawford to his wife, October 22, 1862, in South Carolina Division of the United Daughters of the Confederacy, *Recollections and Reminiscences, 1861–1865 through World War I,* 9 vols. to date (n.p.: South Carolina Division, UDC, 1990 –), 2: 189; Jesse Steed McGee to My dear Mollie, September 24, 1862, in E. D. Sloan, ed., *McGee-Charles Family Papers (1852 –1924)* (Greenville, S.C.: by the editor, [1996]), 58; Walter Battle to his mother, September 29, 1862, in Walter Raleigh Battle, "The Confederate Letters of Walter Raleigh Battle of Wilson, North Carolina," ed. Hugh Buck Johnston (Wilson, N.C.: typescript by the editor, ca. 1977), unpaginated [letters arranged chronologically]; [An English Combatant], *Battle-Fields of the South, from*

Bull Run to Fredericksburgh: With Sketches of Confederate Commanders and Gossip of the Camps [1864; reprint, Alexandria, Va.: Time-Life, 1984), 492–93.

45. Tia Atwood, ed., *Prologue: Portrait of a Family* ([Enis, Tex.]: by the editor, 1980[?]), 105; William H. S. Burgwyn, *A Captain's War: The Letters and Diaries of William H. S. Burgwyn, 1861–1865,* ed. Herbert M. Schiller (Shippensburg, Pa.: White Mane, 1994), 20 [entries for September 20, 21, 1862]; Fisher, "Travels of the 13th Mississippi," 310; Sanford W. Branch to his mother, September 23, 30, 1862, in Mauriel Phillips Joslyn, ed., *Charlotte's Boys: Civil War Letters of the Branch Family of Savannah* (Berryville, Va.: Rockbridge Publishing Co., 1996), 132–33; Ansel Sterne to Dear Friend, September 28, 1862, in William H. Davidson, ed., *War Was the Place: A Centennial Collection of Confederate Letters* (n.p.: Chattahoochee Valley Historical Society, Bulletin 5 [November 1961]), 73–74; William J. Evers to his wife, September 30, 1862, in Georgia Division UDC, *Confederate Reminiscences and Letters,* 6:207.

46. James P. Crowder to his mother, October 5, 1862, in Ray Mathis, ed., *In the Land of the Living: Wartime Letters by Confederates from the Chattahoochee Valley of Alabama and Georgia* (Troy, Ala.: Troy State University Press, 1981), 49; William Stillwell to his wife, September 18, 1862, in Lane, *Dear Mother,* 185.

47. Daniel Harvey Hill, whose division defended the Sunken Road at Antietam, later wrote about the "demoralized condition of the army" during the Maryland campaign. "No one not with our Army at that time & not cognizant of its deplorable condition," he stated in a revealing letter to Robert Lewis Dabney on July 19, 1864, could understand how vulnerable Lee's force had been in mid-September. (The letter is in the Robert Lewis Dabney Papers, Special Collections, Union Theological Seminary, Richmond, Va.)

48. Letter from "A Private," September 20, 1862, printed in Richmond *Enquirer,* October 14, 1862; William Dorsey Pender to Fanny Pender, September 19, 1862, in William Dorsey Pender, *The General to His Lady: The Civil War Letters of William Dorsey Pender to Fanny Pender,* ed. William W. Hassler (Chapel Hill: University of North Carolina Press, 1965), 175; Alexander Cheves Haskell to his parents, September 23, 1862, in Louise Haskell Daly, ed., *Alexander Cheves Haskell: The Portrait of a Man* (1934; reprint, Wilmington, N.C.: Broadfoot, 1989), 84.

49. Sanford W. Branch to his mother, September 30, 1862, in Joslyn, *Charlotte's Boys,* 133; Edgar Richardson to his mother, October 1, 1862, in Lane, *Dear Mother,* 192; Ujanirtus Allen to Susan Fuller Allen, in Allen, *Campaigning with "Old Stonewall,"* 165; James A. Graham to his mother, September 21, 1862, in Graham, *Papers,* 132.

50. John W. Hodnett to Miss Mary Hodnett, October 1, 1862, in Davidson, *War Was the Place,* 75; Thomas J. Goree to Sarah Williams Kittrell Goree, October 10, 1862, in Thomas J. Goree, *Longstreet's Aide: The Civil War Letters of Major Thomas J. Goree,* ed. Thomas W. Cutrer (Charlottesville: University Press of Virginia, 1995), 99; Draughton Stith Haynes, *The Field Diary of a Confederate Soldier, Draughton Stith Haynes, While Serving with the Army of Northern Virginia C.S.A.,* ed. William G.

Haynes Jr. (Darien, Ga.: Ashantilly Press, 1963), 22 [entry for October 18, 1862]; Reuben A. Pierson to his father, October 26, 1862, in Thomas W. Cutrer and T. Michael Parrish, eds., *Brothers in Gray: The Civil War Letters of the Pierson Family* (Baton Rouge: Louisiana State University Press, 1997), 130–31.

51. Alexander S. Pendleton to his mother, October 8, 1862, quoted in William G. Bean, *Stonewall's Man: Sandie Pendleton* (Chapel Hill: University of North Carolina Press, 1959), 81; John William McLure to his wife, October 2, 1862, in Sarah Porter Carroll, ed., *Lifeline to Home for John William McLure, CSA, Union County, S.C.* (Greenville, S.C.: A Press, 1990), 108.

52. Walter H. Taylor to Mary Louisa Taylor, September 21, 1862, in Taylor, *Lee's Adjutant,* 45; William R. Montgomery to his brother, October 4, 1862, in William R. Montgomery, *Georgia Sharpshooter: The Civil War Diary and Letters of William Rhadamanthus Montgomery, 1839–1906,* ed. George Montgomery Jr. (Macon, Ga.: Mercer University Press, 1997), 72; Jesse S. McGee to My dear Mollie, September 24, 1862, in Sloan, *McGee-Charles Family Papers,* 59; letter from an unidentified officer in the 1st Georgia Regular Infantry, September 23, 1862, printed in Macon *Daily Telegraph,* October 1, 1862.

53. On Lee's reputation in 1862, see Gary W. Gallagher, "The Idol of His Soldiers and the Hope of His Country," in Gary W. Gallagher, *Lee and His Generals in War and Memory* (Baton Rouge: Louisiana State University Press, 1998). For the argument that many soldiers considered Lee to be a stand-in for Johnston, see William Garrett Piston, "Lee's Tarnished Lieutenant: James Longstreet and His Image in American Society," 2 vols. (Ph.D. diss., University of South Carolina, 1982), 1:175–76.

54. John W. Harrison to his mother, September 9, 1862, Confederate Miscellany, IA, folder 3, Robert Woodruff Library, Emory University, Atlanta, Ga.; letter signed "G," October 16, 1862, printed in Athens (Ga.) *Southern Banner,* December 3, 1862; Theodore Fogle to his parents, September 28, 1862, in Lane, *Dear Mother,* 190; John Hampden Chamberlayne to his mother, September 22, 1862, Chamberlayne to Lucy Parke Chamberlayne, October 13, 1862, in Chamberlayne, *Ham Chamberlayne,* 114, 125–26.

55. William Dorsey Pender to Fanny Pender, September 7, October 24, 1862, in Pender, *General to His Lady,* 173, 185; William Nelson Pendleton to My Darling Wife, September 28, 1862, William Nelson Pendleton Papers, Southern Historical Collection, Wilson Library, University of North Carolina, Chapel Hill. For other criticism of Lee, see Kean, *Inside the Confederate Government,* 91. On August 13, 1863, Kean compared Lee's conduct at Gettysburg with that at Sharpsburg: "The fact stands broadly out that, as at Sharpsburg, the enemy were more vigorous than he calculated and were amongst his troops before he was aware of their near approach."

56. James W. Lineberger to his wife, in James Wellington Lineberger, *Letters of a Gaston Ranger: 2nd Lt. James Wellington Lineberger, Company H, 49th North Caro-*

lina Regiment, Ransom's Brigade, C.S.A., ed. Hugh Douglas Pitts (Richmond, Va.: by the editor, 1991), 23; Shepherd G. Pryor to his wife, in Pryor, *Post of Honor,* 269; John Hampden Chamberlayne to Lucy Parke Chamberlayne, in Chamberlayne, *Ham Chamberlayne,* 125.

57. Lee's report of the Sharpsburg campaign, in Robert E. Lee, *The Wartime Papers of R. E. Lee,* ed. Clifford Dowdey and Louis H. Manarin (Boston: Little, Brown, 1961), 312–13. Dated August 19, 1863, Lee's report succinctly lays out his reasons for invading Maryland. See also William Allan, "Memoranda of Conversations with General Robert E. Lee," in *Lee the Soldier,* ed. Gary W. Gallagher (Lincoln: University of Nebraska Press, 1996), 13, for Lee's postwar summary of the Sharpsburg campaign.

58. R. E. Lee to George W. Randolph, October 8, 1862, Randolph to Lee, October 8, 1862, in U.S. War Department, *The War of the Rebellion: A Compilation of the Official Records of the Union and Confederate Armies,* 127 vols., index, and atlas (Washington: GPO, 1880–1901), ser. 1, vol. 19, pt. 2:656–57 (hereafter cited as *OR;* all references are to ser. 1).

59. For Lee's requests for supplies, see his letters to Jefferson Davis on September 21, to Quartermaster General A. C. Myers on September 21, to Secretary of War George W. Randolph on September 21, to Davis on September 23, 28, to Randolph on September 29, 30, and to Davis on September 30, in *OR* 19(1):142–43, (2):614, 622–23, 633, 637, 643–44.

60. R. E. Lee to Jefferson Davis, September 21, 1862, R. H. Chilton to Generals Longstreet and Jackson, September 22, 1862, Lee to George W. Randolph, September 23, 1862, in *OR* 19(1):143, (2):618, 622. William Dorsey Pender joined Lee in excoriating soldiers who plundered. He informed his wife on September 19 that his men had "lost all honor or decency, all sense of right or respect for property. I have had to strike many a one with my saber." Pender, *General to His Lady,* 175.

61. Lee, *Wartime Papers,* 299–300 (text of the proclamation); Robert E. Lee to George W. Randolph, September 30, Lee to Jefferson Davis, October 2, 1862, in *OR* 19(2):636–37, 644.

62. *OR* 19(1):142–43; (2):622, 626–27.

63. Robert E. Lee to Gustavus W. Smith, September 24, 1862, in *OR* 19(2):624–25.

64. Walter H. Taylor to Mary Louisa Taylor, September 28, 1862, in Taylor, *Lee's Adjutant,* 45–46. For typical descriptions of tearing up railroads, see Ujanirtus Allen to his wife, October 24, 1862, in Allen, *Campaigning with "Old Stonewall,"* 176; Capt. H. W. Wingfield's diary entries for October 18–29, 1862, in W. W. Scott, ed., *Two Confederate Items* (Richmond: Virginia State Library, 1927), 18; and Joseph Head to Luckie Head, October 29, 1862, in Georgia Division UDC, *Confederate Reminiscences and Letters,* 6:232.

65. Robert E. Lee to Jefferson Davis, September 21, 1862, in *OR* 19(1):143.

66. General Orders No. 116, dated October 2, 1862, in *OR* 19(2):644–45.

BROOKS D. SIMPSON

General McClellan's Bodyguard

The Army of the Potomac

after Antietam

As night fell across the fields and farms surrounding Sharpsburg, Maryland, on September 17, 1862, officers and men of the Army of the Potomac who had survived that day's bloody work paused to reflect on what they had endured. Brig. Gen. Marsena R. Patrick, whose brigade of New Yorkers had battled across David Miller's cornfield that morning, surveyed the battlefield with Brig. Gen. Oliver O. Howard, only recently recovered from his wound at Seven Pines. Patrick judged the day's battle "one of the severest ever fought" and remarked on the dead bodies that covered the ground. It was not clear what the morrow would bring. No one knew if the slaughter would lead to anything. But Patrick offered posterity a glimpse into what he expected when he commenced his diary entry for September 18: "We were not attacked last night, & this morning Sumner told me that McClellan's orders were '*not* to attack' & if possible have re-inforcements come up—It seems to be fairly understood, that only Madcaps, of the Hooker stripe, would have pushed our troops into action again without very strong re-inforcements—We had all that we could do to hold our ground yesterday & if we had attempted to push the enemy, today, with the same troops, we should have been whipped." Tomorrow, reinvigorated by rest and reinforcements, would be the day to push ahead.

During the 18th, Patrick learned that a good friend, Col. Henry W. Kingsbury, had fallen while directing the men of the 11th Connecticut to advance against the Lower Bridge the previous day. "The loss of no one has affected me so deeply," Patrick mourned. "He was a noble fellow! His poor Mother will feel that life is now valueless." Kingsbury's ghost haunted the brigade commander that night as he struggled to sleep. "I prayed much of the night—prayed for my country—prayed for my children—prayed for myself—It was a night of wrestling with God—Did he hear?" Dawn came, bringing news that the Confederates were nowhere to be found. Eventually Patrick received orders to march, but after a series of stops and starts his men covered less than two miles before setting up camp for the night in an open woods. Patrick slept well that night.[1]

Patrick's experience is revealing to students of the operations of the Army of the Potomac during and after the Antietam campaign. Recent scholarship has reemphasized the army's failure to build on what it had gained on September 17 by dealing a death blow to Robert E. Lee's Army of Northern Virginia. "The salient feature of the entire Maryland campaign . . . was McClellan's opportunity to inflict a catastrophic defeat on Lee's army," observed Gary W. Gallagher, summarizing the conventional wisdom, in 1989. "No other commander on either side during the Civil War enjoyed a comparable situation." Nowhere was this opportunity more evident than on September 18: "But once again McClellan lacked the fortitude to let his loyal soldiers seek complete victory. . . . The Army of the Potomac possessed the requisite elements to deliver the fatal blow."[2] But did it? Was the Union failure to close out the war in the East in September and October 1862 simply attributable to the shortcomings of its commander? Or was there something deeper, more problematic about that army's psychology, that, whatever McClellan's contributions to shaping it, transcended him?

Considerable evidence suggests that in the seven weeks between Antietam and McClellan's removal from command the qualities of hesitation, intrigue, and wariness toward civil superiors epitomizing the general were characteristic of his army as a whole. If T. Harry Williams is correct in labeling McClellan "the problem child of the Civil War," perhaps it is only fair to add that the Army of the Potomac remains the problem army of the Civil War. Certainly Bruce Catton erred in titling the first volume of his trilogy on that organization *Mr. Lincoln's Army,* unless he did so with tongue in cheek, for to some extent it always remained General McClellan's army. John Pope discovered as much during the Second Manassas campaign and claimed that the failure of McClellan's generals to cooperate with him contributed decisively to that campaign's sad outcome (this also conveniently concealed Pope's own bumbling). Some two years later, Ulysses S. Grant would also learn what it was like to be an outsider when he traveled east to oversee the army's operations while at the same time assuming the responsibilities of general-in-chief. By then changes in personnel meant that a good number of the soldiers who had served under McClellan were no longer with the army, and the majority of the men who voted in 1864 cast their ballots for Lincoln. That did not surprise one western general who visited Grant's headquarters: "The men are right in sentiment, though many leading officers are McClellanized."[3] The distinction was important. To a large extent the officer corps of the Army of the Potomac was as much a reflection as it was the creation of the army's first commander.

Perhaps McClellan impressed on his army the peculiar qualities of his personality and character, but it would be wrong to hold him entirely responsible for the attitudes of his officers and soldiers. Rather, many of his men shared his perspectives toward war and politics. A good number of them demurred on the question of whether to renew the attack on September 18, and more than a few actually expected Lee to strike back. Nor was there much dissent expressed about the army's failure to launch a vigorous pursuit. During the next seven weeks, many generals, officers, and enlisted men complained about the pressure placed on them by the public, press, and president to do something. It was not unusual to hear that the army had become the plaything of politicians, editors, and other incompetents. Strong political overtones surfaced in the army's response to Lincoln's preliminary emancipation proclamation and to McClellan's removal on the heels of the fall elections. It is worth noting that other major Union field armies experienced their share of friction and internal rivalries. In the Army of the Tennessee, for example, the presence of generals who were politicians or had close political connections shaped relations among its leading officers. But no one ever expressed concern that any Union force except the Army of the Potomac might actually march on Washington to protest administration decisions, or worried that any other army's leadership conspired to thwart the administration's prosecution of the war. If the problem with the Army of the Potomac resided merely with George B. McClellan, it would be easy to remedy; however, many Republicans and others in the North suffered anxious doubts precisely because the problem extended far beyond army headquarters.

One might excuse Marsena Patrick and his fellow officers and men for their hesitation to renew the offensive on September 18. Few soldiers in the Army of the Potomac had ever seen anything resembling the battlefield at Antietam. The area stretching from the Miller Cornfield to the Bloody Lane proved especially disturbing. Rufus Dawes of the 6th Wisconsin characterized the scene as "indescribably horrible," the worst of the war. Untold others agreed. "The slaughter upon both sides is enormous," Lt. Frank A. Haskell of the newly christened Iron Brigade told the folks back home in Wisconsin. "All hands agree that before they had never seen such a fearful battle," affirmed Haskell. "I hope you may never have occasion to see such a sight as it is. I will not attempt to tell you of it." Brig. Gen. Alpheus S. Williams, interim commander of the Twelfth Corps, was staggered by the number of dead bodies he encountered in riding over the field. William H. Powell, viewing bodies so black that they might be mistaken for African Americans, turned away from the "marred and bloated remains" and concluded that "this was war in all its hideousness." A Connecticut soldier, recalling the horrors of the battlefield after the sun set on September 17, remarked, "Of all gloomy nights, this was the saddest we ever experienced."[4]

What the officers and men of the Army of the Potomac experienced that night and the following day was indeed unusual. Because while most of the army was composed of combat-hardened regiments, few veterans had previously found the opportunity to explore a battlefield immediately after fighting ceased. In most of its earlier engagements—including the recent battles of Second Manassas and South Mountain—the army had either retreated or, less frequently, advanced immediately after the struggle. McClellan's decision to remain in place along Antietam Creek meant that his soldiers saw up close the carnage resulting from the war's bloodiest single day of combat. The experience stayed with them. Although the Army of the Potomac would see action on many another battlefield, its veterans invariably singled out as especially memorable what they saw, heard, and smelled on the night of September 17 and the following days.

If many observers found the sight of mangled corpses repulsive, they nonetheless were encouraged by the fact that a large proportion of the grotesque forms wore gray uniforms. The vast majority of McClellan's men believed that they had more than held their own against Lee's veterans on September 17, and a good number declared that they had won a victory. "We feel that a death blow has been given the rebel army of Virginia," a private enthused, adding that at last the Confederates "found that they are not invincible." George W. Whitman of the 51st New York, one of the two regiments that had taken what was to become known as Burnside's Bridge, agreed. "[A]s near as I can find out the rebels have been terribly cut up within the past few days," wrote the New Yorker. He added that Confederate prisoners, confessing that "the late raid into Md. was a desperate thing," offered that "they had to do something as they were in such a bad fix in Virginia that the war will soon have to be brought to a close." Oliver W. Norton, a private

Civilians gawk at Antietam's human wreckage while northern burial
parties labor to clean up the battlefield.
Frank Leslie's Illustrated Newspaper, October 18, 1862

in the 83rd Pennsylvania, cheered, "The victory is ours, and the enemy took advantage of an armistice granted them to bury the dead and care for the wounded, to ingloriously retreat across the river."[5]

McClellan's men debated the need for additional Union attacks. Few had the stomach to contemplate an immediate renewal of operations; only in hindsight did some second-guess McClellan. "Now that it is all over you will hear that we ought to have advanced the next day," observed staff officer Alexander S. Webb. "Well I say that myself but no one thought so at the time." George G. Meade, commanding the First Corps in place of the wounded Joseph Hooker, told his wife that "our army was a good deal broken and demoralized—so much so that it was deemed hazardous to risk an offensive movement" until reinforcements arrived.[6]

Lee's departure changed matters. General Williams anticipated the commencement of a new campaign: "If it goes on with the same bloody issues as the past two weeks have seen, there will be nothing left from privates to generals."[7] Learning that Lee had recrossed the Potomac, Lt. Elisha H. Rhodes exclaimed, "Thank God Maryland is clear and free from the Rebel Army. The old Army of the Republic can fight after all, and I think that the Rebels found it out this time." Two days later, however, he added, "Oh, why did we not attack them and drive them into the river?" A few soldiers actually argued that they would not need to fight again. "The impression among our soldiers is that the war is finished," observed one New York private, who arrived just days after the battle. "They think the battle of Wednesday [September 17] the greatest of the war and decisive." That impression quickly dissipated. As September drew to a close, the New Yorker noted that "everyone is surprised that McClellan does not move faster. We want to finish up everything before going into winter quarters"— of course, if everything was "finished up" there would be no need for winter quarters.[8]

Once it became clear that Lee had gone away only to fight another day, officers and men began to review the management of the battle in an effort to discover whether more could have been accomplished. Able at last to reflect on recent events, Alpheus Williams, with memories of his post-battle inspection still fresh in his mind, concluded that "we punished the Rebels severely in the last battle." But that did not satisfy him. Someone had blundered: "If McClellan's plan had been carried out with more coolness by some of our commanding generals, we should have grabbed half their army. But we threw away our power by impulsive and hasty attacks on wrong points." That it was the commanding general's responsibility to ensure that such things did not happen escaped Williams. "Our men fought gloriously and we taught the rascals a lesson, which they much needed after Pope's disaster," the general wrote. "They out-numbered us without doubt, and expected to thrash us soundly and drive us all pell mell back to Washington."[9]

After several weeks of gathering and weighing information, Charles S. Wainwright, Hooker's chief of artillery, concurred that any blame for failing to seize the opportunity presented at Antietam lay in the fumbling execution of McClellan's plan by his subordinates. Hooker had blundered by precipitating a skirmish on the evening of the 16th, then by oversleeping the following morning, and finally by advancing without waiting for Edwin V. Sumner's Second Corps to move into position—"an attempt to get all the glory himself." In turn, Sumner failed to deploy his men in timely fashion. "There seems to be no doubt that if McClellan's orders had been carried out," maintained Wainwright, "had Sumner been on time, and Hooker not too anxious to do it all himself, the attack would have been so complete a success that but little of the rebel army would have escaped." Finally, Burnside's inability to do anything until the afternoon allowed Lee to shift his men back and forth to check the piecemeal assaults. "Antietam was a victory, and a glorious one when you consider that but seventeen days before this army was running most disgracefully from the same troops over which they were now victorious," the artillerist concluded. "Why it was not a more complete victory

Marylanders in Frederick cheer McClellan as he leads his army in pursuit of the rebels
prior to Antietam. The battle did little to dim the heroic image of their commander
held by many officers in the Army of the Potomac.
Frank Leslie's Illustrated Newspaper, October 4, 1862

seems to me to be owing to the three cases of disobedience of orders on the part
of corps commanders, especially to Sumner." [10]

Not everyone agreed. Lt. Robert Gould Shaw, who participated in the advance
across the Miller Cornfield, was a bit bemused. "The result of the battle was, that
we remained in possession of the field, and the enemy drew off undisturbed," he
informed his father. "Whether that is all we wanted, I don't know; but I should
think not." Nevertheless, he was not anxious to hold McClellan responsible:
"[T]he enthusiasm of the troops for him is great, and that they will fight under
him better than under any one else, is proved by the difference between this battle
and those around Manassas." Perhaps, he conceded, "Little Mac" was not "a
very great general," but "he is the best we have." [11]

Joseph Hooker offered a typically vigorous opinion. Recovering from a wound suffered as he directed operations on the Union right during the battle's initial phase, Hooker freely voiced his belief that had he not been hit, "he could have driven the enemy into the river." The general also spoke harshly of McClellan's failure to renew the offensive on September 18. He was not alone in this. An officer in the 57th New York expressed astonishment that "the whole line was not engaged simultaneously." This man deplored the fact that the Union offensive followed "the old McClellan method of fighting in detail, one corps at a time, the rest of the army looking on." Although he judged the result a Union victory, he was surprised that McClellan did not renew the battle on the 18th: "Lee's army ought not to have gotten away so easily, but should have been pushed to the wall, and fought without mercy every day. From experience, however, we know that General McClellan is not equal to great occasions, and therefore it is useless to expect brilliant results while he is in command." Hooker's criticism might have carried more weight but for his reputation as a braggart who often deprecated the accomplishments of others. "I wish I could tell when Hooker is really speaking the simple truth," remarked Wainwright, "but he so universally finds fault with everybody, not under himself, that one can attach but little consequence to what he says. From what I can learn, nearly if not quite all our other generals expected Lee would make an attack on us yesterday. They say too that our men were used up, and that they could not have been got up to attack with any hope of success."[12]

Much of this exercise in hindsight was to be expected, as second-guessing is inherent in assessing military operations. A good number of officers and soldiers wondered why Lee was not decisively defeated on September 17 or brought to battle again on September 18–19; far fewer blamed McClellan for what happened. Oliver W. Norton, tired of press criticism directed at the army's commander, contemplated resorting to fisticuffs with the general's stay-at-home critics, admitting that he would "lay myself liable to indictments for assault and battery pretty often" if there were as many critics as he had been told. It would be far better if the folks at home left the fighting to the generals and the soldiers rather than to the editors and the politicians. General Meade concurred. "Now, if there is any common sense in the country," he observed, "it ought to let us have time to reorganize and get into shape our new lines, and then advance with such overwhelming numbers that resistance on the part of the enemy would be useless."[13]

On September 22, 1862, Abraham Lincoln issued a proclamation declaring that on January 1, 1863, he intended to free all slaves living in areas under Confederate control. The proclamation horrified McClellan. "I cannot make up my mind to fight for such an accursed doctrine as that of a servile insurrection—it is too infamous," he told his wife. He was finding it "almost impossible . . . to retain my commission & self respect at the same time," especially while Lincoln kept Edwin M. Stanton as secretary of war and Henry W. Halleck as general-in-chief. Little Mac also found repulsive Lincoln's September 24 declaration suspending the writ of habeas corpus, which "at one stroke of the pen" rendered the republic a "despotism." If anyone harbored doubts about supporting the cause, it was the commander of the Army of the Potomac. General William F. Smith, who loved to tell embarrassing stories about his superiors, later claimed that McClellan had drafted a letter of protest to the president, destroying it only after Smith opposed the idea. Although one might question Smith's account, McClellan had shared with Lincoln his opinions on civil policy when the president paid a visit to Harrison's Landing in July. It is not altogether unlikely that he contemplated doing it again.[14]

In later years much would be made of how officers and soldiers responded to news of the preliminary emancipation proclamation. Fitz John Porter, commander of the Fifth Corps and McClellan's close friend, informed Manton Marble, editor of the Democratic *New York World,* that "[t]he proclamation was ridiculed in the Army—caused disgust, discontent, and expressions of disloyalty to the views of the administration and amount, I have heard, to insubordination."[15]

The document undoubtedly sparked controversy, but not nearly as much as Porter and some later observers would suggest. Moreover, it would be a mistake to suppose that the response was overwhelmingly negative; far more soldiers questioned the measure's utility. One officer in the Iron Brigade reported that the proclamation took "well with the army here." General Williams, for one, "was prepared to sustain any measure" that "would help put an end to this cursed rebellion." "There is no fear, however, that slaves will be freed any faster than our troops get possession of Rebel territory, and this was the case before the proclamation," stated Williams. "I don't think matters are much changed by that document." Oliver Norton, who believed that McClellan would do his duty regardless of his political sentiments, approved of the proclamation but did not "think it is going to scare the South into submission." George Whitman agreed, pointing out that the president "has got to lick the south before he can free the niggers." Writing from the camps of the 2nd Massachusetts, Lieutenant Shaw, son of two abolitionists, concurred. "For my part, I can't see what *practical* good it can do now," he told his mother. "Wherever our army has been, there remain no slaves, and the Proclamation won't free them where we don't go. . . . I don't mean to say that it is not the right thing to do, but that, as a war measure, the evil will overbalance the good for the *present.*" In fact, believed Shaw, it might cause the Confederacy to intensify the war effort and make this "a war of extermination" by punishing Yankee prisoners. Wainwright, himself no advocate of emancipation (he thought it one of the Radical Republicans' "vile notions"), remarked that although he heard little discussion of the proposal, "all think it unadvised at this time; even those most anti-slavery." [16]

More problematic was the suspicion that politicians stood ready once more to interfere with military affairs. A meeting of northern state governors at Altoona, Pennsylvania, to discuss war measures provoked considerable alarm. Many of those who traveled to Altoona were unhappy with the Lincoln administration, in part because it was not earnest enough in striking against slavery. In issuing the preliminary proclamation, the president muffled criticism of his policy, but some soldiers were convinced that deeper forces were at work. They cursed "fearfully" over the assemblage of "Abolition" governors, aware that at least some of them desired McClellan's removal. "They believe with all their hearts in McClellan," one new recruit remarked of the men loyal to their commander, "and are unwilling to be slaughtered in the experiment of muddle headed politician generals." What would the politicians ask for next? The immediate resumption of military operations? Robert Shaw declared that "the army certainly needs rest," adding, "Heaven preserve us from a winter campaign!" Should editors continue to cry "On to Richmond," Shaw thought it would be best to let them "come down and try it themselves." [17]

There were sound reasons for a short-term delay. Immediately after the battle the army welcomed new regiments to the fold. It would take time to absorb them and commence their field training—and at these tasks McClellan reputedly excelled. "Gen. McClellan is an indefatigable officer in organization," noted Williams, who had thirteen rookie regiments to handle. "Nothing seems to escape his attention or his anticipation," wrote Williams approvingly. "Every endeavor is made, and constantly kept up, to enforce drill and discipline and to create an *esprit de corps* and confidence. I have met no officer at all his equal in this respect." [18]

Whatever the merits of pausing to train raw troops, within less than ten days after the battle a careful observer could detect the excuses that would be raised to justify inaction during the next five weeks. First was the issue of comparative army strengths. The impression prevailed in the army that the contending forces were at best "about equal," as Wainwright estimated it; others argued that Lee and his men significantly outnumbered Little Mac. Second was the army's need to be resupplied. Officers repeatedly complained that they were running short of essentials and that the replenishment promised by headquarters—or by Washington—had not materialized. This was the beginning of a long-term problem that plagued the army for the next six weeks. Richard B. Irwin, a staff officer, recalled that the army "needed nearly *everything* before beginning a fresh campaign of its own choice." In Irwin's eyes, the fault lay with the authorities in Washington, who wanted McClellan to take the offensive without providing him with the means to do so — or at least to succeed.[19]

If some of the officers and the men of the Army of the Potomac thus distrusted the government's willingness to send supplies needed to win on the battlefield, a growing number of administration officials were concerned that McClellan's subordinates had no intention of moving in any case. A comment by Maj. John M. Key, who worked in the War Department, gave plausibility to this impression. In conversation following the battle, Major Key responded to a query concerning McClellan's failure to pursue the rebels. Such a movement "is not the game," remarked Key, because it would run contrary to a plan to exhaust the resources of both sides as a prelude to a negotiated peace that would preserve slavery and reunite the Republic. Normally listeners would treat this as nothing more than an idle, if careless and rash, comment, but Key's brother, Col. Thomas M. Key, was on McClellan's staff. Maj. Levi C. Turner shared Key's response with others. For anyone predisposed to wonder about the Army of the Potomac's behavior, Key's conversation quickly raised questions about exactly what was going on. On the evening of September 25, Lincoln confided to his private secretary, John Hay, that "he had heard of an officer who had said they did not mean to gain a decisive victory but to keep things running so that they, the Army, might manage things to suit themselves." Lincoln stated further that he "should have the matter examined and if any such language had been used, his head should go off."[20]

The next day Lincoln wrote Key, asking him to confirm or deny the story in the presence of both the president and Major Turner. On September 27 the two officers appeared at the White House. Turner repeated his story, adding that he nevertheless believed Key was loyal to the Union. Key affirmed his loyalty but did not contradict Turner. A dissatisfied Lincoln ordered Key dismissed from the army, adding if there was any "game" being played "to have our army not take an advantage of the enemy when it could, it was his object to break up that game."[21]

That very day, after discussing the incident with Lincoln, Postmaster General Montgomery Blair decided to warn McClellan about Key. The president, he wrote, was deeply disturbed by Key's assertion that "the plan was to withhold your resources so that a compromise might be made which would preserve Slavery & the union at the same time." Both Blair and his father, the aged Francis Preston Blair, urged McClellan to accept emancipation as a product of the war, but the general ignored them. Instead he gathered several generals to discuss the matter, claiming that political advisers and army friends were asking him to come out in open opposition to the policy. It was a strange conversation, for those assembled immediately pointed out that if McClellan followed such advice, he would find himself in Key's shoes, accused of insubordination—if not treason. Besides, they added, any portrayal of the army as united in anger over the proclamation was clearly overdrawn, and precious few would support any formal protest. Backing down, McClellan sought to cover his tracks by saying that he would ponder what to do.[22]

Lincoln did not worry that McClellan would turn the army on Washington. The same hesitation that had sacrificed the fruits of victory at Antietam would suffice to safeguard the Republic. There was disgust and disdain but not concern in his observation that the general "was doing nothing to make himself either respected or feared." Yet Lincoln thought it best to see things for himself, and so on the morning of October 1 he headed toward Harpers Ferry, arriving at noon. McClellan joined him there in the afternoon to review soldiers. The next day Lincoln traveled north to visit McClellan's headquarters, where he alternated between conferring with the general and his corps commanders and visiting portions of the army. Wainwright was disappointed to see the "great Mogul" arrive in an army ambulance "with some half-dozen Western-looking politicians." The sight prompted the New York aristocrat to snarl: "Republican simplicity is well enough, but I should have preferred to see the President of the United States traveling with a little more regard to appearances than can be afforded by a common ambulance, with his long legs doubled up so that his knees almost struck his chin, and grinning out of the windows like a baboon. Mr. Lincoln not only is the ugliest man I ever saw, but the most uncouth and gawky in his manners and appearance." A private in the 20th Maine seemed equally unimpressed, reporting that "old Abe Lincoln was . . . [as] homely as a stump fence."[23]

The president toured the battlefield with McClellan as his guide. Perhaps he did not understand the slight to his host when he appeared less than attentive as the general pointed out the features of the field from his command post at the Pry House, but Lincoln made matters worse when he finally piped up, "Let us go and see where Hooker went in"—as if he wanted to explore in detail where a fighting general led his men, instead of remaining distant from the field with a commander who pretended to direct matters. That Hooker's criticisms of McClellan's handling of operations were well known served to increase Little Mac's ill-concealed annoyance with his superior. Even more frustrating, when McClellan and his escort arrived at the location of the Union right flank, the president had disappeared. McClellan dispatched one staff officer after another to find the errant chief executive; as dusk came, the general finally discovered that "Mr. Lincoln had suddenly changed his mind, and driven back to camp."[24]

Lincoln's behavior also annoyed other officers. Patrick noted that the entire

First Corps—none other than Hooker's command—had waited all afternoon to be reviewed. At last, John Reynolds, the new corps commander, and Meade attempted to "hunt up" the president, only to learn that after his abbreviated battlefield tour he had "ran away, in an Ambulance, & drove to Sharpsburg, without putting off the Review, or saying a word to McClellan." Four hours of waiting thus went for naught, and the men "marched hungry and thirsty back to camp." The president kept Hooker's heroes waiting the following day as well, finally arriving some four hours after he was scheduled to appear. His actions were inexcusable. Whatever his problems with McClellan, his erratic behavior was unfair to the soldiers, who expressed exasperation with such "damn *foolishness!*" [25]

Lincoln's actions left a bad impression with McClellan's supporters, although perhaps they were beyond influencing in any case. It is unclear exactly what the president sought to find out during his visit. Anything more than a cursory review of the army would have revealed that the men needed supplies, especially shoes and clothing, but Lincoln's later comments suggest that he was not concerned with such things. Although he allowed himself to be photographed with detective Allan Pinkerton, who helped provide McClellan with information that bolstered the general's extravagant estimates of Confederate numbers, the president made his own assessment of McClellan's strength, which he concluded exceeded 88,000 men (he excluded the Twelfth Corps from his estimate). [26]

Meade thought that Lincoln's purpose in paying a visit "was to urge McClellan on, regardless of his views, or the condition of the army. I think, however, he was informed of certain facts in connection with this army which have opened his eyes a little, and which may induce him to pause and reflect before he interferes with McClellan by giving positive orders." Alpheus Williams came away from a conversation with the chief executive rather pleased. "He really is the most unaffected, simple-minded, honest, and frank man I have ever met," Williams confided to his wife. "I wish he had a little more firmness, though I suppose the main difficulty with him is to make up his mind as to the best policy amongst the multitudes of advisers and advice." Williams thus distinguished between Lincoln the man and Lincoln the leader; perhaps, he concluded, Lincoln was not quite up to negotiating the disagreements between military leaders and politicians. [27]

Lincoln's visit to the front would later become the subject of political attack when Democrats claimed that he cracked jokes and asked others to sing merry songs as he passed by the site of the late battle. For many scholars, however, the most revealing moment of the visit came when Lincoln looked over the tents surrounding army headquarters early one morning. Illinois secretary of state Ozias Hatch, who cast his eye over the same scene, was surprised when Lincoln asked him what he saw. Why, responded a somewhat puzzled Hatch, he supposed it

Lincoln and McClellan confer during the president's visit to the Army
of the Potomac in early October 1862.
Library of Congress

was the Army of the Potomac. "No, you are mistaken," Lincoln replied; "that is General McClellan's bodyguard."[28]

Most scholars have interpreted the remark as a dig against McClellan, but in fact the comment applied just as truly to the entire army. The president sensed that he was not in altogether friendly territory. Bodyguards, after all, protect people from all threats. Lincoln's visit represented one of these threats; so, in a larger sense, did an anxious administration and the army's critics among Republican politicians and editors. Officers and men knew that McClellan's precarious standing with his superiors prior to Second Manassas had not improved appreciably because of what had happened in September. They knew as well that pompous John Pope, with his ideas of taking the war to the southern people, more closely fit Lincoln's idea of a general. They resented Pope for nearly destroying the army (or so its members thought) and for sacrificing McClellan's favorite volunteer brigade of New York Zouaves at Second Bull Run. From the president's perspective, his comment betrayed a sense of uneasiness that the army gave its primary loyalty to McClellan and not to the Republic, an understandable attitude in light of recent events, especially the Key incident.

The encounter between Lincoln and McClellan neither resolved their mutual distrust nor cleared up misunderstandings and miscommunication. McClellan believed that he had explained the problems he confronted in preparing to take the offensive, and he later claimed that Lincoln was willing to allow him time to prepare. Thus he must have been unnerved when just two days after the president left he received an unequivocal wire from General Halleck: "The President directs that you cross the Potomac and give battle to the enemy or drive him south. You must move now, while the roads are good." Obviously something had gone seriously awry, for the condition of the roads was irrelevant to an army whose soldiers lacked shoes. Had Lincoln not seen the condition of the men? Did he not understand the need to rest and refit?[29]

McClellan might have protested that Lincoln and his advisers were being unreasonable in their demands, but he found another way to strike back—a way that could serve only to increase the obstacles to cooperation between the capital and headquarters. The lack of soldiers' comment about the president's emancipation edict during his visit suggested that whatever controversy it had sparked, much of it had died down. Nor had the president heeded McClellan's advice to pursue "a conservative course" on the issue. In the wake of Halleck's October 6 telegram, McClellan decided to lash back. On October 7, after consultation with William H. Aspinwall, a businessman and Democratic supporter who advised the general on political matters, he issued General Orders No. 163, reminding his officers and men that they were to obey the decisions of civil authorities and that continued discussion of the wisdom of such measures served only "to impair and destroy the discipline and efficiency of troops. . . . The remedy for political errors, if any are committed, is to be found only in the action of the people at the polls." A copy of the order went to Lincoln, who knew, as did McClellan, that in a week voters would travel to the polls in Iowa, Ohio, Indiana, and Pennsylvania. Little Mac's sense of timing was deliberate and his message loud and clear: the army was not happy with emancipation, but the voters would have to do something about it.[30]

"Jeb" Stuart's Confederate cavalry soon blunted whatever force McClellan's message may have had. Stuart had decided it was time to ride around the Army of the Potomac again, and on October 10 his troopers crossed the Potomac, reaching Chambersburg, Pennsylvania, that night. The following day they destroyed stores and railroad equipment. That done, Stuart dashed back across the Potomac on October 12, completing his circuit around the befuddled Federals. The exploit embarrassed McClellan and angered Lincoln, who needed no such incident on the eve of the fall elections. Still, McClellan did not move; again he called for supplies, including remounts for his cavalry, which had struggled to corner Stuart. Betraying impatience, Lincoln offered a lengthy reply. Reminding McClellan that during their conference he had warned the general of his "over-cautiousness," the president asked: "Are you not over-cautious when you assume that you can not do what the enemy is constantly doing? Should you not claim to be at least his equal in prowess, and act upon the claim?" Lincoln then offered a series of observations on the military situation, each of which was designed to convince the general that he could achieve something, but only if he moved. "It is all easy if our troops march as well as the enemy," concluded Lincoln, "and it is unmanly to say they can not do it."[31]

Although Lincoln thought it was time for the army to do something, not everyone agreed. To be sure, some generals were beginning to have second thoughts. Writing of McClellan, George Meade observed, "I think myself he errs on the side of prudence and caution, and that a little more rashness on his part would improve his generalship." But Meade considered Stuart's raid to be more than an embarrassment. The rebel cavalry had destroyed "a large amount of clothing destined for this army, which the men are greatly in need of, and without which they can hardly move." Other commanders seemed content with what McClellan had achieved. "I hope we shall not have a second Antietam immediately," Alpheus Williams wrote, "unless the salvation of the Union depends upon it. I think we are fighting and have fought battles enough to save this Union, if they had been properly directed." Most officers and men welcomed the chance to refit and rest as they occupied the appropriately named Pleasant Valley, which nestled between

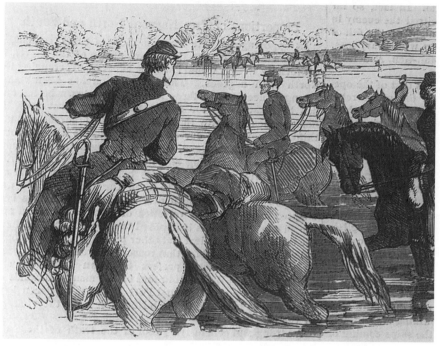

This northern engraving portrayed "Stuart's rebel cavalry, after their
successful raid into Pennsylvania."
Frank Leslie's Illustrated Newspaper, November 1, 1862

Elk Mountain and the South Mountain range just northeast of Harpers Ferry.
Some men pointedly noted that they lacked sufficient clothes, shoes, and blankets, but, asserted an optimistic Lieutenant Rhodes, "we do not complain, as it is
all for the Union." Rumors of battles and movements reverberated through the
ranks, but aside from efforts to check the progress of Jeb Stuart's cavalrymen as
they rode circles around the army, little happened. "We only half believe any
thing we hear down here, unless we see for ourselves," a new recruit noted. "Any
little thing serves to start great stories." [32]

"With all our efforts it seems almost impossible to get the troops into good condition for the field," Williams observed. "Old regiments are much reduced and
disordered, if not demoralized by loss of officers, by battle and disease. Majors
are commanding brigades and lieutenants, regiments. While this lasts an efficient
force cannot be made, and if we advance we shall soon retrograde." For the time
being, thought Williams, it was best to sit in place. "Yet I see by the newspapers
that an uneasy and impatient public are demanding an immediate advance," con-

tinued Williams. "[T]hese anxious souls know nothing of our preparations, nothing of the force or resources of the enemy. It would seem as if they thirsted for blood; for stirring accounts of great battles. No sooner is one story of bloody fights grown cold than the outcry is for another." A few days later, the general observed that "the public pressure is terrible" to do something. "The public knows nothing of our actual strength or preparation," he growled. "If we fail, that same dear public will howl our condemnation." [33]

The concern about refitting the army was justified. "There seems to be an unaccountable delay in forwarding supplies," Williams complained. "We want shoes and blankets and overcoats—indeed, almost everything." But nothing Williams could do hastened their arrival. "I see the papers speak of our splendid preparations. Crazy fools! I wish they were obliged to sleep, as my poor devils do tonight, in a cold, shivering rain, without overcoat or blanket," under a leaky tent; "I wish these crazy fools were compelled to march over these stony roads barefooted, as hundreds of my men must if we go tomorrow. When will civilians who know nothing of our preparation or the force and strength of the enemy learn to leave war matters to war men, who have means of knowing their duties, their capabilities, and their chances?" [34]

Other officers echoed such sentiments. "The papers, I see, are getting very impatient," Charles Wainwright sourly remarked, "and the old cry as to McClellan's slowness is again being raised. I was much surprised at first myself that we did not cross the river at once, but the more I know of the condition of the army, and other matters, the less certain does it appear that we could have done so to advantage." Once more supply shortages were to blame. Wainwright lacked sufficient ordnance, fresh horses, and even horseshoes. Although Meade recognized that McClellan's position was "most precarious," he added, "At the same time they do not, or will not, send from Washington the supplies absolutely necessary for us to have before we can move." His horses needed to be shod and fed; many of his men still lacked shoes. Meade insisted that "it is hard the army should be censured for inactivity, when the most necessary supplies for their movement are *withheld,* or at least not promptly forwarded when called for." [35]

Although some scholars have been all too willing to dismiss McClellan's complaints concerning supply shortages as part of an "old game" of delay, excuse, and procrastination, comments from officers such as Williams, Wainwright, and Meade suggest more than a maladjusted personal psychology at work. Commanders failed to make timely requisitions in anticipation of shortages; in turn, supply lines had become rather tangled, with matériel sitting untouched along the route between Washington and the army. None of this was a tribute to McClellan's reputation as a master of logistics and organization. Still, the general appeared more intent on complaining about circumstances than changing them. Once more it seemed as if he would not move until everything was just right.[36]

Officers and soldiers, smarting under the growing demands of the public and press to do something, snapped back that the folks at home and the politicians in Washington simply did not understand war. "The war will not end until the North wakes up," Rhodes asserted. "As it is now conducted it seems to me to be a grand farce. When certain politicians, Army contractors and traitors North are put out of the way, we shall succeed. General McClellan is popular with the Army, and we feel that he has not had a fair chance." Wainwright agreed. "The papers are full of reports of McClellan's removal, and I fear they will prove only too true," he observed. "His enemies are very bitter, and will see no good in him, though there is not a doubt that no other man in the country could have saved Washington last month." Perhaps Little Mac was no Napoleon, "but I do think he is head and shoulders above any other man we have."[37]

Here and there, however, appeared signs of impatience. "We ought to have force enough now, to go right ahead and balsmather the seceshers," Lieutenant Whitman argued. "I dont like the idea of fighting over the same ground three or four times but I suppose its all right." Joshua L. Chamberlain found it curious that "something seems to strike all the vigor out of our arms just at the point of victory." In a similar vein, Lt. Josiah Favill observed: "The Newspapers are getting anxious about another campaign, and it does look as though we were wasting valuable time, although none of us is particularly anxious for another fight."[38]

In late October, McClellan readied to move but remained concerned about the condition of his cavalry's mounts. He forwarded to Washington a complaint about weary horseflesh, as if to suggest that the supply problems he confronted were not a product of his imagination. What followed demonstrated that his problems with the president were quite real. At last unable to restrain himself, Lincoln issued a sarcastic retort: "Will you pardon me for asking what the horses of your army have done since the battle of Antietam that fatigues anything?" Patiently McClellan explained what his men had done, but Lincoln stood firm, observing that the Confederate cavalry had outperformed their counterparts in blue. The general defended his cavalry again; Lincoln finally backed down, although he made it clear that he was unhappy to hear that McClellan's horsemen needed fresh mounts after the army's "more than five weeks total inaction." Of the first Lincoln telegram, an angry McClellan said, "[I]t was one of those dirty little flings that I can't get used to when they are not merited." He was tired of "the mean & dirty character of the dispatches I receive." Such exchanges revealed that the relationship between Lincoln and McClellan had deteriorated to the break-ing point.[39]

Under such circumstance it was understandable that some soldiers questioned whether McClellan favored offensive operations. "We understand the present ad-vance has been ordered perëmptorily by the President, who is disgusted with McClellan's torpidity, and is bound to make him take the offensive," reported one New York officer. Rumors circulated that Lincoln was on the verge of removing McClellan. "The general has many friends in the army," noted one lieutenant, "who will be sorry to part with him, and even those of us who have no great faith in his abilities, are attracted to him through long association, and will feel the change, as another link broken in the chain of friendship, which, in the army, is highly developed." Civilians behind the lines simply could not understand an army's needs; politicians and editors played upon that ignorance in their unrea-sonable insistence that something be done immediately. "I wish those northern editors, who have been striving to poison the public mind against McClellan, had to sit in my present position to write their infamous editorials," one New York private grumbled. Matters looked far more complex when one was at the front. "No one is better pleased than myself with this advance, but human endurance has its bounds even in this soldier and they have been far overstepped by north-ern civilians when talking about a winter campaign." Charles H. Brewster, an officer in the 10th Massachusetts, agreed. The army lacked supplies; the men had just thrown away that day's rations of "wormy bread and stinking pork"; soldiers needed clothes and shoes. "I wish our dear friends at the North who have forced McClellan to move had to share our comforts with us," Brewster snarled. "I reckon that the US is about played out, as they cannot feed clothe or pay us, but it makes no difference if everyone that remains at home can get a political office."[40]

McClellan's advance proved time-consuming. It was not until November 2 that most of the army was across the Potomac. Lee shifted his men in response to the advance, so that by November 5 Longstreet's corps blocked the Union route to Richmond. If McClellan was eager to get between Longstreet and Jackson, who was still in the Shenandoah Valley, he showed little sign of it. Meade expressed confidence that in light of the superior strength of the Union army, "victory is sure to be ours."[41]

As dusk came on November 7, Charles Wainwright wondered about the out-come of the New York election three days earlier. That state's gubernatorial con-test pitted Democrat Horatio Seymour against Republican James S. Wadsworth, who held a major general's commission and was known to favor emancipation.

"A few days will now show whether they have been waiting until this election is over in order to remove McClellan." Wainwright and others would not have to wait even that long, for later that night Brig. Gen. Catharinus P. Buckingham arrived at army headquarters with orders relieving McClellan and naming Ambrose Burnside as his replacement. Secretary of War Stanton, who had hand-picked the general to perform this task, shared with him his concern about McClellan's patriotism and loyalty. In turn Buckingham exploited the divisiveness in the army's high command by warning Burnside that if he turned down the top spot, it would be offered to Joe Hooker.[42]

The orders Buckingham carried had their origin in a directive issued by Lincoln on November 5—the day after the fall elections. Although that very day the president had reassured a dissatisfied Illinois colonel (who had just been elected to Congress as a Democrat) that "in considering military merit, it seems to me that the world has abundant evidence that I discard politics," he had acted with an eye on the political calendar. Much would be made later of the fact that McClellan was finally advancing and that battle with Lee might soon be joined, but Lincoln had lost all faith in his general. Neither man trusted the other; both were all too willing to ascribe base motives to the other's actions. It is only fair to add that this state of affairs was not entirely due to McClellan. Indeed, there was good reason to question Lincoln's assessment of generals at this time, both his selection of the reluctant Burnside as McClellan's successor and his earlier endorsement of John A. McClernand's project to capture Vicksburg (a plan that was designed to promote McClernand at the expense of Ulysses S. Grant). Far less debatable was the president's October 24 decision to remove Don Carlos Buell from command of the Army of the Ohio, a move that should have placed McClellan on alert.[43]

"The Army is in mourning & this is a blue day for us all," Marsena Patrick sadly noted. "It is known that his removal was planned & to be carried into effect the moment the Elections were over—They did not dare to remove him before the Election." Other officers and soldiers quickly linked the timing of the removal to the political calendar, citing it as yet another example of improper interference in army affairs. Had Lincoln wanted to act on military grounds, observed George Meade, he could have sacked McClellan immediately after Antietam: "This removal now proves conclusively that the cause is political, and the date of the order, November 5 (the day after the New York election) confirms it." Others seconded this assessment. "There are those who insist that it is from incompetence that he has been removed," John Haley of the 17th Maine, a newcomer, observed. "But the soldiers, who are not so steeped in prejudice that they can see nothing but party, claim he had submitted to one reduction after another of his forces until he has a smaller army than Lee although we are the attacking party. The soldiers believe he has accomplished nothing short of a miracle in saving his army." A Pennsylvania infantryman feared the change would "cause much dissatisfaction in the army," adding, "I never saw men have so much confidence in a man as the soldiers have in McClellan." Other critics bluntly voiced their anger. "There is but one opinion upon this subject among the troops and that is the Government has gone mad," reported General John Gibbon, who had just ascended to division command. "It is the worse possible thing that could have been done and will be worth to the south as much as a victory." Few disagreed. "I think everyone in the army regrets it," Robert Shaw noted, "except, perhaps, some envious major-generals." [44]

In expressing regret over McClellan's removal, officers and men did not necessarily argue that he was a great general. Gibbon offered that the men "fight better under him than they do under anybody else"—although the only other general who had directed elements of the army in combat was John Pope. "Perhaps McClellan has too much of the Fabian policy," Alpheus Williams admitted, "but in judging of this one must not forget that he has been placed in circumstances where to lose the game would have been to lose all." Williams knew where to place the real blame: "My idea is that the cursed policy of this war has its origin at Washington. Old fogyism has ruled in every department. Trepidation for the safety of the Capital seems to have paralyzed all faculties of preparation and promptness." Robert Shaw manifested a similar attitude. "The newspapers and other jackasses can talk forever," he wrote home, "but I shall still be persuaded that it is our Government that has failed and not our Generals." [45]

To those officers and men who were critical of political interference, McClellan's removal offered ample confirmation of their belief that Abraham Lincoln was all too willing to make the army the puppet of partisan concerns. To remove the beloved general just as the army commenced an advance suggested just how much Republicans feared what a successful McClellan might do. "The general query is, why was he taken from us at such a time, if at all?" wondered one Wisconsin private. "The prevailing opinion among the officers and men is that the Administration is awfully inefficient, beside having no inclination to do that which would hasten the termination of the war." It was just more evidence that the politicians in charge could not be trusted. "This change produces much bitter feeling and some indignation," commented Elisha Rhodes. "McClellan's enemies will now rejoice, but the Army loves and respects him." But Rhodes would have nothing to do with any movement to keep the general in command: "Like loyal soldiers we submit." [46]

Not everyone was willing to submit. Some talked of turning the army against Washington, but McClellan, his nickname notwithstanding, proved to be no

Napoleon. To equate the demands for action with the Newburgh Conspiracy of the Revolutionary War is to go too far; Lincoln's frequent references to the possibility of mutiny revealed his deep distrust of the officer corps, an understandable but unworthy reaction. One must distinguish between these alarmist reactions and the very real discussions among line officers who were prepared to resign their commissions. Members of some of the army's best regiments counted themselves among the latter, including individuals in the 1st Minnesota and the Iron Brigade's 6th Wisconsin. It was not the prospect of emancipation as a war aim that sparked this response; it was a sense that the administration had played politics once too often with the army. Many officers and men who would have nothing to do with talk of resignation nevertheless agreed that the timing of McClellan's removal indicated that political pressures, not military concerns, explained Lincoln's decision. That it could be a decision undertaken for primarily military reasons but timed according to the political calendar escaped them. When regimental commanders got wind of the intentions of some of their subordinates, they did what they could to dissuade them, and in the end whatever threat existed of the army's dissolving dissipated, leaving only grumbling.[47]

George McClellan left his army as he had led it—deliberately. On November 9–10 he reviewed his command one last time. As the general rode past the long lines, most of the men cheered long and loud. Marsena Patrick, who observed that "the Troops love him with a devotion almost idolatry," called for them to cheer as McClellan reviewed the Provost Guard. Similar scenes occurred down the line, despite orders prohibiting such displays of affection. A private in McClellan's favorite volunteer regiment, the 5th New York, looked at the general, then "felt for the first time in a long while a decided sensation of enthusiasm burning in the ashes of my defunct patriotism." Brig. Gen. Thomas Meagher ordered the flag bearers of his Irish Brigade to fling down their banners as a vivid symbolic protest; McClellan directed them to pick them up, which served to endear him even more to the brigadier. "Ah!" he wrote Democratic adviser S. L. M. Barlow. "If the gentlemen of the White House could have seen what I saw this morning—could have heard the cheers from those 100,000 soldiers which rent the air and deadened the artillery itself as the parting salute was fired—they would have felt that a mistake or crime has been committed by them, which the Army of the Union will never forgive." Such comments—as well as the person to whom they were directed—suggest that a good number of the army's generals were already immersed in politics, perhaps too much so for their own good. Other observers drew a different lesson from the review. As one lieutenant, no fan of McClellan's, sadly observed, "The parade showed up a wonderfully fine looking body of men which, under a capable leader, could do almost anything."[48]

Artist Alfred A. Waud sketched McClellan, accompanied by his successor, Ambrose E. Burnside, waving his hat as he reviewed his troops in the field for the last time.
Library of Congress

Stories would circulate for years that McClellan discouraged efforts to protest his removal. Talk of a march on Washington was just that, nothing more, and in any case, in light of the army's past track record one wonders whether the dissenters would have soon found themselves explaining their failure to move against a superior opponent and expressing a preference for a spring campaign. Talk of mass resignations in several regiments posed a more serious threat. By staying around to participate in final reviews, McClellan allowed his men to vent their displeasure and cool off. Many officers and men remained bitter about the administration and the press, but they decided to stay and stick it out. Still, many of them smarted under the impression that they served in a "shamefully abused army." A member of the Iron Brigade remarked, "The last time Abraham visited his children, they gave him a very cool reception, but I venture the next will be more so."[49]

Circumstances reinforced the impression held by many officers that it was politics, not military performance, that led to Little Mac's removal. The train designated to take him away from the army had carried General James S. Wadsworth, Seymour's defeated rival, to camp. McClellan had devotedly hoped for the general's defeat, for he possessed a thorough "contempt for the man" and regarded him as "a vile traitorous miscreant." Wadsworth, whose abolitionist sentiments and closeness to Lincoln were known throughout the army, reported that he was going to advise the new army commander. "Well!" Patrick exclaimed in disgust. "Perhaps it is all right, but I think the Administration adds insult to injury." The next day Fitz John Porter took his leave of the army to answer charges of insubordination pressed by Pope; his replacement as Fifth Corps commander was none other than Joe Hooker, perhaps McClellan's most vocal uniformed critic.[50]

The shadow of McClellan's removal (and the reaction to it) lingered long over the army. Andrew A. Humphreys was a case in point. He had let others know of his unhappiness over the removal; nevertheless, the following month, at Fredericksburg, he led his division with courage and skill against Marye's Heights. For that he expected to win promotion to major general. Burnside urged the promotion on Lincoln, who apparently consented. When nothing happened, however, Humphreys took it upon himself to visit Lincoln, only to find that the president had no recollection of the conversation with Burnside. Humphreys concluded that Republican senators would have nothing to do with confirming the promotion of a McClellanite. After Gettysburg he reluctantly accepted a position as Meade's chief of staff, convinced that politics blocked his chance to become a corps commander.[51]

Humphreys's experience was typical of officers identified as McClellan men. For the remainder of the war, those who had been warm supporters of the general wondered whether it cost them professionally—among them John Sedgwick, Gouverneur K. Warren, and Winfield Scott Hancock. Those three men commanded the army's infantry corps when it marched forth in the spring of 1864, a fact that helps one assess the validity of their concerns. For at least one of them, McClellan became the symbolic victim of political interference by an unreasonable president and a carping press that simply did not understand the realities of war. About the time Joseph Hooker assumed command of the army in January 1863, Warren wrote a lengthy essay in which he attributed reports of the demoralization of the army to the failure of Burnside and Hooker to shower all of the troops with the same love and devotion they reserved for their old commands. McClellan had done so, he said, but "those who live in Washington city, who have never heard the hiss of an enemy's bullet, who live in an atmosphere of envy, malice, and all uncharitableness" had failed to appreciate what manner of man they had in McClellan.[52]

So it would always be, to some extent, with the Army of the Potomac. Not everyone who served in its ranks would have welcomed Lincoln's characterization of the army as "McClellan's bodyguard," but they would have interpreted the president's remark as a caustic comment typical of a man who did not understand war. What shaped the peculiar character of this army was not simply the imprint of the character and personality of its first commander. The legacy of that general's troublesome relationship with the authorities in Washington also played a role, as did a pervasive belief that Republican newspaper editors and, to a lesser extent, the northern public held unreasonable expectations for the army. Many generals, officers, and men shared McClellan's reluctance to renew battle along Antietam Creek on September 18; many echoed his complaints about the feebleness of resupply efforts during October; many agreed that a winter campaign was out of the question; and a good number questioned the degree to which political demands influenced military decisions. McClellan may have reinforced these tendencies, but they endured long after he left. Perhaps so many members of the Army of the Potomac cherished their association with George B. McClellan in part because he was indeed one of them.

NOTES

1. Marsena R. Patrick, *Inside Lincoln's Army: The Diary of Marsena Rudolph Patrick,* ed. David S. Sparks (New York: Yoseloff, 1964), 150–52.

2. Gary W. Gallagher, "The Maryland Campaign in Perspective," in *Antietam: Essays on the 1862 Maryland Campaign,* ed. Gary W. Gallagher (Kent, Ohio: Kent State University Press, 1989), 89–90.

3. T. Harry Williams, *Lincoln and His Generals* (New York: Knopf, 1952), 25; Bruce Catton, *Grant Takes Command* (Boston: Little, Brown, 1969), 383. It is worth noting that Grenville M. Dodge, who served in the Western Theater, used the term "McClellanized" to indicate an outlook grounded in certain political sympathies. John Y. Simon offers a different understanding of the term in "Grant, Lincoln, and Unconditional Surrender," in *Lincoln's Generals,* ed. Gabor S. Boritt (New York: Oxford University Press, 1994), 170, 181, although he fails to define exactly what he means by the expression (which Grant himself did not employ).

4. Bruce Catton, *Mr. Lincoln's Army* (Garden City, N.Y.: Doubleday, 1951), 316, 318–19; Haskell to "Dear Brothers, and Sisters," September 22, 1862, in Frank L.

Byrne and Andrew T. Weaver, eds., *Haskell of Gettysburg: His Life and Civil War Papers* (1970; reprint, Kent, Ohio: Kent State University Press, 1989), 48; Alpheus S. Williams, *From the Cannon's Mouth: The Civil War Letters of General Alpheus S. Williams,* ed. Milo M. Quaife (Detroit: Wayne State University Press, 1959), 130; William H. Powell, *The Fifth Army Corps* (1895; reprint, Dayton, Ohio: Morningside, 1984), 302–3.

5. Seymour Dexter, *Seymour Dexter, Union Army: Journal and Letters of Civil War Service in Company K, 23rd New York Volunteer Regiment . . . ,* ed. Carl A. Morrell (Jefferson, N.C.: McFarland and Co., 1996), 107; George Washington Whitman, *Civil War Letters of George Washington Whitman,* ed. Jerome M. Loving (Durham, N.C.: Duke University Press, 1975), 69; Oliver W. Norton, *Army Letters, 1861–1865* (Chicago: O. L. Deming, 1903), 121.

6. Stephen W. Sears, *George B. McClellan: The Young Napoleon* (New York: Ticknor & Fields, 1988), 320; George G. Meade, *The Life and Letters of General George Gordon Meade,* 2 vols. (New York: Scribner's, 1913), 1:311.

7. Williams, *From the Cannon's Mouth,* 133.

8. Elisha Hunt Rhodes, *All for the Union: The Civil War Diary and Letters of Elisha Hunt Rhodes,* ed. Robert Hunt Rhodes (1985; reprint, New York: Vintage, 1991), 73–74; Edward King Wightman, *From Antietam to Fort Fisher: The Civil War Letters of Edward King Wightman, 1862–1865,* ed. Edward G. Longacre (Rutherford, N.J.: Fairleigh Dickinson University Press, 1985), 39, 44.

9. Williams, *From the Cannon's Mouth,* 134–35.

10. Charles S. Wainwright, *A Diary of Battle: The Personal Journals of Colonel Charles S. Wainwright, 1861–1865,* ed. Allan Nevins (New York: Harcourt, Brace & World, 1962), 111–13.

11. Robert Gould Shaw, *Blue-Eyed Child of Fortune: The Civil War Letters of Colonel Robert Gould Shaw,* ed. Russell Duncan (Athens: University of Georgia Press, 1992), 242, 245.

12. Wainwright, *Diary of Battle,* 103–4; Josiah Marshall Favill, *The Diary of a Young Officer* (Chicago: Donnelley, 1909), 188, 191.

13. Norton, *Army Letters,* 123; Meade, *Life and Letters,* 1:311.

14. George B. McClellan to Mary Ellen McClellan, September 25, 1862, McClellan to William H. Aspinwall, September 26, 1862, in George B. McClellan, *The Civil War Papers of George B. McClellan: Selected Correspondence, 1860–1865,* ed. Stephen W. Sears (New York: Ticknor & Fields, 1989), 481–82; William F. Smith, *Autobiography of Major General William F. Smith,* ed. Herbert M. Schiller (Dayton, Ohio: Morningside, 1990), 57–58. Smith shared the story during the war; eventually it made its way to the ears of Lincoln's private secretary, John Hay. See John Hay, *Lincoln and the Civil War in the Diaries and Letters of John Hay,* ed. Tyler Dennett (New York: Dodd, Mead, 1939), 216–18. The story in Hay's diary differs in marked particulars from that in Smith's autobiography, offering grounds to treat it with skepticism.

15. Sears, *McClellan*, 325.

16. Lance J. Herdegen, *The Men Stood Like Iron: How the Iron Brigade Won Its Name* (Bloomington: Indiana University Press, 1997), 199; Williams, *From the Cannon's Mouth*, 142; Norton, *Army Letters*, 125; Whitman, *Civil War Letters*, 71; Shaw, *Blue-Eyed Child of Fortune*, 245; Wainwright, *Diary of Battle*, 109, 113.

17. William B. Hesseltine, *Lincoln and the War Governors* (New York: Knopf, 1948), 253–61; Wightman, *From Antietam to Fort Fisher*, 44–45; Sears, *McClellan*, 324; Shaw, *Blue-Eyed Child of Fortune*, 244.

18. Williams, *From the Cannon's Mouth*, 135–36.

19. Wainwright, *Diary of Battle*, 107, 108; Richard B. Irwin, "The Removal of McClellan," in *Battles and Leaders of the Civil War*, ed. Robert Underwood Johnson and Clarence Clough Buel, 4 vols. (New York: Century, 1887–88), 3:102–3.

20. Hay, *Lincoln and the Civil War*, 50–51.

21. Abraham Lincoln, *The Collected Works of Abraham Lincoln*, ed. Roy P. Basler, 9 vols. (New Brunswick, N.J.: Rutgers University Press, 1953–55), 5:442–43.

22. Stephen W. Sears, *Landscape Turned Red: The Battle of Antietam* (New York: Ticknor & Fields, 1983), 322–23.

23. Hay, *Lincoln and the Civil War*, 51; Wainwright, *Diary of Battle*, 109; Wightman, *From Antietam to Fort Fisher*, 48; Alice Rains Trulock, *In the Hands of Providence: Joshua L. Chamberlain and the American Civil War* (Chapel Hill: University of North Carolina Press, 1992), 79.

24. Wainwright, *Diary of Battle*, 110.

25. Patrick, *Inside Lincoln's Army*, 155–56; Herdegen, *Men Stood Like Iron*, 200; Alan D. Gaff, *On Many a Bloody Field: Four Years in the Iron Brigade* (Bloomington: Indiana University Press, 1996), 197.

26. "Memorandum," October 1–3, 1862, in Lincoln, *Collected Works*, 5:448.

27. Meade, *Life and Letters*, 1:317; Williams, *From the Cannon's Mouth*, 136.

28. Don E. Fehrenbacher and Virginia Fehrenbacher, eds., *Recollected Words of Abraham Lincoln* (Stanford: Stanford University Press, 1996), 201.

29. Irwin, "Removal of McClellan," 103.

30. Warren W. Hassler Jr., *General George B. McClellan: Shield of the Union* (Baton Rouge: Louisiana State University Press, 1957), 302–3. Most accounts fail to note the sequence of events during the first week of October, tending to treat separately the army's discussion about emancipation, culminating in the McClellan order, the Lincoln visit, and the Halleck telegram. However, the origins of McClellan's order and the role that Democratic political adviser William Aspinwall had in its issuance were known in Washington almost immediately. See Gideon Welles, *Diary of Gideon Welles*, ed. Howard K. Beale, 3 vols. (New York: Norton, 1960), 1:163.

31. Hassler, *McClellan*, 303–5; Lincoln to McClellan, October 13, 1862, in Lincoln, *Collected Works*, 5:460–61.

32. Meade, *Life and Letters*, 1:319; Williams, *From the Cannon's Mouth*, 137;

Rhodes, *All for the Union,* 76; Joel Molyneux, *Quill of the Wild Goose: Civil War Letters and Diaries of Private Joel Molyneux, 141st P. V.,* ed. Kermit Molyneux Bird (Shippensburg, Pa.: Burd Street Press, 1996), 43.

33. Williams, *From the Cannon's Mouth,* 138–39.

34. Ibid., 140.

35. Wainwright, *Diary of Battle,* 114–15; Meade, *Life and Letters,* 1:320–21.

36. Sears, *Landscape Turned Red,* 326–27; Joseph T. Glatthaar, *Partners in Command: The Relationship between Leaders in the Civil War* (New York: Free Press, 1994), 88–92; Sears, *McClellan,* 332–33; Kenneth P. Williams, *Lincoln Finds a General,* 5 vols. (New York: Macmillan, 1949–59), 2:466–67.

37. Rhodes, *All for the Union,* 76; Wainwright, *Diary of Battle,* 115–16.

38. Whitman, *Civil War Letters,* 72; Trulock, *In the Hands of Providence,* 86; Favill, *Diary of a Young Officer,* 196.

39. Abraham Lincoln to George B. McClellan, October 25, 26, 27, 1862, in Lincoln, *Collected Works,* 5:474, 477, 479; McClellan to Lincoln, October 25, 26, 1862, in McClellan, *Civil War Papers,* 508–9; McClellan to Mary Ellen McClellan, October 26, 29, 1862, in ibid., 511, 514–15.

40. Favill, *Diary of a Young Officer,* 198–99; Dexter, *Seymour Dexter,* 111; Charles Harvey Brewster, *When This Cruel War is Over: The Civil War Letters of Charles Harvey Brewster,* ed. David W. Blight (Amherst: University of Massachusetts Press, 1992), 188–89 [letter dated November 5, 1862].

41. Meade, *Life and Letters,* 1:324.

42. Sears, *Landscape Turned Red,* 340.

43. Abraham Lincoln to William R. Morrison, November 5, 1862, in Lincoln, *Collected Works,* 5:486.

44. Patrick, *Inside Lincoln's Army,* 173; Meade, *Life and Letters,* 1:325; John W. Haley, *The Rebel Yell and the Yankee Hurrah: The Civil War Journal of a Maine Volunteer,* ed. Ruth L. Silliker (Camden, Maine: Down East Books, 1985), 50; Frederick Pettit, *Infantryman Pettit: The Civil War Letters of Corporal Frederick Pettit,* ed. William Gilfillan Gavin (Shippensburg, Pa.: White Mane, 1990), 36; John Gibbon, *Recollections of the Civil War* (1928; reprint, Dayton, Ohio: Morningside, 1988), 96; Shaw, *Blue-Eyed Child of Fortune,* 255.

45. Gibbon, *Recollections,* 99; Williams, *From the Cannon's Mouth,* 151; Shaw, *Blue-Eyed Child of Fortune,* 259–60.

46. Herdegen, *Men Stood Like Iron,* 214; Rhodes, *All for the Union,* 80.

47. Michael C. C. Adams, *Our Masters the Rebels: A Speculation on Union Military Failure in the East, 1861–1865* (Cambridge: Harvard University Press, 1978), 117–23; Richard Moe, *The Last Full Measure: The Life and Death of the First Minnesota Volunteers* (New York: Henry Holt, 1993), 204–5; Herdegen, *Men Stood Like Iron,* 212–13; Gaff, *On Many a Bloody Field,* 201–2.

48. Patrick, *Inside Lincoln's Army,* 174; Thomas P. Southwick, *A Duryee Zouave*

(1930; reprint, Brookneal, Va.: Patrick A. Schroder Publications, 1995), 93; Sears, *Landscape Turned Red,* 342–43; Favill, *Diary of a Young Officer,* 201.

49. Herdegen, *Men Stood Like Iron,* 214.

50. Sears, *Landscape Turned Red,* 332; Patrick, *Inside Lincoln's Army,* 174–75.

51. Henry H. Humphreys, *Andrew Atkinson Humphreys: A Biography* (Philadelphia: John C. Winston, 1924), 173, 200–202; Abraham Lincoln to Ambrose E. Burnside, January 28, 1863, in Lincoln, *Collected Works,* 6:81.

52. Emerson Gifford Taylor, *Gouverneur Kemble Warren: Life and Letters of an American Soldier* (Boston: Houghton Mifflin, 1932), 100.

WILLIAM A. BLAIR

Maryland, Our Maryland

Or How Lincoln and His Army
Helped to Define the Confederacy

The Army of Northern Virginia entered Maryland as self-proclaimed liberators. As they crossed the Potomac on September 4, 1862, soldiers sang "Maryland, My Maryland"—an anthem that pledged retribution for the repression of Confederate sentiment by the northern government. Four days later Robert E. Lee issued a proclamation that announced the army's mission as one of liberty for the citizenry rather than conquest. Among the violations of rights by the Union, Lee listed military occupation, arrests of legislators and citizens without warrants or charges, and suppression of newspapers and free speech. The northern government was guilty as charged: Lincoln had employed all of these measures in trying to keep Maryland in the Union. The general told residents of the state that his army was "prepared to assist you . . . in regaining the rights of which you have been despoiled." People throughout the South shared this perspective, with many hoping the army would ignite an uprising that would cause Maryland to join the Confederacy or send men from the state rushing into the ranks.[1]

We know that the uprising did not materialize and that the army gained, but did not swell, from an infusion of new recruits. To readers today, it seems obvious that citizens in the border region would stay with the Union rather than support the Confederacy. Most people no longer even consider Maryland a southern state, yet in the mid-nineteenth century this was not the case. The Mason-Dixon line — or the boundary between Pennsylvania and Maryland — formed the eastern border between North and South, with slavery as a key component delineating the two regions. Marylanders often viewed themselves as southerners, even though portions of the state had assumed commercial ways that made it appear more northern. Regardless of this sometimes ambiguous position between free and slave state, events during the first eighteen months of war convinced Lee's army that in 1862 it marched onto friendly soil containing fellow southerners held under the heel of a tyrant named Lincoln.

The violation of civil rights in Maryland demonstrated to southerners, especially those who had waffled through the sectional crisis, that secessionists had accurately gauged the extralegal motivations of Republicans. Lincoln's policies persuaded many that a defense against oppression lay at the heart of the conflict, a cause that could unite both slaveholders and nonslaveholders.[2] As studies of Confederate nationalism and the reasons for fighting have demonstrated, once the war began, the southern people needed a broader issue to rally behind than the slavery controversy that had brought on the war. The South quickly adopted the posture of a nascent nation fighting to avoid oppression — a populace conducting a defensive struggle for existence against an unconstitutional aggressor. Such a cause not only forged internal unity but also presented a stronger case for soliciting foreign support from antislavery nations such as Britain and France. Through measures conducted by the Union in Maryland (and elsewhere, for that matter), Confederates could build a persuasive image of themselves as a liberty-loving people struggling to maintain the heritage of the American Revolution.[3]

The Antietam campaign served as a turning point in the southern view of Maryland citizens. After the autumn of 1862, the state's reputation declined because it became clear Marylanders would not join the Confederacy. Even this, ironically, helped in the construction of a Confederate identity by providing a negative image against which people contrasted the positive aspects of a true Confederate. Marylanders were accused of being Yankee southerners, or the speculators and extortionists who grew rich from other people's suffering. They also could remain out of the army because the southern government considered them aliens. Hostility against Marylanders festered the strongest in Virginia, a congregating point for refugees from the Old Bay State. Although it never completely left the thoughts of the Confederate public, Maryland later failed to inspire the same affection that marked the warm September days when the Army of Northern Virginia stepped onto the northern shore of the Potomac.

Although the South of the mid-nineteenth century was a clearly defined entity because of slavery, the region had evolved in distinct ways that affected the position of its white residents during the secession crisis. The Deep South consisted of the seven states that seceded first and formed the Confederate States of America in February 1861. These states had the most commitment to King Cotton, slave owning, and the Democratic Party. The other eight slave states constituted the Upper South, which featured a more diverse economy, fewer slaves as a percentage of the population, smaller farms, and thriving two-party politics. They also contained more northern immigrants and, in the eastern states from Maryland through North Carolina, significant numbers of pacifist religious groups that had migrated into the western Piedmont during the colonial period. Secession proved a much more ticklish matter in states where the nonslaveholding population outnumbered the planters, may have come from the North, and did not grow as much tobacco or other plantation staples. The region also realized that war would come first on its soil, meaning that its leaders did not have the luxury of favoring heart over head like their fire-eating cousins farther south. The border prided itself on moderation—a section of calm, rational thinkers living between emotional extremes.

Reflecting its geographic position between North and South, Maryland was a complex hybrid of slave and free state. By 1850, it consisted of two sections with different economic and social compositions. Northern Maryland lay above and west of the fault line and featured a diverse ethnic population with a thriving commercial interest. The six counties in this zone, which included the city of Baltimore, were mostly white and free with a black population of 16 percent and only 5 percent slave. Immigrants from Ireland and Germany in particular lived here. In the decade from 1844 to 1854, the state had experienced a fivefold increase in immigration. Most of the newcomers settled in this part of the state, which also contained the most population overall. In the western region could be found a polyglot group of coal miners, railroad workers, and pacifist German Dunkards. The recent immigrants entered through the port of Baltimore, a commercial city thriving on trade and linked to the western regions by the Baltimore & Ohio Railroad. Baltimore had become the third-largest city in the country with a population exceeding 200,000. The South had nothing else quite like it. The city contained a contentious working class and artisans prone to violent protest, which occurred frequently because of economic and social changes in the 1850s.[4]

The most secession-minded people lived, appropriately enough, in the southern part of the state on both sides of the Chesapeake. The Eastern Shore contained a mix of people and economy, with its secessionist residents occupying the plantations that hugged the bay. Across the bay, the western shore most resembled the Deep South, with the residents referred to as "Old Society." Called variously southern or lower Maryland, the six counties located below Baltimore comprised 36 percent of the state's slaveholders. In this region, slaves constituted 44 percent of the population, and black people were a majority at 54 percent. A traveler through the region in the 1840s observed that he had met only two white persons during a fourteen-mile ride. Tobacco continued as a major crop, although some planters supplemented their staples with corn and wheat. From lower Maryland came the most agitation for secession, volunteers to the Confederate army, and smugglers who ferried spies and goods to and from Virginia during the war.

As the Confederate army would learn during the Antietam campaign, the geography of southern loyalties would be described roughly by a rectangle extending from southern Maryland upward to Baltimore and westward to Frederick. In the northwest lived the most Union-minded people, although the pacifist sects like the Dunkards may more accurately be described as neutral. Baltimore featured a northern commercial character carving itself out of a southern, slaveholding society. Many residents in Baltimore, however, took offense at being called northerners. "The ambivalence between a Northern life style and southern sentiment," one historian has written, "always plagued Baltimore—and Maryland as a whole—whenever the sectional crisis became acute." [5]

Throughout the secession winter, the state's hesitancy to enter the Confederacy caused little alarm because it behaved no differently than the rest of the Upper South. The Deep South was frustrated by the passivity of the other slave states but found it easy to excuse Maryland. For one thing, the blame for inaction fell more on Virginia. Residents in the Cotton South viewed the Old Dominion as the dominant force in the border region and expected the Upper South to follow its lead. Suspicion also existed that Republicans prevented Maryland from acting freely. Governor Thomas H. Hicks became a principal scapegoat. Planters had petitioned the governor to convene the legislature—dominated by the plantation interests of the southern section—so that a convention could decide on secession. A strong Unionist, Hicks refused to do so, becoming a hero for the North and a villain for the South. It was easy for the rest of the South to view the state as led by a Tory in league with Black Republicans who prevented the people from following their natural, legal course. [6] When Virginia passed its ordinance of secession on April 17, Maryland might have lost luster by not joining the Confederacy; however, events reinforced the portrait of southern sympathizers held in the Union against their will.

It all began with a riot on April 19 that indicated secession sentiment lived within the state. On the day before the riot, following a series of secession meetings, citizens had marched through the streets of Baltimore to harass more than six hundred Union soldiers passing through town to make their railroad connection. The crowd waved Confederate flags and yelled acclaim for Jefferson Davis and South Carolina. The police did nothing, claiming that citizens had the right to express their views. No serious violence occurred. The same could not be said for April 19, as horses hauled the 6th Massachusetts Infantry in streetcars to another railroad line. Crowds obstructed the ninth car, then hurled taunts and stones at the troops who had to make their way on foot. Knots of men castigated the "northern scum," shouting, "You Yankee dogs you'll never go back." Coal, stone jars, bottles, dishes, and other debris descended on the soldiers from windows above the street. Some in the crowd became so frenzied that they tore open shirts, exposing breasts and daring the "Yankee hirelings" to shoot. The soldiers eventually complied. Sixteen people died, four of them soldiers. Scores more were wounded on both sides. As violence continued that night, the mayor and police chief convinced Governor Hicks to allow the burning of bridges north of the city to prevent more troops from coming in. In the process, telegraphic communications were cut, isolating the capital and placing Washington in a siege mentality. Lincoln temporarily suspended shipment of troops through the city. After extensive negotiating with civic authorities, the president finally declared martial law on April 27.[7]

To the rest of the South, this was heady stuff. Finally, Marylanders had shown they might not submit to coercion. Lincoln also had revealed his true colors as a person who paid only lip service to protecting the Constitution. A Richmond newspaper praised the residents for their honor and courage, adding: "The only regret that we feel on the subject is that they did not succeed in exterminating the last one of these wretches—as just vengeance for a lawless invasion of a free people, and as a warning to their brethren for all time."[8] Anxious to learn more, Virginia authorities dispatched James M. Mason to assess the condition of Maryland. After talking to prominent people around the state, Mason reported on May 6 that he believed the Maryland legislature would unite with the Confederacy except for certain obstacles. Foremost was the lack of organized military effort. Mason had advised the formation of a public safety committee to begin arming for defense but feared these efforts would be overwhelmed shortly by Federal soldiers. At the least, he hoped the South would smuggle in guns to prepare "large bodies in that State, acting as Guerillas, of infinite value when the struggle comes."[9]

How much support to give Maryland—covert or otherwise—was not an easy decision. Although southerners did not want to appear as aggressive as the Lincoln government, some urged that the Confederacy adopt a more active role in helping secession. Yet even among the latter group there was waffling on the issue

The 6th Massachusetts fires into the mob in Baltimore on April 19, 1861.
Confederates interpreted this event as evidence that Marylanders
opposed the United States government.
Collection of the editor

of taking action. More than ten days after the riot, for example, the Richmond correspondent for the Charleston *Mercury* observed that Baltimore and eastern Maryland were "sound." But he was not sure this support could last without help from the Confederate government: "We are looking every day for President Davis, confident that he will answer this question satisfactorily." In a dispatch on May 4, the same reporter changed his mind about intervention because he saw no nucleus of military organization in Maryland. Secessionists had adapted too easily to martial law. "While our forces would sustain that State," he continued, "they will not assume to lead or force that State to an attitude of opposition, and so, for the present at least, Maryland would seem to be out of view." In Virginia, planter Edmund Ruffin was of the same mind, writing off Maryland for the time being because its legislature did not invite the Confederate forces in. The new southern government was trying to portray itself as a protector, not an invader.[10]

Confederate sympathy grew for Maryland as the repression escalated. Lincoln believed he needed to keep the state in the Union, no matter how stern the measures. Without it, the capital would become surrounded by the Confederacy. The loss of Maryland also jeopardized command of Chesapeake Bay. Beginning on April 27 when Lincoln ordered martial law, the military moved to quash secession sentiment in the state. Arrests fell into two broad patterns: activity from May through July to solidify the state and calm passions in Baltimore, and a tighter reign from September through November to eliminate opposition within the legislature and secure the state elections for Unionists.

Military occupation consolidated by mid-May 1861 under the auspices of Maj. Gen. Benjamin F. Butler. As he did so often in the war, Butler pushed the issue before his superiors wanted. The general had crept closer to Baltimore with the troops under his command until, by May 5, he controlled the railroad lines leading into the city. This much was within his orders. Then Butler pushed the limits of his authority and, under cover of a stormy night, occupied the city of Baltimore on May 13. An incensed Winfield Scott demanded that his subordinate explain the move, then chastised Butler: "It is a God-send that it [the occupation] was without conflict of arms." He also ordered the general not to issue any more proclamations. Butler had announced to the people of Maryland that he had taken possession of the city because of reports that a riot greeted recruitment officers and rumors that secessionists had hidden arms for use in treasonous activity. He promised no disruption of civil authority but prohibited displays of banners, flags, or other signs of the rebellion.[11]

Troops also had arrested Ross Winans, a member of the Maryland House of Representatives. The exact reason for imprisonment remains unknown, but Winans provided ample cause. His desire for secession was well known. He had formed part of a delegation to Harpers Ferry that informed Stonewall Jackson of the legislature's attempt to force the governor to call a convention to discuss breaking from the Union. Winans was released on parole in a day or so, but his arrest and the occupation of the city fostered the belief that the state was held in the Union through force, even though attitudes were far from unanimous within Maryland at the time. Without weapons, the citizens could not resist this military demonstration. Judith McGuire, an observant diarist in Richmond, saw Maryland and Kentucky as sharing these circumstances. "I believe that the very best people of both States are with us," she noted, "but are held back by stern necessity. Oh that they could burst the bonds that bind them, and speak and act like freemen!" A day later she observed about the Federal troops quartered in Maryland: "The North has its heel upon her, and how it grinds her."[12]

The grinding continued with a major civil liberties case involving a showdown between a Supreme Court justice and the president. On May 25, troops arrested

John Merryman, a Maryland landowner and a lieutenant in a secessionist company that had burned bridges after the Baltimore riot. As usual, he was held without charges. Another Maryland resident, Chief Justice Roger B. Taney, heard an appeal as the senior judge of a federal circuit court that had jurisdiction over the case. As he had with the Dred Scott decision in 1857, Taney proved sympathetic to the southern cause. When Union authorities refused to produce Merryman and list the charges against him, Taney castigated Lincoln for arbitrary arrests in general. In an opinion titled *Ex parte Merryman,* the judge accused Lincoln of overstepping his constitutional limits by suspending habeas corpus, noting that only Congress could enact this order. Lincoln did not necessarily disagree with Taney's interpretation of the law. The president, however, ignored the justice's ruling and later convinced Congress that he had acted appropriately in choosing to protect the whole Union rather than one law.[13]

Maryland's travails did not convince every southerner that the state was worth worrying about. The Lower South in particular was suspicious about the political influence that the border region could exert. With greater population and a location near Richmond, the Border States might dominate government patronage.[14] The commercial nature of Maryland also created mixed feelings. A correspondent for the Charleston *Mercury* articulated this ambivalence when he noted that if Maryland joined the Confederacy it would inevitably monopolize manufacturing. This would repress such economic development elsewhere. Yet if the state failed to join the Confederacy, the South needed to encourage manufacturing and, more distressing, free labor to accomplish it. The correspondent guessed the government would need to attract skilled workers—the kind that caused so much trouble in Baltimore. "Pauper labor" would in turn try to "make our institutions suit them," which meant having an equal say with planters on issues such as slavery. So the problem was a complicated one. The Confederacy needed the manufacturing that Maryland could offer. But if the state joined the southern cause, then manufactures might bypass the Lower South. If the state stayed in the Union, then the Confederacy needed to open its doors to immigrants who might undermine the slaveholding elite. The South might gain manufacturing but, in its eyes, lose democracy. Neither option appealed to this correspondent.[15]

The riot in Baltimore heightened unease among southern elitists who wondered about how to control the lower class, especially one so prone to violence. John B. Jones, a clerk in the War Department in Richmond, criticized the attack on the Union troops because it was carried out by a common rabble incited by "animal, and not intellectual or patriotic instincts. Baltimore has better men for the strife than bar-room champions."[16] Snobbery against working rabble accounted for the low opinion that Mary Chesnut's friends from the slaveholding elite held of the state. They saw Marylanders as weak-willed people afraid of secession—not of the right southern stuff. If the upper crust were that way, what could be said for the common person? Baltimore, they sniffed, contained street thugs who practiced murder as a fine art.[17]

Continued Union repression eventually overrode this ambivalence. By the summer, Union major general Nathaniel P. Banks, now in charge in the state, brought fresh attention to Baltimore as he arrested the marshal of police and four members of the police board. The War Department ordered the action through General-in-Chief Scott to suppress southern sentiment among public officials in sensitive positions. Police Marshal George P. Kane had helped persuade the governor to burn bridges leading into the city during the April disturbances. Since then, he and the police board rarely had cooperated wholeheartedly with federal authorities, although they had not resisted openly. They dragged their feet when asked to help stifle Confederate sentiment. Federal officials also suspected that the police board had amassed weapons and aided other surreptitious activity. On June 27, officials whisked Kane to Fort McHenry, disbanded the local police, and placed a colonel of the state militia in charge of law and order as the city's provost marshal. The four members of the police board followed Kane to jail on the night of July 1, as federal authorities pounded on doors between 2:00 and 3:00 A.M. to seize the men under cover of darkness. The arrests sent a message to secessionists about the fate that awaited resistance.[18]

Protests against the arrests came to naught, although they revealed that the president supported the action. Maryland's House of Representatives sent a memorial to the U.S. Congress demanding release of the men or at least an explanation about the reasons for the arrests. The legislature, ironically, attempted to portray Maryland as a loyal Union state treated with undue harshness by the federal government. The memorialists denied that the police board or the marshal had obstructed justice. Petitioners pointed out that civil cases had gone on undisturbed and dared the government to name a specific example to the contrary. The petition also defended the cache of arms held by the police as weapons either to protect the peace or to prevent their unlawful seizure. Congress forwarded the material to Lincoln for an explanation, only to be refused with the terse explanation that no grounds for the arrests could be given because "it is judged to be incompatible with the public interest at this time to furnish the information called for by the resolution."[19] Lincoln would not back down.

The arrests not only failed to end dissent but also infused a new spirit of resistance in the secessionist population. Congressman Henry May of Maryland visited Virginia to consult with Jefferson Davis after the police board was disbanded. He presented a rather bizarre picture, as he spoke publicly about his concerns to Confederate citizens in a speech around the Fourth of July. Here was a member of the federal government standing in a rebel state and criticizing his president. A correspondent was impressed with May's comments, which fostered this impression about the North: "A party who will use its power to make unauthorized war to suspend the civil rights of its own people, to establish a military dictatorship in defiance of law, and to trample upon the decisions of the Chief Justice of the United States will stop short of nothing in their career of despotism to accomplish their ends." After sharing the tale of the nighttime arrests of the police board, the correspondent concluded: "The fate of Maryland would have been the fate of Virginia, had she not seceded; and the Old Dominion was well nigh being placed in such a situation through her submissionists and the Yankee population which has become mixed in with the chivalrous race."[20] Maryland thus provided proof of Lincoln's tyranny and a reason for staying out of the Union.

Events on the battlefield emboldened southern sympathizers in Baltimore. The defeat of the Union army at First Manassas on July 21 caused the city to teem with people cheering the results. A Unionist woman wrote a friend: "We have thousands upon thousands sympathizing with the South who have lost their love for the Union (they say the Union is broken up) and who would this day array themselves against it if they had the power." She confided that she hoped Federal troops would remain because she had no faith in the city's loyalty.[21] Increased friction occurred in the streets as Union soldiers brushed against civilians and sometimes confiscated rebel paraphernalia. Some women literally wore their loyalties on their sleeves. *Harper's Weekly* carried a cover illustration of a Baltimore woman wearing a dress patterned from the first national flag of the Confederacy, known as the Stars and Bars. The editor made light of the incident, portraying the young lady as delighting soldiers with her costume and then ignoring them. Taunts from other women who shouted "Hurrah for Jeff Davis" and "How about Bull Run?" were supposed to have amused the Union soldiers.[22]

Although such incidents seem quaint, they were watched closely by Confederates. When Union soldiers lost patience and either returned the taunts or snatched rebel colors from women, word spread throughout the South. A woman in North Carolina could not comprehend the despotism that encouraged soldiers to seize not only Confederate flags but also children's socks and ladies' bonnets that contained the colors. At the least, the rough treatment of civilians indicated to the rest of the South that the Union government considered Maryland as unfriendly soil.[23] But this treatment of women and children, no matter how minor to us today, spoke volumes to Confederates about the caliber of the enemy they faced. Simply put, Union authorities were barbarians who preyed on helpless civilians.

Further repression dwarfed these events. The rising intransigence of the secession element worried northern officials as the elections for General Assembly neared. By September, the legislature contained a significant number of members planning to push for a resolution supporting secession during a session scheduled to open on the 17th in Frederick. This position would embarrass the Lincoln administration and possibly affect the election. The orders came down from the War Department on September 11 for the army to prevent passage of a pro-secession resolution. General Banks complied by arresting Congressman May and about thirty members of the Maryland legislature. Also taken was the mayor of Baltimore, who had been a thorn in the side of Union military officials since the occupation. Twenty-nine of the public officials went to prison. Most remained until at least beyond the election, although a number stayed in jail until February or longer. Although no one had official charges lodged against him — or a hearing of any kind — authorities claimed that the men had conspired to promote secession.[24]

As important for chilling dissent, the government shut down two newspapers in Baltimore, the *Exchange* and the *South*. Both had professed Confederate sympathies. Military authorities hauled into prison four men who worked on these newspapers. Francis Key Howard, identified as an editor of the *Exchange,* created the most controversy. He was the grandson of Francis Scott Key, who had composed "The Star-Spangled Banner" during the War of 1812 after the British had bombarded Fort McHenry — the very same place that had become a Federal holding tank for secessionists. Howard was arrested on September 12 for being in sympathy with the rebels. Authorities portrayed his arrest as a military precaution, claiming his written material "might at any time burst into a flame of discord and insurrection." Despite repeated protests, he was held for more than a year in four different prisons until finally released in November 1862.[25] Confederates watching these events likened the time to a reign of terror, comparing the Lincoln administration to the excesses of Robespierre during the French Revolution. No one, not even a person with a pedigree like Howard's, was safe from a tyrant like Lincoln.

Armed intervention continued as the November election neared and the government moved to ensure that the voting favored the Union. The officer in charge of the state explained the mission of the military to one of his subordinates in this manner: "You will bear in mind that we are on the eve of an election in Maryland of vital importance. The preservation of this state is indispensable to the safety of the capital." He urged discretion in arrests, "but while all the just rights of those who are disloyal should be respected, they should be made to feel that no act of open hostility to the Government will be tolerated for one moment."[26] The military focused on southern Maryland, where most of the secessionists lived. Officers who would make their fame later in the war directed the efforts. Brig. Gen. Oliver Otis Howard supervised five arrests, including a local official who used treasonable language and brandished a knife. Brig. Gen. Joseph Hooker sent four companies of Indiana cavalry to polling places, instructing them to arrest a tavern owner who ran as a secession candidate. He also "invited" his troopers to attend a secession barbecue scheduled for election day as a show of force.[27]

In the end the government preserved Maryland as a Union state, although its methods provided Confederates with additional ammunition about why their nation needed to succeed in its struggle for existence. The arrests clearly appalled southerners. In Virginia, Edmund Ruffin took note of the imprisonment of the mayor, legislators, and editors. He wondered: "Can such pitiful & contemptible, as well as galling, tyranny be tolerated long?" Many shared the opinion of the South Carolinian who told a Baltimore resident "that a Georgia negro was now freer than a Maryland legislator."[28]

By the fall of 1861, southerners began to favor an invasion of Maryland. Ever since the victory at Manassas, the Confederate high command had deliberated what should occur next. No one liked the idea of merely assuming a defensive position in northern Virginia and waiting for the Union to strike the next blow. Gen. P. G. T. Beauregard and other officers strongly urged Jefferson Davis to allow the army to cross the Potomac, threaten Washington, and force the Union to fight. Davis was not against the idea but believed it a luxury that might waste resources at the expense of other places, especially Tennessee. He also was conscious of living up to the Confederacy's proclaimed reason for fighting—to defend against aggression and tyranny.[29]

Throughout September and October the debate continued about whether to conduct an "On to Washington" campaign. Some saw the actions by the Union government as ample cause for an incursion into Maryland. These same advocates typically urged much broader action, using Maryland as an excuse for an invasion of Pennsylvania and Ohio. Southerners—especially Virginians—had grown sensitive to the cry of northern newspaperman Horace Greeley for the Union to press "On to Richmond." They hoped the Confederate army would scare northern civilians. Others took a more cautious approach. The editor of the Richmond *Examiner* at first argued against a push into Maryland because of the questionable loyalties of the state. He sympathized with the hardships endured by the people but added: "They must work out their own salvation. Maryland has not seceded. She must first give some tangible proof of her devotion to the South ere we cross her borders." Five days later, the same editor deemed it intolerable to wait for the enemy to attack. Like others in the South, he began to see the best defense as a good offense. The writer also argued that entering Maryland would not be an invasion at all "but, on the contrary, going where we shall meet hosts of warm and true friends." Editors characterized the state as containing slave-holders, "bone of our bone" and "flesh of our flesh."[30] Although events dictated that the South delay this campaign, when Lee finally turned the army northward and crossed the Potomac the following year, he fulfilled a commonly held desire within the Confederacy.

By the time the Army of Northern Virginia was ready to march into Maryland, the state's southern sympathizers had been cowed. The arrests from the summer through autumn of 1861 made an impact. Full-fledged political opposition against the Union effectively died. Resistance in the state continued, but in a more muted and individual fashion. Southern sympathizers cut Unionists from social calendars or stalked out of church when the inevitable prayer came on behalf of the president of the United States. Others fled the state, continuing a consistent trickle of refugees that had begun with the opening of the conflict, with most settling in Virginia. Still others operated illicit trade with the Confederacy, helping exchange contraband through an underground railroad that operated on the waters surrounding Chesapeake Bay and never ceased throughout the war. Despite these activities, Confederate-minded Marylanders for the most part resigned themselves to remaining in the Union, even if they were unhappy about it.

Ironically, as fatalism lowered the spirits of Maryland secessionists during the winter of 1861–62, the South elevated the people as symbols of the struggle for independence. A testament to the impact of Maryland in the southern mind lies in the popular culture manufactured within the early Confederacy. A host of patriotic poetry was churned out that often formed the lyrics adapted to popular airs. These texts traveled the South in broadside form, with Baltimore presses churning out some of them even after the height of political repression.[31]

The most widely known example is "Maryland, My Maryland." James R. Randall of Baltimore had composed the original poem in honor of a friend who survived a wound during the riot of April 19. The lyric opened with "The despot's heel is on thy shore" and continued with specific references to the wrongs enacted against the citizenry by the government. The poem perhaps was a little too local in orientation, referring to prominent families such as the Carrolls, former governor Enoch L. Lowe, and Congressman May. By March 1862 the song had undergone changes that eliminated the more arcane local references in favor of broadening its appeal. The names of Maryland citizens had disappeared, along with specific references to the Baltimore riot. The later version was perhaps more generic but also far more aggressive, with the opening proclaiming: "To arms! to arms! defend the soil, / Of Maryland, dear Maryland!" Like the original, the lyric promised liberation of the state by a southern army, with the last stanza capturing the sentiment with which the Army of Northern Virginia entered the state during the Antietam campaign:

> But hark! the tramps of Southern braves!
> Maryland! My Maryland!
> For you they come, your homes to save,
> Maryland! My Maryland!
> Hark! the shouts of victory!
> See them in their majesty!
> Thy Shackles fall, and thou art free!
> Maryland! My Maryland![32]

Put to the music of "Oh, Tannenbaum," the song ranked second only to "Dixie" as a popular Confederate tune. "We are glad to see this Maryland song so enthusiastically received by the Southern people," a reporter wrote in early 1862, adding, "To the gallant exiles of Maryland, who are shedding their blood for our cause upon every battlefield, the fact that this air occupies the first place among the 'Songs of the War,' will be taken as a grateful earnest of the resolution which animates the masses of the South, that, sooner or later, Maryland shall be free."[33]

The song was only one of many tributes to Maryland, all of which defined the Confederate cause as a noble one of resisting Union tyranny that treated white Marylanders no differently than slaves. Each composition invariably portrayed the state as waiting for the South to liberate it. A poem called "Oh Jeff! Why Don't You Come?" perfectly captures this posture, while using the events in Baltimore to illustrate how the public suffered in a Yankee hell:

> Jeff Davis are you coming? We'll be glad to see you here!
> We'll give you a hearty greeting, you'll be welcome everywhere!
> You'll find a subjugated set, appeals are all in vain!
> They've disbanded all our police, and arrested Marshal Kane.[34]

Baltimore and the behavior of its southern ladies served as a subject worthy of its own patriotic poetry. A composition titled "How They Act in Baltimore" celebrated the defiance of women against northern soldiers. The composer used their example of resistance to shame men into similar attitudes: "If this hate the women feel / . . . Brothers, lovers reap the wind, / And the pride of all their scorn, / Be the bleeding, mangled form / Of some loved and cherished friend." Similarly, the song "Baltimore" repeated the themes of a city oppressed by vandals and mercenaries. Southern honor demanded retribution, especially for the wrongs against women. Finally, the poem "There Is Life in Old Maryland Yet" asked how the South could doubt the fealty of the Old Bay State, promising:

> This life still breathes, and up will spring,
>   When we can once more rise;
> Then like an eagle on the wing,
>   'Twill pierce the very skies!
> Remember! think! consider well,
>   'twill save the South regret,
> To know that 'tis truth we tell,
>   There's life in Old Maryland yet![35]

These texts spread across the Confederacy. A few months later, as Stonewall Jackson outmaneuvered Federal generals in the Shenandoah Valley, a North Carolina woman heard rumors that a campaign into Maryland might be imminent. The thought of this sparked memories of these lyrics, causing her to muse playfully, "[S]o we shall see whether or not 'There is life in the Old Land Yet,' or whether the 'Despot's Heel' has crushed it entirely out of 'Maryland, My Maryland.'"[36]

The moment to test this faith came in September 1862. Lee informed Jefferson Davis on the 3rd about the reasons for the campaign. Opportunity lay to the North. He could not stay where he was and feed his soldiers. Retreat meant inviting the northern vandals to return to Virginia and disrupt the autumn harvest. But Lee used other rationale for crossing the Potomac. Besides the military and logistical value of an offensive, he understood the potential political gain and warmed to this thinking as he corresponded with the president. The time had arrived, according to Lee, to give Maryland the chance to throw off oppression. On September 4, he indicated to Davis that he would begin the offensive unless receiving orders to the contrary. He hoped the president would send the former governor of Maryland, Enoch L. Lowe (he of "Maryland, My Maryland" fame), to act as a guide and mediator with the population. By September 5 at 1:55 P.M., Stonewall Jackson had a division of soldiers on the northern side of the river. The march of the liberators was on.[37]

Soldiers perceived this as a chance to lift the Federal yoke—an impression helped by the sympathizers who greeted the army as it entered the state. A Charleston editor praised the maneuver, noting that "Maryland, from her eastern shore to the Blue Ridge, is throbbing with the hope of an early deliverance, and sits uneasy in her chains." A Virginia editor took a more wait-and-see approach, indicating that "a vast deal now depends on Maryland." He was concerned that the state had experienced so much tyranny for so long that its people would be incapable of rallying to the cause. Another Virginian, however, had more sympathy. Hearing of Lee's crossing, this woman saw connections with her own experience of Union occupation: "[W]ith them I've tasted the bitterness of slavery, with them I've welcomed deliverance which only we could appreciate."[38] Expectations were high that the army could rescue the state.

Davis and Lee had higher stakes in mind than merely the liberation of Maryland. The advance took place in tandem with Braxton Bragg's army heading for Kentucky, but even the prospect of expanding the Confederacy paled next to the overall potential. Lee thought the war could end with this thrust into the North and advised Davis that the government ought to press the Union for recognition. The offer would demonstrate that the South fought only for independence. Refusal would confirm that the North wanted this war of aggression, which could erode support for the Union during the November elections and increase interest on the part of Europe for recognition of the Confederacy. Here was Lee clearly overstepping his military role, but doing it in such a way that Davis accepted the advice without apparent hard feelings.[39]

On September 8, Lee felt compelled to issue his proclamation to the public despite having neither word from the president nor the presence of Lowe as an emissary to the Confederate faithful. The natives, in Lee's opinion, were nervous about the army's intent. He issued his proclamation to alleviate their concerns. The army had come, he stated, to restore "the inalienable rights of freemen." Those who wanted to support the Confederacy would be protected by southern arms. Yet he quickly reassured Marylanders that no force would be used against civilians — each person could exercise free will. "It is for you to decide your destiny freely and without constraint," he wrote. "This army will respect your choice, whatever it may be; and while the Southern people will rejoice to welcome you to your natural position among them, they will only welcome you when you come of your own free will."[40]

Lee issued a moderate statement partly because he could not afford to have civilians hindering the acquisition of food. He had crossed into Maryland acutely aware that severe logistical deficiencies plagued the army. He hoped to feed off the countryside while letting Virginia agriculture recover, but the mood of the state was more complicated than the Confederate public had believed. Residents welcomed the army as long as it was in the southern sections of the state, but nowhere did they part with provisions readily. Payment in Confederate money

A northern reaction to Lee's proclamation, showing Marylanders forced into the
Confederate army and otherwise intimidated by rebel "liberators."
Harper's Weekly, September 27, 1862

held little appeal, especially because the civilians would need to spend this currency in a Union state when the southern army left. As to an uprising of the
people: none occurred.

Lee was not totally surprised by these events. When Lowe failed to arrive in
camp, the general sought advice from Bradley T. Johnson, a prominent Marylander in the army. Johnson counseled the general not to expect the uprising
promised in songs and poetry. Geography provided part of the reason. The army
spent most of its time in the Unionist portion of the state. Johnson also warned
that the citizens had experienced military rule for fifteen months. They would not
consider armed resistance to the Union without assurances that a Confederate
government would offer permanent protection.[41] By the time he issued the
proclamation, Lee knew what to expect from the civilian population.

The army lagged only slightly behind Lee in learning about the limits of Maryland's support. Cavalry changed impressions faster because they covered ground
more rapidly and could see the shift in temperament as they roamed farther
northward. Just below Frederick, a cavalry officer found a hospitable public, but
in the town and slightly to the north he encountered a different reception. Frederick itself was extremely divided. Soldiers on both sides claimed it as loyal or
disloyal, with no seeming consistency. Confederates reacted favorably when
residents of Frederick treated Lee with fine southern hospitality and presented

Jackson with a horse. But despite the good reception, the longer the soldiers stayed, the more their faith in the population declined.[42]

Some soldiers wisely questioned whether they could ever gauge the true feelings of residents in the Border States. John Hampden Chamberlayne noted that the people treated Confederate soldiers kindly, but he did not believe the sentiment was heartfelt. He could see fear in the faces and claimed they looked upon the army as potential "Vandals and Huns." Civilians were being nice, he reasoned, to protect themselves from harm. Furthermore, traveling through the state convinced Chamberlayne that no political union with the South would occur. His own ethnic prejudice led him to believe the people in the northwestern part of the state could never be true Confederates. The German residents there consisted of a lower class—"dutch" and "Yankee blood," people "among whom a republic is impossible."[43] In a similar vein, Lafayette McLaws thought it wise to suspect people living on the border who had suffered no property damage. He interpreted this as a sign of Unionism, or of persons who cared for neither side as long as they could protect themselves. Although they treated the Confederates well, McLaws expected that they did the same for the enemy.[44]

It would be a mistake to say that Confederate soldiers became completely disenchanted with the civilian population. Some obviously did, but more were inclined to excuse Marylanders for failing to throw off their oppressor. As long as the Confederate army could not establish a permanent garrison, Maryland's secessionists faced a hard choice between accepting the Union's dominion or leaving home as exiles. One captain wrote his sister that the army did reasonably well with recruiting under the circumstances. After all, fate had placed the fighting within the Unionist strongholds, places settled by people from Pennsylvania. "Maryland is all right," he wrote, "but we have bad people among us." Confederate newspapers offered estimates ranging from 300 to 1,500 new soldiers for the cause.[45] Some of Lee's soldiers still identified with the southern sympathizers and worried about them as the army withdrew across the Potomac. The people who had helped the Confederates would now be vulnerable to retribution from the Union.[46] Although they did not agree on whether to absolve the civilians, the soldiers returned with one fairly widespread idea—Maryland was a hopeless cause unless a Confederate army could be garrisoned in the state. A northern editor reached the same conclusion when noting that "Whatever the opinions of the Marylanders may be—and we hope they are sound and loyal—they had no more chance of 'rising' than the convicts in a well-ordered penitentiary."[47]

Southern civilians underwent a similar metamorphosis in their feelings about Maryland. At first, the public believed the campaign had gone quite well because of the victory at Harpers Ferry on September 15. Southerners also appreciated the reception given by the citizens of Frederick, relishing the hospitality showered upon Lee and Jackson. Rumors fed by early newspaper reports also raised hopes that citizens from the state flocked to the colors. Accounts went further by alleging that men in the southern regions had risen up and butchered Union provost marshals. The newspapers were fulfilling the prophecy of popular poetry and songs, but they were also inventing more outrageous stories. One of the more ludicrous rumors indicated that women with shaved heads had greeted the army joyfully. According to the account, they had cropped their hair "to make themselves hideous in the eyes of Yankee officers." While the cavalry skirmished, the women reputedly climbed into the stirrups to shower officers with kisses. "Alas! for the poor privates," the editor noted, although he added that the story was probably too good to be true.[48] As they realized that Maryland had not risen up to evict the oppressor, some became disgusted. One woman noted that she and her neighbors were greatly disappointed. "It was thought there would be a great uprising of the people as soon as the Stars and Bars should wave across the Potomac," she noted, adding that nothing of the kind had occurred. Lack of armed rebellion perhaps could be forgiven but not the reality that fewer men than expected had come into the ranks. She washed her hands of the civilians. "Well, let the Old Bay State go, if her people had rather be slaves in the Union than masters in the Confederacy."[49]

Opinions, however, typically mirrored the more moderate sentiments of the soldiers. After initial disappointment, Confederates accepted that an uprising failed because the Army of Northern Virginia had operated in the most Unionist region of Maryland populated by natives of the North or Germany. What else could Confederates expect of Yankees or common Dutch? A Georgia editor commented that just as southerners did not blame Virginia for the actions of the residents of western Virginia, they should not blame Maryland for the people who lived near the northern boundary. "It may become necessary in the course of the war," he reasoned, "to abandon for the present the idea of incorporating Maryland into the Confederacy . . . ; yet let us not judge her people who labor under great difficulties, either hastily or harshly."[50]

Although they could remain forgiving about Maryland, nothing prevented Confederates from judging the exiles from the state. Some Confederate sympathizers had decided that when Lee's army retreated they had better pack their bags and head south. Richmond in particular swelled with these refugees, although small communities set up in other towns such as Lynchburg. The first wave had come early, beginning with the initial signs of repression in May 1861. At least two hundred men met during that month in Richmond to discuss joining the Confederacy. Throughout the first eighteen months of the war, a trickle of

Union soldiers welcomed by civilians in Maryland. Reports of such behavior prompted
many Confederates to denounce Marylanders as unworthy allies.
Frank Leslie's Illustrated Newspaper, November 1, 1862

families relocated themselves in the Old Dominion. These were not rabble. On
the contrary, the refugees came from the best and wealthiest families. And at first
they were welcomed. Relief efforts for exiled Marylanders were held in various
places, and express companies shipped parcels at no charge if they went to the
"Maryland boys" who had left home to fight with the Confederacy.[51] In the southern Congress, representatives expressed their support for the state and promised
not to have a peace settlement before giving residents a chance to join the Confederacy. Sentiment continued for exempting the refugees from taxes and other
laws. One representative from Virginia went so far as to suggest that Maryland
residents be allowed to send nonvoting members to the Congress, a proposal that
died because the state had not instituted a provisional government like Kentucky
and Missouri.[52]

The last wave of immigrants set loose by the Antietam campaign, however,
became notorious to Virginians because many of the men refused to serve in the
military. The suspicion was widespread that young men of military age had fled
to avoid the state draft that Maryland conducted for the Union army. One man
from the state who had volunteered for the southern cavalry in September 1862

was ashamed of his neighbors. Shortly after the Antietam campaign, he heard of sixty men crossing over to Virginia on one night. He ran into nine of them registering at a Richmond hotel and did not appreciate their refusing his pleas to volunteer. "Every young able man in Richmond in citizens clothes is a Marylander," he recorded in his diary. "There is an enormous number of [men] loafing here and all the riots and fights are caused by Marylanders." He added: "They almost all go into some money making business, and then they live idle, simply through the clemency of the Confederacy."[53]

The Alien Enemies Act provided the clemency that allowed Maryland men to remain out of the army. When enacted in August 1861, the law gave citizens forty days to declare their allegiance to the Confederacy or leave, with their remaining property confiscated. Because the fate of the Border States was not yet known, the Congress exempted residents from Maryland, Kentucky, and Missouri. Consequently, young sons of Maryland planters would be considered aliens but allowed to remain in the South with exemption from conscription. As the war exacted greater sacrifices from Virginians, resentment built that these men could stay out of combat while making money from the war. The inevitable happened—brawls broke out, and local people blamed their problems of law and order partly on this foreign element. In a hospital in Richmond, Phoebe Yates Pember noticed the discrimination against Marylanders. They were resented as being rich and able to gain from the war. The soldiers wounded in battle were segregated in the hospital and received poorer attention from the medical staff. Pember believed the allegations unjust. Because of the state's status, forgers used it as the residency on fraudulent passports or exemption papers. This made the public believe that more Maryland residents tried to get around service than was the case. Congress sought in 1864 to close the loophole entirely, but Jefferson Davis used a pocket veto to kill the measure. It was not worth the small numbers that would be conscripted.[54]

Confederates finally wrote the state off as a lost cause after the Gettysburg campaign. A correspondent who traveled with the army captured the change in mood when he reported that "Maryland is neither with us, nor of us—for my part, I say 'let her alone.' I believe 'she is joined to her idols.'"[55] Yet for various reasons interest in Maryland failed to die completely in the Confederate mind. Illicit trade conducted by people from the state continued from the Eastern Shore and southern Maryland throughout the war. Sympathizers also harbored Confederate prisoners escaping from Union hospitals and prisons. Vague rumors about a secret society forming to support the South cropped up in 1863. All of this encouraged hopes that southern sentiment still existed, even if forced underground.[56] Maryland residents also fought and distinguished themselves in the Confederate army and navy. About 4,580 men served in Maryland-designated commands; roughly

20,000 were scattered in other units. Among the notable volunteers were generals such as Arnold Elzey, Bradley T. Johnson, Mansfield Lovell, and George H. Steuart Jr. Charles Sidney Winder lost his life in a key moment that helped save the battle of Cedar Mountain. Isaac R. Trimble led a division during Pickett's Charge at Gettysburg. Arguably the most famous seaman in the Confederacy hailed from the state, Raphael Semmes of the CSS *Alabama*. Where Marylanders fought, they did so with distinction.[57]

In retrospect, though, Maryland's greatest contribution to the southern cause may have been the ideological fortification that helped moderates make the transition from Union to Confederacy. This was especially true for the first two years of war and for people in the Upper South who had suffered the greatest qualms through the secession crisis. Early in the conflict these southerners witnessed the northern measures that seemed an outright attempt to subjugate the South. The suspension of habeas corpus and military arrests convinced all but the most diehard Unionists to become willing Confederates. William Blackford of Lynchburg, Virginia, provides an example. A staunch Unionist in early 1861, he quickly found a home in the Confederacy after learning of the arbitrary arrests, destruction of newspaper presses, and suspension of habeas corpus in Maryland. "Now we may well ask what is wanting to complete the enslavement of the people," he pondered, adding, "Was there any thing worse than this state of things in the despotism of Louis 15." Like many of his comrades noted above, he blamed the infusion of foreigners in places such as Baltimore for corrupting "the spirit of saxon liberty."[58]

Blackford's statement contains the complicated bundle of ideas on which the southern public created a Confederate identity—an identity that Lincoln's actions against Maryland helped to construct. Southerners prided themselves on being a liberty-loving people, yet they understood freedom in terms of slavery. When northern Republicans put people in jail without the chance to defend themselves or when they confiscated property, it seemed that they wanted to exert the control over white southerners that masters enjoyed over slaves. Southerners looked to the Revolutionary past for guidance about how to resist such tyranny, more often citing the American experience with the British than, as William Blackford did, the French example.

The white South also considered itself a superior region because of character traits different from those of the Yankee. Besides the greed and materialism associated with the North before the war, Yankees proved themselves capable of waging war on helpless civilians, especially women. They also did not respect property but robbed civilians and destroyed crops and fences. This behavior was partly attributable to their background. Unlike a white South that was largely

Protestant and English, the North contained Catholics and immigrants who could not conduct themselves properly. The Irish created problems in cities like Baltimore, where they challenged the authority of capital over labor. The Germans seemed to be people living on the margin, isolated because of language and hopeful that they could ride out the war with their property intact. Even the enemies within the Confederacy could be tarred with this brush. Maryland exiles acted like southern Yankees when they tried to sit out the war while capitalizing on misery through speculation in goods. This line of thinking on the part of southerners was, of course, the worst kind of stereotyping built on small grains of truth. But it was compelling stuff that could bind together both slaveholder and nonslaveholder in a war of independence.

Maryland alone was not responsible for the construction of Confederate identity. Union actions elsewhere had a similar effect. But the example of its citizenry came at a crucial time when southerners were trying to justify disunion. Ironically, well after the federal government had smothered secession sentiment in the state, Maryland's ideological importance grew in songs and poems. The soldiers who waded through the waters of the Potomac River may have suspected that the civilians would not flock to the colors, but they could not have known for sure as they sang the final stanza of the second most popular song of the young Confederacy: "She breathes! She burns! She'll come! She'll come! / Maryland, my Maryland!"

NOTES

1. U.S. War Department, *The War of the Rebellion: A Compilation of the Official Records of the Union and Confederate Armies,* 127 vols., index, and atlas (Washington: GPO, 1880–1901), ser. 1, vol. 19, pt. 2:601–2 (hereafter cited as *OR;* unless indicated otherwise, references are to ser. 1).

2. Edward A. Pollard, *Southern History of the War,* 2 vols. in 1 (1866; reprint, New York: Fairfax Press, 1977), 1:74.

3. James M. McPherson, *For Cause and Comrades: Why Men Fought in the Civil War* (New York: Oxford University Press, 1997), 19–21; James M. McPherson, *What They Fought for, 1861–1865* (Baton Rouge: Louisiana State University Press, 1994), 9–25; Drew Gilpin Faust, *The Creation of Confederate Nationalism* (Baton Rouge: Louisiana State University Press, 1988), 7–21; Emory M. Thomas, *The Confederate Nation, 1861–1865* (New York: Harper and Row, 1979), 105.

4. For background on Maryland, see Barbara J. Fields, *Slavery and Freedom on the Middle Ground: Maryland during the Nineteenth Century* (New Haven: Yale Univer-

sity Press, 1985), 6–22; William J. Evitts, *A Matter of Allegiances: Maryland from 1851 to 1861* (Baltimore: Johns Hopkins University Press, 1974), 2–12; Kevin Conley Ruffner, *Maryland's Blue and Gray: A Border State's Union and Confederate Junior Officer Corps* (Baton Rouge: Louisiana State University Press, 1997), 16–33.

5. Evitts, *Matter of Allegiances,* 12.

6. Charleston *Mercury,* January 22, February 4, 12, 28, 1861; George L. Radcliffe, *Governor Thomas H. Hicks of Maryland and the Civil War* (Baltimore: Johns Hopkins University Press, 1902), 20–35.

7. Richmond *Whig,* April 22, 1861; Frank Towers, ed., "Military Waif: A Sidelight on the Baltimore Riot of 19 April 1861," *Maryland Historical Magazine* 89 (Winter 1994): 427–46; Ruffner, *Maryland's Blue and Gray,* 34–36.

8. Elizabeth Van Lew, *A Yankee Spy in Richmond: The Civil War Diary of "Crazy Bet" Van Lew,* ed. David D. Ryan (Mechanicsburg, Pa.: Stackpole, 1996), 31–32; Richmond *Whig,* April 22, 1861.

9. Jefferson Davis, *The Papers of Jefferson Davis,* ed. Lynda Lasswell Crist and others, 9 vols. (Baton Rouge: Louisiana State University Press, 1971–), 7:148–51.

10. Charleston *Mercury,* April 30, May 8, 1861; Edmund Ruffin, *The Diary of Edmund Ruffin,* ed. William Kauffman Scarborough, 3 vols. (Baton Rouge: Louisiana State University Press, 1972–89), 2:14–15.

11. *OR* 2:28–32.

12. *OR,* ser. 2, 1:567–68; Charleston *Mercury,* May 10, 21, 23, 1861; [Judith McGuire], *Diary of a Southern Refugee during the War* (1867; reprint, Lincoln: University of Nebraska Press, 1995), 15.

13. James M. McPherson, *Battle Cry of Freedom: The Civil War Era* (New York: Oxford University Press, 1988), 287–89; *OR,* ser. 2, 1:574–85.

14. John B. Jones, *A Rebel War Clerk's Diary at the Confederate States Capital,* 2 vols. (1866; reprint, Alexandria, Va.: Time-Life, 1982), 1:41.

15. Charleston *Mercury,* May 10, 1861. For a similar opinion, see the Richmond *Whig,* September 14, 1861.

16. Jones, *Diary,* 1:25.

17. Mary Chesnut, *Mary Chesnut's Civil War,* ed. C. Vann Woodward (New Haven: Yale University Press, 1982), 152.

18. *OR* 2:138–39; ser. 2, 1:619–67.

19. *OR,* ser. 2, 1:631.

20. Charleston *Mercury,* July 8, 1861.

21. M. A. Albinson to friend, July 22, 1861, Albinson Letters, Confederate Papers, Miscellaneous, Southern Historical Collection, Wilson Library, University of North Carolina, Chapel Hill (repository hereafter cited as SHC).

22. *Harper's Weekly,* September 7, 1861, 571.

23. Catherine Ann Devereux Edmondston, *"Journal of a Secesh Lady": The Diary*

of Catherine Ann Devereux Edmondston, ed. Beth Gilbert Crabtree and James W. Patton (Raleigh: North Carolina Division of Archives and History, 1979), 83; Charleston *Mercury,* July 6, August 19, 1861.

24. *OR* 5:193–95; ser. 2, 1:619–748, 790–94; Daniel D. Hartzler, *Marylanders in the Confederacy* (Silver Spring, Md.: Family Line Publications, 1986), 55; Charleston *Mercury,* September 18, 1861.

25. For Howard's arrest, see *OR,* ser. 2, 2:778–86. Other arrests are in ibid., 787–90.

26. *OR* 5:620.

27. *OR* 5:640; ser. 2, 1:612–13.

28. *OR,* ser. 2, 1:595; Ruffin, *Diary,* 2:133–34; Chesnut, *Civil War,* 184.

29. William C. Davis, *Jefferson Davis, the Man and His Hour: A Biography* (New York: Harper/Collins, 1991), 363–67.

30. Richmond *Examiner* editorial reprinted in Charleston *Mercury,* September 26, 1861; "On to Washington," editorial from Richmond *Examiner* reprinted in Charleston *Mercury,* October 1, 1861.

31. This analysis is based on a collection of 250 poems and lyrics in the Confederate Broadside Poetry Collection, Rare Book Room, Z. Smith Reynolds Library, Wake Forest University, Winston-Salem, N.C. (collection hereafter cited as CBPC-WF). Accounts dealing with Maryland amount to roughly 20 percent of this collection. Documents were accessed through the Internet via the library's Web page. All references are to the specific address for the document. For a description of the collection, see William Moss, *Confederate Broadside Poems: A Descriptive Bibliography Based on the Collection of the Z. Smith Reynolds Library of Wake Forest University* (London: Meckler, 1988).

32. "Maryland! My Maryland!," new version, http://www.wfu.edu/library/rarebook/broads/Maryla11.jpg, CBPC-WF.

33. Charleston *Mercury,* February 28, 1862.

34. "Oh Jeff! Why Don't You Come?," http://www.wfu.edu/library/rarebook/broads/ohjeff.jpg, CBPC-WF.

35. "An Answer to the Poem Entitled 'How They Act in Baltimore,'" http://www.wfu.edu/library/rarebook/broads/ananswer.jpg; "Song. Baltimore," http://www.wfu.edu/library/rarebook/broads/baltimor.jpg; "There Is Life in Old Maryland Yet," http://www.wfu.edu/library/rarebook/broads/thereis1.jpg, all in CBPC-WF.

36. Edmondston, *Diary,* 184.

37. *OR* 19(2):590–93.

38. Robert J. Trout, ed., *With Pen and Saber: The Letters and Diaries of J. E. B. Stuart's Staff Officers* (Mechanicsburg, Pa.: Stackpole, 1995), 96–97; H. L. P. King diary, September 6, 1862, SHC; Charleston *Mercury,* September 6, 1862; Richmond *Enquirer,* September 9, 1862; Lucy Buck, *Sad Earth, Sweet Heaven: The Diary of*

Lucy Rebecca Buck during the War between the States, ed. William P. Buck (Birmingham, Ala.: Cornerstone, 1973), 141.

39. Emory M. Thomas, *Robert E. Lee: A Biography* (New York: Norton, 1995), 256; Davis, *Jefferson Davis,* 468–69; Stephen W. Sears, *Landscape Turned Red: The Battle of Antietam* (New York: Ticknor & Fields, 1983), 64–69.

40. *OR* 19(2):602.

41. *Southern Historical Society Papers,* ed. J. William Jones and others, 52 vols. (1876–1959; reprint with 3-vol. index, Wilmington, N.C.: Broadfoot, 1990–92), 12:504–5 (hereafter cited as *SHSP*). Although a postwar account, Johnson's story rings true. When Lee issued his report nearly a year after the campaign, he indicated that the Confederacy would not succeed in liberating Maryland unless the South could "give them assurance of continued protection." See *OR* 19(1):144.

42. R. Channing Price to mother, September 10, 1862, in Trout, *With Pen and Saber,* 96; Virginia Bardley, ed., "Frederick Diary: September 5–14, 1862," in *Maryland Historical Magazine* 60 (June 1965): 134–36; Calvin Leach diary, September 11, 1862, SHC; James Munnerlyn to sister, October 9, 1862, Munnerlyn Papers, SHC; W. G. Morris to family, September 7, 1862, Morris to companion, September 23, 1862, William Groves Morris Papers, SHC; Charleston *Mercury,* September 16, 1862.

43. John Hampden Chamberlayne to sister, September 8, 1862, in John Hampden Chamberlayne, *Ham Chamberlayne—Virginian: Letters and Papers of an Artillery Officer in the War for Southern Independence, 1861–1865,* ed. C. G. Chamberlayne (Richmond, Va.: Dietz, 1932), 105.

44. Lafayette McLaws to wife, September 4, 1862, McLaws Papers, SHC.

45. Capt. D. W. Barringer to sister, September 30, 1862, Barringer Papers, SHC. For recruiting estimates, see Davis, *Papers,* 8:411 n. 16.

46. William Machall to Minie, September 26, 1862, Machall Papers, SHC.

47. *Harper's Weekly,* September 27, 1862, 610.

48. Charleston *Mercury,* September 8, 10, 1862; Edmondston, *Diary,* 261 (entry for September 22, 1862).

49. Kate Stone, *Brokenburn: The Journal of Kate Stone,* ed. John Q. Anderson (Baton Rouge: Louisiana State University Press, 1955), 146.

50. Opinion of the Savannah *Republican* quoted in Charleston *Mercury,* October 15, 1862.

51. Charleston *Mercury,* October 28, 1861; Hartzler, *Marylanders in the Confederacy,* 57.

52. *SHSP* 50:222; Wilfred Buck Yearns, *The Confederate Congress* (Athens: University of Georgia Press, 1960), 163.

53. Edmund C. Paca, ed., "'Tim's Black Book': The Civil War Diary of Edward Tilghman Paca, Jr., CSA," *Maryland Historical Magazine* 89 (Winter 1994): 457.

54. Phoebe Yates Pember, *A Southern Woman's Story: Life in Confederate Rich-*

mond, ed. Bell Irvin Wiley (1897; reprint, Jackson, Tenn.: McCowat-Mercer Press, 1959), 61–64; Mary Elizabeth Massey, *Refugee Life in the Confederacy* (Baton Rouge: Louisiana State University Press, 1964), 43–45.

55. Richmond *Enquirer,* July 21, 1863.

56. Charleston *Mercury,* April 28, September 1, 1863.

57. Hartzler, *Marylanders in the Confederacy,* 1; *SHSP* 31:209–14.

58. William Blackford diary, May 8, August 29, 1861, vol. 5, box 2, Blackford Family Papers, Alderman Library, University of Virginia, Charlottesville.

KEITH S. BOHANNON

Dirty, Ragged, and Ill-Provided For

Confederate Logistical Problems in the 1862

Maryland Campaign and Their Solutions

Confederate general John R. Jones claimed in his official report of the battle of Antietam that the Army of Northern Virginia had never been "so dirty, ragged, and ill-provided for" as it was in the 1862 Maryland campaign. Years later, the astute former artillery officer Edward Porter Alexander wrote that "[i]n the matter of shoes, clothing, and food" Robert E. Lee's army was "upon the whole, probably worse off" during the Antietam campaign "than it had ever been before or ever was again."[1] If the statements of Jones and Alexander are true, what were the reasons for this state of affairs? How did these conditions affect Lee's army on the march and in battle? What was the reaction to this situation within the Army of Northern Virginia, the Confederate government, and the southern populace?

Robert E. Lee had a number of reasons for not following his beaten enemy toward Washington in the wake of victory at Second Manassas. He had no intention of attacking or investing the formidable fortifications surrounding the United States capital. Even if the Confederate army possessed ample ammunition to do so, Lee wrote Jefferson Davis on September 3, he would "be unable to supply provisions for the troops." The war had ravaged northern Virginia. In an 1868 letter, Lee asserted that he could not have maintained his army in the immediate environs of Washington, "so barren was it of subsistence, and so devoid were we of transportation." An "expedition into Maryland," as Lee termed his proposed movement, would allow his army to subsist off a countryside untouched by war. With luck, it would also draw the Federal army north of the Potomac River, giving a much needed respite to northern Virginia's farmers and allowing Confederate commissary agents to gather cattle, wheat, and forage from the region.[2]

Lee enjoyed a number of important advantages when his army forded the Potomac River on September 5, 1862. His men were in high spirits after their victories in the Seven Days and Second Manassas campaigns, and the army boasted a cadre of skilled generals. The physical condition of the Army of Northern Virginia was a different matter, as Lee acknowledged in a September 3 communication with Jefferson Davis. "This army is not properly equipped for an invasion of the enemy's territory," Lee noted. It lacked "much of the material of war, is feeble in transportation, the animals being much reduced, . . . the men . . . poorly provided with clothes, and in thousands of instances . . . destitute of shoes." Despite being weaker than his opponents in men and military equipments, Lee considered it important that his command remain on the offensive and that he maintain the initiative.[3]

At the same time that Lee offered Jefferson Davis a frank appraisal of the army's condition, he revealed an uneasiness in regard to his supplies of ammunition and subsistence. His concern about subsistence was warranted, given conditions within the Confederacy in the fall of 1862. Southern reverses in the war's Western Theater in the winter of 1861–62 had resulted in the abandonment of central Tennessee, the largest pork-producing region in the Confederacy. Despite the conversion of much farmland from cotton to foodstuff cultivation, a severe drought in the summer of 1862 nullified any potential to increase food production. Confederate secretary of war George W. Randolph summarized the situation in a mid-November 1862 letter to Lee. "The supply of hogs is 100,000 less than it was last year," wrote Randolph, "[and] the failure of the corn crop in Tennessee and Northwestern Georgia renders even this supply to some extent unavailable." The supply of beef was less than it had been, as was the wheat crop in Virginia. The secretary of war concluded his grim assessment by stating that "the corn crop in the Southern States is unavailable by the difficulties of transportation."[4]

When moving into Maryland, Lee realized that his men would be far from major southern supply depots or railroad routes. He consequently proposed to Davis on September 5 that the army supply itself with provisions and forage taken from the countryside. Confederate soldiers had done this to some extent during the Second Manassas campaign. The diet of green corn, or "roasting ears," and green apples usually associated with the Maryland campaign appears in official reports, newspaper columns, and the diaries and letters of many soldiers in early August 1862 and continues through most of September.[5]

Lee's ordnance situation also merited concern. By the late summer of 1862, the Army of Northern Virginia had obtained sufficient numbers of infantry arms through importation, production at government and local shops, and capture on the battlefield. The army's problems resulted from the quality, not the quantity, of its arms. According to Stonewall Jackson's ordnance officer, William Allan, the infantrymen were armed "in a heterogenous fashion" in the fall of 1862. E. P. Alexander believed that about 30 percent of the foot soldiers carried antiquated .69 caliber smoothbore muskets. Although captured arms from the battlefields around Richmond enabled some commands to exchange their smoothbores for rifle muskets, this process was far from complete as Lee's men marched into Maryland. Allan noted that along with smoothbores, many Confederate infantrymen carried one of three types of .54 caliber muskets: the U.S. Model 1855 "Harper's Ferry" rifle, the U.S. Model 1841 "Mississippi" rifle, or the Austrian Lorenz rifle. Still others carried the .57 caliber 1853 Enfield rifle muskets imported from England or the .58 caliber Springfields.[6]

Fragmentary Confederate ordnance records and receipts confirm the general statements of Allan and Alexander. A fall 1862 requisition for ammunition "for [the] use of General Jackson's Command" filled out by chief of ordnance Maj. George Henry Bier requested forty thousand .58 caliber cartridges, twenty thousand .69 caliber cartridges, and a smaller number of rounds for Burnside, Smith, and Hall carbines. A November 1862 inspection report of Gen. John B. Hood's division revealed that at least two regiments in the Texas Brigade and both regiments present from Evander M. Law's brigade had "mixed arms," some of them in "bad" or "tolerable" order. Armament reports for the brigades of Gens. William Barksdale and Joseph B. Kershaw of Lafayette McLaws's division show that between 20 and 30 percent of the men still carried .69 caliber weapons during the Maryland campaign.[7]

William Allan's observation that most ordnance officers were "anxious to replace the smooth bores with rifles, and especially with calibre .58 [weapons]," held true for most but not all army personnel in the fall of 1862. At least one officer preferred the smoothbores, while others favored the .54 caliber rifles. When Col. William L. DeRosset of the 3rd North Carolina Infantry had the chance after the Seven Days campaign to exchange his regiment's .69 caliber smoothbores for captured Model 1861 Springfield rifles, he declined. He defended his decision by noting that at Sharpsburg the smoothbores "did excellent service, being at very close quarters, not over one hundred yards . . . from the enemy." London *Times* correspondent Francis Lawley claimed that many Confederates preferred

INVOICE of Ordnance and Ordnance Stores turned over by *Capt E. Taliaferro*
Ord. Off. Maj. Genl McLaws ~~Arsenal, to~~ *Div. to Officers*
for immediate Quartermaster C. S. A., for ~~Transportation to~~ *service in*
Battle Sep 17th & 19th 1862

NO.	MARKS.	CONTENTS.	WEIGHT.
	Capt Read	100 rounds 8 inch shell	
		64 rounds Parrot shell	
		200 Friction Primers	
	Lt Allen (Ord off)	4000 Carts Cal 57	
		3000 " Cal 58	
		4000 " Cal 54	
		9000 " Cal 69	
	Lt Colepton	48 rounds Parrot shell & 200 Fr Primers	
	Capt Carter	48 rounds Parrot shell	
		200 Friction Primers	

I CERTIFY, that the above Invoice is correct. *& that the Stores were issued*

E. Taliaferro

Sharpsburg Md ARSENAL,
Sep. 17th 1862.
Shepherdstown Va Sep 19, 1862

Capt & ord off.

This invoice for ammunition issued to William Barksdale's Mississippi brigade and several accompanying artillery batteries "for immediate service" in the battle of Sharpsburg reveals the heterogeneous nature of Confederate armaments in the autumn of 1862.
Edwin Taliaferro Papers, National Archives

"smoothbore rifles" over Enfields or Springfields, noting that the men "seldom fire until within two hundred yards of their enemy." "At this distance," wrote Lawley, "the constant tendency of the rifled musket is to throw its ball too high." An Alabama officer gave a similar statement to a Richmond newspaper correspondent, stating that "in practice, these long-range weapons [Enfields or Springfields] had been found of little or no use, inferior in every way to the Mississippi or Harper's Ferry rifle, especially in warfare against the Yankees, who had been whipped by Lee's army always by bold charges and by firing at close quarters."[8]

The armament situation within the Confederate cavalry was similar to that in the infantry. Artist Alfred R. Waud, trapped briefly behind Confederate lines during the initial stage of the Maryland campaign, noted that the men in the 1st Virginia Cavalry carried "the United States cavalry sabre, Sharp's carbine, and pistols." The carbines, the horsemen told Waud, were mostly captured from the Federals. Henry B. McClellan of Gen. J. E. B. Stuart's staff stated that "breech-loading carbines were procured only in limited quantities, never more than enough to arm one, or at most two squadrons in a regiment." The rest of the troopers usually carried Enfield rifles, the shorter carbine versions if possible.[9]

The varied types of arms carried by Lee's men into Maryland had several important ramifications. Because the smoothbore muskets had an effective range of only about one hundred yards, it remained important to mass men in lines to concentrate their fire. Supplying ammunition to units armed with different caliber weapons created a complex situation for army ordnance officers, many of whom apparently had little experience in their duties. "As a result," wrote William Allan, "little system or order existed in the management or distribution of supplies." Allan admitted that "great waste existed" within the Ordnance Department, but frequent and valuable captures helped avoid serious difficulties.[10]

Lee's army brought approximately 246 pieces of artillery to the field at Antietam, some of the weaker batteries having been left in Winchester or Richmond. Unfortunately for the Confederates, many of the pieces were short-range smoothbore cannon such as the Mexican War–vintage Model 1841 6-pounder guns, inferior in range and hitting power to the more modern Federal guns (Lee's army had 41 of the obsolete Model 1841 6-pounder guns at Antietam; the Federals had none). Of the fifty-nine southern batteries present at Antietam, only five had uniform armaments. This created problems not only in supplying ammunition but also in the tactical deployment of batteries. In many instances, only rifled pieces or sections of batteries could be utilized against the longer-range Federal artillery.[11]

Confederate artillerists also had serious problems with the quality of their fuses and shells. E. P. Alexander found that four-fifths of the smoothbore shells utilizing the Bormann fuse burst prematurely, many of them in the guns. Mullane shells, used in rifled cannon, frequently burst within the barrels of guns or failed to explode in flight. The consequences of utilizing such ammunition became clear during the siege of Harpers Ferry. The Confederate bombardment of the town's Union garrison had far more moral than physical effect. Many of the shells fired by the southern rifled batteries on Loudoun and Maryland Heights failed to burst or exploded prematurely, while others tumbled in flight and missed their targets. "Even the smooth-bore shells," Alexander observed, "often burst near the guns." [12]

The Confederate artillery overcame its handicaps to perform superbly at Antietam. Although the southern batteries had been informally grouped together following the success of such organizations at Second Manassas, many of Lee's artillerists "constantly shifted about" at Antietam, detached from battalions or groups. This tactic allowed the cannoneers to close on the attacking enemy infantry, their main target, while dividing the fire of the superior Federal artillery. At close range, the case and canister of the Confederate 6-pounder guns and light howitzers proved extremely effective against the ranks of Union foot soldiers. [13]

Many southern artillerists and their comrades in the infantry marched onto the field at Sharpsburg poorly clad and shod. Part of the blame lay with the army's commutation system, which required soldiers to furnish their own clothing in quantities stated by regulations in exchange for a biannual fixed sum of money. By late August 1861 it was clear that this system was not adequate, and new legislation in the Confederate Congress called for the secretary of war to furnish, as far as possible, "clothing for the entire forces of the Confederacy." The new law actually expanded the commutation system, requiring the War Department to pay states such as North Carolina that supplied their own troops with clothing. [14]

The establishment by the Confederate Quartermaster Department of clothing depots or bureaus in several major southern cities facilitated the efficient distribution of goods. These depots, one of the earliest and largest of which was in Richmond, served as centers of accumulation of goods obtained by the Confederate government through contracts with private businesses. The depots also turned out finished uniforms and shoes, although production levels remained low early in the war. Union seizures of major depots and production centers in Nashville in February 1862 and New Orleans two months later dealt crippling blows to the Confederate Quartermaster Department, wiping out much of its stock of surplus goods. [15]

Shortages in raw materials such as wool and leather also plagued the Confederate Quartermaster Department. In a January 1863 report of conditions within the Confederacy, Secretary of War James A. Seddon informed President Davis that "reliance has been placed to a considerable extent on foreign supplies, since they [leather and wool] are not adequately furnished within the Confederate States." Seddon admitted that "under the losses and interruptions caused by the Blockade, there has been at times rather scant supplies of Blankets, Shoes, and some other articles of clothing."[16]

Despite the many problems facing the Confederate quartermaster system, Q.M. Gen. Abraham C. Myers wrote Secretary of War Randolph in mid-August 1862 urging that the commutation system be totally abolished. Myers admitted that his department was not "prepared to fully cloth[e] the Army in the field," but he nonetheless argued that "the troops can be more effectually supplied through the [central government] depots than from any other source." Rampant inflation, Myers noted, had made the commutation payment of twenty-five dollars per soldier for six months' worth of clothing "totally inadequate . . . a pair of servicable shoes costing one half of that sum." Soldiers buying clothing on the market competed with purchasers from the Confederate government, driving up the prices set by "traders and speculators." Myers also noted that the frequent and valuable donations of clothing made by private individuals and organizations earlier in the war had nearly ceased by the fall of 1862 because of the "difficulty of safe and prompt transportation, and for the more controlling reason, that nearly all such sources of supply have been made available by the Q. M. Department."[17]

While Quartermaster General Myers argued to end the commutation system, the Army of Northern Virginia engaged in a series of long marches resulting in a Confederate victory at Second Manassas. These movements took an enormous toll on shoe leather, leaving thousands of southern soldiers either barefoot or with only the remnants of shoes. Some army officers, unable to obtain assistance from the Quartermaster Department, tried to alleviate the situation, usually with little success. A detail of men from John B. Hood's division making shoes in Louisa Court House, for example, had only a "scant supply on hand" when an officer arrived to take the footwear to the division.[18]

A reduction in the number of regimental baggage wagons within Lee's army also contributed to the soldiers' woes. On August 6, 1862, Lee ordered three wagons taken from every regiment in the army to provide additional vehicles for hauling subsistence. This order denied the soldiers access to large amounts of spare clothing and blankets and made it impossible for Stonewall Jackson's men to haul away valuable supplies captured at Manassas Junction. Another redistribution of wagons, enjoining infantry officers to haul only "cooking utensils and the absolute necessities of a regiment," occurred on September 4 just prior to the army's crossing the Potomac River into Maryland. The second reduction, like the first, helped free vehicles to carry flour to the army.[19]

Reductions ordered in the personal baggage carried by individual soldiers exacerbated the problems caused by the absence of regimental wagons. Throughout the first several weeks of August, most officers in Lee's army received orders for their men to place knapsacks, tents, and extra blankets in storage and proceed in light marching order. The baggage left behind remained in various locales, including Rapidan, Gordonsville, Charlottesville, and Richmond, until late October or November 1862.[20]

The absence of baggage wagons and personal baggage, together with the inability of the Quartermaster Department to issue clothing or shoes, left Lee's men in dire straits throughout most of August and September 1862. Plundering the dead offered some relief. Lt. George L. P. Wren of the 8th Louisiana Infantry noticed that at Second Manassas he "did not see a man but had been stripped of his shoes.... [They] being a very scarce article, there was a great demand for them." Newspaper correspondent Felix G. De Fontaine concurred, noting with a bit of exaggeration that some southern regiments could "charge and strip every dead Yankee's feet they pass without coming to a halt."[21]

As Lee's men left the Manassas battlefield and marched northward, their commanding officer made preparations to secure his supply lines. On September 3, the Confederates captured the town of Winchester. Although retreating Federals had blown up their magazine and burned several buildings filled with supplies, the southerners captured a quantity of stores, including ammunition, some fine guns, medical stores, tents, and cooking utensils. Lee subsequently designated Winchester an army depot, ordering that stragglers be collected there along with surplus and worn-out animals and wagons. He also specified that the Ordnance and Quartermaster departments establish workshops in the town to repair broken-down wagons and artillery vehicles.

On September 5, the day after Confederates began crossing the Potomac into Maryland, Lee sent Jefferson Davis a telegram describing the army's new supply route. From Culpeper Court House, wagons were to travel westward into the Shenandoah Valley and then proceed by way of Luray and Front Royal to Winchester. An alternate route directed wagons to Staunton and then down the Valley Turnpike to Winchester.[22]

Immediately prior to the Confederate army's passage of the Potomac, Lee issued a general order that he hoped would provide food and forage, clothing, shoes, medical stores, and horses for his command. He instructed quartermaster and commissary officers to purchase from civilians supplies for issuance to their respective commands "upon proper requisition." If unable to pay for necessities, officers were to provide "certificates of indebtedness of the Confederate States for future adjustment." These measures, Lee hoped, would remove all excuses for depredations.[23]

Numerous Confederates testified that Lee's troops exercised restraint while marching through Maryland. J. F. J. Caldwell contended that the men "distinguished themselves by studiously refraining from injury to the persons or property of the people." Caldwell saw thousands of troops pass orchards "without touching a fruit." Another South Carolinian concurred, stating that "not an apple, peach, or plum were allowed to be taken without payment, or at the owner's consent." One journalist informed his readers that "not a pound of hay nor a piece of wood has been consumed without the owner's consent and full compensation."[24]

Other southerners left a different portrait of the army's behavior as it passed through Maryland. John William McLure, a quartermaster in Micah Jenkins's brigade, told his wife that civilians "sometimes object to take Confederate notes in payment for hay and other necessary supplies for our army, which necessitates us to adopt the rather stringent measures of taking the desired articles by force, which process is popularly known in the army by the name of 'pressing.'" An Alabama soldier admitted that Lee's army was "quite as destructive as the Yankees to fences & cornfields," but he justified the actions by arguing that the southerners "distroy from necessity they [the Federals] from the desire to plunder."[25]

Almost immediately after the dramatic crossing of the Potomac by Lee's troops on September 5, Marylanders began witnessing the destruction of their farm fences and cornfields. After reaching the Maryland shore, thousands of hungry rebels went through a familiar series of tasks repeated many times in the following weeks. With no sign of their commissary wagons, the men received orders to move into large fields of corn purchased by Confederate commissary officers. There the soldiers filled their haversacks with instructions to feed any remaining husks and stalks to the horses. Jedediah Hotchkiss, a member of Stonewall Jackson's staff, wrote that his commander "bought rails and ordered the men to have one day's rations of roasting ears cooked and in the haversacks by dawn" the next day. The absence of cooking utensils was a problem in many messes. An artillerist noted that "the man who owned a frying pan, was possessed of no little influence, and various sorts of flattery were frequently resorted to, to gain temporary possession of it." As the soldiers marched away from "Camp Roastangear," as it had been dubbed in the diary of at least one wag in the ranks, Jed Hotchkiss heard a passing soldier wonder aloud if General Jackson "has roasting ears in his haversack too?" The answer came when Stonewall halted for dinner and "took a large roasting ear out of his haversack and deliberately gnawed off the corn." "The whole army," wrote Hotchkiss, "stretched for miles along the road, followed suit."[26]

The diet of green corn and apples, supplemented occasionally by flour and fresh beef, remained a constant for Lee's men throughout the Maryland campaign. A private in the 14th Alabama estimated that "two-thirds of the subsistence our men got in Maryland, was roasting-ears." A company-grade officer wrote home that "many days we had to march without a meal in our haversacks, and when they did feed us it was with beef with no salt and bread the same." A Georgian informed his wife that since leaving Richmond the men had lived "some days on raw baked and roasted apples some times on green corn and some times nothing." Some soldiers, especially officers, enjoyed a more varied diet owing to the efforts of their personal servants. "The great horde of negro cooks and servants that usually followed the army were allowed to roam at will over the surrounding country," noted a South Carolinian.[27]

A halt of several days in the environs of Frederick, Maryland, allowed Lee's men a much needed rest. Stonewall Jackson's troops entered Frederick on September 6, hundreds of soldiers crowding into stores while others took meals in the homes of friendly civilians. Frederick civilian Jacob Engelbrecht estimated in his diary on September 9 that there were "at least ten thousand [Confederates] in town—a complete jam, all the Stores & Shops were sold out, & not the one half supplied." The ragged hordes of rebels received a mixed reception from Frederick's denizens; although many merchants and civilians sold freely and accepted Confederate script from southern soldiers, others did not.[28]

In the hope of bringing order to the streets of Frederick and facilitating the official purchase of supplies, Lee closed off the town on September 9 to all soldiers except those on army business. He later claimed that Confederate quartermasters obtained only a thousand pairs of shoes and some clothing in Frederick, hardly enough to meet the desperate needs in the ranks.[29]

The same day that Lee ordered Frederick off limits, he telegraphed Jefferson Davis to describe the army's supply situation. "We are able to obtain forage and some provisions," Lee wrote, "but there is more difficulty about the latter." Many Maryland farmers had not gotten their wheat out of the fields, Lee explained, adding that there was "a reluctance on the part of millers and others to commit themselves in our favor." Some cattle, "but not great numbers," had been obtained in the countryside.[30]

The Union garrisons at Martinsburg and Harpers Ferry obstructed Confederate supply and communication lines into the Shenandoah Valley. Lee decided while at Frederick that his men must dislodge the two Federal garrisons "in order to open our communications through the Valley for the purpose of obtaining from Richmond the ammunition, clothing, etc., of which we were in great need."

A postwar engraving titled "Rations from the Stalk." Roasted ears of corn were a dietary
staple in the Army of Northern Virginia during the 1862 Maryland campaign.
Robert Underwood Johnson and Clarence Clough Buel, eds., *Battles and Leaders
of the Civil War*, 4 vols. (New York: Century, 1887–88), 2:561

The Confederate commander knew that he could obtain ample supplies of flour
and probably cattle from farmers in the valley.[31]

Lee issued orders on September 9 dividing his army into several parts to facil-
itate the capture of Martinsburg and Harpers Ferry. Stonewall Jackson with three
divisions would march by way of Middletown, Boonsboro, and Williamsport to

Martinsburg "to capture or to drive the force there stationed toward Harper's Ferry." Jackson would then invest and capture Harpers Ferry with the assistance of two divisions under Gens. Lafayette McLaws and John G. Walker, McLaws's command being stationed on Maryland Heights and Walker's on Loudoun Heights. The remainder of Lee's force, under Gen. James Longstreet, would move first to Boonsboro at the western base of South Mountain and then to Hagerstown. Lee hoped that after the fall of Martinsburg and Harpers Ferry the army could be reunited on the Maryland side of the Potomac before it became necessary to give battle to his cautious adversary, George B. McClellan.[32]

Jackson's men occupied Martinsburg on the morning of September 12, capturing "a lot of corn, commissary stores, and military supplies" according to Virginia artillerist William E. Jones. A South Carolinian remembered how "the citizens of the place brought us baskets of food, and invited large numbers of us to go home to dine with them." While the soldiers gorged, having "a sort of repetition of what occurred at Second Manassas," Jackson's commissary and quartermaster officers posted guards at the captured Union army warehouses until the supplies could be inspected and loaded into wagons. When Capt. David G. McIntosh, a battery commander, went into one storehouse to secure a pair of boots, he encountered Jackson's capable chief quartermaster, Maj. John A. Harman. Harman turned McIntosh away, claiming that "nothing could be had except by a regular requisition."[33]

The quantity of material captured by the Confederates at Martinsburg paled in comparison to that seized at Harpers Ferry, where the Union garrison surrendered on September 15 after a three-day siege. The Federal capitulation left Stonewall Jackson's command in possession of roughly 11,000 prisoners and an equal number of small arms, 73 cannon, 200 wagons, and "a large amount of camp and garrison equipage." Out of the limited supply of rations captured in the town, Jackson's commissary officer, Maj. Wells J. Hawks, issued full rations for two days to the prisoners and divided the rest among Jackson's men.[34]

Confederate ordnance officers detailed to secure the captured arms and ammunition at Harpers Ferry had orders to send all suitable ammunition to the main army at Sharpsburg and forward everything else to Winchester. E. P. Alexander, who arrived in Harpers Ferry on September 16, eventually sent forty-nine field pieces, twenty-four mountain howitzers, and a large amount of unsuitable artillery ammunition to Winchester. According to Alexander, none of the artillery or small arms collected at Harpers Ferry reached Sharpsburg in time for the army to utilize them in the battle on September 17.[35]

The failure of these ordnance supplies to reach Lee's army was probably due in part to the incompetence of support personnel. Jackson's chief of artillery

Col. Stapleton Crutchfield reached Harpers Ferry on the evening of September 16 with orders to send captured guns and ammunition to Sharpsburg, "as our ordnance supplies were getting short and our batteries in an inefficient condition from hard marching and previous fighting." At Harpers Ferry, Crutchfield found that the quartermaster assigned to remove the captured artillery had "mismatched the caissons, limbers, and guns to such an extent that after vainly spending half the day at it, I gave up the task of getting together any batteries from among them." Crutchfield assembled fresh horses, ammunition, and new guns for three disabled batteries before starting to the battlefield.[36]

Despite the efforts of quartermasters and commissaries to account for all the property seized at Harpers Ferry, much of it never appeared on official inventories. John A. Harman complained that large amounts of captured property were not turned over to the Quartermaster Department, "especially by the cavalry." In many cases, quartermasters of individual units failed to produce inventories of captured supplies hauled off in new wagons they had exchanged for worn-out vehicles. Even high-ranking officers succumbed to the temptation of plundering. An artillerist noted that Gen. A. P. Hill "appeared to have the contents of an whole sutler's stores in one of his wagons, part of the 'loot' of Harper's Ferry."[37]

Many of Jackson's foot cavalrymen ignored protocol when it came to the captured stores at Harpers Ferry. A Tennessean from Archer's brigade remembered that his unit ostensibly guarded a large warehouse full of supplies but that most of the men spent their time appropriating whatever suited their fancy. A South Carolinian noted that while guarding prisoners the gaunt southerners "fared sumptuously." In addition to "meat, crackers, sugar, coffee, shoes, blankets, underclothing etc.," many of the boys "captured horses roaming at large on whom to transport our plunder." When the South Carolinians of Gregg's brigade fell in to receive rations consisting of "*very fair* bread" cooked on flat rocks, one of their commissary officers noted that the men "stood but little in need" of the ration, "having supplied themselves from captured stores."[38]

Maxcy Gregg's South Carolinians, along with the remainder of A. P. Hill's "Light Division," spent all of September 16 in Harpers Ferry paroling prisoners. The rest of Jackson's command had marched to Sharpsburg the previous afternoon to rejoin Lee's army. During the Light Division's brief rest in the crowded streets of Harpers Ferry, at least two North Carolina regiments of Gen. Lawrence Branch's brigade, and perhaps other units as well, exchanged their smoothbore muskets for captured rifle muskets. Capt. David G. McIntosh, commanding the Pee Dee Artillery, received a complement of two new cannon, as well as new harnesses and "some very fine looking western horses from Chicago." To the regret of McIntosh's artillerists, the horses turned out to be "soft" and "wilted alongside the lean Confederate stock used to hard work and short rations."[39]

Hill's men also took the opportunity at Harpers Ferry to cast off their ragged garments in exchange for Federal uniforms. Capt. Andrew Wardlaw wrote his wife that throughout the Federal camps "the whole ground . . . was pretty well covered in places with old clothes which our soldiers had thrown off, substituting new ones." So many men in Gen. James J. Archer's brigade donned captured clothing that one member claimed that "but for the tattered Battle flags [they] might have been taken for a brand new Brigade from Boston."[40]

In addition to feasting on captured rations and acquiring new garments, Hill's soldiers returned to their old owners hundreds of former slaves (the estimates run from five hundred to twelve hundred) captured at Harpers Ferry. John A. Harman later testified that he took some of the former slaves off the street corners in Harpers Ferry and utilized them as teamsters before their masters took them away. Most of the former slaves had been claimed by September 16; according to North Carolina captain John C. Gorman, many ended up being sent "down South" by their owners.[41]

As Jackson moved against the Union garrisons at Martinsburg and Harpers Ferry, Lee accompanied Gen. James Longstreet's command and the division of Gen. D. H. Hill across the South Mountain range. Hill's division initially remained at Boonsboro to support the Confederate cavalry east of South Mountain, while Longstreet's command marched westward to Hagerstown with the reserve, supply, and baggage wagons of the army to secure supplies and guard against a reported Federal advance southward from Chambersburg, Pennsylvania. The Confederate army's ordnance and other supply trains moved with the reserve artillery between Longstreet and Hill.[42]

Longstreet's veterans received a warm welcome in Hagerstown. Virginian Alexander Hunter remembered that "not only were the men and women outspoken in their sympathy for the Southern cause, but they threw open their hospital doors and filled their houses with soldiers, feeding the hungry, and clothing the naked, as well as their limited means allowed." Journalist Peter W. Alexander informed his readers that most of the Unionists in Hagerstown had fled before the Confederates arrived, while those remaining "who constitute a majority of the town and country, have given us a very cordial reception." Alexander admitted that despite the welcome it remained difficult to pass Confederate currency. "If it were known that the army would remain in Maryland," he wrote, "the people would receive it freely at least they say so."[43]

The supplies of foodstuffs and clothing obtained by the Confederates in Hagerstown failed to meet the needs of Longstreet's ragged and hungry command. Lee informed Davis on September 12 that the army had found about 1,500 barrels of flour in the city and hoped to gather more from nearby mills. This was hardly enough, and Lee told the president that he feared "we shall have to haul [flour] from the Valley of Virginia." The army had obtained only a small amount of beef and no bacon. The 400 pairs of shoes found in Hagerstown combined with 250 pairs found in Williamsport and those obtained in Frederick were scarcely sufficient, Lee acknowledged, to cover the bare feet of his men.[44]

Lee's deep concerns over supply problems came at the same time that the Army of the Potomac began an unexpectedly rapid advance toward the passes in South Mountain, the result of McClellan's possession of Special Order No. 191. Although Lee had not planned to dispute the Federal passage over South Mountain, by the afternoon of September 13 he realized that the mountain passes must be held to ensure the safety of Lafayette McLaws's division, then located in Pleasant Valley as part of the force besieging Harpers Ferry. By daylight on September 14, Lee had D. H. Hill's division defending Turner's and Fox's Gaps while Longstreet's brigades hastened to Hill's assistance from Hagerstown.[45]

At the same time Lee ordered Longstreet eastward to assist Hill, he instructed the portion of the army's wagon train then in Hagerstown to proceed toward Williamsport "with a view to its safety, & if necessary, to cross the [Potomac] river." A reporter accompanying the army noted that such a movement would "give free scope to the army, and prevent the blocking up of roads." On the evening of the 14th, after a day of heavy fighting in the South Mountain passes, Lee decided to concentrate his forces at Sharpsburg. He sent orders for the wagons at Hagerstown to cross the Potomac at Williamsport and proceed through Martinsburg and Shepherdstown, recrossing the Potomac at the latter place to rejoin the army at Sharpsburg.[46]

The crisis at the South Mountain passes prevented the Confederates from detailing a large force to guard their trains at Hagerstown. Only a tiny contingent of infantrymen, composed of two and one-half infantry regiments from the brigades of Robert Toombs and George T. Anderson, and one cavalry regiment accompanied the wagon trains as they moved out of Hagerstown on the road toward Williamsport after dark on September 14. The column of trains "extended for several miles" and numbered, according to one quartermaster in the column, "from 500 to 600 wagons." Most of the guards remained in the rear, "that being the only direction from which an attack was apprehended."[47]

Unfortunately for the southerners, a column of approximately 1,300 Union cavalrymen under the command of Col. Benjamin F. "Grimes" Davis intercepted a portion of the Confederate train approximately two miles northeast of Williamsport before dawn. Having escaped from Harpers Ferry just hours before, the

Federals rode up to wagons and began directing them northward onto the Green-castle Pike. In the darkness, many of the teamsters thought the horsemen were Confederates "and obeyed instructions with their usual cheerfulness." Capt. Francis W. Dawson of Longstreet's staff, one of those captured by the Federals, noted that "as the trains came up they were halted, and the men who were in them were quietly captured." An officer in charge of the fourteen ordnance wagons of Gen. Thomas F. Drayton's brigade rushed to his vehicles when he heard that "the Yankees are on us." He ordered "the teamsters to unhitch and fly but it was too late."[48]

The Federal horsemen eventually captured forty-five wagons loaded chiefly with ammunition and commissary stores, burning five and escorting the rest northward to Greencastle, Pennsylvania. Many of the vehicles had originally belonged to the Union army; a civilian in Frederick had noted a few days earlier that the rebels "seemed to have been largely supplied with transportation from some United States Quartermaster." "Uncle Sam's initials," he continued, "were on many of its wagons, ambulances, and horses." Although E. P. Alexander later commented that the loss of these wagons was "a severe blow at such a distance from our base," the incident received only scant mention in Confederate reports of the campaign. Alexander's reserve ordnance train, numbering eighty vehicles, crossed the Potomac at Williamsport on the morning of September 15 along with several battalions of artillery and the rest of the wagon train, having missed the Federal horsemen by only a short time.[49]

By September 16, Lee had concentrated his army, with the exception of two divisions, on a range of hills east of the town of Sharpsburg facing McClellan's force to the east. Lee realized that a combination of factors, including "great privations in rest and food, and the long marches without shoes over mountain roads," had greatly reduced the number of men in his army's ranks. The inability of many company and regimental grade officers to maintain discipline in the ranks and the resistance of some soldiers to the idea of invading Maryland also contributed to the straggling. At Antietam the Army of Northern Virginia probably had only between 35,000 and 40,000 men to face the far larger Army of the Potomac.[50]

Those men left in Lee's army at Antietam were famished. An Alabamian wrote home that "hunger gnawed on our stomachs mightily." Richard H. Watkins of the 3rd Virginia Cavalry observed that "had it not been for the young corn and apples we could hardly have survived." D. H. Hill noted that since his division's commissary wagons had been sent off to cross the Potomac at Williamsport on September 15, his men "had been sustaining life on green corn and what cattle as they could kill in the fields." In Gen. Richard B. Garnett's brigade, details from each company were sent into cornfields adjacent to the line of battle with orders to gather "roasting ears," each man being allowed eight ears a day. The absence of salt and the scarcity of wood to roast or burn the corn made its preparation a challenge.[51]

By the night of September 16, John B. Hood's division had "been without food for three days, except a half ration of beef for one day and green corn." When the famished men finally went to the rear that evening after skirmishing with the Federals, they found that the supply wagons had not arrived. Capt. James L. Lemon of the Texas Brigade wrote in his diary that "just as we began to cook our rations near daylight [on September 17] we were shelled and ordered into formation." Lemon noted that he had "never seen a more disgusted bunch of boys & mad as hornets."[52]

While men such as those in Lemon's company cursed both their scanty fare and the Yankees, commissary officers in the rear struggled to find and transport foodstuffs to their commands. The ordeal of Maj. John F. Edwards, chief commissary officer for McLaws's division, is probably typical of that endured by many of Lee's logistical officers. During the siege of Harpers Ferry, Edwards obtained only about twenty barrels of flour and a few head of cattle for his command, then located in Pleasant Valley and on Maryland Heights. He also procured some wheat, but the inability to grind it made it impossible to issue. When Harpers Ferry fell, Edwards went into the town but was told by one of Jackson's officers that "neither provisions nor stores of any kind of that captured, could be obtained . . . as the captured stores had been distributed to others." Edwards went into Charles Town with General McLaws, finding after a diligent search a small quantity of flour, but "not enough for one issue." Upon reaching Shepherdstown, Edwards drew rations for his division and had them cooked on the Virginia side of the Potomac but could not issue them to the men until after the battle of Sharpsburg.[53]

Capt. Thomas E. Ballard, commissary officer in Alexander R. Lawton's division under Jackson, faced problems similar to Edwards's in the wake of the battle of Sharpsburg. On September 18, Ballard received orders from Jackson to issue a single day's rations to the men. Ballard took his wagons to the Maryland side of the Potomac and deposited their loads "about two miles from Sharpsburg." Because many of the troops were in line of battle, Ballard was unable to issue all his rations before being ordered to send his trains back across the Potomac.[54]

In contrast to their paucity of rations, many of Lee's men apparently had sufficient ammunition for the September 17 battle. Some units received a fresh supply on the field; others left the firing line after emptying their cartridge boxes, but usually only after sustaining heavy casualties and after the fighting had ended

Despite the logistical breakdown of Lee's army that led to widespread suffering, thousands of Confederate soldiers like William Pinkney Irvin made it to Sharpsburg to participate in the war's bloodiest day of combat. Irvin, a nineteen-year-old member of Company A, 13th Georgia Volunteer Infantry, died in the fighting. Rachael Weitnauer, Atlanta, Georgia

on their sector of the field. Those regiments that left the battlefield passed through Sharpsburg to the ordnance and commissary wagons that filled the road and fields between the town and Boteler's Ford on the Potomac River. The survivors of the 10th Louisiana Infantry went "two miles to the rear for ammunition" after fighting along the Hagerstown Turnpike in the morning. The Louisianians remained in the rear until 7:00 P.M. before being sent forward again. A member of the Washington Artillery noted how the crews in his battery left the field at one point during the day to reload their chests, then "reappeared at two or three different points during the day."[55]

There inevitably were instances in which Confederate infantry commands ran low or completely out of ammunition while fighting, particularly among the fragmentary units engaged on the Piper farm. Although most of the southern artillery batteries conserved rounds by firing only at Federal infantrymen, some ran out of ammunition and left the battlefield. Capt. James Reilly's North Carolina Battery expended 483 rounds during the battle and despite the "greatest exertions" of the captain could not obtain more ammunition. One section of Reilly's battery, composed of 3-inch rifles, remained unengaged during the day because of a lack of ammunition. On the morning of September 18, William M. Owen of the Washington Artillery noted that the ammunition issued to the artillery was "not enough for a long engagement." The ammunition shortage, he surmised, was serious.[56]

Lee chose to maintain his army's position east of Sharpsburg on September 18 despite the horrific casualties sustained the previous day. After a day of inactivity on the 18th, the Confederate commander issued orders that afternoon for the army to withdraw across the Potomac. The movement's success depended on getting the army's extensive trains over Boteler's Ford.

Fortunately for the Confederates, Lee and Jackson had the assistance that evening of Jackson's chief quartermaster, Maj. John A. Harman. Harman's task was daunting. An artillerist noted that the scene that night on the Maryland side of the Potomac "rivaled Bedlam." The wagon train had to negotiate "a very high and almost perpendicular bank, and except for the still greater danger from behind, was such a descent that no prudent wagoner would ever have attempted to make." The combination of staff officers on both banks of the river yelling at teamsters and the teamsters whipping and yelling at their animals combined to produce a "terrible racket."[57]

With assistance from Lee, Jackson, and others, Harman worked through the night to get the wagons across. The worn-out condition of the animals and the deep mud often forced large details of infantrymen to drag the vehicles across the river. Occasionally some of the commissary wagons, overloaded and blocking the road, "would be compelled by impatient cursing from behind, to vomit up their contents." "To see the road strewed with heavy old trunks and useless plunder belonging to a favored few," wrote one artillerist, "was very exasperating, and at the same time much enjoyed by everyone except the owners."[58]

By late morning on the 19th, all of Lee's army, including the wagon trains, was across the Potomac. Several members of Jackson's staff attributed the movement's success to Harman, William Allan noting that the profane quartermaster "swore" the trains across the river. Jackson praised Harman for his "promptitude and success" but did not mention the major's colorful language.[59]

As the Confederates moved into camps north of Winchester near Bunker Hill, Lee admitted to Jefferson Davis on September 21 that the army's efficiency had been "greatly paralyzed by the loss to its ranks of the numerous stragglers." The problem worried Lee because he hoped "to threaten a passage into Maryland, to occupy the enemy on this frontier, and . . . to draw him into the Valley, where I can attack them to my advantage." The army commander hoped that a few days' rest and regular issuance of rations would restore the men's efficiency, and he requested from Davis "reenforcements, clothing, and shoes."[60]

The farms of the lower Shenandoah Valley initially provided adequate, if not

Long lines of wagons, similar to those depicted in this postwar
engraving, accompanied Confederate troops moving from
Sharpsburg toward the Potomac River on September 18, 1862.
Robert Underwood Johnson and Clarence Clough Buel, eds., *Battles and
Leaders of the Civil War*, 4 vols. (New York: Century, 1887–88), 2:189.

abundant, supplies for the gaunt men in Lee's ranks. The army's stationary position also made it easier for wagon trains to reach it from the supply depot at
Staunton. On September 23, Lee reported to Davis that "we have plenty of beef
and flour for our troops, hay for our horses, and some grain." Three days later
Lee tempered his assessment, stating that "forage is not so plentiful." The army
commander feared the consequences if more could not be obtained. "Our horses
have been so reduced by labor and scant food," he warned, that "unless their condition can be improved before winter, I fear many of them will die."[61]

Conditions within the Army of Northern Virginia dictated the impressment of
local resources in the valley. On September 30, Lee informed the president that

the army's chief quartermaster had orders to purchase "all the cloth, leather, shoes &c that can be found in this country." The army commander also ordered the impressment of flour from valley millers. "If millers or owners will not set their flour at a fixed rate," Lee explained, "we are obliged to take it." The question, stated the general, was whether the civilians would take a fair price for their flour or leave it for the enemy once the Confederate army had withdrawn. A Georgia soldier noted the results of Lee's orders, explaining to his hometown newspaper how "the flour mills have been pressed into service in this region, and the wheat, of which most of the farmers have two years crop on hand, is rapidly turning into flour for the use of the soldiers." [62]

The impressment of foodstuffs and other resources in the Shenandoah Valley only partially eased the suffering within the Confederate army. In official correspondence, diary entries, and letters to their loved ones or hometown newspapers, southern soldiers assessed their harsh living conditions. A South Carolinian described the men as "sunburnt, gaunt, ragged, [and] scarcely at all shod." Surgeon Spencer G. Welch wrote his wife that "thousands of our men now have almost no clothes and no sign of a blanket nor any prospect of getting one either. Thousands have had no shoes at all." Lt. William L. Cage of the 21st Mississippi related that his command was "without tents, rather poorly clad, and blankets very scarce." Col. Edward T. H. Warren noted that the men in his 10th Virginia Infantry were "ragged, dirty and full of lice" and that 175 of them were without shoes. Warren remembered how his "heart used to bleed as I would read the account of the sufferings of the patriot army at Valley Forge, and little did I think that the time would come when I would command men in a like destitute condition." [63]

The "emaciated, limping, ragged, filthy mass" of men in Lee's army blamed their woes in part on the shortcomings of logistical officers. Situations like that encountered by Col. Stephen D. Lee, who "failed in several attempts" to obtain desperately needed shoes and blankets from the chief quartermaster, undoubtedly caused anger and frustration. A soldier who identified himself as "Barefoot" in a letter to the Macon *Daily Telegraph* suggested that only "willfull negligence" could have resulted in more than one-third of the men in the army being without shoes. Maj. Franklin Gaillard of the 2nd South Carolina Infantry told his wife that the army's problems with straggling could not be avoided "unless the Government has it in its power to put its Quartermaster, Commissary, and Medical Department in better condition." [64]

Newspaper correspondents and editors also criticized the Confederate government. One correspondent claimed that if the government "had exercised a little foresight last spring and summer, when vessels were running the blockade, with cargoes of calico, linen, and other articles of like importance, a partial supply at least of hats, blankets, shoes, and woolen goods might have been obtained in England." An article titled "Scarcity of Leather" in the Montgomery *Daily Advertiser* speculated that "one half of the hides taken from slaughtered cattle have been lost through improvidence and want of transportation." Whether the high prices of leather were due to army officers neglecting to save hides or tanners holding their hides for purposes of speculation, the writer demanded that "the evil should be corrected." Another army correspondent suggested after writing of the scarcity of leather that "if the General Government fails to take this matter in hand, let the noble women of the land do so . . . let them put in operation the tanneries . . . demand the shoemakers from the army, and shoe their barefoot boys themselves." [65]

In an article titled "Gross Mismanagement," a contributor to the Mobile *Tribune* alleged that government officials had failed to forward donated clothing to soldiers. "There was a letter received by a soldier," a writer to the Columbia *Guardian* noted, "stating that he was suffering greatly—barefoot and almost naked—but he did not want any more sent until there is a provision made to take them safely from Richmond to camp, as there is clothing and shoes there now if he can get them." Many government officials, the *Guardian* contributor claimed, appropriated the railways for their own purposes of speculation, while "many more were simply both insolent and careless." [66]

Some soldiers and civilians tempered their criticism by acknowledging the enormous handicaps under which their government operated. Franklin Gaillard admitted that the Confederacy might be unable to provide much more logistical support, "cut off as it is from the world with undeveloped manufacturing resources." An editor for the Selma *Reporter* expanded on Gaillard's argument, stating that "with blockaded ports, the Mississippi River in general possession of the enemy, and [the] fewness of manufactories . . . , few people properly estimate the difficulties that impede the most faithful and energetic efforts to obtain full supplies of clothing." This writer pointed out the manufacture of large quantities of clothing at numerous points throughout the Confederacy, adding that "contracts for the importation of goods from abroad (necessarily uncertain), have been made to an amount which repel the flippant accusation of a want of foresight and energy on the part of the Quartermaster's Department." An editor of the Macon *Daily Telegraph* verified that important contracts for shoes and clothing had been let in several cities throughout Georgia but that "the material has pretty much run out. There is little or no cloth or leather in market." [67]

Many white southerners blamed the scarcity of goods on businessmen or "speculators" who hoarded raw materials and amassed large profits from their ventures. A writer in the Montgomery *Weekly Advertiser* contrasted the barefoot soldiers "charging over the flinty surfaces of a macadamized road, marking their course with their blood," with the "thousands of slick speculators" who had bought up all the leather in the Confederacy while sporting "$20 calf skin boots and resting at night on the downy beds of ease." The outraged writer asked why "vampires and blood-suckers" were protected while "those who stand a living wall between us and our enemies are permitted to go barefooted and their families allowed to suffer the common necessities of life?" A soldier writing to the Atlanta *Southern Confederacy* pointed out how "men of wealth are erecting new mills, tan-yards, shoe-shops, &c., and are filling them with their sons." If this trend continued, the soldier opined, "the army will be composed of poor men exclusively," whose families would "be left to the scanty charities of Extortion and Speculation."[68]

The apparent inability of the Confederate government to control speculation or improve conditions within the army prompted calls for private donations. A Richmond correspondent for the Memphis *Daily Appeal* suggested that "every family in the Confederacy determine to supply one two or three soldiers with shoes and blankets." In the previous year, the writer noted, "there was a very general and lively industry among the fair women of the South in the manufacture of socks for the army and many hundreds of thousands of pairs were made." "Are you weary of the good work, my sisters?" asked the correspondent rhetorically, answering that he was "sure that you are not." A member of the 17th Mississippi Infantry wrote from Virginia that "in the forced marches recently made, all the clothing and many of the blankets of the soldiers were lost." "Something must be done," he demanded, "either by the government or the people at home." A "poor country girl" wrote the editor of the Columbus *Daily Sun,* reminding women that "God has given you the work to do; it is a sacred duty, and it matters not if no relation or dear friend appeals to you for help, all are brothers, friends, in the common cause." A contributor to the Montgomery *Daily Mail* claimed that "the only thing that can be done is to set to work, and endeavor to atone for the remisness of the Government."[69]

The most widely read appeal for assistance to Lee's army came from one of the Confederacy's premier newspaper correspondents, Peter Wellington Alexander, or "P. W. A." Alexander's graphic writing style and the abundance and reliability of the information presented in his letters resulted in their widespread circulation in papers across the South. After accompanying Lee's troops through the Maryland campaign, Alexander wrote an article dated September 26, 1862, titled, "Our Army, Its Great Deeds, Its Trials, Its Sufferings, and Its Perils in the Future," in which he called on the southern people to supply clothing and shoes to the soldiers for the upcoming winter. Alexander knew that the women of the South would respond to his call because they were God's "holy oracles in this day of trial and tribulation." He also addressed the problem of speculation, arguing against "violent measures" but warning that no one should be allowed to hoard leather and cloth. "If they neither clothe the naked, nor feed the hungry, who are fighting for their freedom, and for their homes and their property," Alexander wrote about the speculators, "what right have they to expect anything but eternal damnation, both from God and man?"

Alexander wondered in the conclusion of his piece what effect Lee's army would have if it marched "from Richmond to the Mississippi." Civilians would see soldiers "ragged and almost barefoot and hatless, many of the men limping along and not quite well of their wounds and sickness . . . their clothes riddled with balls and their banners covered with the smoke and dust of battle, and shot to tatters." The sight of such an army, Alexander insisted, "would produce a sensation that has no parallel in history since Peter the Hermit led his swelling hosts across Europe to rescue the city of the Holy Sepulchre."[70]

Alexander's dramatic appeal elicited widespread notice across the Confederacy. The editor of the Richmond *Dispatch* praised the piece as "true eloquence, coming from the heart of a man who not only sees what he describes, but is himself a participant." An officer in the 3rd Georgia Infantry hoped that "every body in Georgia has read P. W. A.'s letter." "Even the speculator," the officer continued, "souless and shameless as he is, could not but pause and reflect on his infamous course, could he but see Gen. Lee's ragged and barefooted army." A notice from the assistant quartermaster of Edward L. Thomas's brigade asking the public for donations of clothing referred readers to Alexander's article, which "describes truly the situation of our soldiers." The editor of the Atlanta *Southern Confederacy,* after noting Alexander's "stirring appeal," reminded readers that "the plea that the Government ought to provide for the soldiers, affords them but little comfort while they stand guard in the frosts and snows . . . without a sufficiency of clothing to cover their bodies."[71]

Confederate and state government officials responded to Alexander's article by admitting their inability to supply the army with necessities. When questions arose concerning the accuracy of Alexander's article and the true level of need, Secretary of War George W. Randolph responded by stating, "We desire all the assistance . . . that can be furnished." North Carolina governor Zebulon B. Vance proclaimed that his state would be unable to clothe and shoe its soldiers "without again appealing to that overflowing fountain of generous charity—the private contributions of our people." Vance declared that if every farmer tanning hides would spare one pair of shoes and every mother knit one strong pair of thick cotton or woolen socks, the army would be "abundantly supplied." Blankets were also in great need, and the governor urged their donation as well as carpet substitutes. If owners did not feel able to donate items, Vance assured them that "a liberal price will be paid for everything." Above all, the governor implored his citizens not to sell to a speculator; "though he offers you enormous prices spurn him from your door. . . . [J]ust think for a moment of the soldier and what he is doing for you." [72]

While central and state government officials asked constituents to sacrifice for the cause, civilians in turn demanded legislative action to impress needed goods such as wool and leather and to exempt tailors, tanners, and shoemakers from military service. The editor of the Columbus *Daily Sun* called for government agents to seize the large quantities of leather being hoarded by speculators. "Let societies be formed and canvassing committees be appointed in every county and militia district in the state," the editor demanded, "and then every family will have an opportunity to contribute its mite." Across Georgia, women signed petitions to the governor calling on him to seize the cotton and wool factories from their "stony hearted owners" and operate them for the benefit of soldiers and needy citizens. [73]

Such calls for government action indicate that by the fall of 1862 many white southerners probably believed in increased government control of the burgeoning Confederate war industry. An unsigned editorial in the Macon *Daily Telegraph* suggested this by arguing that while "we have been snuffing danger from centralization of the Confederate Government — the army has got out of shoes — out of clothes — out of bacon and out of nearly everything else but strong hearts and sturdy patriotism." The writer urged readers to reconsider "the old dreams of a simple pastoral and planting life in which we are to exchange raw crops for all we want to wear and a good part of what we eat." [74]

Some white southerners believed that the logistical crisis facing the Confederate armies in the fall of 1862 also called for sacrifices from the slave population. As one contributor to the Memphis *Appeal* argued, "[T]here is no negro in the South who is not better off . . . than some of the best soldiers and first gentlemen in all the land." A planter in middle Georgia argued that slave owners "can well afford to let their negroes go barefooted for one season" in order to send shoes to the army. In a letter to the Montgomery *Weekly Advertiser*, "Lowndes" said that planters should give up a portion of their "negro cloth" and instruct their wives to dye it gray for army uniforms. Shoes, he continued, should be given only to slave men doing outdoor work. Slave women and girls could remain barefoot indoors spinning and weaving. [75]

The myriad calls to assist Lee's men elicited patriotic responses from all classes of white people. When women working in a factory in Tallassee, Alabama, learned that members of the 13th Alabama Infantry from their community needed assistance, they formed a committee to raise funds for clothing. The women, all of whom "support themselves by the labor of their own fair hands," raised five hundred dollars within two days. One hundred mechanics in Columbus, Georgia, donated five dollars each for soldier relief and challenged other workingmen to do the same. Responding to Governor Vance's appeal, Fayetteville, North Carolina, resident E. J. Hale contributed 100 pairs of shoes and his wife 250 pairs of socks. Jane Robinson of Robinson Springs, Alabama, sent a woolen coverlet and bed quilt to the army. Across the Confederacy, state and local relief organizations and church congregations pooled their resources to send money, clothing, blankets, medicine, and other supplies to Virginia.[76]

State governments pledged their support to assist their soldiers serving in Lee's army. The governor of Alabama announced in November 1862 that a large amount of clothing, much of it produced by Ladies' Aid Societies, had been issued to soldiers by the state Quartermaster Department. Florida legislators appropriated $75,000 to purchase shoes and uniforms for the state's soldiers. The Georgia State Legislature passed a resolution in late November 1862 warning proprietors of factories and tanneries who refused to sell their products to the state at reasonable prices that the government would "appropriate their whole products for army use." In October 1862, the quartermaster general of South Carolina sent 7,000 coats, 2,000 overcoats, 3,000 pairs of pants, and 6,000 blankets to the Palmetto State troops in Lee's army. The result, according to Confederate quartermaster general Myers, was that "all the South Carolina troops have been supplied with blankets and clothing, received from the State."[77]

The number of uniforms and blankets sent to the Army of Northern Virginia by private citizens and state governments paled in comparison to the supplies eventually delivered by the Confederate government. On September 25, 1862, Quartermaster General Myers informed the secretary of war that despite leather shortages in the Richmond shoe shops, 7,000 pairs of shoes had already been sent to the army and 10,000 more had been ordered to Virginia from storehouses in Chattanooga. Twenty thousand suits of clothing had been "put up" for Lee's men, with an initial shipment going to the army the next day. Blankets were particularly hard to procure; by mid-November, Myers admitted that it was "not possible to procure blankets in the Confederacy, except by introducing them in exchange for cotton on the Mississippi."[78]

Peter W. Alexander reported the results of government efforts in a column dated October 18, 1862. He had recently visited the Confederate Clothing Bureau in Richmond, a large complex that employed 58 tailors and roughly 2,700 women in the production of uniforms. Although supplies of "officer's cloth" had been exhausted for some time, there remained on hand "a considerable stock of coarse strong cloth . . . being made up for the troops as rapidly as possible." An officer in the bureau claimed that it assembled clothing at the rate of 9,000 garments a week and that it had sent than 33,000 uniforms to Lee's army within the past twenty days.[79]

Alexander also noted that the Confederate Congress had detailed soldiers to increase shoe production. By mid-November, more than 250 shoemakers who had been serving under Lee received orders to report to government workshops in Richmond, Atlanta, and Columbus. At the same time, quartermasters began issuing large numbers of imported English shoes to the troops. Alexander believed such efforts should have been made earlier. "It is now too late to procure supplies of leather, thread, and pegs," he wrote, "and even if we had an abundant supply of each, it would be months before a sufficient number of shoes could be manufactured to meet the present needs of the army." A soldier writing to the Columbia *Daily Southern Guardian* agreed, noting that although several thousand shoes had been distributed within his army corps by mid-October, there remained double that number of barefoot men.[80]

As late as November 17, Lee informed the secretary of war that although the army had recently received approximately 5,000 pairs of shoes and a commensurate number of uniforms and blankets, there remained around 2,000 barefoot men in the ranks and 3,000 more "whose shoes are in such a condition that they will not last longer than another march." By December, the Quartermaster Department had forwarded to Lee's army all the shoes on hand in Richmond and at Lee's suggestion had started impressing large lots of shoes held by speculators.[81]

The Confederate Quartermaster Department's issuance of clothing to the army came in haphazard fashion, the garments often varying widely in quality. Sometimes the allotments were pathetically small; Colonel Warren of the 10th Virginia Infantry wrote that there were "not more than ½ doz pair of socks being sent to the regiment for distribution at one time." While some soldiers received garments from relief associations or families and friends, others like Pvt. Eli P. Landers waited to draw government clothing promised since the revocation of the commutation system by the Confederate Congress to date from October 8, 1862. Landers told his mother that although soldiers paid a high price for government clothing, "it would be better to pay . . . for them here than to send some to me and I not get them." The periodic return to the army throughout the fall of 1862 of regimental and personal baggage, in storage since August, undoubtedly thrilled thousands of soldiers like Landers who were without blankets or changes of clothing.[82]

As army quartermasters scrambled to provide sufficient clothing for the upcoming winter, they faced another crisis in regard to the army's supply of horses. Constant service involving extraordinary exertions and insufficient forage had resulted in great numbers of lame or broken-down mounts. To make matters worse, an epidemic known as "sore tongue" began infecting many animals. By early November 1862, a more serious affliction referred to as "greased heel" or "soft hoof" had broken out, afflicting roughly three-fourths of the animals according to a report from Gen. J. E. B. Stuart. The greased heel epidemic almost cut in half the number of cavalrymen capable of performing mounted duty in Gen. Fitzhugh Lee's brigade and necessitated the establishment of a horse hospital near Culpeper Court House.[83]

Solving the problems plaguing Lee's horse supply proved difficult. Most of the stricken animals belonged to individual cavalrymen who were responsible by law for replacing them. The government provided compensation to those who lost horses, but only at the value appraised when the men mustered into service. By the winter of 1862–63 this allowance proved insufficient because of the depreciation of Confederate currency. The inflated cost of horses made it difficult for Virginia troopers who were close to home to find new mounts and nearly impossible for cavalrymen from the Deep South. This inability to procure mounts, combined with the scarcity of forage in central Virginia, elicited great concern from Robert E. Lee throughout the fall of 1862 and the following winter.[84]

Despite the difficulties plaguing Lee's Quartermaster and Commissary departments, a series of important internal reforms that offered hope for improvements took place within the army and Confederate government during the fall of 1862 and the following winter. The artillery arm underwent a reorganization necessitated by the greatly reduced numbers of men and horses; at least eighteen understrength batteries ceased to exist after being consolidated with stronger units. The formal practice of assigning individual batteries to infantry brigades also ended, batteries instead being grouped together into battalions. Each of the army's two corps received a number of artillery battalions, with all battalions in a corps falling under the command of a corps chief of artillery. Those batteries not directly assigned to one of the two army corps constituted a general reserve.[85]

A desire for more and better-trained artillery ordnance officers led to the issuance, in September 1862, of a general order by the Confederate Adjutant and Inspector General's Office establishing examinations to test applicants' knowledge of field manuals and to examine their credentials and prior service. By January 1863, many applicants with high scores on the examinations had received appointments. Secretary of War Seddon believed that the new ordnance officers "rendered the distribution of munitions and the supply of arms and artillery more regular and complete and . . . promoted economy in consumption, care in preservation, and greater efficiency in use."[86]

Reforms instituted within Lee's infantry commands also bore fruitful results. The positions of army corps chief of ordnance and division ordnance officer had apparently only existed since April 1862, both being appointed posts involving no formal process of review. The position of brigade ordnance officer had been created in July 1862 and also apparently involved no examinations. Many of the officers subsequently assigned to ordnance duty undoubtedly lacked the requisite knowledge or training and ended up like Peyton Thompson Manning of James Longstreet's staff. Francis W. Dawson, another officer in Longstreet's entourage, claimed that Manning "knew comparatively little of his work as Ordnance officer, and was unable to write an official letter correctly." Practical experience in the field for officers such as Manning, coupled with the appointment of additional ordnance officers at the brigade level and a new Ordnance Bureau rule that ordnance officers maintain a "daily journal of their operations, embracing everything that comes within their observation," undoubtedly improved matters.[87]

Incompetence regarding ordnance matters was not confined to nascent staff officers. A September 25, 1862, army special order admitted that "it does not appear to be generally understood by commanders of companies that they are responsible for the arms and accoutrements of their men." Jackson's ordnance officer, William Allan, agreed, claiming that the inspection of ordnance supplies in the hands of the troops had been "irregular and imperfect."[88]

The Army of Northern Virginia's high command addressed problems of ordnance accountability within the infantry by issuing a spate of orders directed at company and regimental grade officers. On September 22, Lee directed Jackson and Longstreet to instruct company commanders to inspect their soldiers on a daily basis to account for all arms and equipment. Those men lacking arms or equipment would be resupplied and anything lost through carelessness or neglect charged to the individuals responsible, the replacement cost of the item or items being deducted from their pay. Weekly inspections would assure that arms were clean and cartridge boxes full. Every other week, regimental commanding officers would be required to turn in reports stating the number of arms and accoutrements in the hands of the men in their commands.[89]

By the first week of October 1862, the stockpiles of arms and accoutrements captured at Second Manassas and Harpers Ferry had been distributed throughout the Confederate army. These issuances, along with the probable distribution during the winter of 1862–63 of additional weapons brought in through the blockade, resulted in the exchange of smoothbore muskets for rifles in most southern infantry regiments by the spring of 1863. According to E. P. Alexander, "about nine-tenths" of the Confederate infantrymen who fought at Gettysburg carried .58 or .54 caliber rifle muskets.[90]

The field pieces captured at Harpers Ferry could fill only some of the demands within Lee's artillery arm. As late as December 5, Lee argued that despite the acquisition of heavier guns, the increased skill of his artillery personnel, and the more careful preparation of ammunition, a great disparity still existed between his artillery and that of the enemy. Lee stated that more long-range pieces were urgently needed, arguing that the best cannon for field service were the 12-pounder Napoleons, 10-pounder Parrotts, and 3-inch rifles. Josiah Gorgas, the Confederacy's impressive chief of ordnance, responded by pointing out that the personnel at Richmond's Tredegar ironworks already had instructions to labor night and day to turn out the requested guns and that lighter guns had been sent from the army to Richmond for recasting into heavier pieces.[91]

Changes within the Confederate Quartermaster Department in the fall of 1862 and the following winter also boded well for Lee's army. On October 1, Quartermaster General Myers wrote an angry letter to the secretary of war regarding the supply situation in the Army of Northern Virginia. The army's quartermasters, Myers contended, had failed to send requisitions through proper channels. Myers subsequently learned about the army's supply crisis from letters Lee had written to Davis and the secretary of war that were forwarded to the quartermaster general. In a statement that seems disingenuous given the publicity directed at the topic, Myers told the secretary of war that "the troops, as far as I am informed, are not in need."[92]

Myers expanded on the shortcomings of army quartermasters in another letter to the secretary of war dated November 22, 1862. The quartermaster general found reprehensible the common practice of army quartermasters going to Richmond under orders from their commanding officers to obtain supplies. Such trips involved unnecessary expenses and kept the quartermasters from assigned posts, "where their services are constantly required." All army quartermasters should be aware, Myers stated, "that nothing can be accomplished by their presence at the seat of government, beyond what is attained by their remaining at their posts, and making regular requisitions."[93]

Robert E. Lee had undoubtedly been aware of the problems mentioned by Quartermaster General Myers. On September 22, he sent orders to Jackson and Longstreet requiring quartermaster and commissary officers "to remain with their trains," knowing that "their accounts will be examined, [and the] property on hand inspected." Violations of these orders, including evidence of misappropriation of property, would be reported to the army's commanding general.[94]

The Confederate Adjutant and Inspector General's Office also addressed the quartermaster general's concerns, issuing a series of general orders in December 1862 and January 1863 that delineated official channels for the requisitioning of clothing. Company commanders could procure clothing only by making the proper requisitions through their commanding officers to the Quartermaster Department. A January 1863 order specified that Confederate quartermaster depots were under "the special control of the Quartermaster General." Issuances from depots would occur only after officers sent their requisitions to their army's chief quartermaster, who would in turn forward the requests to the quartermaster general in Richmond.[95]

Other changes established in the spring of 1863 by Quartermaster General Myers improved his department's efficiency and helped channel the Confederacy's domestic resources toward supplying the armies. Myers reorganized his department's procurement wing, dividing every southern state into districts, each in charge of a principal purchasing officer. In many locales, the Quartermaster Department established a near monopoly on scarce goods such as wool and leather. In other cases, such as the cotton textile industry, Myers exercised a limited degree of control to ensure that the clothing bureau's needs would be met.[96]

The Commissary Department implemented a series of changes similar to those in the Quartermaster Department. In response to the extreme shortage of foodstuffs within the Confederacy during the fall of 1862 and the following winter, Commissary General Lucius B. Northrop reorganized the purchasing arrangements of his department. Northrop partitioned each state into districts under district purchasing commissaries. The districts were then divided into subdistricts under subcommissaries and agents. Chief commissaries controlled all the operations within a state and forwarded monthly reports to the commissary general's office. The plan centralized the Commissary Department's purchasing arrangements, removing the responsibility from the field commanders. Unfortunately for Northrop, who wanted complete control over the collection of subsistence within the Confederacy, the distribution of foodstuffs was not centralized. Chief commissary officers of armies sent their requisitions to the chief commissaries of the states in which the armies operated or intended to move through.[97]

The creation of the tax in kind, or tithe, created a powerful new tool for the beleaguered Commissary Department. This measure, wrote a leading historian of the subject, "cut through the Gordian knot of inflation, speculation, impressment, and hoarding by simply taking a portion of the subsistence stocks of the country as taxes." The tax in kind, part of a tax bill passed by the Confederate Congress in late April 1863, called for local tax assessors to establish at market time the quantity owed the Confederate Government by every producer. After reserving a certain amount of his food for himself, the farmer was to deliver one-tenth of his taxable field crops and one-tenth of his hogs in the form of cured bacon to a government depot. Administration of the tithe fell to a new group of Quartermaster Department officials known as post quartermasters.[98]

Commissary Department reforms involving the tax in kind and the centralization of purchasing operations provided hope for improved conditions, but subsistence problems persisted within the Army of Northern Virginia. Lee's troops had gotten through the fall of 1862 on foodstuffs gathered from the countryside, bacon shipped by railroad, and flour accumulated by impressment. When complaints among army officers became widespread regarding insufficient rations for their men, Lee consulted with his chief commissary and increased the flour and beef rations. Secretary of War Randolph eventually questioned Lee about this action, prompting the general to defend his decision in a November 17, 1862, dispatch noting that other portions of the official ration, including vegetables, were unavailable at the time. After consulting with Commissary General Northrop, Randolph ordered Lee to enforce the reduced rations stipulated by the War Department.[99]

Lee's men continued on short rations until the late spring of 1863. While encamped in the war-ravaged environs of Fredericksburg, the Army of Northern Virginia remained dependent on the efficient use of the railroads. Unfortunately for the army, the railroad owners responded to the crisis with an assertion of their individual rights and a failure to give government shipments high priority. The consequent unreliability of the railroads made it nearly impossible to ship perishable portions of the official ration over long distances.[100]

Although numerous problems continued to plague the Army of Northern Virginia in the spring of 1863, the situation had improved dramatically since the 1862 Maryland campaign. Reforms instituted within the army's supply bureaus, particularly the Quartermaster and Ordnance departments, led to greater professionalization and accountability for scarce resources. The broader enactments of the supply bureaus established the basic policies for domestic procurement and production that would be pursued, with only slight modification, for the remainder of the Civil War.[101]

Much of the impetus for change came as a result of the outcry from southern soldiers and civilians over the abysmal conditions within Lee's army. Peter W. Alexander, who had done as much as anyone else to publicize the Army of Northern Virginia's plight, undoubtedly echoed the opinions of many southern civilians and soldiers in his assessment of that army's performance in the campaigns of the summer and fall of 1862. "No army on this continent," Alexander wrote, "has ever accomplished as much or suffered as much as the Army of Northern Virginia within the last three months." At no time in the Revolutionary War, he continued, "even at Valley Forge — did our forefathers in arms encounter greater hardships or endure them more uncomplainingly."[102]

ACKNOWLEDGMENTS

The author would like to thank the following individuals for their assistance in providing source material and advice for this essay: Peter S. Carmichael, Earl J. Coats, Gary W. Gallagher, Robert E. L. Krick, Robert K. Krick, Joni Mabe, Eric Minck, Michael P. Musick, Robert O'Neill, James Ogden III, and Stephen Scarpero.

NOTES

1. U.S. War Department, *The War of the Rebellion: A Compilation of the Official Records of the Union and Confederate Armies,* 127 vols., index, and atlas (Washington: GPO, 1880–1901), ser. 1, vol. 19, pt. 2:1007 (hereafter cited as *OR;* all references are to ser. 1); Edward Porter Alexander, *Military Memoirs of a Confederate: A Critical Narrative* (New York: Scribner's, 1907), 223.

2. Randolph Abbott Shotwell, *The Papers of Randolph Abbott Shotwell,* ed. J. G. de Roulhac Hamilton, 3 vols. (Raleigh: North Carolina Historical Commission, 1929–36), 1:307; *OR* 19(2):590, 591.

3. *OR* 19(2):590.

4. Richard Goff, "Logistics and Supply Problems of the Confederacy" (Ph.D. diss., Duke University, 1963), 89, 172–75; *OR* 19(2):590, 716–17.

5. *OR* 19(2):594, 678–79; James M. Folsom, *Heroes and Martyrs of Georgia* (Macon, Ga.: Burke, Boykin, and Co., 1864), 15; J. F. J. Caldwell, *The History of a Brigade of South Carolinians, Known First as "Gregg's," and Subsequently as "McGowan's Brigade"* (Philadelphia: King & Baird Printers, 1866), 86; Mills Lane, ed., *"Dear Mother: Don't grieve about me. If I get killed, I'll only be dead." Letters from Georgia Soldiers in the Civil War* (Savannah, Ga.: Beehive Press, 1977), 185; J. Cutler Andrews, *The South Reports the Civil War* (Princeton, N.J.: Princeton University Press, 1970), 198, 202.

6. Goff, "Logistics and Supply Problems," 134; William Allan, "Reminiscences of Field Ordnance Service with the Army of Northern Virginia—1863–'5," in *Southern Historical Society Papers,* ed. J. William Jones and others, 52 vols. (1876–1959; reprint, with 3-vol. index, Wilmington, N.C.: Broadfoot, 1990–92), 14:139 (hereafter cited as *SHSP*); Alexander, *Military Memoirs,* 223.

7. Compiled Service Record (hereafter cited as CSR) of George H. Bier, M331, National Archives, Washington (repository hereafter cited as NA); *OR* 19(2):718–19; "Invoice of Ordnance and Ordnance Stores turned over by Capt E. Taliaferro Ord Off.

Maj Genl McLaws Divn to officers for immediate service in battle Sept 17th & 19th 1862," "Report of Armament of Kershaw's Brigade, Dec 30th, 1862," and "Armament of Barksdale's Brigade," in Edwin Taliaferro Papers, RG 109, War Department Collection of Confederate Records, box 1, folder titled "Taliaferro Papers," entry 134 A, NA. See also list of items for John B. Hood's division "expended and lost in battle of Fredericksburg" in CSR of Beverley Randolph, M331, NA, for evidence that many men in that organization carried .69 caliber smoothbore muskets in late 1862.

8. Allan, "Reminiscences of Field Ordnance Service," *SHSP* 14:140; Greg Mast, *State Troops and Volunteers: A Photographic Record of North Carolina's Civil War Soldiers* (Raleigh: North Carolina Department of Cultural Resources, 1995), 113; "The Southern Confederacy," from "Our Special Correspondent" [Francis C. Lawley], London *Times,* December 1, 1862; "Our Richmond Correspondence," letter dated February 12, 1864, from GAMMA [Dr. George W. Bagby], Mobile *Advertiser and Register,* February 21, 1864.

9. "The First Virginia Cavalry," *Harper's Weekly,* September 27, 1862; Henry B. McClellan, *The Life and Campaigns of Major General J. E. B. Stuart* (Boston: Houghton Mifflin, 1885), 260; *OR* 12(2):733. For efforts to obtain carbines for the cavalry after the Maryland campaign, see *OR* 25(2):820; Janet B. Hewett et al., eds., *Supplement to the Official Records of the Union and Confederate Armies* (Wilmington, N.C.: Broadfoot, 1994), pt. 1, vol. 3:484 (hereafter cited as *ORS;* all references are to pt. 1). Col. Thomas T. Munford stated in his report of the September 14, 1862, battle of Crampton's Gap that his horsemen fought "with pistols against rifles," although he also mentions the existence of a small group of sharpshooters within his brigade. The sharpshooter parties in Munford's and Fitzhugh Lee's brigades had a combined strength of roughly one hundred men. *OR* 19(1):826–27.

10. Allan, "Reminiscences of Field Ordnance Service," *SHSP* 14:137.

11. Curt Johnson and Richard C. Anderson Jr., *Artillery Hell: The Employment of Artillery at Antietam* (College Station: Texas A&M University Press, 1995), 5, 40–41; Alexander, *Military Memoirs,* 223; Edward P. Alexander, "Confederate Artillery Service," *SHSP* 11:109.

12. Alexander, "Confederate Artillery Service," *SHSP* 11:104; Alexander, *Military Memoirs,* 235.

13. *OR* 19(1):854, 858, 910, 926, 1010, 1022, 1026. Jennings C. Wise argued that the Confederate batteries at Sharpsburg "were more effective individually than grouped" because concentrations of guns drew the overwhelming fire of the Federal guns. Jennings C. Wise, *The Long Arm of Lee; or, The History of the Artillery of the Army of Northern Virginia . . .,* 2 vols. (Lynchburg: J. P. Bell, 1915), 1:257, 323–26.

14. Goff, "Logistics and Supply Problems," 35, 57, 82; Abraham C. Myers to George W. Randolph, August 16, 1862, Letters and Telegrams Sent by the Confederate States Quartermaster General to the Secretary of War (hereafter cited as CSQM to SW), RG 109, M900, reel 6, 075-06, NA.

15. Leslie D. Jensen, "A Survey of Confederate Central Government Quartermaster Issue Jackets, Part I," *Military Collector and Historian* 41 (Fall 1989): 110; Goff, "Logistics and Supply Problems," 35, 82, 123, 142.

16. James A. Seddon to Jefferson Davis, January 3, 1863, Letters Sent by the Confederate Secretary of War to the President, 1861–65, vol. 1 (chap. 11, vol. 39), RG 109, M523, reel 1, NA.

17. A. C. Myers to G. W. Randolph, August 16, 1862, CSQM to SW, M900, reel 6, 075-075, NA; Caldwell, *History of a Brigade,* 52. J. F. J. Caldwell wrote that the commutation payment "was hardly enough to cover one's nakedness, for prices were at least treble the peace standard."

18. Jeffrey Stocker, ed., *From Huntsville to Appomattox: R. T. Coles's History of the 4th Regiment, Alabama Volunteer Infantry C.S.A.* (Knoxville: University of Tennessee Press, 1996), 58–59.

19. General Orders 101, August 6, 1862, General Orders, Army of Northern Virginia (hereafter cited as GO-ANV), RG 109, M921, reel 1, NA; *OR* 12(2):555, 559; 19(2):595, 641; Charles R. Schrader, "Field Logistics in the Civil War," in Jay Luvaas and Harold W. Nelson, *The U.S. Army War College Guide to the Battle of Antietam* (New York: Harper and Row, 1988), 272. Lee's efforts to reduce the number of wagons in his army were typical of efforts made by Civil War army commanders on both sides.

20. William P. Pigman diary, August 18, 1862, Georgia Historical Society, Savannah; Alexander Hunter, "A High Private's Account," *SHSP* 10 : 504; James L. Clements to wife, October 21, 1862, James L. Clements Collection, Arkansas Historical Commission, Little Rock; Caldwell, *History of a Brigade,* 86; William E. Jones diary, September 7, 1862, James Schoff Collection, University of Michigan Special Collections, Ann Arbor (repository hereafter cited as UM); "S. L. W." [member of Co. B, 17th Mississippi Infantry], "Virginia Correspondence, Winchester, October 14, 1862," Memphis *Daily Appeal,* October 28, 1862; Andrew B. Wardlaw to wife, October 5, 1862, bound vol. 206, Fredericksburg and Spotsylvania National Military Park Library, Fredericksburg, Va. (repository hereafter cited as FSNMP); Donald E. Reynolds, ed. "A Mississippian in Lee's Army: The Letters of Leander Huckaby, Part I," *Journal of Mississippi History* 46 (May 1974): 167; John W. Harrison to mother, September 9, 1862, Confederate Miscellany 1A, folder 3, Emory University Special Collections, Atlanta (repository hereafter cited as EU); William Allan, "Reminiscences of Field Ordnance Service," *SHSP* 14 : 141; Special Orders 239, November 11, 1862, Special Orders, Army of Northern Virginia (hereafter cited as SO-ANV), RG 109, M921, reel 1, NA. Some accounts state that soldiers threw their knapsacks and blankets away in order to travel light.

21. George L. P. Wren diary, August 31, 1862, EU; Andrews, *South Reports the Civil War,* 198. See also "Condition of the Army," Richmond *Whig,* October 2, 1862; *OR* 19(1):1022; Joseph B. Polley, *Hood's Texas Brigade* (New York: Neale, 1910), 115; John D. Chapla, "Quartermaster Operations in the Forty-second Virginia Infantry

Regiment," *Civil War History* 30 (March 1984): 10, 19; Ray Mathis, ed., *In the Land of the Living: Wartime Letters by Confederates from the Chattahoochee Valley of Alabama and Georgia* (Troy, Ala.: Troy State University Press, 1981), 49; Greenlee Davidson, *Captain Greenlee Davidson, C.S.A.: Diary and Letters, 1851–1863,* ed. Charles W. Turner (Verona, Va.: McClure Press, 1975), 50; William S. Ricketson to father and mother, September 21, 1862, original in possession of Joni Mabe, Athens, Ga.

22. *OR* 19(1):139; (2):59–64.

23. *OR* 19(2):595–96.

24. Caldwell, *History of a Brigade,* 69; D. Augustus Dickert, *History of Kershaw's Brigade* (Newberry, S.C.: Elbert H. Aull Co., 1899), 146; Peter W. Alexander, "Our Army Correspondence," Mobile *Advertiser and Register,* September 24, 1862. See also William Allan, *The Army of Northern Virginia in 1862* (Cambridge, Mass.: Riverside Press, 1892), 325.

25. Sarah P. Carroll, ed., *Lifeline to Home for John William McLure, CSA, Union County, S.C.* (Greenville, S.C.: A Press, 1990), 110–11; Kent M. Brown, "The Confederate Soldier," *Virginia Country's Civil War* 3 (1985): 32.

26. *ORS* 3:497; Isiah Fogleman diary, September 5, 1862, bound vol. 113, FSNMP; Napier Bartlett, ed., *Military Record of Louisiana* (Baton Rouge: Louisiana State University Press, 1964), 133; Robert T. Mockbee, "'The Sun never shined on a braver & truer Set of Soldiers': The 14th Tennessee Infantry Regiment," *Civil War Regiments* 5 (1996): 20; Henry C. Wall, *Historical Sketch of the Pee Dee Guards* (Raleigh: Edwards, Broughton, & Co., 1876), 42.

27. Marshall B. Hurst, *History of the 14th Regiment Alabama Volunteers* (1863; reprint, Tuscaloosa, Ala.: Confederate Publishing Co., 1982), 14; [Probably Lt. George E. Hayes, Company K, 3rd Georgia Infantry], "Camp near Winchester, Va., Oct. 16, 1862," Athens *Southern Banner,* December 3, 1862; Lane, *Dear Mother,* 185; Dickert, *History of Kershaw's Brigade,* 151–52.

28. William R. Quynn, ed., *The Diary of Jacob Engelbrecht,* vol. 3, *1858–1878* (Frederick: Historical Society of Frederick County, 1976), entries for September 6, 1862; [Captain in the 15th Alabama Infantry], "The 15th Ala. at Sharpsburg—Desperate Fighting," Columbus *Daily Sun,* October 6, 1862; *ORS* 3:497.

29. *OR* 19(2):603–5.

30. *OR* 19(1):602.

31. Shotwell, *Papers,* 1:307; *OR* 19(2):603.

32. Allan, *Army of Northern Virginia,* 333–34.

33. William E. Jones diary, September 12, 1862, UM; Caldwell, *History of a Brigade,* 70; David G. McIntosh, "The Maryland Campaign of 1862," David G. McIntosh Papers, sec. 6, Virginia Historical Society, Richmond (repository hereafter cited as VHS); *OR* 19(1):961.

34. *OR* 19(1):951, 961. Receipts in the papers of Major Hawks show that the Confederates also purchased foodstuffs in Charles Town to supplement the stores captured in

Harpers Ferry. Thomas J. Jackson Papers, 18-A, box 2, Southern Historical Collection, Wilson Library, University of North Carolina, Chapel Hill (repository hereafter cited as SHC).

35. Alexander, *Military Memoirs,* 242, 272.

36. *OR* 19(1):962.

37. *OR* 19(1):960–61; William Miller Owen, *In Camp and Battle with the Washington Artillery* (Boston: Ticknor, 1885), 162.

38. Mockbee, "Sun never shined," 21; Caldwell, *History of a Brigade,* 72; Andrew B. Wardlaw diary, September 13, 1862, bound vol. 206, FSNMP.

39. Ordnance Returns for Lane's brigade dated April 3, 4, 1863, vol. 59, Bryan Family Papers, SHC; Walter Clark, comp., *Histories of the Several Regiments and Battalions from North Carolina in the Great War 1861–'65,* 5 vols. (Raleigh: E. M. Uzzell, 1901), 1:372, 2:32 (hereafter cited as Clark, *N.C. Regiments*); McIntosh, "Maryland Campaign of 1862." Despite the exchange at Harpers Ferry of smoothbores for rifles within the 7th and 18th North Carolina regiments, the regiments in James Lane's brigade still carried a large number of smoothbores as late as April 1863.

40. Andrew B. Wardlaw diary, September 13, 1862, bound vol. 206, FSNMP; Mockbee, "Sun never shined," 21; John Keely, "Narrative of the Campaigns of the 19th Georgia Volunteer Infantry," Atlanta *Constitution Magazine,* March 15, 1931; *OR* 19(1):468. The Union uniforms worn by many of A. P. Hill's men at the battle of Sharpsburg caused momentary confusion among the Federals fighting in the Otto, or "40-acre," cornfield.

41. Letter from "G" [probably Lt. John C. Gorman, Company B, 2nd North Carolina Infantry] to wife, dated September 21, Raleigh *Standard,* October 1, 1862; Andrew B. Wardlaw diary, September 13, 1862, bound vol. 206, FSNMP; CSR of Charles J. Taylor, M331, NA; *ORS* 3:501.

42. Allan, *Army of Northern Virginia,* 333–34; *OR* 19(2):603.

43. Alexander Hunter, "A High Private's Account of the Battle of Sharpsburg," *SHSP* 10:511; Peter W. Alexander, "Our Army Correspondence," Mobile *Advertiser and Register,* September 24, 1862.

44. *OR* 19(1):604–5.

45. Allan, *Army of Northern Virginia,* 343–46.

46. *OR* 19(1):142; Personne [Felix De Fontaine], "Our Army Correspondence," Charleston *Daily Courier,* September 29, 1862.

47. *OR* 19(1):142, 891, 911; [Acting Quartermaster of James's S.C. Infantry Battalion], "A Disaster," Charleston *Daily Courier,* October 1, 1862; Kitrell J. Warren, *Muster Roll and History of the Eleventh Regiment, Georgia Volunteers* (Tyler, Tex.: Lee & Burnett Printers and Binders, 1903), 36. The five companies of the 11th Georgia Infantry had been detached to guard Gen. D. H. Hill's commissary train.

48. James Murfin, *The Gleam of Bayonets: The Battle of Antietam and Robert E. Lee's Maryland Campaign, September 1862* (1965; reprint, Baton Rouge: Louisiana

State University Press, 1982), 192–95; Francis W. Dawson, *Reminiscences of Confederate Service,* ed. Bell I. Wiley (1882; reprint, Baton Rouge: Louisiana State University Press, 1985), 64; "A Disaster," Charleston *Daily Courier,* October 1, 1862.

49. Alexander, *Military Memoirs,* 242; *OR* 19(1):830; Richard Harwell, ed., *The Union Reader* (New York: Longmans, Green, 1958), 170. Although the captured wagons apparently belonged to Longstreet's command, that officer made no mention of the incident in his report of the campaign.

50. *OR* 19(1):151; Stephen W. Sears, *Landscape Turned Red: The Battle of Antietam* (New York: Ticknor & Fields, 1983), 175–76, 389.

51. Richard H. Watkins to wife, September 23, 1862, Richard H. Watkins Letters, VHS; *OR* 19(1):1025; "Joe" [member of the 3rd Alabama Infantry] to father, "Letter from a Mobile Rifleman," Mobile *Advertiser and Register,* October 18, 1862; Shotwell, *Papers,* 1:345.

52. *OR* 19(1):922; James L. Lemon diary, September 18, 1862, extracts in 18th Georgia Infantry file, Antietam National Battlefield Park, Sharpsburg, Md.

53. John F. Edwards, "Atlanta, October 11, 1885," box 1, folder titled "McLaws' Division," Antietam Studies, NA; Albert W. Henley memoir, 38, bound vol. 125, FS-NMP; "S. L. W." [member of Co. B, 17th Mississippi Infantry], "Letter from Our Virginia Army," Memphis *Daily Appeal,* October 13, 1862. Some of the men in McLaws's division went into the Federal camps at Harpers Ferry and took captured rations.

54. CSR of Thomas E. Ballard, M331, NA.

55. George M. Neese, *Three Years in the Confederate Horse Artillery* (1911; reprint, Dayton, Ohio: Morningside, 1988), 125; Clark, *N.C. Regiments,* 1:187; Bartlett, *Military Record,* 44, 140; James M. Garnett and Alexander Hunter, "The Battle of Antietam or Sharpsburg," *SHSP* 31:35–36.

56. Robert Underwood Johnson and Clarence Clough Buel, eds., *Battles and Leaders of the Civil War,* 4 vols. (New York: Century, 1887–88), 2:669; Clark, *N.C. Regiments,* 1:573–74; Owen, *In Camp and Battle,* 158.

57. Bartlett, *Military Record,* 140; Owen, *In Camp and Battle,* 162.

58. Folsom, *Heroes and Martyrs of Georgia,* 15; Bartlett, *Military Record,* 140.

59. William Allan memoir, 158, vol. 8, William Allan Papers, SHC; *ORS* 3:502; *OR* 19(1):957; W. G. Bean, "John A. Harman: Jackson's Logistical Genius," *Augusta Historical Bulletin* 8 (Fall 1972): 39; James I. Robertson Jr., *Stonewall Jackson: The Man, the Soldier, the Legend* (New York: Macmillan, 1997), 620.

60. *OR* 19(1):143.

61. *OR* 19(2):622, 633; "Burr" [member of the 44th Georgia Infantry], letter dated October 3, 1862, Macon *Daily Telegraph,* October 10, 1862.

62. *OR* 19(2):637, 633, 699; "Letter from Kenan, Winchester, Va. Oct. 3d, 1862," Macon *Daily Telegraph,* October 14, 1862; Richard Goff, *Confederate Supply* (Durham, N.C.: Duke University Press, 1969), 78. At the same time Lee began im-

pressing wheat in the valley, Secretary of War George W. Randolph closed the borders of Virginia to further exports of flour by either the government or private citizens.

63. Caldwell, *History of a Brigade,* 86; Spencer G. Welch, *A Confederate Surgeon's Letters to His Wife* (New York: Neale, 1911), 31; T. Harry Williams, ed., "The Civil War Letters of William L. Cage," *Louisiana Historical Quarterly* 39 (1956): 127; Terrence V. Murphy, *Tenth Virginia Infantry* (Lynchburg, Va.: H. E. Howard, 1989), 55.

64. Caldwell, *History of a Brigade,* 86; Stephen D. Lee to William N. Pendleton, September 26, 1862, William N. Pendleton Papers, SHC; "Barefoot" to editor, September 27, 1862, Macon *Daily Telegraph,* October 7, 1862; Fred E. Gaillard, ed., *Franklin Gaillard's Civil War Letters* (n.p.: n.p., 1941), 24.

65. "P. W. A." [Peter W. Alexander], "Our Army, Its Great Deeds, Its Suffering, and Its Perils in the Future," Augusta *Daily Constitutionalist,* October 4, 1862; "Scarcity of Leather," Montgomery *Daily Advertiser,* November 26, 1862; Felix De Fontaine, "Our Army Correspondence," Charleston *Daily Courier,* October 3, 1862.

66. "Gross Mismanagement," Memphis *Daily Appeal,* October 21, 1862. See also "Destitution in our Armies," Montgomery *Daily Advertiser,* November 5, 1862; Reverend H. H. Parks, "To the People of Columbus," Columbus *Enquirer,* October 7, 1862.

67. Gaillard, *Civil War Letters,* 24; "Clothing for the Army," Selma *Reporter,* December 11, 1862; "Clothing for the Army," Macon *Daily Telegraph,* October 4, 1862. See also "Clothing the Army," Columbus *Daily Sun,* October 10, 1862.

68. "Destitution in our Army," Montgomery *Weekly Advertiser,* October 8, 1862; "A Soldier," "Are We Whipped? Must We Give Up?" Atlanta *Southern Confederacy,* October 30, 1862.

69. "Dixie," "Letter from Richmond," Memphis *Daily Appeal,* October 17, 1862; "S. L. W." [member of Co. B, 17th Mississippi Infantry], "Virginia Correspondence," Memphis *Daily Appeal,* October 28, 1862; "S. C. B.," "An Appeal of a Lady for the Soldiers," Columbus *Daily Sun,* October 15, 1862; "Destitution in our Army," Montgomery *Daily Mail,* November 5, 1862.

70. Andrews, *South Reports the Civil War,* 50, 217; "P. W. A.," "Our Army, Its Great Deeds." Alexander's article appeared in many newspapers across the Confederacy.

71. Andrews, *South Reports the Civil War,* 218; [Probably George E. Hayes, Co. K, 3rd Georgia Infantry], "Camp near Winchester, Va., Oct. 16, 1862," Athens *Southern Banner,* December 3, 1862; Assistant Quartermaster John T. Brown, "Special Notice to the Family & Friends of the Soldiers belonging to the 14th, 35th, and 49th Regiments," Atlanta *Southern Confederacy,* October 17, 1862; "Our Needy Soldiers," Atlanta *Southern Confederacy,* November 2, 1862.

72. "Clothing for the Soldiers—Dispatch from the Secretary of War," Montgomery *Weekly Advertiser,* October 29, 1862.

73. "Clothing for the Army," Columbus *Daily Sun,* October 10, 1862; "Petition

from the Ladies of Bartow County," October 10, 1862, Georgia Governor's Papers, box 58, Telamon Cuyler Collection, University of Georgia, Athens; "Various Items," Montgomery *Weekly Advertiser,* October 18, 1862.

74. "The Arts of Independence," Macon *Daily Telegraph,* October 2, 1862.

75. "The Soldier's Necessities," Memphis *Daily Appeal,* October 29, 1862; "A Planter," "It Must be Done," Macon *Daily Telegraph,* October 8, 1862; "Lowndes," "Mr. Advertiser," Montgomery *Weekly Advertiser,* October 22, 1862. See also Catherine Ann Devereux Edmondston, *"Journal of a Secesh Lady": The Diary of Catherine Ann Devereux Edmondston, 1860–1866,* ed. Beth Gilbert Crabtree and James W. Patton (Raleigh: North Carolina Division of Archives and History, 1979), 282.

76. "Tallassee," "Tallassee, Ala., November 20, 1862," Montgomery *Daily Advertiser,* November 26, 1862; "A Mechanic," "A Proposition," Columbus *Daily Sun,* October 14, 1862; "Contributions to the Cause," Raleigh *Semi-Weekly Standard,* October 24, 1862; Jane E. Robinson, letter dated October 20, 1862, Montgomery *Weekly Advertiser,* October 25, 1862; "Our Hospitals in Virginia," Charleston *Daily Courier,* October 9, 1862.

77. "Governor's Message, Executive Department, Montgomery, Ala., Nov 10th, 1862," Selma *Reporter,* November 13, 1862; "Copy of A Resolution," November 25, 1862, Atlanta *Southern Confederacy,* January 1, 1863; Ron Field, *The Hampton Legion* (Gloucestershire, England: by the author, 1994), 43; *OR* 19(2):718; Knox Mellon Jr., ed., "A Florida Soldier in the Army of Northern Virginia: The Hosford Letters," *Florida Historical Quarterly* 46 (January 1968): 248.

78. A. C. Myers to G. W. Randolph, September 25, 1862, CSQM to SW, RG 109, M900, reel 6, 075-06, NA; *OR* 10(2):718.

79. P. W. Alexander, "Help Needed at Once! Let No One Wait!," Atlanta *Southern Confederacy,* October 29, 1862.

80. Ibid.; Special Orders, November 15, 1862, SO-ANV, RG 109, M921, reel 1, NA; C.S. Quartermaster Department, Clothing Account Book, 7th Louisiana Infantry, RG 109, chap. 5, vol. 205, NA; "Clarence," October 14, 1862, Columbia *Daily Southern Guardian,* October 29, 1862.

81. *OR* 21:1016, 1045, 1097–98; Goff, "Logistics and Supply Problems," 146.

82. Murphy, *Tenth Virginia Infantry,* 55; Leslie D. Jensen, *Thirty-second Virginia Infantry* (Lynchburg, Va.: H. E. Howard, 1990), 98; Michael Shuler diary, October 12, 14, 23, November 4, 21, 1862, bound vol. 67, FSNMP; General Orders 100, December 8, 1862, *General Orders from Adjutant and Inspector-General's Office, Confederate States Army, in 1862* (Charleston: Evans & Cogswell, 1863); Eli Pinson Landers, *In Care of Yellow River: The Complete Civil War Letters of Pvt. Eli Pinson Landers to His Mother,* ed. Elizabeth W. Robertson (Gretna, La.: Pelican Publishing Co., 1997), 100–101; Robert J. Driver, *Fifty-eighth Virginia Infantry* (Lynchburg, Va.: H. E. Howard, 1990), 37; James J. Kirkpatrick diary, November 15, 1862, bound vol. 131, FSNMP; Special Orders 239, November 11, 1862, SO-ANV, RG 109, M921, reel 1, NA.

83. Charles W. Ramsdell, "General Robert E. Lee's Horse Supply, 1862–1865," *American Historical Review* 35 (July 1930): 760–61; *OR* 19(2):701, 709; H. H. Matthews, "Pelham-Breathed Battery—From the Valley to Fredericksburg—Part VII," Saint Mary's (Md.) *Beacon,* February 9, 1905; Heros von Borcke, *Memoirs of the Confederate War for Independence* (Edinburgh: William Blackwood and Sons, 1866), 326. Stuart's staff officer von Borcke claimed that the greased heel epidemic cost the cavalry and artillery more than one-fourth of their horses and mules.

84. Ramsdell, "General Robert E. Lee's Horse Supply," 760–61; Wise, *Long Arm of Lee,* 1:329–30. Lee issued a general order on October 1, 1862, that established strict regulations for the use and care of horses in an effort to curb past abuses.

85. Allan, "Reminiscences of Field Ordnance Service," *SHSP* 14:140; *OR* 19(2): 646, 647–52; D. S. Freeman, *Lee's Lieutenants: A Study in Command,* 3 vols. (New York: Scribner's, 1943), 2:447–50.

86. General Orders 68, September 17, 1862, General Orders 12, January 28, 1863, *General Orders from Adjutant and Inspector-General's Office;* James Seddon to Jefferson Davis, January 3, 1863, Letters Sent by the Confederate Secretary of War to the President, 1861–65, vol. 1 (chap. 11, vol. 39), RG 109, M523, reel 1, NA; Wise, *Long Arm of Lee,* 1:338. Jennings C. Wise points out that many trained and able subalterns in the field artillery could not be induced, even with the promise of advanced rank, to leave their batteries for other duties.

87. Dawson, *Reminiscences of Confederate Service,* 63; General Orders 24, April 16, 1862, General Orders 46, July 1, 1862, *General Orders from Adjutant and Inspector-General's Office;* "War Department, Ordnance Bureau, Richmond, September 22, 1862, Order No. 6," folder 12, Edward P. Alexander Papers, SHC. For an excellent discussion of the early problems and evolution of the staff system within the Army of Northern Virginia, see Freeman, *Lee's Lieutenants,* 2:433–43.

88. Special Orders 201, SO-ANV, September 25, 1862, RG 109, M921, reel 1, NA; Allan, "Reminiscences of Field Ordnance Service," *SHSP* 14:138.

89. Allan, "Reminiscences of Field Ordnance Service," *SHSP* 14:138; *ORS* 3: 483–84. For evidence of the new regulations enacted regarding ordnance stores and equipment, see the official correspondence of Edwin Taliaferro, ordnance officer for Lafayette McLaws's division, in the White, Welford, Taliaferro, and Marshall Papers, M-1300, SHC, and Lafayette McLaws to E. P. Alexander, October 18, 1862, folder 12, E. P. Alexander Papers, SHC. Lee's September 22, 1862, order also specified that inspectors regularly examine company and regimental papers to "see that a proper system of accountability prevails." *OR* 19(2):618.

90. *OR* 19(2):593–94; *ORS* 3:483–84; Alexander, *Military Memoirs,* 370. See also A. J. L. Fremantle, *Three Months in the Southern States: April–June 1863* (New York: John Bradburn, 1864), 225. For an example of a southern infantry regiment that received captured rifle muskets from Harpers Ferry, see William A. McClendon, *Recollections of War Times by an Old Veteran* (Montgomery, Ala.: Paragon Press, 1909), 155.

91. *OR* 21:1046–47; Wise, *Long Arm of Lee,* 1:340–41.

92. A. C. Myers to G. W. Randolph, October 1, 1862, CSQM to SW, RG 109, M900, reel 6, 075-06, NA; Goff, "Logistics and Supply Problems," 146.

93. A. C. Myers to James Seddon, November 22, 1862, CSQM to SW, RG 109, M900, reel 6, 075-06, NA.

94. *OR* 19(2):618.

95. General Orders 100, December 8, 1862, *General Orders from Adjutant and Inspector-General's Office.*

96. Goff, "Logistics and Supply Problems," 160, 167.

97. Goff, *Confederate Supply,* 84–85.

98. Ibid., 85–86.

99. Goff, "Logistics and Supply Problems," 173–75; *OR* 21:1016.

100. Edward Hagerman, *The American Civil War and the Origins of Modern Warfare* (Bloomington: Indiana University Press, 1988), 121; Goff, *Confederate Supply,* 105–7.

101. Goff, "Logistics and Supply Problems," 198.

102. "P. W. A.," "Our Army, Its Great Deeds."

D. SCOTT HARTWIG

Who Would Not Be a Soldier

The Volunteers of '62 in

the Maryland Campaign

"Then, after the leaving the turnpike, filing to the left across the fields, and wading or jumping a small running stream, the column is halted, and for the first time the Ninth regiment men receive orders to load. Some have never before loaded a gun, few have ever loaded with a ball cartridge, and many must be shown the whole process."[1]

It was September 14, 1862, and soldiers of the 9th New Hampshire Infantry were preparing to enter battle for the first time at South Mountain. Their utter lack of preparation for combat, short of being issued uniforms, equipment, muskets, and ammunition, was not unique in the Army of the Potomac that Maj. Gen. George B. McClellan led into Maryland that fateful September. Green troops innocent of the training and discipline vital to perform effectively on a battlefield made up nearly one-quarter of McClellan's infantry. Yet they participated in fighting throughout the Maryland campaign, frequently with grimly predictable consequences. More often than not they proved to be a hindrance in combat, and despite enthusiastic courage they proved largely detrimental to Union success.

The large number of green Union regiments in the Maryland campaign resulted indirectly from an order issued by Secretary of War Edwin M. Stanton on
April 3, 1862, closing recruiting stations across the North. McClellan had landed
the Army of the Potomac on the Virginia Peninsula; the war was progressing satisfactorily in the West, and it seemed as if the force at hand could bring the rebellion to a close that summer. But then came Shiloh, and McClellan's soldiers were
felled by the hundreds when they encountered the climate of the Virginia Peninsula. McClellan's defeat in the Seven Days battles soon followed, and with it the
realization that the war would not end that summer. The government needed
more soldiers, and quickly. Lincoln held a hurriedly assembled meeting of northern governors in New York on July 2, after which he issued a call for 300,000 volunteers. But men did not flock to the colors as they had in 1861. To stimulate en-
listments, Congress authorized payment of a bounty of twenty-five dollars to
three-year volunteers and on July 17 passed the Militia Act of 1862. This legislation empowered the president to call the state militia into Federal service for a
period of up to nine months. On August 4, the government announced an additional levy of 300,000 nine-month militia. In a sense this was a draft; however,
Lincoln neatly sidestepped a potentially volatile issue by leaving it up to the states
to mobilize their manpower. The militia call-up was further softened by a provision that allowed each three-year volunteer raised under the July 2 call to count as
four men against the nine-month militia quota.[2]

Northern governors found it easiest to raise volunteers by organizing new regiments. Enlisting recruits for veteran regiments in the field would have been
infinitely more efficient but far more difficult to accomplish because it lacked any
incentives. With each new regiment came thirty-four officers' commissions to be
awarded to those who helped raise the unit. No such plums could be awarded for
recruiting men to join existing regiments. So throughout the month of July northern cities, villages, and towns appealed to the patriotism of their men and asked
them to volunteer. But the hard battles of 1861 and 1862 had dampened the military ardor of the North's male population, or at least provided it with a dose of the
reality of soldiering. Abner R. Small, who had been promised a captain's commission if he recruited a company for what would be the 16th Maine Infantry, recalled that "recruiting was a discouraging business. I called up all the eloquence
of my ancestors, if they had any; I pleaded, cried, swore, and prayed, yet only two
patriots were enrolled to my credit." In Redfield Corner, Maine, Small "painted
the town red with patriotic posters" yet managed to enlist only one minor, whom
his father led away by the ear while threatening to make Small "a dead hero" if
he remained in town.[3] Some states resorted to offering bounties, in addition to
the Federal bounty, to those who volunteered. Although the entire recruiting

effort suffered from numerous defects, it somehow managed to raise thousands of new troops.

The new regiments were needed at the front as quickly as they could be organized and equipped. The capital's garrison had been reduced to reinforce Maj. Gen. John Pope's Army of Virginia, as had the garrisons at the strategic points of Winchester, Harpers Ferry, and Martinsburg, Virginia. In mid-August, when many of the newly organized regiments began arriving in Washington, the situation along Pope's front was active, but the garrisons were quiet—making the latter ideal locations for raw soldiers to gain seasoning and begin their training. By the beginning of September, green troops accounted for more than half of the garrison at Harpers Ferry. In uniform barely three weeks, these men remained untrained and unprepared for combat except in spirit. Martinsburg boasted a smaller garrison of entirely green troops. By September 6, thirty-six new regiments, more than 30,000 men, camped within the capital's defenses. Had Pope been able to check Lee in northern Virginia, this crowd of civilians in uniforms could have completed their training and by autumn would have represented a formidable reinforcement to the Union army. But Pope did not hold Lee in check, and the Union strategy in the East collapsed like a house of cards when his army suffered its bruising defeat at Second Manassas. By September 2, the Army of Virginia and Army of the Potomac had retreated into the capital's defenses. Lee planned to give them no opportunity to rest and reorganize. His intelligence sources told him that 60,000 new troops had arrived in Washington, and he determined to invade Maryland and force the Federals to react before these raw soldiers could organize and train.[4]

Lee's army began crossing the Potomac near Leesburg, Virginia, on September 4, creating a crisis for the northern government and a need to field an army immediately. Maj. Gen. George B. McClellan would command this army. He had a sizable force at his disposal, but the summer's campaign had left many veteran formations completely used up, particularly those that had served with Pope. Combat losses had been heavy in some units, and there were thousands of non-battle casualties, victims of incessant marching and Pope's miserable logistical support. An enormous number of men also had absented themselves from their units. Brig. Gen. Alpheus S. Williams, a division commander in the Twelfth Corps, described the service his command had endured in a letter to his daughter: "Suffice it to say that for over three weeks we have been scarcely a day without marching—for at least seven days without rations." Brig. Gen. George Sykes's excellent division of regular troops, which had seen hard fighting at Second Manassas as well as during the Seven Days battles, reported only 3,985 of 6,995 men present for duty on August 31. Those missing were absent or sick or

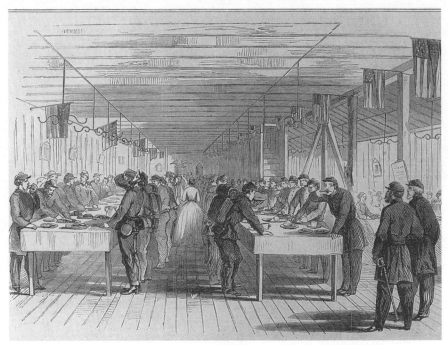

New troops on their way to join McClellan's army enjoy themselves at
a "Union refreshment saloon" in Philadelphia.
Frank Leslie's Illustrated Newspaper, September 27, 1862

had deserted. The Second Corps, which had seen no fighting at Manassas, counted 6,905 men absent out of a total of 24,652. The Twelfth Corps presented the most deplorable picture. Its two divisions contained only 4,000 effectives, and one of its brigades reported just 629 men present for duty. To reinforce his depleted brigades, McClellan had little choice but to use the new regiments, whose full ranks at least represented a substantial increase to his manpower.[5]

In the early days of the Maryland campaign, Federal intelligence remained uncertain whether the entire Confederate army had invaded Maryland. Some reports suggested that a large force remained on the south bank of the Potomac. McClellan thus had to allocate a strong force to man the defenses of Washington. He selected the Third, Fifth, and Eleventh Corps to form the bulk of the capital's garrison, while he led the First, Second, Sixth, Ninth, and Twelfth Corps, together with Sykes's division of the Fifth Corps and Maj. Gen. Darius N. Couch's division of the Fourth Corps, in pursuit of the Confederate invaders. The field army had an effective strength of approximately 60,000 men. On September 6–7, McClellan assigned twenty-four new regiments to his field army, distributing them unequally among his corps, with the Second, Ninth, and Twelfth receiving the largest number. Only eighteen regiments, numbering about 15,000–16,000 men, actually accompanied the army, the others being unable to join their assigned brigades before the army moved. In addition, several thousand volunteers who had been recruited for veteran regiments joined their commands in the days before the army marched, raising the number of recruits in the field to approximately 20,000. This meant that nearly one-quarter of McClellan's infantry had undergone little or no training. Historians of the Maryland campaign frequently stress McClellan's advantage in strength over Lee but almost never address this important point. The number of green infantry units that accompanied the army into the field significantly affected its mobility and combat effectiveness. Col. Ezra A. Carman, who led the 13th New Jersey at Antietam and later became the battle's most thorough historian, believed that McClellan lacked confidence in his army's combat capabilities and hoped to avoid a showdown with Lee in Maryland. Instead, he preferred to maneuver the enemy out the state. The green troops alone did not shape the Federal commander's strategic planning, but they undoubtedly contributed to it.[6]

McClellan has often been criticized for the slowness of his army's advance from Washington to Frederick in the opening stages of the campaign. Although logistical problems, which are beyond the scope of this essay, prevented his moving anywhere rapidly, the large number of new troops also hampered the army's mobility. Marching places severe demands on new troops. The British military observer and historian G. F. R. Henderson wrote that "an ill-disciplined army lacks mobility. Marching . . . makes the greatest demand on the subordination of the men and exertions of the officers." McClellan's new regiments lacked discipline; most of their company and many of their field officers were unfamiliar or uncomfortable with their duties and responsibilities. Some officers exhibited incredible ignorance of elementary commands and duties—especially considering that they and their men would be in combat in a matter of days. On September 7, Colonel Carman described in his diary an encounter with Col. Samuel Croasdale of the 128th Pennsylvania. "The Col was evidently green on military matters as he asked me how to form line of battle," wrote Carman, "not knowing himself and giving as an excuse that he had no time since being commissioned to buy a copy of tactics." Col. Eliakim Sherrill, commander of the 126th New York at Harpers Ferry, freely confessed "that he knew nothing about military; that he made no pretensions to military; that he was just in the field and green." Such officers, no matter how brave (both Sherrill and Croasdale were courageous men), lacked the training and experience to move large numbers of troops long distances and deliver the maximum number of men to the critical point. The ultimate purpose of marching is to bring men to the battlefield, and it is possible that the generally short marches McClellan's army made from Washington to Frederick stemmed partly from the commander's desire to give the new recruits some seasoning.[7]

The 16th Connecticut made nearly a twenty-mile march on a brutally hot and dusty September 7. The regimental historian recorded with pride that the men covered nineteen miles in eight and one-half hours. "This was good marching for new troops, and showed what we would be equal to when necessity required," he wrote. Indeed it was, but the historian neglected to mention that comparatively few men completed the march. Jonathan E. Shipman of the 16th informed a friend that in his company "only between 20 and 30 answered roll call." About fifty others subsequently caught up, "but a number we have not yet seen," observed Shipman five days later. Nearly every new regiment shared a similar experience. Lt. Albert A. Pope of the 35th Massachusetts recorded in his journal on September 6 that his regiment marched from 5:00 P.M. until 1:00 A.M. "It was a hard march," noted Pope. "The men were falling out of the ranks all along the road. I fell out about a mile behind the regiment and slept on the porch of a house." Sebastian Duncan of the 13th New Jersey admitted that "one-third of the regiment gave out" in their first march. The next day was intensely hot, added Duncan, with "the dust often so thick that we could scarcely breathe, or even see before us. Many had fallen out the night before, but now they began to wilt by the dozens & when we halted at noon we had not more than half a company." The historian of the 118th Pennsylvania related a similar experience during that unit's march from Washington on September 12:

> Wholly unused to such fatigues, and totally unacquainted with reducing their loads to the minimum by dispensing with useless appendages and trappings, the march told upon the men severely. . . . Overburdened, worn and weary, man after man, yielding to the inevitable, had dropped by the wayside, or straggling, broken and dejected, was struggling to reach the goal of his apparently endless journey. The sergeant and the color-guard fell in complete exhaustion, and colonel himself bore the standard to the bivouac. Three men to a company, as the "strength present for duty," was a most creditable showing when the final halt was made.

When a thoroughly exhausted, disgusted, and demoralized private of the regiment encountered Maj. Gen. George W. Morrell, he inquired, "General, can you tell me where the 118th Pennsylvania is?" Morrell replied, "Certainly, my man, everywhere between here and Washington."[8]

Foraging became another problem with the new regiments. Maryland offered a countryside rich in good things to eat. A combination of loose discipline and bad army food, and often not enough of the latter, prompted green soldiers to seek out the bounty of Maryland's farms. Lt. Albert Pope noted in his diary on September 8 that "all the hens within a mile have been bagged by our men. One man in the vicinity had forty hens, and the boys took them all besides a pig." Andrew Tehrune and his comrades in the 13th New Jersey found foraging a frolic. He wrote to his cousin on September 9, "[W]e have bully times out here[.] [W]e went out yesterday and caught four hogs and skinned them and roasted them over the coals[.] [T]his morning we fetched in another hog and some ducks and chickens[.] [W]e live first rate out here. . . . Who would not be a soldier." Tehrune would sing a different tune after his first dose of combat on September 17.[9]

Sometimes officers behaved as badly as their men. Jonathan Shipman, with the 16th Connecticut, complained that when a farmer invited soldiers from his regiment into his orchard to pick some fruit, Col. Francis Beach rode up and struck one of the men with his sword—"a favorite game" of the colonel's. "He and all the other officers steal everything they want to eat," claimed Shipman; "the other night he took a chicken away from a man who had bought it." Foraging with the tacit permission of officers weakened the bonds of discipline vital to survival in combat.[10]

As the army advanced toward Frederick, each day of marching grew slightly easier than the one before. Frederick Hitchcock, the adjutant of the 132nd Pennsylvania, recalled: "[A]n interesting feature of our first two days' march was the clearing out of knapsacks to reduce the load. . . . After the second day's march, those knapsacks contained little but what the soldier was compelled to carry, his rations, extra ammunition, and clothing." Each day of marching also brought the men closer to possible combat. On September 13, as the 14th Connecticut marched into Frederick City, they passed an old engine house where some Confederate prisoners were being held. One Confederate called out, inquiring what regiment the New Englanders belonged to. "The 14th Wooden Nutmeg," the men replied. To this, recalled the regimental historian, the "audacious prisoner answered, 'You will soon get your heads grated.'"[11]

By the time of this humorous exchange, green troops garrisoning Harpers Ferry had already seen the elephant. Their experience was an unhappy one, particularly for the 126th New York Infantry, which became one of the principal scapegoats of the disaster at Harpers Ferry. Commanded by the woefully unprepared Col. Eliakim Sherrill, the 126th arrived in Harpers Ferry on August 28, about two weeks after they had been organized in New York. Numbering 1,031 officers and men, the regiment was the largest of the garrison. They received orders on September 12 to reinforce the defenders of Maryland Heights, who faced the Confederate brigades of Gens. Joseph B. Kershaw and William Barksdale of

Maj. Gen. Lafayette McLaws's division. The regiment had done some drilling since its arrival on the 28th and had started to learn the manual of arms, but they had never loaded or fired their muskets before being ordered up to face McLaws's veterans. En route to the summit of the heights, five companies of the regiment were detached to perform picket and skirmish duty. The remaining five companies, accompanied by their colonel, continued on to the mountain's summit, beyond a rude breastwork of logs and abatis of trees and brush that had been felled in front of the Union position.

The time was about 5:30 P.M. Colonel Sherrill instructed his companies to form a line of battle in rear of skirmishers from the veteran 32nd Ohio, who were trading shots with skirmishers of Kershaw's brigade. About the time Sherrill's New Yorkers arrived, the South Carolinians pressed the Federal line. On rugged ground covered by thick vegetation, particularly mountain laurel, men in the 126th could see few enemy soldiers. Sherrill permitted them to open fire, however, and also sent for two of his detached companies to bolster his firing line. The Confederate skirmishers sought merely to test the Union strength, and the crash of hundreds of muskets from the 126th let them know numerous Federals lay ahead. Darkness soon fell across the mountain and firing ceased.[12]

The 126th were ordered to rest on their arms in line but not to sleep. The Confederates lay a mere one hundred yards away — so close that the regiment's major, William H. Baird, testified, "[W]e could hear the enemy in pretty large force, by their talk, as I judged." Lt. Samuel A. Barras, the regimental adjutant, recalled that he "heard several remarks made as to what they were going to do in the morning."[13]

Early on September 13, Colonel Sherrill detailed Company B to the skirmish line. Some dismounted Maryland cavalry under Maj. Charles H. Russell soon joined them. As the Federal troopers made their way forward, a Confederate skirmisher put a bullet through the leg of a cavalry sergeant. A considerable part of Company B witnessed this event, unnerved by the first casualty they had ever seen. Russell observed that a large part of the company "broke and ran" back toward the main line of battle. The major deployed his men under cover to respond to the Confederate fire, then went back to the New Yorkers "and begged the officers to bring their men forward again." They did so, and Company B resumed its place on the skirmish line. Both sides traded shots for a few minutes until the South Carolina skirmishers withdrew. Believing they had repulsed an attack, Company B raised a shout of relief and victory, soon taken up by the other companies of the regiment in line of battle to their rear. Minutes later the long roll sounded on a drum from the direction of the Confederate line, followed by shouts of "forward" by southern officers and the sound of a heavy line of battle making its way through the dense undergrowth.[14]

Before the Confederates became visible, Company B broke again and ran back to the line of battle. According to Major Russell, some of the men sprinted all the way to the breastwork. The six companies of the regiment in the general line of battle stood their ground, and when the main body of Confederates appeared, the companies opened what Major Baird described as a fire by file. Combined with the musketry of more experienced regiments on their flanks, the 126th's effort checked the enemy advance for nearly fifteen minutes. Owing to cover provided by the woods, the regiment suffered relatively few casualties, but several wounded passed through the 126th's line, creating some unsteadiness. The conduct of Major Baird did not provide encouragement. He apparently dodged from tree to tree while his men traded fire with Kershaw's Confederates. One of Major Russell's lieutenants suffered what must have been a particularly unnerving wound—Russell did not relate whether he was killed—because it caused all but two companies of the 126th to fall into disorder and start for the rear. Major Baird led the way.[15]

Colonel Sherrill and Lieutenant Barras dashed back to head off their retreating men and managed to beat them to the breastwork. Hoping to avoid struggling through the thick mountain laurel, most of the men in the 126th had crowded on a trail that led from the main line to the breastwork. Sherrill met them with drawn revolver as they came up to the work. What the colonel did not understand about tactics he attempted to compensate for with pure courage. With Barras's help, and sheer will, Sherrill managed to rally about two-thirds of his men. The rest passed over the breastwork and slipped down the mountain and out of the fight.[16]

The retreat of the greater part of the 126th unhinged the forward Union line, which soon withdrew to the breastwork. There the companies of several regiments, including the 126th, were arranged without regard to regimental integrity. Kershaw's men soon came up against this line, and the fight resumed. Protected by the log breastwork, the 126th fought effectively, delivering a murderous fire that helped bring the South Carolinians to a standstill. Capt. Charles M. Wheeler, commanding Company K, observed that the men "were very cool indeed, as a rule; dropping behind the breastwork to load, and then rising and firing coolly over the breastworks." The same soldiers who had fled from the early morning skirmish now fought bravely and stubbornly. The reason was simple. In the open their lack of drill and discipline caused the regiment to fall into confusion whenever they attempted to maneuver, particularly in the thick woods on Maryland Heights. Their inexperience, notably among the officers, also created a general uneasiness and lack of confidence in the face of a disciplined enemy such as Kershaw's brigade. The breastwork offered a fixed position upon which they could form. With maneuver unnecessary, the men only had to load and fire. This behavior of green troops also would be common at Antietam; regiments that pushed straight ahead, loading and firing, maintained far greater cohesion and effectiveness than regiments that tried to maneuver.[17]

Colonel Sherrill's dynamic leadership also contributed to the 126th's rising courage. He may not have known tactics, but he knew how to inspire men. During the fight he climbed on the log works, recklessly exposing himself to animate his men and direct their fire. "I never saw a braver man than Colonel Sherrill in my life," Lieutenant Barras testified. But a single bullet popped the regiment's newfound confidence like a balloon. A South Carolinian fired a shot that struck Sherrill in the face, knocking out several teeth, tearing his tongue, and producing a very bloody wound. The effect was demoralizing. One officer at the breastwork testified that after Sherrill went down "his men mostly fell back in spite of all we could do," adding that they "were in the utmost confusion." Not everyone from the 126th left the breastworks at this time, but the regiment was finished for the day as an organized force.[18]

In October 1862, the army held an extensive investigation into the humiliating surrender of the Harpers Ferry garrison. The final report singled out the 126th New York for special criticism. "The Commission calls attention to the disgraceful behavior of the One hundred and twenty-sixth New York Infantry," the document read. Only Colonel Sherrill, Adjutant Barras, and several other officers of the regiment, whom the commission did not name, were spared censure. This report left a stain on the regiment's reputation that it would not erase until Gettysburg. Under the circumstances, the commission had little choice but to censure the 126th. They could not condone such behavior—even on the part of a green regiment. Yet the regular officers on the commission likely knew that any regiment as green as the 126th would have performed similarly.

In fact, with the exception of the 9th Vermont Infantry, which did well at Harpers Ferry, nearly every green regiment in the garrison failed to stand fire during the siege. The 125th New York, commanded by Col. George L. Willard, a West Pointer, broke under the Confederate artillery fire that struck their position near Bolivar Heights on September 14. Charles W. Belknap, a captain in the regiment, recorded in his journal that "they began to shell our regiment which produced quite a panic. The men rushed without order for their arms and then started off at a pretty good speed for a ravine back of the hospital. I thought it was too bad to see the men run in such confusion when there was no great danger." When a brigade commander later asked Willard to advance to support a regiment

A photograph taken from the base of Maryland Heights looking across the Potomac River toward Harpers Ferry. Fighting on Maryland Heights and elsewhere during the siege of Harpers Ferry underscored the vulnerability of green Federal units.
National Archives

engaged at the front, the colonel replied that his soldiers were so panic-stricken that "he could not hold them together to face the enemy." Other green regiments defending Bolivar Heights had behaved in the same manner when exposed to Confederate artillery fire. Lacking discipline and training, and never having been subjected to an artillery bombardment, they behaved like the crowd of civilians they still were, dashing helter-skelter for cover and reforming only after considerable effort by their officers.[19]

Although Union leadership at Harpers Ferry left much to be desired, it is doubtful that any officers could have averted the surrender of a force that included so many inexperienced units. In his testimony to the commission, Col. William H. Trimble, who led a brigade in the garrison, responded to a question as to whether the Federals could have made an effective resistance to a Confederate attack on Bolivar Heights. "There were some regiments there that would have stood until they were cut to pieces," he stated, "but some of those new regiments, not three weeks from home, could not have been expected to stand. . . . Like wild asses or colts, they would have run into danger rather than out of it, there." Colonel Willard had so little confidence in the fighting ability of the troops that he doubted they could have held Bolivar Heights against a determined Confederate assault for more than three minutes. The problem lay not with the men or their officers, most of whom were brave enough and ready to do their duty, but with their lack of confidence, which training and discipline could have instilled. Regiments like the 126th New York did not have an opportunity to build this confidence. They could do little beyond loading and firing their weapons. Maneuvering was impossible. Either officers did not know the proper commands, or, if they did, their men did not know how to execute them. The results were both predictable and unfortunate.[20]

On September 14, the main body of the Army of the Potomac engaged Confederates defending the gaps of South Mountain in an attempt to hold off Federals until Harpers Ferry could be reduced. Three of McClellan's five army corps participated in this action: the Sixth at Crampton's Gap; the Ninth at Fox's Gap, five miles to the north; and the First near Turner's Gap, a mile north of Fox's. Green regiments fought only at Fox's Gap. At Crampton's, Maj. Gen. Henry B. Slocum, commanding the Sixth Corps division that spearheaded the Union assault, wisely held his single new regiment, the 121st New York, out of the action. The First Corps left the 16th Maine, its only new regiment, behind at Ridgeville, Maryland, because the rookies could not keep up with their veteran comrades. Abner Small considered this a sound move, recalling that his men were "fairly well drilled in the manual of arms, and were able to perform creditable evolutions of squad and company, and doubtless could have got through a gap in a fence without breaking ranks; but we were not ready to meet the requirements of a battle except in resolution. We realized this and dwelt constantly upon the thought." And the 16th's training was superior to that of the 126th New York at Harpers Ferry, which offers some idea of how ill prepared that regiment had been to clash with Lee's veterans.[21]

Three green regiments faced their baptism of fire with the Ninth Corps at Fox's Gap—the 9th New Hampshire, 35th Massachusetts, and 17th Michigan. The first two arrived near the close of heavy fighting at the gap, and neither distinguished itself. Ordered to relieve the 46th New York, the New Hampshire men, according to the 46th's commander, "commenced firing before they had taken our position, thereby greatly endangering the lives of our soldiers, who only saved themselves by throwing themselves down on the ground." The 35th Massachusetts also fired into their own men a short time later. They and the other regiments of their brigade, a tough group of veterans commanded by Brig. Gen. Edward Ferrero, had taken position in a small square pasture, since called Wise's field, at the summit of Fox's Gap. The veteran 51st New York and 51st Pennsylvania occupied the front line, with the 21st Massachusetts in their rear and the 35th behind the 21st. Ferrero previously had sent the 35th into nearby woods to scout for the enemy. Why he did not select one of the veteran regiments for this important work is unknown. The 35th reported finding no enemy troops nearby and took their place in the brigade formation.

For some reason, the 35th failed to detect the advance of Brig. Gen. John B. Hood's Confederate division. Just at dusk, and minutes after the 35th left the woods, Hood's men came up and opened fire on Ferrero's men in Wise's field. "The surprise was complete," recalled the 35th's historian; "the darkening forest was lined with flashes of the hostile guns, and their bullets cut the earth about our feet.... Instantly some of the men threw forward their rifles and returned the fire, aiming over the heads of the line in front." The 51st Pennsylvania, part of the "line in front," recalled it differently. The rookies' fire did not pass over the Pennsylvanians' heads but came through their line. "The 51st was in between two lines of musketry, and getting shot down like dogs," recorded Thomas Parker. "Had not the 51st N.Y. interfered and threatened to fire on the 35th if they did not cease firing," Parker insisted, "God only knows when the slaughter would have ceased." This would not be the last time in the campaign that green regiments would fire upon comrades.[22]

In contrast to the 9th New Hampshire and 35th Massachusetts, the 17th Michigan had acquitted itself well earlier in the afternoon during bloody fighting with Brig. Gen. Thomas F. Drayton's brigade. There was a distinct difference between the 17th and the other two green regiments. The latter pair were raw and undrilled, barely three weeks from their camps of rendezvous. The 17th had commenced forming in late May 1862 and spent the summer drilling under Col. James E. Pittman, the state paymaster. Although not mustered into Federal service until August 21, the Michiganders should not be considered true rookies. Pittman's drill and discipline left the regiment in a "very creditable condition," well prepared for the action on September 14 that highlighted the difference training made in combat effectiveness. Col. Benjamin C. Christ, their brigade commander, reported that the 17th, facing Drayton's Georgians and South Carolinians, "moved steadily forward until they arrived within good range, and then opened a fire on the enemy with terrible effect, piling the road and field with his dead and wounded, and finally completely routing him." Even the veterans of the 79th New York, who supported the 17th, applauded their midwestern comrades' courage. Wrote William Todd, the 79th's historian, "[T]he Michigan troops, wherever engaged, displayed a bravery that was seldom equalled and never surpassed."[23]

The Union army beheld a sobering scene after the Confederate retreat from South Mountain. That September 15 proved to be especially disconcerting for the rookie soldiers. A member of the 9th New Hampshire who traversed the ground at Fox's Gap wrote: "Looked over a part of the battle-field, and oh, it was horrible beyond description." Another soldier in the same regiment observed, "I have seen all of war ever wish to. The thing is indescribable. Oh, horrors!" Sgt. Benjamin Hirst of the 14th Connecticut, whose regiment arrived too late to take part in the fighting, awoke at 5:00 A.M. and walked some of the battleground "to see what war was without romance. I cannot describe my feelings, but I hope to God never to see the like again." Three days later Hirst and thousands of untrained, raw soldiers like himself would see the like again, except it would be more frightening and horrible than any of them could imagine.[24]

By the evening of September 16 even the rawest soldier knew that a major battle was imminent. Fred Hitchcock of the 132nd Pennsylvania recalled, "[T]he camp was ominously still this night. . . . Unquestionably, the problems of the morrow were occupying all breasts. . . . I can never forget the words of Colonel Oakford, as he inquired very particularly if my roster of the officers and men of the regiment was complete, for, said he, with a smile, 'We shall not all be here to-morrow.'" The Twelfth Corps, with 4,000 raw soldiers constituting about half its strength, crossed Antietam Creek after midnight on September 17 and massed on the George Line farm, about one mile in rear of Maj. Gen. Joseph Hooker's First Corps. The First Corps already had made contact with the enemy, and the Twelfth Corps would support Hooker's men when the battle opened in the morning. Sebastian Duncan Jr. of the 13th New Jersey revealed his feelings about the pending battle in a letter to his father: "The sight of the wounded and dead, with the knowledge that you may yourself be in a similar condition in twenty four hours does not seem to produce the slightest effect. I suppose that mingling with the old soldiers who have repeatedly gone through these ordeals in safety tend[s] very much to remove fear from the minds of the boys. . . . I can truly say that as yet I have not felt the slightest fear." Of course, no one had yet fired at Duncan with the intent to kill him. For officers such as Col. Samuel Croasdale, it must have been an anxious night. Eight days earlier he had not even known the proper commands to form his regiment into line of battle. Now he would have to lead it against a skilled and disciplined enemy.[25]

Brig. Gen. Alpheus S. Williams, commanding the First Division of the Twelfth Corps, reported that the corps moved toward the front at the sound of the "first cannon at daylight." The time was probably shortly before 6:00 A.M. The corps chief, Maj. Gen. Joseph K. F. Mansfield, an older regular officer, had assumed command on September 15, and in this, his first test of combat, he fussed over every detail. Williams considered his superior a gallant soldier, but "he had a nervous temperament and very impatient manner." Mansfield insisted that the corps move toward the action—which was steadily increasing in sound and fury—in a close column of companies. This meant that each regiment would present a front of one company, with the other companies following behind at a distance of six paces between each. "When so formed a regiment looks like a solid mass," wrote Williams. Before the dense formation had covered one hundred yards, shell and solid shot began to fly "thick over and around us." Any artillery round that struck in the moving mass of soldiers would kill and maim dozens of men. Williams feared the effect such a calamity would have on his five new regiments. He rode to Mansfield and begged him "to let me deploy them in line of battle, in which the men present but two ranks or rows instead of twenty, as we were marching, but I could not move him." Mansfield "was positive that all the new regiments would run away," wrote Williams, and refused to alter the formation.[26]

As the mass of Twelfth Corps soldiers continued forward, sounds of a furious battle assailed them. "The cannonading and musketry kept up a constant roar more terrific than the most violent thunder storm I every heard," wrote Sebastian Duncan to his mother. Soon the Federals began to encounter large numbers of wounded making their way to the rear. On any fresh battlefield, the maimed always frighten new soldiers more than the dead. The dead are silent—the wounded are not. E. Livingston Allen, an enlisted man in the 13th New Jersey, recalled passing a wounded soldier of the 107th New York, another untested unit, who had both arms broken by a solid shot: "[H]e, in his agony, knowing death must soon come, was calling, Mother! Mother! MOTHER! Brave hearts trembled—strong men wept—indescribable emotions swept over mind and heart." Another member of the 13th, Charles N. Ritchie, wrote in his diary that the sights as they came upon the rear of the battle were "sickening, men lying wounded in every conceivable form, and praying for some kind hand to put them out of their misery; others just breathing their last and lisping the holy name of 'mother.'" In the East Woods, Duncan found a soldier with one leg shot off and the other shattered. The man was "fairly shrieking with pain." Although his suffering no doubt moved the soldiers of the 13th, his presence threatened to be demoralizing. Colonel Carman ordered several shirkers from the earlier fighting, whom Duncan wrote were "all around us skulking behind trees," to carry the wounded soldier away.[27]

When the 124th Pennsylvania came up near the David Miller farm, Sgt. William W. Potts recalled how a colonel or general (he could not remember which) rode up to their line asking them to hurry forward, "as his men were getting cut to pieces." Potts was not inspired. "Feeling that we might experience the same, I had no desire to accept this invitation," he wrote. Neither did his company commander, Capt. Frank Crosby. When the bullets began to crack nearby, Crosby announced that it was too hot for him, "and if we wanted to go we might, but he would be —— if he would, and he retired to the rear." No one stepped forward to assume command—apparently the lieutenants were as frightened as everyone else—so Potts, who had been the drillmaster, took charge.[28]

There were a number of Crosbys, both enlisted men and officers, in all the new regiments of the Twelfth Corps, but those who remained in line outnumbered them. Although frightened, the latter chafed to go forward. After the men in the 13th New Jersey began to realize that every shell they heard was not going to hit them, they became "decidedly too anxious to get up and see what was going on." Getting them into the fight proved something of a task. Mansfield fell mortally wounded minutes after his corps came under small-arms fire, which left Williams in command. He immediately started to deploy the new regiments. Williams took the 128th Pennsylvania, Colonel Croasdale's regiment, and told Gens. Samuel W. Crawford and George H. Gordon to form two others. "I got mine in line pretty well by having a fence to align it on," wrote Williams. He ordered Croasdale to advance and "open fire the moment he saw the Rebels." Croasdale did as instructed, leading his men up toward the infamous Miller Cornfield. His big regiment instantly drew fire from Confederates in the Cornfield and East Woods. Croasdale was killed, the lieutenant colonel wounded, and the regiment thrown into disorder. "The trouble with this regiment and the others," wrote Williams, "was that in attempting to move them forward or back or to make any maneuver they fell into inextricable confusion and fell to the rear, where they were easily rallied. The men were of excellent stamp, ready and willing, but neither officers nor men knew anything, and there was an absence of the mutual confidence which drill begets. Standing still, they fought bravely."[29]

Some veteran sergeants from the 28th New York and Col. Joseph Knipe of the 46th Pennsylvania helped rally the 128th Pennsylvania and reform its line. Knipe suggested to Maj. Joel B. Wanner, upon whom command had devolved and who had no idea what his men should be doing, that an advance might be better than standing still and taking fire. Wanner accepted the colonel's advice, moving his regiment into the Cornfield. The men cheered as they went forward, but when they reached the southern boundary of the corn, Confederate infantry blasted them, scattering the regiment and rendering it noneffective for the remainder of the day.[30]

The experience of the 13th New Jersey resembled that of the 128th Pennsylvania. After being moved from one point to another, the 13th eventually received orders to assist the veteran 2nd Massachusetts in recapturing the West Woods, which had been lost minutes earlier when John Sedgwick's division of the Second Corps was driven out. The two regiments crossed the Cornfield and entered the Hagerstown Pike, where they came under fire from Confederates in the woods. Both Union regiments returned the fire, and for several minutes the two sides blazed away at each other. Finally, an officer who appeared to the men of the 13th to be a Federal rode forward and cried out, "For Gods sake stop; you are shooting your own men!" According to Sebastian Duncan, this "created considerable confusion" in the ranks of the 13th, and some men ceased firing. Suddenly, the Confederates rushed from the woods, so near, according to Charles Morse of the 2nd Massachusetts, that "you could easily distinguish the features of the men." The 2nd stood firm and gave the southerners a solid volley that sent them back into the cover of the trees. But the undrilled 13th, Morse observed, "without any cause . . . bolted, officers and men, and we were left alone." Duncan wrote that "some of the officers who had *driven* us in now [were] *leading* us out."[31]

The 13th tumbled back to the shelter of the East Woods, where they were rallied and reformed. Brig. Gen. George H. Gordon, the 13th's brigade commander, rode up and addressed the regiment, asking them whether they would again follow their colors into the woods. "We replied with hearty cheers," wrote Duncan. But the regimental color-bearer did not share his comrades' enthusiasm. No doubt he had learned while under fire at the Hagerstown Road that colors attracted fire from enemy riflemen. As the cheers died out, he announced that he would not carry the colors into battle again. Col. Ezra Carman called for a volunteer. According to Duncan, "there was a moment's silence when a man stepped forward & desired to take them." The regiment returned to the fray, this time entering the West Woods around the Dunker Church. As they took position, officers warned the men to hold their fire until they saw a clear target. The Confederates soon made their appearance, and the 13th blazed away with the other regiments that held a tenuous foothold in the West Woods. "We were doing very well," wrote Duncan, "when the order was given 'cease firing.'" In what was either a ruse to gain advantage or simply the inexperience of the 13th, someone announced that the Confederates in front were carrying their weapons at "trail arms" and wanted to surrender. The 13th's adjutant and a captain walked forward to receive the enemy's "surrender." Meanwhile, Confederates who had maneuvered to gain both flanks of the 13th raised their weapons and delivered a terrible volley into the ranks of the Jerseymen. Somehow the adjutant and captain were unscathed, but many others were less fortunate. Without waiting for orders, the 13th fled the trap that was swiftly closing upon them. "But we got great praise for not being captured," wrote Charles Ritchie. "There is no doubt if we had been disciplined enough to await orders before running we would have been all gobbled up." By day's end, the regiment tallied its losses at 101 killed, wounded, and missing. Considering that they were little more than an armed mob, the 13th had done reasonably well. Even the demanding General Gordon thought they had performed satisfactorily in what he deemed a battle "unparalleled in this war in severity and duration."[32]

The same could be said of every new regiment in the Twelfth Corps. Under the circumstances they had all fought bravely and done the best that could be expected. Against Lee's veterans their best simply was not enough. But what a difference their large numbers would have made had they received sufficient training before their baptism of fire.

Of the ten regiments in the Second Corps division of Brig. Gen. William H. French, four were composed of new recruits who represented more than half of the division's combat strength. Fortunately for these regiments, the battle they engaged in at the Sunken Lane unfolded as precisely the type in which untrained soldiers could perform successfully—a static slugfest where soldiers had only to load and fire. Lt. Frederick L. Hitchcock, the adjutant of the 132nd Pennsylvania, described the nature of the battle: "We were ordered to lie down just under the top of the hill and crawl forward and fire over, each man crawling back, reloading his piece in this prone position and again crawling forward and firing."[33]

Under these circumstances, and despite frightful losses, the rookies fought quite well. "When I went into the engagement at the Battle of Antietam I thought I was a coward," John S. Weiser of the 130th Pennsylvania informed his mother a month after the battle, "but that fear left me in five minutes after we received the first fire from the Gray Backs and then I thought of nothing but loading and firing."[34]

Left: Monument to the 130th Pennsylvania Volunteer Infantry dedicated on September 17, 1904, to commemorate the regiment's role in the fighting at the Sunken Road. Together with the 132nd Pennsylvania, the 130th suffered the heaviest losses among the green Pennsylvania regiments at Antietam.
Pennsylvania Antietam Battlefield Memorial Commission, *Pennsylvania at Antietam* (Harrisburg: Harrisburg Publishing Co., 1906), opposite p. 153

Right: Monument to the 132nd Pennsylvania Volunteer Infantry dedicated on September 17, 1904, a short distance from the 130th's monument.
Pennsylvania Antietam Battlefield Memorial Commission, *Pennsylvania at Antietam* (Harrisburg: Harrisburg Publishing Co., 1906), opposite p. 185

On the extreme southern end of the battlefield, the 16th Connecticut's first battlefield experience proved less successful and had serious consequences for the army. As part of Brig. Gen. Isaac P. Rodman's Third Division of the Ninth Corps, the 16th had crossed Antietam Creek at Snavely's Ford around 1:00 P.M.— about the time troops of Brig. Gen. Samuel D. Sturgis's division were attacking and finally carrying the Rohrbach bridge (thereafter known as Burnside's Bridge). During the next two hours the Ninth Corps massed its strength on the west bank of Antietam Creek in preparation for a general attack against the Confederate right. The attack pushed off at 3:00 P.M., initially making good progress against the weak Confederate line. In the process of advancing, the 16th ended up on the extreme left of the Ninth Corps, and thus of the entire army. Their movement led them into farmer John Otto's 40-acre cornfield, planted on steeply rolling ground at the southern end of the battlefield. Amid the tall corn, the regiment could not see "twelve feet ahead" and remained completely ignorant of what transpired around them.[35]

Conditions beyond the 16th Connecticut's severely limited view were changing rapidly. Confederate major general A. P. Hill's "Light Division," just arrived on the battlefield after a grueling seventeen-mile march from Harpers Ferry, was deploying to smash the left flank of the Ninth Corps. The 16th Connecticut stood in Otto's cornfield, unaware of the storm sweeping upon them. The regiment's story was a familiar one on this bloody day. They had been in service for three weeks. They had loaded their muskets for the first time on September 16, the day they had finally overtaken and joined their brigade. Lt. B. G. Blakeslee noted in his diary that "neither line-officers nor the men had any knowledge of regimental movements." Two times during the movements preceding the Ninth Corps attack, a member of the 4th Rhode Island complained that the 16th had "crowded through our regiment and stampeded." Why the regiment had even been brought under fire is unbelievable. They could serve as no more than cannon fodder. Yet now they found themselves in a critical position at a crucial moment of the battle.[36]

The 16th stood quietly in line within Otto's cornfield, listening to the battle that raged beyond them. On a hill that rose up beyond their left flank, the Connecticut men caught sight of troops forming into line with "the utmost order and coolness." It was the 1st South Carolina Rifles of Brig. Gen. Maxcy Gregg's crack South Carolina brigade, deploying to attack the left of the 16th. Other regiments of Gregg's brigade, unseen because of the corn, advanced upon the front of the 16th. Such was the depleted condition of Gregg's brigade that its four regiments probably did not greatly outnumber the 16th. The 1st Rifles, who would inflict the greatest damage to the 16th, carried only 194 officers and men into action. But the combination of experience and position proved decisive. The Rifles delivered a murderous volley into the 16th before the Connecticut boys realized what was happening. The 16th gamely tried to return the fire, but their lack of discipline caused them to crowd to their left into the 4th Rhode Island, which had been advanced to their support. The 1st Rifles continued to pour their fire into the mass of Connecticut soldiers in their front. "So great was the confusion caused by our fire, this large, well equipped regiment failed to rally, broke and fled from the field," reported Lt. Col. James M. Perrin, commander of the Rifles. Berry Benson, a member of the 1st South Carolina Infantry (not to be confused with the 1st South Carolina Rifles), recalled that his regiment found the 16th in a "crouching, disorderly line" and that they poured repeated volleys into the Federals. The return fire against Benson's regiment was so ineffectual that the South Carolinians were able to direct methodical volleys by wing into the hapless Connecticut rookies.[37]

The 16th suffered terribly in the unequal contest, quickly losing 42 men killed and 143 wounded. Many fell to Confederate muskets as they attempted to escape the fire. The regiment dissolved, leaving the 4th Rhode Island to bear the brunt of the attack, which soon broke their line as well. Units on the left flank of the Ninth Corps toppled like dominoes under the attack of Hill's division. Although ultimately checked, Hill's division had stopped Ambrose Burnside's offensive. The last opportunity for the Army of the Potomac to carry the day had been lost. The 16th Connecticut by no means bore sole responsibility for this failure—Hill's opportune arrival and skillful deployment of his division against the Federal left flank were the key factors—but it had been the weak link in the line. Unable to maneuver or fight effectively, it proved more of a hindrance than a help, just as many other green regiments had been that grim day. A comparison of casualties suffered by the 16th and its adversaries sharply illustrates the advantage Lee's veterans enjoyed over the Union greenhorns in fluid combat. The 1st Rifles and 1st South Carolina, the two regiments principally engaged with the 16th, lost 12 and 34 killed and wounded, respectively, and most of these losses were probably suffered in combat with the 4th Rhode Island. The South Carolinians had very likely inflicted casualties of eight or nine to one in their engagement with the 16th.[38]

Apart from their generally good performance in the fighting at the Sunken Lane, McClellan's green regiments had been little more than cannon and musketry fodder on September 17. Thirteen brand new regiments had been committed to battle. They lost 1,737 killed, wounded, and missing (most of them killed or wounded), or 14 percent of the army's entire loss at Antietam (see table). It was

GREEN REGIMENTS ENGAGED AT ANTIETAM

Regiment	Corps	Strength*	Killed	Wounded	Missing	Total	% Loss
132nd Pa.	2nd	985	30	114	8	152	15
14th Conn.	2nd	957	20	41	48	156	16
108th N.Y.	2nd	952	26	122	47	195	20
130th Pa.	2nd	1,005	32	146		178	17
17th Mich.	9th	966	18	89		107	11
9th N.H.	9th	964	10	49		59	6
35th Mass.	9th	1,018	48	160	6	214	21
16th Conn.	9th	949	42	143		185	19
124th Pa.	12th	974	5	42	17	64	6
125th Pa.	12th	963	28	115	2	145	15
128th Pa.	12th	950	24	86	6	118	12
13th N.J.	12th	899	7	75	19	101	11
107th N.Y.	12th	1,031	7	51	5	63	6
Total		12,613	297	1,233	158	1,737	13

Source: OR, ser. 3, 3:204–5, 760–79.

*Strength is regiment's muster-in strength. All carried fewer men into action on September 17; therefore, the percentage loss would be higher in each case.

the costliest "training" program the United States Army conducted during the war. Had McClellan attacked again on the 18th, a major element of his attacking force would have been the newly arrived division of Brig. Gen. Andrew A. Humphreys, which consisted of seven raw regiments and one trained regiment, hardly an assault force to give a commanding general confidence.

All of the green regiments eventually received proper drill and discipline and acquitted themselves well on subsequent battlefields. But in September 1862 their presence in such large numbers proved a mixed blessing to the Army of the Potomac. At Harpers Ferry they were an absolute detriment. Although they added enthusiastic and motivated manpower to the army, their lack of training and discipline reduced the army's mobility on the march and its offensive capability in battle. It may be that McClellan achieved as much as possible with the material at hand on September 17. The fact that so many new regiments saw combat before they were ready speaks to the success of Lee's strategy, which was to draw the Union army and its new levies out of Washington before they had been prepared for active campaigning.

For the rookie soldiers, their abrupt entry into combat came as a rude shock. "Who would not be a soldier," Andrew Tehrune of the 13th New Jersey had written eight days before Antietam. Tehrune apparently decided that he would not be a soldier after his first taste of battle. On September 17, he joined his brother and several other men from the regiment in deserting. Tehrune would return to service in 1863, but his brother would not. Yet the post-battle letters and diaries of most of the new men reveal a strong devotion to duty and a patriotic ardor, despite their rough handling. Samuel Fisk of the 14th Connecticut may have summarized the green soldiers' experience at Antietam best in a letter to his hometown newspaper after the fight: "The battle itself was a scene of indescribable confusion. Troops did not know what they were expected to do, and sometimes, in the excitement, fired at their own men. But in the main for green troops I think we behaved well." [39]

NOTES

1. Edward O. Lord, *History of the Ninth Regiment New Hampshire Volunteers in the War of the Rebellion* (Concord, N.H.: Republican Free Press, 1895), 71.

2. James G. Randall and David Donald, *The Civil War and Reconstruction* (Lexington, Mass.: D. C. Heath, 1969), 312–13.

3. Abner Small, *The Road to Richmond: The Civil War Memoirs of Maj. Abner R. Small of the 16th Maine Vols,* ed. Harold Adams Small (Berkeley: University of California Press, 1959), 36.

4. U.S. War Department, *The War of the Rebellion: A Compilation of the Official Records of the Union and Confederate Armies,* 127 vols., index, and atlas (Washington: GPO, 1880–1901), ser. 1, vol. 19, pt. 2:590 (hereafter cited as *OR;* unless indicated otherwise, all references are to ser. 1).

5. Alpheus S. Williams, *From the Cannon's Mouth: The Civil War Letters of General Alpheus S. Williams,* ed. Milo M. Quaife (Detroit: Wayne State University Press, 1959), 119; *OR* 12(2):781; 19(2):223–24.

6. McClellan probably left the Third, Fifth, and Eleventh Corps in the capital's defenses because they had done some of the hardest fighting at Second Manassas. The Third and Fifth also had seen hard service on the Peninsula. Still, all of them were in better condition than the Twelfth Corps; its inclusion in the field army is something of a mystery. For strength returns, see *OR* 12(3):781; 19(2):197–98. The strength of the eighteen regiments that accompanied the army into the field is an estimate, as many of the regiments were below 1,000 men by the time they were assigned to a brigade. The men recruited for veteran regiments were principally from New York and Massachusetts. The approximate number that reached the army is derived from a statement of men furnished to old regiments in the field. See *OR,* ser. 3, 2:861.

7. G. F. R. Henderson, *The Civil War: A Soldier's View, a Collection of Civil War*

Writings, ed. Jay Luvaas (Chicago: University of Chicago Press, 1958), 145; Ezra A. Carman diary, New Jersey Historical Society, Newark (repository hereafter cited as NJHS); *OR* 19(1):672.

8. B. F. Blakeslee, *History of the Sixteenth Connecticut Volunteers* (Hartford, Conn.: Case, Lockwood & Brainard Co., 1875), 9; Jonathan Edward Shipman to friend Hubbard, September 14, 1862, bk. 5, Lewis Leigh Collection, United States Army Military History Institute, Carlisle Barracks, Pa. (repository hereafter cited as USAMHI); Albert A. Pope diary, Civil War Times Illustrated Collection, USAMHI; Sebastian Duncan letterbook, September 9, 1862, entry, NJHS; Survivors Association, *History of the Corn Exchange Regiment 118th Pennsylvania Volunteers* (Philadelphia: J. L. Smith, 1888), 29–30.

9. Albert A. Pope diary, USAMHI; Andrew Tehrune to cousin, September 9, 1862, bk. 27, no. 56, Lewis Leigh Collection, USAMHI.

10. Jonathan Edward Shipman to friend Hubbard, September 14, 1862, bk. 5, Lewis Leigh Collection, USAMHI.

11. Frederick L. Hitchcock, *War from the Inside* (Philadelphia: Lippincott, 1904), 37–38; Charles D. Page, *History of the Fourteenth Regiment, Connecticut Vol. Infantry* (Meriden, Conn.: Horton Printing Co., 1906), 27.

12. *OR* 19(1):607; Arabella M. Willson, *Disaster, Struggle, Triumph: Adventures of 1000 "Boys in Blue," from August, 1862, to June, 1865* (Albany, N.Y.: Argus Co., Printers, 1870), 58.

13. *OR* 19(1):567, 607; Lt. Richard A. Bassett to his wife, September 22, 1862, Richard A. Bassett Collection, Ontario County Historical Society, Canandaigua, N.Y.

14. *OR* 19(1):607, 727.

15. *OR* 19(1):570, 727, 607, 672, 676.

16. *OR* 19(1):568, 601, 608, 727.

17. Willson, *Disaster, Struggle, Triumph,* 61.

18. *OR* 19(1):680, 571, 733–34. The testimony given during the Harpers Ferry Court of Inquiry does not support the 126th's historian, who asserted that members of the regiment were emboldened by the fall of their colonel.

19. *OR* 19(1):798, 540, 744; Charles W. Belknap journal, Civil War Miscellaneous Collection, USAMHI.

20. *OR* 19(1):744–45, 565. Nearly all of the green Harpers Ferry regiments went on to compile solid combat records later in the war.

21. Small, *Road to Richmond,* 46.

22. *OR* 19(1):442; Regimental Association, *History of the Thirty-fifth Regiment Massachusetts Volunteers* (Boston: Mills, Knight & Co., 1884), 29–30; Thomas H. Parker, *History of the 51st Regiment of P.V. and V.V.* (Philadelphia: King and Baird, Printers, 1869), 225–26.

23. Ida C. Brown, *Michigan in the Civil War* (Ann Arbor: University of Michigan Press, 1966), 374–75; *OR* 19(1):437; William Todd, *The Seventy-ninth Highlanders,*

New York Volunteers in the War of the Rebellion, 1861–1865 (Albany: Brandon, Barton & Co., 1886), 233.

24. Lord, *Ninth Regiment New Hampshire,* 89–90. Benjamin Hirst quoted in Page, *Fourteenth Regiment, Connecticut,* 27–28.

25. Hitchcock, *War from the Inside,* 55–56; Sebastian Duncan to mother, September 21, Duncan to father, September 16, 1862, NJHS; Ezra A. Carman diary, NJHS. Twelfth Corps division commander Brig. Gen. Alpheus S. Williams wrote that when his troops arrived on the Line farm it was difficult to get them into position: "It took a long time as I had five new regiments who knew absolutely nothing of maneuvering." Williams, *From the Cannon's Mouth,* 125.

26. Williams, *From the Cannon's Mouth,* 125.

27. Sebastian Duncan to mother, September 21, 1862, NJHS; "A Newark Soldier in the Civil War," Newark *Evening News,* July 8, 1903; E. Livingston Allen, *Both Sides of Army Life: The Grave and the Gay* (Poughkeepsie, N.Y.: privately printed, 1885), 2.

28. Robert M. Green, comp., *History of the One Hundred and Twenty-fourth Regiment Pennsylvania Volunteers in the War of the Rebellion, 1862–1863* (Philadelphia: Ware Bros., 1907), 120–21. Captain Crosby was discharged on September 24, 1862.

29. Duncan to mother, September 21, 1862, NJHS; Williams, *From the Cannon's Mouth,* 126.

30. Oliver C. Bobyshell, *Pennsylvania at Antietam* (Harrisburg: Antietam Battlefield Memorial Commission, 1906), 149–50; Hugh A. Jameson (28th New York) to John M. Gould, [n.d.], John M. Gould Antietam Collection, Dartmouth College, Hanover, N.H.

31. Sebastian Duncan to mother, September 21, 1862, NJHS; Charles Morse to mother, September 21, 1862, Charles Morse Papers, Massachusetts Historical Society, Boston.

32. Sebastian Duncan to mother, September 21, 1862, NJHS; *OR* 19 (1):502 (Carman's report), 495–97 (Gordon's report). Colonel Carman charitably reported that the color-bearer had been disabled. The soldier who took the colors was Pvt. James Kilroy of Company G. He was severely wounded later in the action. See "A Newark Soldier in the Civil War," Newark *Evening News,* July 15, 1903.

33. Hitchcock, *War from the Inside,* 59.

34. John S. Weiser to mother, October 13, 1862, copy provided to the author by Frederick S. Weiser.

35. John Burnham to mother and family, October 4, 1862, Connecticut Historical Society, Hartford (repository hereafter cited as CHS).

36. Blakeslee, *Sixteenth Connecticut,* 11; John R. Bartlett, *Memoirs of Rhode Island Officers Who Were Engaged in the Service of Their Country during the Great Rebellion of the South* (Providence: Rider, 1867), 235; Blakeslee quoted in Stephen Sears, *Landscape Turned Red: The Battle of Antietam* (New York: Ticknor & Fields, 1983), 288.

37. John Burnham to mother and family, October 4, 1862, CHS; *OR* 19(1):455–56, 993–95; Berry Benson, *Berry Benson's Civil War Book: Memoirs of a Confederate Scout and Sharpshooter,* ed. Susan W. Benson (Athens: University of Georgia Press, 1962), 27–28.

38. *OR* 19(1):197, 989.

39. Page, *Fourteenth Regiment, Connecticut,* 48.

LESLEY J. GORDON

All Who Went into That Battle Were Heroes

Remembering the 16th Regiment
Connecticut Volunteers at Antietam

On October 11, 1894, a small group of survivors, family members, and friends of the 16th Regiment Connecticut Volunteers gathered at Antietam to dedicate a monument to their unit. Former lieutenant colonel Frank Cheney was one of several speakers at the ceremony. "Comrades," he began, "[w]e made our first pilgrimage to this spot five years ago to decorate the graves of our companions in the National Cemetery." Now, they had decided to have "their own graveyard . . . where our regiment stood the brunt of its first battle." Cheney remarked that many knew the "general history of the Battle of Antietam" but that each man who experienced the battle had his own personal story to tell:

> The story of each man's own life is the only atom of history he has knowledge of at first hand,—what he knows about himself and his companions at arms; how they came to be soldiers; how they lived and looked in camp and on the march, in winter and summer, in storm and sunshine, at rest and in the thick of the fight; alive—full of courage and high hopes; then dead on the field or sadder yet, in the hospital; the hurried burial or the slow funeral march, the last volley over the grave and the march back to

quick time. These war scenes come rolling over you with that bloody day
at Antietam thirty two years ago.[1]

The 16th Connecticut's "bloody day at Antietam" was unforgettable. In their
first and only large-scale combat experience, its men broke ranks and ran off
the field within a matter of minutes. Members of the regiment tried soon after the
battle to describe what happened in an effort to make sense of the chaos. By the
time survivors returned to Antietam in 1894, they had commenced reconstruct-
ing their own "atom of history" into something courageous rather than cowardly,
admirable rather than embarrassing, meaningful rather than pointless.

When the 16th Connecticut came into existence in the summer of 1862, no
one could have predicted the fate that awaited it on September 17. In mid-
summer 1862, the Union's war effort abruptly lost momentum with the indecisive
results of George B. McClellan's Peninsula campaign. The conflict seemed to
have reached yet another impasse, and President Abraham Lincoln needed more
men. On July 1, 1862, he issued a call for 300,000 volunteers; two days later Connecticut's governor, William Buckingham, added his own exhortation. Lofty and
urgent declarations stirred enlistment, but so did high bounties. The 16th Connecticut began accepting enlistees soon after Buckingham's proclamation and by
the end of August numbered more than 1,000 men and officers.[2]

The 16th drew solely from Hartford County, one of the most prosperous areas
in Connecticut. Volunteers' occupations reflected the economic diversity of the
region, ranging from farmers to machinists, artisans to teachers. Muster rolls list
some of the state's best-known and oldest family names, in addition to a spatter-
ing of recent immigrants. A number of the men were single and young, many just
eighteen and nineteen years old.[3]

Married men also joined in high numbers. At one rally in Bristol, a bookish
and well-educated geology professor returned to his childhood home to encourage others to enlist and found himself so caught up in the crowd's excitement that
he impulsively joined and was immediately made captain. Newton Manross told
his anxious wife: "You can better afford to have a country without a husband than
a husband without a country."[4]

Encamped in Hartford through the end of August, the unit showed little re-
semblance to a military organization. For the first several days men lacked uniforms and guns, and their colonel did not arrive until midmonth. Visitors roamed
through the camp at all hours of the day and night, bringing homemade food,
clothing, and personal effects for family members and friends. Crowds watched
excitedly as militia officers led crude drill exercises, marching men up and down
a dusty parade ground and teaching them company formation. Despite the initial

Colonel Francis Beach
Connecticut State Archives, RG 69:23,
box 10, folder B, MCH copy negative

informalities, new recruits began the often difficult transformation from free citizen to soldier. Bernard Blakeslee recalled these early days in camp as a "shock to most of the men" and a "complete revolution in their method of life." It was an exceptionally hot summer, and many recruits unaccustomed to outdoor living succumbed to heat exhaustion and sun poisoning.[5]

The arrival of Col. Francis Beach on August 15 radically changed camp routine. An 1857 graduate of West Point, Beach was the son of prominent Hartford banker George Beach. He had served in Utah and on the western plains fighting Indians, and when civil war broke out, many had high expectations for the promising young officer. His men would soon find him a stern disciplinarian, too recently removed from West Point to realize that troop formations always moved more crisply and cleanly in textbooks than in battle.[6]

The ragtag appearance and disorganized behavior of his unit appalled Beach, who immediately demanded improvements. He issued polish to brighten brass and blacken shoes. Uniforms and equipment soon arrived, although weapons were conspicuously absent. Beach also instituted strict restrictions on travel and visitations. When he ordered a review and inspection of the regiment, Beach angrily blasted the troops for their shortcomings and vowed that such sloppy soldiering would not continue under his command. Frustrated and furious with raw volunteers, he allegedly was unable to give orders without swearing. Pvt. George

Robbins recalled that for men who had known great personal autonomy in their daily lives, "[e]ach day brought some restraint on our freedom." Some felt depressed and surprised, no longer could they easily slip away from camp to visit friends and family. A few openly threatened the "unfeeling" Beach, boasting that once they were in battle they would "fill his back full of lead."[7]

As the men grudgingly endured Beach's command, rumors circulated that they were going to the front. On August 24, 1862, the regiment was formally mustered into United States service for three years. Four days later it left for Washington, D.C. As the men marched to the city wharf, enthusiastic crowds lined the streets, and Governor Buckingham fell in step in front of the regiment. The unit boarded two steamers and traveled down the Connecticut River, cheered by people lining the riverside. It was an emotional and exciting send-off.[8]

On board the steamers the enlistees discovered another startling reminder of their new military identity. When a few of the wealthier privates tried to pay for cabin berths and staterooms, orders were issued stipulating that only officers could be above deck. The gulf between officers and men had further widened.[9]

On their journey to the nation's capital, the regiment maintained relatively high spirits. Rumors continued to spread that they would soon head directly to the front to participate in the final, major battle of the war. In Elizabethport they changed from boats to a cramped, dirty train and arrived in Washington on August 31. No crowds greeted them in the nation's capital, and the men spent the night sleeping in the open on muddy ground. On September 1, they marched into Virginia to Fort Ward, meeting ambulances piled high with dead and dying soldiers from the battle of Second Manassas. The unit's first encounter with battlefield death shocked many of the men. Pvt. William Relyea recalled that their previously "exuberant spirits" were "completely subdued." Some wounded called out to the green recruits: "God speed you," and "You are wanted bad at the front." Lieutenant Colonel Cheney excitedly pledged that the 16th Connecticut would make the rebels pay for their suffering.[10]

The regiment spent one week at Fort Ward, some five or six miles from Washington, D.C. The men finally received arms—Whitney rifles and "made over Belgian muskets" described as "[v]ery nasty and dirty"—but apparently performed little drill in their use. Mainly the regiment did "fatigue duty," building breastworks and cleaning their guns, practicing their aim, but learning next to nothing of battlefield commands and military movements.[11] A Connecticut soldier informed the *Hartford Courant* that the men at Fort Ward were "very cheerful and healthy, and do not complain." To friends and family this same man confessed: "We know as little and perhaps less, [about] what is going on about us than you do at home," adding, "as far as I am concerned I do not feel as anxious here and eager for news as I did at home." Jacob Bauer painted a less sanguine picture of the 16th Connecticut at Fort Ward. "We have our guns now rubber blankets and everything necessary to go into battle," he observed, "but we are not drilled enough with the guns to do any mischief." The transformation from citizen to soldier remained incomplete, and Bauer noted "a kind of despondency and fear of being led into battle before we are fit which can not be overcome." [12]

On September 7, the 16th Connecticut received orders to proceed immediately to the Army of the Potomac, where it would join Brig. Gen. Isaac P. Rodman's division of the Ninth Corps. The regiment would become part of Col. Edward Harland's 2nd Brigade, which also included the 8th and 11th Connecticut and the 4th Rhode Island. The regiment had been away from Hartford a week, and, as one historian of the unit noted, "it had received no drill, no discipline, few instructions even in marching. It was little more than a crowd of earnest young Connecticut boys." A difficult march took the regiment to the front. Still unused to the rigors of soldiering, many of the men suffered from exhaustion. For nine days the unit kept at a hurried pace, with little clear idea of where they were going. The days were hot and the roads dry and dusty. One soldier remembered how difficult it was to see the file in front of him; another described the roads as "ankle deep in dust." The regiment marched between twelve and fourteen miles a day and lost numerous stragglers.[13]

Rations during the march were either of poor quality or poor quantity. Men foraged in nearby fields, orchards, and farmhouses. But officers seemed to be eating just fine. As with the episode involving accommodations on the steamer that had carried the 16th from Hartford to Elizabethport, at least some enlisted men resented what they perceived to be unfair advantages officers enjoyed in finding food. Colonel Beach struck some men as especially high handed in his efforts to supply his table.[14]

Although resentment toward Colonel Beach had not abated since leaving Hartford, other officers were rising in stature among the soldiers. Young Captain Manross of Company K stood out during the march because of his concern for the men. He constantly encouraged his company, helping them forget their physical pain and discomfort. For those who faltered, he offered to carry their guns until they felt strong enough to bear the weight again.[15]

As they tramped through the Virginia and Maryland countryside, men witnessed not only the destructive results of an army on the move but also the results of recent combat. "You can have no possible idea of the desolation of Va," Robert Kellogg wrote his parents; "the fences are gone, trees cut down, grass eat up for forage, *and* the country cut up by military roads." Army wagons, ambulances, and multitudes of marching troops crowded roads. The Connecticut men occasionally heard distant artillery fire and spotted bullet-ridden fences, houses, and trees. At Frederick, Maryland, they were stunned to encounter a group of ragged and emaciated Confederate prisoners who stared hollow eyed and silent at the green bluecoats. Near the South Mountain battlefield, dead bodies littered the roadside, and wounded filled churches and private homes. "You in Hartford," a member of the regiment wrote his hometown paper, "have no idea of what war is, or of the life of a soldier." [16]

Despite the tiring journey and sobering sites, the regiment arrived at the foot of South Mountain in fairly good spirits. Excitement electrified the air as word circulated that a major fight was at hand. Still, when orders confirmed that the regiment was heading to the front, Lieutenant Blakeslee remembered, "This took us a little by surprise as we did not expect to go into battle so soon." [17]

By dusk on September 16, the Connecticut unit had marched to a line of battle behind the Rohrback farm on the Army of the Potomac's far left flank. Hungry and tired, and without ration wagons to feed them, the men devoured corn and green fruit from nearby orchards and fields. Regimental historian Bernard Blakeslee later alleged that it was on this night that the men loaded their muskets for the first time. [18] Officers prohibited fires and ordered quiet in the camp. The men slept fitfully on their arms in a light drizzle, awakened throughout the night by false alarms and nervous sentries. [19]

Early in the morning of September 17, soldiers awoke to find Confederate batteries shelling their position. The entire brigade moved to a safer location, gaining a "magnificent view" of the battlefield. The battle of Antietam had commenced, and men had to shout to be heard over the noise of musketry and artillery fire. By now most of the unit realized combat was imminent, but they had little idea what their part would be. The anticipation drove several to distraction. A few restless souls wandered off to pick peaches. Many others suddenly felt faint and weak, departing for the rear when noon sick call came. Private Relyea noted that many of those so conveniently ill stood among the loudest braggarts. "Rid of regimental rubbish," Relyea commented, the 16th was then "free from everything that would or could tarnish our good name clear of all weakening influences now ready for the ordeal that awaited us." [20]

But they were not ready for what they would soon face. By late afternoon of September 17, the 16th was sent to try to outflank the Confederates and find a usable ford on Antietam Creek. The men crossed the creek about a mile below Burnside's Bridge, holding their guns and cartridge boxes high over their heads. Some described the water as shoulder deep. After hurrying up the side of a hill to support a Union battery, officers ordered the men immediately to hit the ground.

Corporal Oscar Weil (left) and Sergeant Robert Kellogg
Connecticut State Archives, RG 69:23, box 10, folder W, MCH copy negative

Rebel cannon took deadly aim on their position, pounding them with canister, marbles, and railroad iron. The hill's crest protected most of the unit, but about a dozen men suffered injury from the artillery fire. A few privates joked nervously, seeking to break the thickening tension. Colonel Beach barked impatiently at the jokesters, silencing any attempts at levity.[21]

It was sometime between 3:30 and 4:00 P.M., and Colonel Harland impatiently awaited the advance of the 16th Connecticut and the 4th Rhode Island. The 8th Connecticut had already moved forward some distance to the right of the two regiments, creating a gap between the units. Colonel Harland sent an aide to push the remainder of his brigade forward, and Brigadier General Rodman went personally to hasten the men along. Rodman discovered the 16th Connecticut still on the ground, near the edge of a cornfield. As Rodman conversed intently with Beach, he detected enemy movement to the left of the cornfield. Rodman rushed back to find the 4th Rhode Island, and Beach quickly ordered the 16th into formation.

Because the color-bearer forgot to take the state flag out of its dark glazed bag, the regiment entered its first battle essentially waving a black flag—which provided an eerie premonition of what was to come.[22]

"Attention!" Colonel Beach screamed, trying frantically to shift half of the regiment to refuse its left and protect the exposed flank. Suddenly a wave of bullets whizzed through the ranks. Maneuvering men under fire is difficult for any officer, but directing undrilled, undisciplined troops like the 16th Connecticut was impossible. Line officers were as green and confused as the privates. One officer cried out in desperation: "Tell us what you want us to do and we'll try to obey you." Beach replied: "I want my men to face the enemy." The tall, uneven cornfield compounded the chaos. Men could see only a small portion of their line at a time. A few fell out of formation, losing track of their companies. Nearing a wooden fence, officers issued conflicting orders—"tear the fence down" and "never mind the fence."[23]

The few minutes that had passed seemed like an eternity. As officers struggled to find some order and direction, Confederate troops unleashed a deadly crossfire into the regiment. "So dense was the corn," wrote South Carolinian James F. J. Caldwell, "that the lines sometimes approached within thirty to forty yards of each other before opening." Some members of the 16th Connecticut recalled firing only one round; others alleged that they launched a counterattack against the South Carolinians. Some recalled hearing orders to "fall back," but it is unclear whether any officer gave formal instructions to retreat. Whatever the truth, the 16th Connecticut could not bear the enfilade fire and broke and fled in wild panic. The 4th Rhode Island, which had come up on the 16th's left, held a little longer before they also retreated in confusion.[24]

A member of the 1st South Carolina recalled running through the corn, shooting a "galling fire into the fleeing foe." Berry Benson saw bunches of frightened bluecoats crowded into a small hollow at the bottom of the hill, afraid to cross the open slope behind them. "Grouped here in a crouching disorderly line," Benson remembered, "we poured into them volley after volley, doubtless with terrible execution." Other Federals huddled behind a stone fence, sporadically breaking away from the fence, in small groups and individually, to flee to the rear.[25]

Caught up in the swarm of panicked soldiers, Beach stubbornly fought to regain control. He desperately tried to rally a small remnant of the 16th with parts of the 11th Connecticut and redraw a battle line. But most of the 16th Connecticut were dead, wounded, or gone from the field. Dropping from mental and physical exhaustion, stragglers slept the night of September 17 under fences, on rocks, and in thickets. Wounded remained on the field into the next day, moaning and crying for water.[26]

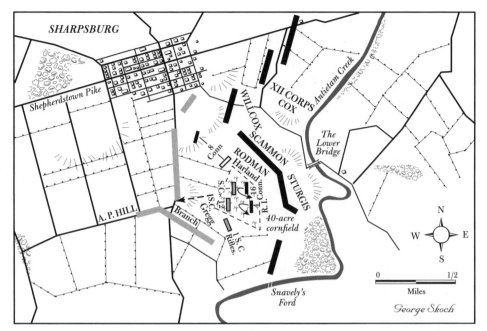

The 16th Connecticut at Antietam

Total casualties for the 16th Connecticut surpassed 25 percent. Of an estimated 940 soldiers engaged, the regiment lost 43 killed, 164 wounded, 20 captured, and 19 desertions.[27] One lieutenant and three captains lay dead, including young Manross, whose last words were, "O my poor wife, my poor wife!" Lieutenant Colonel Cheney, Maj. George Washburn, two captains, and one lieutenant were wounded. Division commander Rodman died attempting to rally the Union flank. Soldiers hastily buried 40 of the regiment's dead in a mass grave near the cornfield. Later these remains were removed to the Antietam National Cemetery or transported north to Connecticut.[28]

Less than one-third of the regiment answered morning roll call on September 18. Throughout the day 200 more men stumbled into camp, groggy, disoriented, and fatigued. Over the next two weeks, one soldier recalled, only a few hundred could be mustered for service. The difficult and abrupt change from civilian life and the strenuous march to the front had taken an initial toll on the ranks; the shock and stress of combat, particularly under such negative circumstances, proved to be too much for many of the Connecticut men. Days after the battle, straggling continued to be a serious problem. On September 23, Garett B. Holcombe wrote his sister that there remained "roughs" in the regiment who would "skedaddle if they had a chance." Holcombe counted 60 guards "around

Private F. Dixon Tucker, one of the
two soldiers who fled to England.
Connecticut State Archives, RG 69:23,
box 10, folder T–U, MCH copy negative

our little camp" who treated everyone as a potential deserter. October regimental
returns listed 28 men as deserters; most had left the day of battle, but 3 had disappeared earlier and 7 after Antietam. Two soldiers fled not only the 16th Connecticut but also the United States, escaping to England.[29]

Official reports of the battle did not entirely explain the regiment's poor performance. Col. Frank Beach described the regiment enduring enemy artillery fire
all day, "until about 5 o'clock when we were brought against the extreme right of
the rebel infantry." He made no mention of his exasperated efforts to refuse his
flank or of the embarrassing retreat. Beach stated simply: "I transmit the casualties. There were probably about twenty taken prisoner. The missing are constantly coming in and it is impossible to give a correct list of them."[30]

Lt. Col. Joseph B. Curtis of the 4th Rhode Island maintained that the 16th
Connecticut's collapse shattered his regiment's ranks. Curtis explained that when
the Rhode Islanders moved forward in support of the Connecticut unit, he
"found the Sixteenth Ct giving way and crowding upon its right compelling" his
men "to move to the left, and rendering it almost impossible to dress the line."
When he tried to rally his troops for an attack, he was unable to find any officer
of the 16th to support the assault. Curtis cried out to his colonel: "[W]e must de-
pend upon ourselves." A few moments later the 16th Connecticut lost all cohe-

sion, and his regiment soon followed. Curtis defended his Rhode Islanders for fighting well throughout the day. "[T]hat they finally broke, under such a severe fire, and the pressure of a broken regiment is not surprising," he concluded, "although much to be regretted." [31]

Only Col. Edward Harland attempted to explain the debacle. He reported his frustration that the Connecticut regiment failed to advance and recalled sending an aide to rally both the 16th Connecticut and the 4th Rhode Island. Harland confirmed that General Rodman himself went to hasten the two regiments forward, but he did praise Beach for his attempts to turn the regiment's front and meet the enemy attack. Harland's report stressed the difficult terrain, poor visibility, and deadly effectiveness of enemy fire. In the end, these men who were under fire for the first time "could not be held," Harland observed, and their rout hastened the disintegration of the 4th Rhode Island and eventually the 8th Connecticut. [32]

Individual soldiers groped for their own explanations of what happened during those few terrible moments in the Cornfield. Members of the 16th filled private letters and diaries with descriptions and questions, trying to make sense out of the chaos and confusion. Reactions ranged from relief to rage to humiliation to shock. Soldiers' blunt honesty, especially during those first few days after the battle, is striking. Twenty-nine-year-old William Relyea wrote his family that he did not consider running until he looked around and "saw only dead men." At that moment, he confessed, "I very quickly decided it was no place for me." He struggled to describe combat to his wife: "Alas I cannot[.] Words are inadequate to the task. Piles of heads, arms, legs and fragments of other portions of humanity all thrown together promiscuously." "It is over now," Relyea concluded, "and we laugh at our fears, that is human, so am I." William Drake was just as candid when he told his cousin that "there was some pretty tall running in the 16th and I guess that I made myself scarce rather fast." Eighteen-year-old George Robbins suffered a minor injury and fell out of formation, losing track of the regiment in all the confusion. He did not run "until the rest did," hiding in the woods until rejoining the 16th the next morning. Leland O. Barlow thought it was a "wonder that any of us got away." Grateful that he and most of his company withstood the ordeal, Barlow stated simply: "It was a hard day for the 16th Reg." The vivid memory of Antietam made one soldier sick. For the next six months, wrote this individual, "everything I eat, drink or smelled had an odor of dead men." Elizur D. Beldon's diary described the fight in the cornfield as a "scene of terror, every man for himself." Beldon was slightly wounded during the frenzied retreat and fell into a "small gutter" with several other men: "[T]here I lay not daring to stir until dark when the firing ceased." [33]

Members of the regiment blamed unnamed officials who ordered them into a critical point of battle without preparation or adequate support. Several alleged that the 4th Rhode Island retreated before they did. "We were murdered," Robert Kellogg bitterly wrote his father.[34] Some blasted the enemy, accusing Confederate troops of trickery for wearing blue uniforms, waving the United States flag, and yelling, "Don't fire on your own men."[35]

An edgy humor also mixed with the anger and disappointment. William Relyea recalled a lieutenant who showed signs of "getting behind a tree" and ranted that the battle was the "biggest 4th of July" he had ever seen. Relyea stumbled over a wounded 8th Connecticut soldier who pleaded: "Don't run boys—give the S—— B——hell." The man's cries meant nothing to the exhausted private, who had no energy to run. Relyea reasoned that he "may as well die walking as running." Another soldier, referring to the two men who fled to England, noted that "some of these heroes in their fight got to running so fast that they could not stop. One who somehow ran across the ocean and arrived in due time in England, as we have never heard from him since he is supposed to be running yet."[36]

Pvt. John B. Cuzner of Company B assured his fiancée, Ellen, on September 21 that some members of the regiment "did not frighten" but he was not one of them. "As for myself," he confessed, "I am a big coward." He claimed that he only "ran when they gave the order to retreat" and then hid behind a stone wall. The regiment, Cuzner wrote, was "cut off most shockingly" after having "few drills and no experience." The seriousness of the regiment's loss did not sink in until roll call, when Cuzner realized how many of his comrades were gone. Still, he was not tired of the soldier's life; he had a good rifle and knew "how to use it." Ten days after the battle the eighteen-year-old Cuzner reassured Ellen that the army experience was making him a better person. But he would say no more about Antietam: "I could fill sheets about it all, but you wouldn't like to read about the horrible sights I saw after the Battle."[37]

Lt. Col. John Burnham authored one of the most revealing letters about the battle. On October 4, he informed his mother about the "big fight," its "severe cost," and his deep regret that the 16th was unable to resume the contest and pursue the fleeing rebels. He tried to record his own memory of the battle, recalling little leading up to the attack. He had been too busy to think about personal danger until he spotted the enemy on his left forming with calm intrepidity, methodically planting a battery in close range to the regiment. At that moment, Burnham wrote, "I am frank to confess that although I had no idea of running away—I trembled. You may call the feeling fear or anything you choose for I don't deny that I trembled and wished we were out of it." Despite the terrible panic and disorganized retreat, Burnham attested: "I tried to do my duty and am satisfied."[38]

Burnham admitted that he would not be sorry to see the war end, but like other members of the 16th he wanted one more chance to prove himself, one more opportunity to get it right. The next time, he believed, "I should be considerably cooler I have no doubt." If battle came again, Burnham told his mother, "I hope as I always have, that I may have the courage to do my duty well, not recklessly but with simple bravery and fidelity so that if I fall you may have the consolation of knowing that I not only lose my life in a good cause but die like a man." For the time being, Burnham and the rest of the 16th Connecticut could only wait restlessly for that second chance to prove themselves in combat.[39]

Pvt. Jacob Bauer told his wife, Emily, three days after the battle that he was surprised he survived. Like Cheney, he too was battle-weary and wished the "war would cease this very hour." Bauer reflected candidly on that "dreadful hour" in the cornfield, conceding that he could recall no thoughts of his wife or of his own safety. Instead, his "only thought and word was forward, forward, forward, which I could think of and sing out." He fired one shot and ran with the rest of the regiment in "Bull Run Fashion."[40]

After a few weeks had passed, Bauer, like many of his comrades, changed his mind about both the regiment's performance at Antietam and the war as a whole. On October 2, he was "feeling first rate and glad that I can do my duty" and professed to "really love" soldiering. The man who unabashedly stated that he and the rest of the 16th fled from the field in "Bull Run Fashion" started thinking dramatically differently about the rout. If he survived the war, he confided to his wife, he would return to Antietam and show her where "the heros [*sic*] rest side by side." The 16th had its share of cowards, Bauer wrote, but he was not one of them. Cowards were the ones who cursed the most, he maintained, "and they were the ones who stayed back in the hour of trial."[41]

Hometown ministers strove to paint the 16th Connecticut's stunning losses in commendable terms and to reaffirm soldiers' and civilians' faith in the regiment and the war. The Reverend A. W. Ide assured grieving friends and family of slain Lt. William Horton that the young husband and father "proved himself a true and brave man." Ide quoted letters from members of Horton's company who last saw their lieutenant "surrounded by rebels, defending himself most valiantly" with his sword. Ide asked Connecticut soldiers attending the funeral to relay a message from home to men at the front: "Tell them that from the steps of the house of God, we give praise and honor to the brave of the 11th and 16th Conn. Regiments— both to the living and the dead." At the funeral of seventeen-year-old Roswell Morgan Allen, the Reverend W. H. Gilbert censured regimental officers for abuse of duty and lack of sensitivity to the men in the ranks. "You all know," Gilbert told his congregation, "how, at the very outset of their career as soldiers,

First Sergeant Jacob and Emily Bauer
Connecticut State Archives, RG 69:23, box 10, folder B, MCH copy negative

[t]his regiment worn by exhaustive marches, was thrust into the very heat of the awful battle of Antietam." Although escaping injury at Antietam, Allen fell seriously sick immediately after the battle. He later died in a Washington hospital. Gilbert read from a letter written by members of Allen's company who praised their dead comrade, and he comforted mourners that the patriotic private "ever remained as pure and noble as when he left home."[42]

Contemporary newspaper accounts of the 16th's performance at Antietam contained remarkably few critical or negative sentiments. The *Hartford Courant* had repeatedly reported that the regiment was in fine condition and high spirits during the days leading up to the battle. On September 12, the paper proclaimed: "A better regiment of men never left the State than the 16th Conn." Six days later, before news of the battle reached Hartford, the paper described the regiment as withstanding the march to the front "bravely, very few giving out." Although Beach had expressed concerns about his men's lack of preparedness, the paper reported that "they were thoroughly drilled, and now the Colonel feels safe in taking them into battle." "Connecticut troops always have fought well," the *Courant* assured readers, "and we have no fears of the brave Sixteenth." Letters from Connecticut soldiers published in the papers after Antietam did not contradict these glowing assessments. Recognizing the regiment's high losses, one infantryman maintained: "There was no faltering or flinching, but simple confusion." Another soldier, identified only as "J. M. B. MC.," wrote that "[t]he Sixteenth sustained unbroken ranks under the most destructive fire for an hour, when they fell back, having suffered severely." The paper agreed, announcing on September 23 that Connecticut should be proud of all its troops: "The universal testimony is that they fought desperately and bravely, the new troops as well as the old. Although terribly cut up, there was no flinching."[43]

Postwar histories of the regiment added to these positive portrayals. Regimental historians, themselves veterans, described the unit as inherently brave but unfairly victimized at Antietam. Bernard Blakeslee's 1875 regimental history stressed how unprepared the men were and asserted that the regiment held firm until ordered to retreat. "It was indeed a fearful day for the Sixteenth," stated former first sergeant Blakeslee. "Without having time allowed to learn even the rudiments of military science, it was hurried forward and was formed in regimental line almost for the first time on the battlefield at Antietam, the bloodiest day America ever saw."[44]

William Relyea's unpublished history also defended the regiment in its brutal baptism of fire. Relyea firmly believed that he and his comrades were unfairly and prematurely forced into combat and had been "compelled to retire" from the field. Five decades after the battle, he recalled: "In less than one month from the home circle and without due preparation they were hurled as it were into a carnival of destruction and death that appalled the stoutest heart." Relyea emphasized both the men's innocence and their cool resolve. "Having no realizing sense of the dread carnage of war," he stated somewhat awkwardly, "the regiment went into this fiery vortex with calm serenity of purpose that contrasted strangely with their conduct in after battles." Because of their experience at Antietam, the men in subsequent battles were "sure to have a clearer vision of what was before them and were cautious though just as brave." Relyea admitted that the regiment suffered from a small number of shirkers, listing twenty-one men whom he claimed exhibited cowardice in the presence of the enemy. But he insisted that these recreants had left the ranks long before their comrades engaged the rebels on September 17, adding, "I have no special tales of heroism to tell for all who went into that battle were heroes, our list of dead and wounded amply testify to this." "Pure gold," he wrote, "were those who withstood the ordeal, and living or dead are honored as brave men." Reflecting back on that terrible day, Relyea declared those dead to be "as grand a body of men as ever the body produced." They gave their lives "for the salvation of their country"; their blood "helped to wash away the dark stain of slavery"; their efforts helped clean "the nation of its foul polution [*sic*]." Relyea summed up Antietam as "an epoch in the history of the 16th C.V. never to be effaced."[45]

George Robbins's postwar narrative stressed not only the inexperience of the troops but also the appalling conditions they faced at Antietam. Robbins refused to "undervalue the courage and willingness of the men of the 16th Connecticut Infantry under the most trying conditions; veterans have had to yield under similar circumstances and what could have been expected of raw troops, with no drilling, no instruction in loading and firing, and in less than two weeks since the arrival on the soil of Maryland, all of which time had been spent in marching to the front." He continued to believe, as did many soldiers right after the battle, that someone somehow had blundered, but it was not the 16th.[46]

The 16th Connecticut never got a chance to prove itself in another large-scale battle. It stood in reserve at the battle of Fredericksburg, with "nothing to do but witness the contest raging in front of us which was fearful." On February 6, 1863, the regiment left for Newport News, Virginia, ending its tenure with the Army of the Potomac. That spring it participated in the defense of Suffolk, then spent the following year on the Virginia and North Carolina coast, seeing only sporadic fighting. In April 1864, nearly the entire regiment suffered capture at Plymouth, North Carolina. Most of the soldiers went to Andersonville, where hundreds died in the notorious Georgia prison.[47]

The 16th Connecticut's bad luck followed them to their final day in uniform. In June 1865, survivors returned to Hartford earlier than planned, only to discover that the 18th Connecticut had just arrived and was enjoying a festive reception. When news spread that the 16th was also home, townspeople hastily prepared breakfast and rushed to meet them at the train depot. As the 130 veterans, many only recently released from prison, marched through the streets, their depleted ranks shocked onlookers. Tears mixed with cheers, and one officer's wife learned for the first time that her husband was dead. She was so distraught that friends had trouble getting her into a carriage to take her home.[48]

Lt. Col. John H. Burnham addressed his fellow survivors on June 29, 1865. "Although a less amount of glory in the field has fallen to our lot than to some others," he said, "no regiment from the State has been subjected to so much suffering." Connecticut historians W. A. Croffutt and John M. Morris agreed: "This regiment saw little but misfortune." Regimental historian Bernard Blakeslee concluded that "The Sixteenth was always called an *unfortunate regiment;* for if there was any special hardship to endure the regiment was sure to be called on to experience it, either by accident or otherwise. It was our bad luck."[49]

Words of praise and admiration supplemented these honest assessments of the unit's hapless and disappointing wartime experiences. Mayor Ezra Hall gave a speech on June 30, 1865, reviewing the regiment's experiences. He greeted them proudly as "[h]eroes of many a hard-fought battle, and worthy veterans of a redeemed country!" Recalling their origins, he noted how "hard [it was] to leave your situations, your homes, and those you loved." Putting aside their doubts, the men of the 16th had resolved to do their duty, and Hall declared that "no braver regiment ever went from our city & state." On September 17, 1862, Hall told the men, "[Y]ou first realized war, and stood on the fated field of death. That was a sad day for the 16th CT." And it was a terribly sad day for Hartford. Hall remembered vividly the grief that swept the city as news spread of the battle's outcome. Glossing over the fiasco at Antietam, he hailed each member of the regiment, alive and dead, as a hero "covered with honor and glory." "Your thinned ranks" and "your torn colors give convincing proof of your deeds of bravery." The "martyred dead," Hall acclaimed, must be remembered for the sacrifice they made "for the country, for the restoration of law and order, for the complete emancipation of race and for the eternal principle of liberty." He assured the crowd that history would keep their memory alive.[50]

Year after year survivors of the 16th Connecticut commemorated the anniversary of Antietam, unable or unwilling to let go of the memory. One aging veteran admitted that the "chief pleasure left to us now is the getting together once a year

Lieutenant Bernard F. Blakeslee
Connecticut State Archives, RG 69:23,
box 10, folder B, MCH copy negative

to shake hands, look each other in the face, listen to the old familiar voices (which never *change*) and recall the past." But recalling the past did change. By the time a small remnant of the unit returned to Antietam in 1894 to dedicate the granite monument at the place where they broke and fled, members spoke only of glory and sacrifice. Chaplain P. V. Finch reminded listeners that "all the good we have or enjoy comes to us through the suffering of others; that the very life which we now have is the result of material anguish." Former regimental surgeon Nathan Mayer recited a poem titled "Antietam," which tried to explain in chivalrous terms what happened on September 17. Mayer maintained that every Federal soldier fought to save the country and that no Union deaths were in vain. But the 16th Connecticut, "brave and untried," Mayer declared, were a "martyr band" thrust into the war's bloodiest battle by "stern duty" to meet their fate.[51] Although freely admitting the regiment's lack of experience, no one at the ceremony openly discussed individual or unit cowardice or fear. There seemed no place for realistic or critical appraisals of their past; veterans publicly adopted indiscriminate, celebratory sentiments that obscured their painful yet distinctive wartime experience.

Survivors continued to promote these distorted versions of their past, and many were gratified to see popular acceptance of their flattering portraits. In

1896, Robert Kellogg wrote a former comrade: "It pleases me no little to see that our 16th C.V. men are appreciated that they have held their own so well all these years, and stand so high in public esteem." In 1907, on the forty-fifth anniversary of the battle, the *Hartford Courant* announced that "all historians agree that the members of the old Sixteenth did their work [at Antietam] in a noble" fashion. Six years later the Hartford *Times* published similar sentiments: "That the regiment did nobly is the verdict of all who witnessed its heroism on the battlefield." By 1931, when only five members of the regiment were well enough to attend their annual reunion, a Connecticut paper called them the "Fighting Sixteenth Regiment of Volunteers." The article notified readers that at Antietam "[m]en fell by the score, but the green Connecticut soldiers carried themselves like veterans."[52]

But the 16th Connecticut neither fought like veterans nor behaved admirably or courageously at Antietam. Hampered by bad luck, ill preparation, individual cowardice, and poor leadership, the regiment failed to accomplish noble deeds. Nonetheless, veterans, public officials, ministers, and newspapers all contributed to distorting the hard truth and fashioning a fictionalized, romanticized memory of battle. Survivors eventually deemed themselves heroes for merely wearing the victor's uniform. Regimental and individual identities became subsumed by a national, corporate identity that had little room for variations or ambiguity. The 16th Connecticut's unique, unheroic "atom of history" was lost under a larger body of glorified Civil War mythology.[53]

NOTES

1. Frank Cheney, "Address," in *Souvenir of Excursion to Antietam and Dedication of Monuments of the 8th, 11th, 14th, and 16th Regiments of Connecticut Volunteers* (New London, Conn.: n.p., 1894), 48 (hereafter cited as *Excursion to Antietam*).

2. Connecticut had a quota of 7,155 men and by the end of August had surpassed that number. See William A. Croffutt and John M. Morris, *The Military and Civil History of Connecticut during the War of 1861–65* (New York: L. Bill, 1868), 223–29. Motivations for enlistment varied among Civil War soldiers, but recently James M. McPherson has argued that ideology and patriotism strongly induced the first two years of volunteer enlistment and kept men in the ranks through the entire conflict. See James M. McPherson, *For Cause and Comrades: Why Men Fought in the Civil War* (New York: Oxford University Press, 1997).

3. Croffutt and Morris, *Military and Civil History of Connecticut*, 227–29; Bernard Blakeslee, *History of the Sixteenth Connecticut Volunteers* (Hartford, Conn.: Case, Lockwood and Brainard Co., Printers, 1875), 5; *Catalogue of the 14th, 15th, 16th, 17th,*

18th, 19th, 20th, and 21st Regiments and the Second Light Battery Connecticut Volunteers; and the 22d, 23d, 24th, 25th, 26th, 27th, and 28th Regiments Connecticut Volunteers for Nine Months. Compiled from Records in the Adjutant-Generals Office 1862 (Hartford, Conn.: Press of Case, Lockwood and Co., 1862), 47–67; "Muster and Descriptive Rolls, 16th Regiment Connecticut Volunteers," Records of the Military Department, Connecticut Adjutant General's Office, RG 13, Connecticut State Library, Hartford (repository hereafter cited as CSL).

4. Croffutt and Morris, *Military and Civil History of Connecticut*, 276.

5. Blakeslee, *Sixteenth Connecticut*, 5; George Robbins, "Recollections," George Robbins Papers, Connecticut Historical Society, Hartford (repository hereafter cited as CHS); William H. Relyea, "History of the 16th Connecticut Volunteer Infantry," 3–4, William H. Relyea Papers, CHS; Robert H. Kellogg to father, August 19, 1862, Robert H. Kellogg Papers, CHS; Charles Gilbert Lee diary, August 20–23, 1862, CHS. See also Croffutt and Morris, *Military and Civil History of Connecticut*, 229.

6. Relyea, "History of the 16th Connecticut," 3; *Hartford Courant*, August 9, 15, 1862; John C. Kinney, "The Memorial History of Hartford," in *The Memorial History of Hartford County, Connecticut, 1633–1884*, 2 vols., ed. J. Hammond Trumbull (Boston: Edward L. Osgood, 1886), 2:98 n. 1.

7. W. H. Gilbert, *Sermon Delivered in Granby, Conn., Jan. 4, 1863, at the Funeral of Roswell Morgan Allen, Private in Co. E, 16th Reg't. C.V., Who Died at the Hospital near Washington, Sunday, Dec. 28, 1862* (Hartford, Conn.: Charles Montague, 1863), 12; Robbins, "Recollections," CHS; Relyea, "History of the 16th Connecticut," 4; Croffutt and Morris, *Military and Civil History of Connecticut*, 228–29; Blakeslee, *Sixteenth Connecticut*, 6.

8. Relyea, "History of the 16th Connecticut," 4; Croffutt and Morris, *Military and Civil History of Connecticut*, 229; Blakeslee, *Sixteenth Connecticut*, 6.

9. Relyea, "History of the 16th Connecticut," 6.

10. Ibid., 10; R. H. Kellogg to Hattie Kellogg, September 5, 1862, Robert H. Kellogg Papers, CHS. See also *Hartford Courant*, September 1, 5, 1862.

11. Quotations from Relyea, "History of the 16th Connecticut," 11–12. Robert Kellogg and Charles Gilbert Lee claimed that the regiment received Whitney rifles. See Lee diary, September 3, 1862, CHS, and Robert H. Kellogg to father, September 6, 1862, Robert H. Kellogg Papers, CHS.

12. J. H. B. to "Editor of the *Courant*," *Hartford Courant*, September 10, 1862; Jacob Bauer to Emily Bauer, September 5, 1862, typescript copy of original, folder titled "16th Regiment Connecticut Volunteers," Antietam National Battlefield, Sharpsburg, Md. (repository hereafter cited as ANB). See also Blakeslee, *Sixteenth Connecticut*, 8; Croffutt and Morris, *Military and Civil History of Connecticut*, 237.

13. Croffutt and Morris, *Military and Civil History of Connecticut*, 260; Blakeslee, *Sixteenth Connecticut*, 8; Relyea, "History of the 16th Connecticut," 14–15; Lee diary, September 7, 1862, CHS; Robbins, "Recollections," CHS. See also "Monthly Re-

turns, 16th Regiment Connecticut Volunteers, September 1862," Records of the Military Department, Connecticut Adjutant General's Office, RG 13, CSL.

14. For an anecdote concerning Beach's taking food from an enlisted man, see note 10 in the preceding essay. On the subject of how the men ate while on the march, see also Croffutt and Morris, *Military and Civil History of Connecticut,* 265.

15. Robbins, "Recollections," CHS.

16. Robert H. Kellogg to father and mother, September 10, 1862, Robert H. Kellogg Papers, CHS; *Hartford Courant,* September 12, 1862. See also Robbins, "Recollections," CHS; Blakeslee, *Sixteenth Connecticut,* 9–10; Relyea, "History of the 16th Connecticut," 16–20.

17. Blakeslee, *Sixteenth Connecticut,* 11. See also Croffutt and Morris, *Military and Civil History of Connecticut,* 265; Relyea, "History of the 16th Connecticut," 21; Robbins, "Recollections," CHS.

18. Accounts vary as to when the men actually learned to load and fire their weapons. Blakeslee may have asserted that they loaded their muskets for the first time the night before Antietam to underscore their poor preparation and thereby lessen criticism for their poor performance on the 17th. Charles Gilbert Lee recorded learning to load and fire guns on September 9; William Relyea attested that the regiment first fired their muskets on September 12, but he added that they had no time to practice. Blakeslee, *Sixteenth Connecticut,* 11; Lee diary, September 9, 1862, CHS; Relyea, "History of the 16th Connecticut," 16.

19. John Niven, *Connecticut for the Union: The Role of the State in the Civil War* (New Haven: Yale University Press, 1981), 216; Croffutt and Morris, *Military and Civil History of Connecticut,* 265; Bernard Blakeslee, "The Sixteenth Connecticut at Antietam," in *Excursion to Antietam,* 13.

20. Robbins, "Recollections," CHS; Relyea, "History of the 16th Connecticut," 22–24; Croffutt and Morris, *Military and Civil History of Connecticut,* 265.

21. Relyea, "History of the 16th Connecticut," 24–26; Robbins, "Recollections," CHS; Blakeslee, *Sixteenth Connecticut,* 14–16; Niven, *Connecticut for the Union,* 220.

22. Relyea, "History of the 16th Connecticut," 42–43; Niven, *Connecticut for the Union,* 220–22; Croffutt and Morris, *Military and Civil History of Connecticut,* 271; Blakeslee, *Sixteenth Connecticut,* 16.

23. Relyea, "History of the 16th Connecticut," 26–27; Robbins, "Recollections," CHS. See also Blakeslee, *Sixteenth Connecticut,* 16.

24. J. F. J. Caldwell, *The History of a Brigade of South Carolinians, Known First as "Greggs," and Subsequently as "McGowan's Brigade"* (Philadelphia: King & Baird, Printers, 1866), 46–47; Niven, *Connecticut for the Union,* 222; Blakeslee, *Sixteenth Connecticut,* 16; Blakeslee, "Sixteenth Connecticut at Antietam," 19; Robbins, "Recollections," CHS; Relyea, "History of the 16th Connecticut," 27.

25. Berry Benson memoirs, 18, Robert S. Brake Collection, USAMHI.

26. Niven, *Connecticut for the Union,* 222–23; Blakeslee, *Sixteenth Connecticut,* 17.

27. Casualty figures vary from source to source. These numbers are abstracted from *Adjutant-General Record of Service of Connecticut Men in the Army and Navy of the United States during the War of the Rebellion* (Hartford, Conn.: Press of the Case, Lockwood & Brainard Co., 1889), 619–39 (hereafter cited as *Adjutant-General Record of Service*). The 1894 Antietam monument lists 779 engaged, 43 killed, and 161 wounded.

28. Croffutt and Morris, *Military and Civil History of Connecticut,* 276; Blakeslee, *Sixteenth Connecticut,* 18; Blakeslee, "Sixteenth at Antietam," 21; Garett B. Holcombe to sister, September 23, 1862, ANB; *Hartford Courant,* September 25, 1862.

29. Garett B. Holcombe to sister, September, 23, 1862, ANB; "Monthly Returns, 16th Regiment Connecticut Volunteers, October 1862," Records of the Military Department, Connecticut Adjutant General's Office, RG 13, CSL; Blakeslee, *Sixteenth Connecticut,* 17–19; Robbins, "Recollections," CHS; Lee diary, September 18, 1862, CHS. Henry Rhodes and F. Dixon Tucker, both of Company A and natives of New England, fled to Britain for the duration of the war. See "F. Dixon Tucker," in "Military and Biographical Data of the 16th Connecticut Volunteers," George Q. Whitney Papers, RG 69, CSL.

30. Francis Beach to J. D. Williams, September 19, 1862, copy of original, ANB.

31. Report of Lt. Col. Joseph B. Curtis, in U.S. War Department, *The War of the Rebellion: A Compilation of the Official Records of the Union and Confederate Armies,* 127 vols, index, and atlas (Washington: GPO, 1880–1901), ser. 1, vol. 19, pt. 1:455–58 (hereafter cited as *OR;* all references are to ser. 1).

32. Report of Col. Edward Harland, in *OR* 19(1):452–54.

33. Relyea, "History of the 16th Connecticut," 35, 43–44; William H. Relyea to wife, September 26, 1862, Letterbook, CHS; William H. Drake to Timothy Loomis, September 29, 1862, Civil War Letters Collection, CHS; George Robbins to sister, September 23, 1862, CHS; Leland O. Barlow to sister, September 19, 1862, ANB; Elizur D. Beldon diary, September 19, 1862, CHS.

34. Robert H. Kellogg to father, September 20, 1862, Robert H. Kellogg Papers, CHS.

35. A. P. Hill's men may have been wearing blue uniforms captured at Harpers Ferry earlier in the day. It is also possible that the blue flag Connecticut men mistook for the Federal flag, or the Ohio state flag, was the 2nd South Carolina's banner. One officer contended that the corn was too high to permit the 16th's soldiers to make out the enemy's uniforms. See James V. Murfin, *The Gleam of Bayonets: The Battle of Antietam and the Maryland Campaign* (New York: Yoseloff, 1965), 282; Lt. Col. Joseph B. Curtis's report in *OR* 19(1):456; Relyea, "History of the 16th Connecticut," 27; Robert H. Kellogg to father, September 20, 1862, Robert H. Kellogg Papers, CHS; Robbins, "Recollections," CHS; George Robbins to sister, September 23, 1862, CHS; Stephen W. Sears, *Landscape Turned Red: The Battle of Antietam* (New York: Ticknor & Fields, 1983), 319.

36. Relyea, "History of the 16th Connecticut," 33–34, 43–44, 24.

37. John B. Cuzner to Ellen, September 21, 27, 1862, typescript copies of originals, ANB.

38. John Burnham to "My Dear Mother and Family," October 4, 1862, copy of original, ANB.

39. Ibid. William Relyea also spoke of the mortification he and other men felt when they learned that there would be no chance to redeem themselves on the 18th. See Relyea, "History of the 16th Connecticut," 29.

40. Jacob Bauer to Emily Bauer, September 20, 1862, ANB.

41. Ibid., October 2, 1862, ANB.

42. A. W. Ide, *Sermon Preached Oct. 8, 1862 at Stafford Springs, at the Funeral of Lieut. William Horton, of Co. I, 16th Conn. Regt. Volunteers, Who Was Killed at the Battle of Antietam, Sept. 17, 1862* (Holliston, Mass.: E. G. Plimpton, Printer, 1862), 14–15, 17; Gilbert, *Sermon,* 12, 22.

43. *Hartford Courant* September 12, 18, 22, 23, 1862.

44. Blakeslee, *Sixteenth Connecticut,* 17.

45. Relyea, "History of the 16th Connecticut," 22, 27, 34, 22.

46. Robbins, "Recollections," CHS.

47. Blakeslee, *Sixteenth Connecticut,* 28–30; Croffutt and Morris, *Military and Civil History of Connecticut,* 816; Niven, *Connecticut for the Union,* 186–87.

48. Blakeslee, *Sixteenth Connecticut,* 110; Croffutt and Morris, *Military and Civil History of Connecticut,* 815–16; *Hartford Courant,* June 30, 1865.

49. Blakeslee, *Sixteenth Connecticut,* 115, 108–9; Croffutt and Morris, *Military and Civil History of Connecticut,* 816.

50. Blakeslee, *Sixteenth Connecticut,* 111–14.

51. Robert H. Kellogg to George Q. Whitney, July 24, 1912, George Q. Whitney Collection, RG 69, CHS (italics in original); P. V. Finch, "Prayer," in *Excursion to Antietam,* 45; Nathan Mayer, "Antietam," in *Excursion to Antietam,* 52.

52. Robert H. Kellogg to George Q. Whitney, April 7, 1896, George Q. Whitney Collection, RG 69, CSL; *Hartford Courant,* September 17, 1907; Hartford *Times,* August 29, 1913 (the *Times* quoted verbatim from Bernard Blakeslee's 1889 essay in the *Adjutant-General Record of Service,* 617); undated and unnamed newspaper clipping, Robert H. Kellogg Papers, CHS.

53. Historians have shown increasing interest in the role of memory during the Civil War era. Two recent studies that deal with Union veterans' memories are Earl J. Hess, *The Union Soldier in Battle: Enduring the Ordeal of Combat* (Lawrence: University Press of Kansas, 1997), 158–90, and Stuart McConnell, *Glorious Contentment: The Grand Army of the Republic, 1865–1900* (Chapel Hill: University of North Carolina Press, 1992).

ROBERT E. L. KRICK

Defending Lee's Flank

J. E. B. Stuart, John Pelham, and Confederate

Artillery on Nicodemus Heights

The artillery arm of the Army of Northern Virginia consistently encountered superior weapons and ammunition during the Civil War. In most situations R. E. Lee's cannon crews could hope, at best, to hold their own. From friction primers to horseflesh, in cannon tubes and case shot, southern gunners labored at a disadvantage. They necessarily fought battles of containment.

Second Manassas and Chancellorsville are oft-cited exceptions to that standard story. In those battles, and perhaps at the Crater, Confederate gunners combined favorable terrain, good tactics, and obliging opponents to influence positively the battle and contribute significantly to final victory. Historians long have applauded the work of Confederate cannon at Sharpsburg, too, but only in a vague, anecdotal fashion. John Pelham, J. E. B. Stuart (moonlighting as an artillerist), and "Stonewall" Jackson's artillery in general made invaluable contributions on the northern end of that famous field. Lost amid the welter of publicity concerning Stephen D. Lee's guns and their "artillery hell" is the vital work of Pelham, Stuart, and a collection of minor officers who anchored the army's flank and helped stifle Union advances all day on September 17.

For the purposes of this essay, the northern end of the battlefield is defined as the area north of Stephen D. Lee's guns on the conspicuous ridge in front of the Dunker Church. The story is not as limited as its geographic boundaries might suggest. During the dozen hours in which it was engaged, Confederate artillery in that region substantially changed targets and positions four times. At least ten batteries came under Jackson's aegis, many of them from organizations not normally affiliated with his wing of the army. Improvisation and initiative became Confederate watchwords that day. "Necessity developed a mobility among the light batteries which was surprising," noted the historian of the army's artillery.[1]

That surprise had its roots in the hidebound policies of the artillery through the summer of 1862. Less than three months before Sharpsburg the "long arm" of the Army of Northern Virginia had suffered what would be its worst day of the war. At Malvern Hill on July 1, batteries reached the field sporadically, in disorder and confusion, and most literally were destroyed one section at a time. As each of Jackson's batteries reached its position, "before it could be turned and un-limbered the whole thing would be torn all to pieces. This was given up as a bad job." The inability of most southern artillery even to contribute to the battle allowed Union gunners undisturbed hegemony over the slopes of Malvern Hill. The 5,000 Confederate casualties accumulated that afternoon testified most vividly to the crucial importance of having competitive artillery on the battlefield.[2]

The chaos at Malvern Hill resulted in part from the inferior weight of most Confederate ordnance. Six-pounder smoothbores were obsolete weapons in 1862, yet there were dozens of them in Lee's army. More important, the Confederate practice of attaching batteries to brigades and allowing the infantry commander to wield the cannon as an extension of his force proved ruinous. Not only were most infantry brigadiers ill suited to post cannon, but this system invariably dispersed firepower and allowed the artillery to be overwhelmed individually. Confederate batteries had demonstrated the advantages of massed artillery at First Manassas, and Federal guns reprised the point at Malvern Hill. Even as Lee moved north in August 1862, key artillerists in his army began tinkering with the organization in the hope of avoiding another disaster.

At Second Manassas Lee saw the first fruits of this labor. Massed guns at Groveton on August 30 shredded Federal infantry and simultaneously mustered enough strength to contain Union batteries. The defensive posture adopted by Jackson and Longstreet made the experiment easier, but that circumstance hardly reduces the importance of the event.

Armed with the lessons of Malvern Hill and Second Manassas, the army entered Maryland with most divisions controlling indigenous artillery, supervised by a chief of artillery who served on the division commander's staff. With five or six batteries to a division, generals now had enough firepower to support infantry and could profit from a seasoned artillerist to advise them. This system was not universally implemented at Sharpsburg, and consistency in matters of supply and transportation remained a problem. Even in its imperfect state this revised organization greatly improved the efficiency of Lee's army.[3]

In contrast to their Federal counterparts, typical Confederate batteries were composed of mixed sizes and weights of ordnance. It was not uncommon for a battery to have all four of its cannon of different sizes. Many captains had to deal with the pernicious 6-pounders. Others found themselves saddled with howitzers. John B. Brockenbrough's Maryland battery, which played an important role in the fighting north and west of the Dunker Church, illustrates this observation. Its armament on September 17 apparently consisted of one 3-inch rifle, one 10-pounder Parrott rifle, one 12-pounder Blakely rifle, and one 12-pounder iron howitzer. This arrangement was not unusual for the Confederate artillery of that period. One can imagine the difficulties of supplying or even deploying such a mismatched combination of guns. Its dissimilar composition ensured that the battery could rarely fight together as a unit.[4]

Despite the wretched 6-pounders, the Confederates otherwise were not as outgunned as tradition suggests. More than 40 percent of Lee's pieces were rifled at Sharpsburg, compared with only about 60 percent of McClellan's. The Federals, however, could turn to their reliable Napoleons for midrange work, and many southern batteries could not.[5]

The battalion and battery commanders under Stonewall Jackson have not, on the whole, come down through history as an especially distinguished group of men. Stapleton Crutchfield was the chief of artillery for Jackson's wing of the army. The twenty-seven-year-old Crutchfield was by no means inept, yet an unmistakable air of lassitude surrounds his reports and operations during the war. He missed the battle of Sharpsburg because he was in Harpers Ferry vainly attempting to refit some batteries and forward them to the battlefield.[6]

The next layer of command below Crutchfield consisted of a pair of majors, Alfred R. Courtney and Lindsay M. Shumaker. Both men commanded battalions during the Maryland campaign, but neither ever demonstrated the necessary tools to manage a half dozen batteries simultaneously. In some quarters at least, Shumaker was an unpopular officer. Ned Moore of the Rockbridge Artillery labeled him "officious," "insolent," "ostentatious," and "bombastic," all in the space of a few sentences. Courtney's performance at Sharpsburg was awful, as will be seen subsequently.[7]

The most significant officers in the artillery that morning proved to be the battery commanders. Some of the more prominent were William T. Poague, John B. Brockenbrough, and John C. Carpenter. The reduction of Harpers Ferry and the

Major John Pelham
Jennings C. Wise, *The Long Arm of
Lee*, 2 vols. (Lynchburg, Va.: J. P. Bell,
1915), 2: opposite p. 512

attendant confusion diminished the number of batteries available to Jackson at
Sharpsburg. In addition to companies commanded by the three men listed above,
he marshaled five others from the two battalions. During the course of the morning additional guns were plucked from other commands and hustled to the northern end of the field, giving Jackson some forty guns at the battle's height.

John Pelham, James Breathed, and the Stuart Horse Artillery constituted the
final element of Jackson's artillery collection. They, of course, had no official connection with the infantry's guns, but Sharpsburg was a decidedly noncavalry
battle. In the absence of Jackson's usual artillery subordinates, the twenty-four-
year-old Major Pelham assumed Crutchfield's responsibilities and tactical control
of Jackson's cannon. Pelham's boyish looks and delicate features had earned him
the nickname "Sally" in school, but a genius for battle displayed during the Seven
Days (particularly at Gaines's Mill) quickly established his martial credentials.
Command of Pelham's horse artillery thus fell to Jim Breathed, destined to become one of the army's hardest-fighting young officers. He had been born in
Maryland in 1838, so Sharpsburg was on his native soil. These were the men, together with Jackson's own captains, who were to anchor the left flank of Lee's
army and play such a sizable role in his successful defense. Three of the five primary Union attacks of the battle came directly at or past their few dozen cannon.[8]

The distinctive terrain on Jackson's front was a vital factor in the triumphs of his artillery. Across Antietam Creek to the east, McClellan's long-range rifled cannon swept the battlefield from atop the Porterstown Ridge. Not only did that commanding position dominate most of the battlefield, but few (if any) Confederate cannon had the range and location to reply. West of Antietam Creek the ground gradually ascended to the ridge along which the Hagerstown Turnpike ran. From the vicinity of the famed Dunker Church all the way to the far south end of the battlefield, Confederate artillery occupied positions either on or east of the turnpike's ridge. In every case they were within comfortable range of the big guns on the Porterstown Ridge.

Only one acceptable artillery position existed on the upper end of the Confederate line, and it proved to be essential to Jackson's defense. West of the turnpike and running parallel to it was yet another spiny ridge. From its considerable height Confederate artillerists had easy angles of fire into the North Woods, the East Woods, the Miller Cornfield, and the West Woods. The most substantial section of the ridge loomed directly west of the Cornfield and was known as Nicodemus Heights. The Nicodemus house stood at its base. A long, low depression running between the ridge and the turnpike made the position deceptive, obscuring the fact that the top of Nicodemus Heights was the same elevation as the center of the Cornfield. The high ground continued south for several hundred yards until bisected by an east–west ravine. The ground then rose again immediately to the south, the ensuing hill being named Hauser's Ridge after the farmhouse at the foot of its eastern slope. Hauser's Ridge was only ten feet lower in elevation than Nicodemus Heights. Occasional knobs provided ideal artillery positions on both ridges.

These were the only spots on the battlefield entirely immune to the plunging fire of the Federal guns on Porterstown Ridge some two and one-half miles away. Nowhere else could the Confederates realistically hope to achieve tactical control of the field with their artillery. The crucial importance of the ground became evident when Union attacks began on the morning of September 17.[9]

By the time Joseph Hooker's First Corps crossed Antietam Creek and began skirmishing with Confederate infantry in the twilight of September 16, a battery or two of Confederate artillery already occupied Nicodemus Heights. Their presence seems to have had little impact on Hooker's men, and even less on Hooker's appreciation of the situation. The tiny infantry divisions making up Stonewall Jackson's wing of the army could stretch no farther than the northern end of the West Woods, leaving the critical high ground lightly defended. There is no evident explanation why Hooker did not take the elevation above the Nicodemus house that evening or the next morning, apart from the disorientation normally

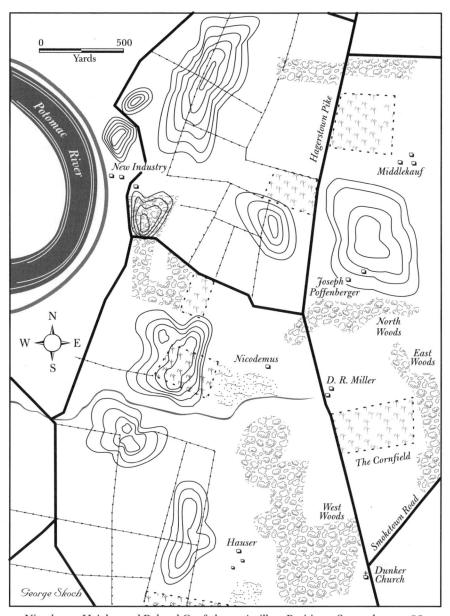

0   500
Yards

Potomac River

New Industry

Hagerstown Pike

Middlekauf

Joseph Poffenberger

North Woods

N
W   E
S

Nicodemus

East Woods

D. R. Miller

The Cornfield

West Woods

Hauser

Smoketown Road

Dunker Church

George Skoch

Nicodemus Heights and Related Confederate Artillery Positions, September 17, 1862 felt by commanders when they encounter new terrain. Hooker later toyed with the truth by officially reporting that Jackson had only moved into position overnight on the 16th and had "at the same time . . . planted field batteries on high ground on our right and rear." Even if this had been true, it was no excuse for not occupying ground that offered a front-row view of his flank.[10]

Nicodemus Heights held wonderful potential as an offensive location for the Confederates. Perceiving that dawn of the 17th would bring battle, Jackson demonstrated that he clearly recognized the importance of the high ground, especially as protection for his (and the army's) vulnerable northern flank. A brigade of J. E. B. Stuart's cavalry had been assigned responsibility for that area on the 16th, and sometime that day Jackson apparently gave Stuart complete control of the area for the next morning's battle. The cavalryman spent the afternoon posting batteries and "riding about the field in every direction." He stopped at his headquarters at the Grove house after dark, and then only briefly, before returning to the ground around the West Woods in the middle of the night.[11]

Despite Stuart's presence, Confederate artillery preparation for the next morning's battle appears to have been haphazard. Some of Jackson's batteries straggled into the West Woods on the 16th and camped wherever it suited them. "Old Jack" himself found the Louisiana Guard Artillery in the middle of the West Woods shortly after midnight and ordered it out, saying it was no place for artillery. After sorting out the situation there, Jackson rode back to Stuart's headquarters at the Grove house and spent the few hours before dawn slumbering on a couch. Perhaps Jackson and Stuart took turns supervising the deployment of troops north of Sharpsburg. At least one of them seems to have been on the ground at all times on the night of the 16th.[12]

John Pelham's Stuart Horse Artillery bedded down on the reverse slope of Nicodemus Heights, not far from Fitzhugh Lee's cavalry brigade. Pelham was with the battery that night and was, as events showed, badly informed on Hooker's dispositions. Robert M. Mackall of the battery recalled being awakened in the middle of the night "by the tramp of a horse near my head." Mackall angrily asked the horseman what business he had riding through sleeping men and found that it was General Stuart, looking for Pelham. Finding the major asleep alongside a post-and-rail fence, Stuart woke him. Mackall overheard Stuart say in his customary bantering tone: "My dear fellow, don't you know that the corn field at the foot of the hill is full of Yankees? and that you ought to have your guns in position now, for if you wait until daylight the hill will be swarming with blue coats." A chastened Pelham roused his company, and together they pushed the battery's guns to "the *highest* point" of Nicodemus Heights before dawn. Stuart condensed

Major General James E. B. Stuart leading his troopers in the field, sketched at about
the time of the Antietam campaign by British artist Frank Vizetelly.
Illustrated London News, November 4, 1862

his night's work into a succinct sentence: "I . . . crowned a commanding hill with
artillery, ready for the attack in the morning."[13]

Across the fields to the northeast less than a mile distant, Joe Hooker's artillery
spent the night parked on the Joseph Poffenberger farm, north of the North
Woods. The ten batteries attached to his corps were about evenly mixed between

Napoleons and ordnance rifles. They were unaware of Confederate artillery preparation that night, and if any of the battery officers had recognized the value of Nicodemus Heights in the gloaming the evening before, they kept their discovery to themselves. Pickets from the 10th Pennsylvania Reserves advanced as far as the eastern base of Nicodemus Heights, pushing up the lane to the house. The Nicodemus family prudently abandoned their farm that night, and the 10th "received this family within our lines." Apparently nobody reported the Confederate artillery only a few yards away on top of the hill.[14]

Earliest light revealed several Confederate batteries already in position atop the various knobs of Nicodemus Heights, all supervised by John Pelham. This force certainly included Pelham's own Stuart Horse Artillery (Va.) and three guns of the Staunton (Va.) Artillery. The Alleghany (Va.) Artillery and the Danville (Va.) Artillery probably unlimbered nearby, giving the force a respectable total of about fifteen guns. All but the Stuart Horse Artillery had been guided to Nicodemus Heights by Stuart's couriers in the predawn hours. The Staunton company found itself short handed from an imperative summons: "It being still dark many of the men were not found and were left lying in the woods still asleep." The remaining men dragged their guns into position at "barely sunrise." The familiar sight of John Pelham on the hill cheered them. He had drilled the battery at Harpers Ferry in 1861. "I think my battery opened the fight," wrote Lt. Asher W. Garber after the war. "I didn't hear any other guns before I opened."[15]

When the morning mist and half-light dissolved, it brought into focus an attractive target. Half a mile distant Hooker's corps dozed unaware. W. H. Humphrey of the Second U.S. Sharpshooters realized the danger when he heard a bugle sound from the opposite heights, followed shortly by the sight of a "rebel battery then in the act of unlimbering." Rhode Island artillerist George Sumner "awoke with a start" just about daylight when the first shell whirled past overhead, ringing in the most violent day in American history. One of the first shots cut the throats of two horses in Frederick M. Edgell's New Hampshire Battery, "struck the ground bounded over our heads [and] then there was lively work falling in." It took some time for Sumner and his drowsy comrades to awaken fully. When they had "recovered from their astonishment," they rushed to their own pieces, faced to the southwest, and established a modest counter–battery fire. Some of the Federal brigades found themselves trapped between the dueling guns and hugged the ground for protection from both. Pelham continued to deliver "a stream of shells" toward Hooker's guns.[16]

The little cornfield and pasture occupied by Pelham's men offered scant cover, and its elevation actually was lower than the ridge where Hooker's artillery sat. The only advantage to the Nicodemus Heights position during the dawn fight was its sharply defined, irregular profile. Federal artillerists had to make a perfect shot to achieve results, while even the most careless gunnery by Pelham's men likely would hit something in Hooker's densely packed campsites.

Capt. J. Albert Monroe of Abner Doubleday's division countered the "exceedingly brisk" Confederate fire with his own batteries. An occasional shot took effect from Monroe's Napoleons. Invisible at the western base of Nicodemus Heights, Fitzhugh Lee's cavalry brigade nominally guarded the army's northern flank. Federal shells that overshot Pelham's position began to drop among the cavalrymen. One of the very first to reach the horsemen "at early dawn" hit a woodpile and exploded with great force beside a cluster of officers. Dirt showered George W. Beale of the 9th Virginia Cavalry and fatally wounded Lt. Col. John T. "Jack" Thornton of the 3rd Virginia Cavalry. "One fragment tore his saddle to pieces, inflicting an irreparable shock on his body," reported his eulogist, "while another crushed his arm almost from the hand to the shoulder." A hasty amputation failed to resuscitate Thornton, who died that evening. The same shell wounded one other man in the regiment. There were no further losses in the 3rd Virginia Cavalry the entire day, although some of the other cavalry regiments incurred sparse casualties under similar circumstances. More than two and a half years later R. E. Lee, ever solicitous of his soldiers' families, interrupted the agony of his final week as army commander to visit Thornton's widow in Farmville on April 7, 1865.[17]

John Pelham managed his guns on the hill above the Nicodemus house with a free hand granted him by General Stuart. Although most of the guns belonged to Jackson, there is no evidence that the infantry general ever visited Nicodemus Heights during the battle. Such inattention to detail was in contrast to Stonewall's customary intrusive tactical management on most battlefields. Its genesis lay in the surprisingly close relationship between the no-nonsense Jackson and his ebullient friend Stuart. It is certain Jackson had weighty concerns of his own; knowing control of the artillery rested in the hands of someone he trusted must have been a relief. The fight for the army's northern flank would be Stuart's.

While the opposing cannon traded rounds in the vague light of early morning, Joe Hooker formed his troops for the main movement. His two-division front would advance mostly southward, toward the West Woods, Dunker Church, and Mumma house. There were several apparent problems affecting Hooker's route, including the good cover enjoyed by Jackson's infantry and the converging defensive fire it would bring to bear. Hooker could rely on the heavy guns east of Antietam Creek as a palliative. In theory they would suppress most of the Confederate batteries and considerably ease the burdens of the Federal First Corps. But the big guns held no sway over Nicodemus Heights. Pelham's tenacity in adhering to that ridge despite counter–battery fire from the nest of Federal guns at Joseph Poffenberger's began to pay off. Hooker soon diverted more of his batteries to provide close tactical support for the advancing foot soldiers, leaving Pelham with virtually uncontested access to Hooker's flank. Oft-quoted artillerist E. Porter Alexander once termed a situation of this sort, when gunners could fire at will into defenseless, tightly packed infantry, as "pie." "One has usually had to pay for this pie before he gets it," remarked Alexander, "so he has no compunctions of conscience or chivalry." When Hooker attacked down his narrow chute toward the Dunker Church, he left his western flank entirely exposed and created one of those rare "pie" moments for John Pelham's artillery.[18]

Having already perfected their distances, the Confederate cannoneers at once began to irritate and damage the infantry forming around the North Woods. Lt. Col. Edward S. Bragg's 6th Wisconsin Infantry was hit hard: "No sooner was the column in motion than the enemy opened fire on us with artillery, and so accurate was his range that the second shell exploded in the ranks, disabling 13 men." Maj. Rufus R. Dawes of the same unit thought it was the third round that did the damage, but he agreed on the casualty figure. The well-aimed percussion shell had struck one of Alfred Poffenberger's threshing machines. Flying shards of farm equipment dismembered at least two unfortunate men. This regiment was of Doubleday's division. Off to its left men from other divisions absorbed similar punishment. The 9th Pennsylvania Reserves emerged from the North Woods but hastily stepped back into the trees "owing to the enemy's battery on the right having obtained our range." The 12th Massachusetts Infantry suffered from "that dreadful battery on our right," whose shells continually were "ploughing through our ranks."[19]

The shelter of the North Woods proved illusory. Pelham's explosives followed the Unionists into the trees. Solid shot dropped among the infantry, "cutting off limbs which fell about us." The searching shells even reached as far as Col. William A. Christian's brigade. As the 88th Pennsylvania sorted itself into formation for the advance, Confederate missiles were "shrieking and flying all around, striking the ground in a wicked manner and throwing up the dirt and dust in great clouds as high as the trees." The 88th suffered "a number" of killed and wounded while forming up, and the "hideous noise made by these projectiles as they screamed through the air" had a sobering effect on the men. It looked to John Vautier as if "all the devils infernal had been incarnated and assembled on this horrible field." The vigorous shelling induced brigade commander Christian to flee the field in terror. Credit for part of this impressive display may belong to other Confederate guns farther south, but some of the iron came from Nicodemus Heights.[20]

Not every Federal regiment had to endure the bombardment. Because of anomalies in the terrain and other considerations, some units entered the infantry fighting untouched. Isaac Hall of the 97th New York testified later that he did "not think a man in Duryea's brigade on that day, was hurt by a cannon shot."[21]

To solve this problem, Hooker's men needed to advance quickly southward, closing the gap between themselves and the southern infantry. The nearer they drew to the West Woods, the narrower Pelham's target became. But to reach that acute angle the First Corps had to traverse the deadly Cornfield, exposing itself to a textbook example of enfilade fire. Pelham's hilltop perch atop Nicodemus Heights was exactly opposite the Cornfield and enjoyed an unobstructed view of Hooker's vulnerable flank.

Hooker, Monroe, and other Federal decision makers had too many options for their own artillery. Confederate targets in three different directions all demanded attention. Pelham's batteries visibly threatened the flank, but Stephen D. Lee's battalion was perfectly situated to blast Hooker's infantry as it advanced head-on, and suppressing Stonewall Jackson's infantry in between required a steady dose of shells. Hooker could not pull together enough guns to meet his obligations. For once the artillery-rich Army of the Potomac found itself short at a crucial point.

The singular opportunity enjoyed by Pelham from Nicodemus Heights, marvelous as it was, did not blind J. E. B. Stuart to the burgeoning danger on that wing. It became apparent that once Abner Doubleday's division reached the latitude of the Cornfield, his infantry would be close enough to molest the Confederate artillery with small-arms fire. To discourage that development, Stonewall Jackson pulled Gen. Jubal A. Early's Virginia brigade from behind the West Woods and dispatched it to Stuart. Early chose an extended route that protected him from hostile fire until he reached the southwest base of Nicodemus Heights. His brigade loitered there in case Federal infantry drew too close, but they apparently had little to do during the earliest action.[22]

A bold battery on the southern end of Pelham's artillery line especially pestered the Federal infantry. Its presence triggered a series of inefficient orders not untypical on Civil War battlefields. Brigade commander Marsena Patrick had discovered the pesky artillery and reported its presence to Joe Hooker, who in turn ordered Abner Doubleday to deal with it. Doubleday predictably turned to General Patrick, who of course knew all about it, and ordered him to divert a regiment westward to keep an eye on the guns. A densely layered command structure seems to have choked some First Corps operations that morning. Patrick chose the 23rd New York to "watch and check the movement" of the troublesome battery.[23]

The confusion did not end with Patrick's order. The 23rd had scarcely taken its watchdog position north of the West Woods before the 10th Pennsylvania Reserves arrived as relief from a different division altogether. That regiment had been preparing to advance into the fray when one of Hooker's staff officers raced up to Lt. Col. A. J. Warner of the 10th "and said Gen. Hooker had received information that the Enemy was trying to reach our right flank"—ignoring the fact that Pelham had been there all along. The Pennsylvanians were hauled out of the column and ordered to move "at once, double quick, to our right and front, and find out what the Enemy was doing . . . and to protect our flank." Crossing the Hagerstown Pike a few yards north of David Miller's farmhouse, Warner soon spotted the offending guns less than five hundred yards distant, "firing heavily into the exposed flank of Hooker's corps." Relieving the 23rd New York, Warner took vigorous action to seal that flank. Deploying sharpshooters in the brushy fields southwest of the Nicodemus house, the regiment soon began "picking off cannoneers." [24]

At this stage of the fight Stuart's grip on the northern flank began to weaken. By all accounts the remaining Union batteries on Joseph Poffenberger's farm zeroed in on the crest of Nicodemus Heights, forcing Pelham to concentrate more on counter–battery fire and somewhat less on aiding Jackson's hard-pressed troops. Federal guns "poured" shells into the Staunton Artillery from both front and flank. Empty limber chests caused a few guns to abandon the field. Others jumped from position to position to avoid the Federal fire. Some of the guns repeatedly rolled down behind the protection of the ridge, only to be pushed back up to fire a few more shells into the infantry before sliding back for shelter.[25]

For the first time enemy infantry occupied positions within rifle range. Jackson's brigades in the West Woods began to waver. Worst of all, the Federal advance had sliced so deeply into the Confederate defense that the angle of fire for Pelham's guns became unsafe. Any round not taking effect among Hooker's masses certainly would endanger Confederate infantry in the Cornfield, in the pasture to its south, or among Stephen D. Lee's artillery battalion opposite the Dunker Church. Eventually Pelham's gunners could not even identify Jackson's line in the smoky distance and ran the risk of causing needless casualties with every round. These disadvantages accumulated during the first ninety minutes of the fight and finally forced Stuart to abandon Nicodemus Heights. Major Pelham passed the word to break off the engagement. His batteries left behind dead horses, splintered carriages, and shattered equipment.[26]

Hauser's Ridge offered the next logical position for Stuart's artillery. From there the guns would be well sited to play upon the enemy with, in Stuart's words, "still more terrible effect than before." With customary promptness, Stuart had Pelham reconcentrate the guns along the various knobs behind the Hauser house.

The batteries no longer had an unrestricted view of the Miller Cornfield, it was true, but under the circumstances Hauser's Ridge enjoyed at least four critical advantages over Nicodemus Heights.

The new position lay almost entirely out of range for the Federal batteries. Even their far-reaching rifled pieces at Poffenberger's could not search out this new collection of Confederate ordnance except on the far northern shoulder of the ridge. If the situation continued to deteriorate, Hauser's Ridge also stood much closer to the escape route toward the Potomac River, offering better hope for saving Jackson's guns in a catastrophe. Third, the artillerists had a shorter trip to the rear to refill depleted limber chests. Nearly every battery had to make that trip at least once during the day, often at crucial times. The greatest benefit of Hauser's Ridge was that it made an admirable backstop to Jackson's increasingly concave line. The more Stonewall's infantry line bulged inward, the closer it came to the base of Hauser's Ridge. Every backward step by that infantry improved the field of fire from Stuart's new position. William Allan cogently argued in his classic history of the army in 1862 that Hauser's Ridge was "the key to the whole of Jackson's position," because of its sweeping command of everything west of the turnpike. "Its retention," Allan maintained, "was vital to the Confederates."[27]

Stuart's switch to Hauser's Ridge seems to have occurred sometime just before or during the attack of the Union Twelfth Corps. The role of the cannon in the repulse of that corps has been exaggerated by scholars over the years. Jennings C. Wise's *The Long Arm of Lee* is the standard handbook for students of Confederate artillery in the East. He credits the Stuart/Pelham cluster of guns on Hauser's Ridge with enjoying almost complete dominance over the northern end of the battlefield in general, and over the Twelfth Corps in particular. "No troops, however brave, could cross the space which Pelham's group so perfectly commanded," wrote Wise. Well-known 1940s historian Joseph Mills Hanson echoed Wise's interpretation, writing that Pelham's guns "swept the entire terrain over which Mansfield's attack would have to pass."[28]

This was a geographic impossibility east of the turnpike. The imposing density of the West Woods stood squarely between Hauser's Ridge and most of the Twelfth Corps. Even stipulating that Pelham's gunners could see all of Mansfield's men, which is doubtful, geometry would have interfered. Pelham had to avoid hitting Jackson's men while lobbing his shells over the West Woods and landing them on a narrow target. It is true that the northwesternmost units in Mansfield's corps took an occasional shell from Pelham's direction, but only at the beginning of their advance above the Cornfield. John M. Gould, a soldier with the 10th Maine of Samuel W. Crawford's brigade in the East Woods, devoted countless hours after the war to studying the battle and corresponding with other

Brigadier General Jubal A. Early, whose infantry supported Confederate horse artillery on September 17. Robert Underwood Johnson and Clarence Clough Buel, eds., *Battles and Leaders of the Civil War*, 4 vols. (New York: Century, 1887–88), 4:529

veterans. His regimental history asserts that "three-quarters of us are ready to testify . . . we were not under artillery fire at all till the very last part of our engagement." Firsthand sources from George S. Greene's Twelfth Corps division also are uniformly silent about artillery fire from the west. It is quite plain that whatever shelling Mansfield's soldiers encountered from their right that morning—if any at all—had little effect on the course of their advance.[29]

The scene on Hauser's Ridge at this point must have been chaotic. Some of the batteries from the army's artillery reserve began arriving from south of Sharpsburg. Other divisions contributed a few pieces to the collection, joining the remnants of the batteries from Jackson's two divisions. This force, assembled under the exigencies of the moment, defies organizational labeling. At least J. E. B. Stuart and John Pelham were there to provide tactical leadership and to assume responsibility for movements. Some of the new cannon came from John B. Brockenbrough's Baltimore Artillery, which had seen action already between the West Woods and the turnpike. Col. Stapleton Crutchfield thought well of that battery, calling it "one of our best companies." Its four guns anchored the northern flank of Hauser's Ridge and joined the four guns of the Lee Battery (Va.) to the south. Parts of the Rockbridge (Va.) Artillery and Louisiana Guard Artillery also were posted on the ridge somewhere.[30]

A desperate situation confronted the infantry in front of Hauser's Ridge. Jackson's division, commanded that morning by John R. Jones, was greatly attenuated even before the fight commenced. Jones claimed after the war that "[t]he whole division was a mere skeleton—about 2300 men to go into action." That puny figure had been pruned drastically during the action in the West Woods. Jones disappeared early in the fight, as was his custom. His replacement, William E. Starke, was killed west of the turnpike shortly afterward. That left Mexican War veteran Col. Andrew J. Grigsby commanding remnants that could not have numbered much more than a few hundred dispirited men. Capt. Robert W. Withers, the senior officer in one of Grigsby's brigades by that time, painted a bleak picture of his men's condition, reporting that they were "broken down from loss of sleep and forced marching" and out of ammunition. Withers's weary troops "paid but little attention to details, and cared but little whether we lived or died."[31]

Most of Jubal Early's brigade stood in front of Hauser's Ridge near Grigsby. When Stuart ordered the abandonment of Nicodemus Heights, Early had taken six of his seven regiments to the West Woods line and left them there while he assumed command of a division in lieu of the wounded Alexander R. Lawton. Early consented to leave one regiment to protect the guns at Hauser's Ridge. That unit was the 13th Virginia Infantry, numbering fewer than one hundred men itself.[32]

The vulnerability of Jackson's punched-in line at that time would be hard to exaggerate. Grigsby's handful of men occupied the Alfred Poffenberger buildings just west of the West Woods, with the artillery on the hill behind them. Nothing more stood between the Union infantry and the rear of Lee's army. When John Sedgwick's division of the Union Second Corps pushed into the West Woods in a decisive midmorning probe, Pelham's guns were well placed to offer their most important contribution of the day.

General Stuart did several things in preparation for Sedgwick's attack. Seeing the inevitability of close-quarters work, Stuart anxiously assembled whatever short-range guns he could find. The entire Louisiana Guard Artillery was engaged in resupplying itself when "we were called upon by Genl J. E. B. Stuart for a howitzer which was at once rushed forward." His sphere of influence extended beyond just Hauser's Ridge. When the batteries of Lafayette McLaws's division approached the field in advance of their infantry, Stuart collared the Troup (Ga.) Artillery and posted its three cannon in the yard of the Dunker Church, despite McLaws's protests. In the process Stuart's horse was shot, one of his couriers was killed, and eighteen of the battery's horses were destroyed. Union artillery soon knocked out all three guns after they had combined to fire only 109 rounds.[33]

Stuart brought one other influence to the fight against the Second Corps: the force of his personality. As the situation grew more perilous the general appeared with increasing frequency among the men. Heros von Borcke and William W. Blackford, both of Stuart's staff, testified to his activity. "I was in constant anxiety for the life of my general, who was always where the carnage was greatest," wrote von Borcke. Blackford agreed: "He was constantly riding over the field watching the progress of the action." One of the general's couriers remembered that Stuart "reviewed the whole Sharpsburg battle ground under Yankee fire" on the morning of the 17th. Richard Channing Price, also of Stuart's staff, spent the day looking for his general, but "so rapid & vague are his movements" that Price could not find him "until late in the day." The worn-out men of the Louisiana Guard Artillery were cheered by Stuart's presence during a hot point of the fight; so, too, were the handful of men left to work the guns of the Staunton Artillery. The courier killed at Stuart's side at the Dunker Church was only one of two such fatalities that morning. H. B. McClellan reported aptly that Stuart was "ceaselessly active."[34]

The guns Stuart arranged spent only a few minutes face to face with Sedgwick's three brigades, yet that quarter hour, seen in retrospect, looms largest on the list of Stuart's feats that day. Pushing through the West Woods, Sedgwick's Federals reached the tree line looking out on the Poffenberger farm. In the middle distance they could see Hauser's Ridge. Soon they felt the lash of the guns atop it. The poor alignment of Sedgwick's division put Willis A. Gorman's brigade alone in front, where it bore the brunt of the fire from both artillery and infantry. At least one section of Confederate guns managed to find a position in front of Hauser's Ridge near its northern end. That section enjoyed an oblique fire on the West Woods and greatly annoyed Gorman's regiments. The 15th Massachusetts suffered in particular. Like most soldiers, Roland Bowen of that regiment felt as though the section was firing directly at his company. He dutifully discharged his rifle at Grigsby's men in front but continued "keeping my eye on them guns so as to *drop*" when they fired. Lt. Col. John W. Kimball of the 15th estimated the distance to the guns at six hundred yards, but that almost certainly is too far, especially since he claimed to have driven the guns off on two separate occasions with rifle fire. The 1st Minnesota and 82nd New York complained about the cannon fire as well. General Gorman lamented his brigade's losses from a "most terrific fire of grape and canister."[35]

Sorting out which Confederate batteries occupied each wrinkle of Hauser's Ridge—and with how many cannon—is impossible. Renowned 1890s historian Ezra Carman is a nearly irrefutable source on troop placements. His excellent maps locate twenty-four Confederate cannon engaged west of the turnpike during Sedgwick's adventure in the West Woods. Those guns are shown at seven distinct locations. Insufficient evidence exists to contest any of Carman's conclusions, but he seems to have been very conservative in interpreting primary evidence, and there may well have been parts of several other batteries engaged in Sedgwick's defeat. The Alleghany Artillery, for instance, assisted in repulsing

Union infantry that had advanced "within a stone's throw" sometime during the day. Only at Hauser's Ridge did Federals get that close, leading to the deduction that the Alleghany Artillery was somewhere on the northern end of that ridge during the crisis. Thomas A. Graham of Ross's Georgia battery wrote that two guns from that unit "received an order from Gen. Stewart to move . . . to his assistance on our left." H. M. Ross of that battery confirmed fighting "on our left" and serving "with Gen. J. E. B. Stewart's command through out the day." Confronted with such vague information, and unable to identify their positions more accurately, Carman chose to leave Ross's battery and the Alleghany Artillery off the Hauser's Ridge maps entirely. So the conglomeration of Confederate guns on and around that crucial hill may have been even larger than anyone has thought.[36]

The fight against Sedgwick was not as one sided as had been the earlier action against Hooker. Gorman's brigade and other scattered units could bring small-arms fire to bear on nearly every Confederate battery. While the Louisiana Guard Artillery peppered Sedgwick's men with canister, sharpshooters posted in the scattered trees between the Nicodemus and Hauser farms "gave us a good deal of worry." Stuart watched the Louisianians toil at their guns for a time, as did Stonewall Jackson himself. "This was a very hot place and kept the men at the Battery, hard at work," reminisced John T. Block. Edwin Marks of the same battery also remembered seeing Stuart and Jackson with the guns and agreed that "it required active work of all engaged to repel" Union infantry working around the flank of Hauser's Ridge. "The Confederate line was thin at that point," explained Marks.[37]

The tiny 13th Virginia Infantry was thin, too, but under Stuart's guidance it made the most of its position in the low ground under Hauser's Ridge. Sam Buck relished his regiment's success "as foot cavalry." At one point the men even assumed the role of horses, helping John Pelham drag two guns of the Stuart Horse Artillery up a steep hill. "The horses could not pull them over the plowed fields and up the hill so every fellow . . . took hold and almost carried both pieces into position." The guns roared into action against Sedgwick's flank, "aiming and firing each piece as fast as the men could load," while the 13th kept up a steady fire with its muskets. Each sortie from the wood line earned the Federals double charges of canister.[38]

Elsewhere on the ridge the Alleghany Artillery and the Staunton Artillery approached the end of their effectiveness. The latter battery had been engaged intermittently since dawn and had so few men on hand that its officers and Pelham himself were serving the guns. "The men had almost given out by hard and double work and [were] almost on verge of giving away," recalled cannoneer John W. Bryan, "when Gen. J. E. B. Stuart rode up to us and with his hat in his hand and in his pleasant way said: 'Boys hold them down for one hour longer and the day will be ours.'" Not far distant the Alleghany Artillery had only two pieces still in action by then. It was one of the few batteries within reach of Hooker's rifled artillery. Once the Virginians unlimbered, a terrific salvo of shells landed among the guns. "We were almost completely demolished," wrote C. A. Fonerden. Capt. John C. Carpenter, commander of the battery, fell with a badly mangled leg. The carnage was so great that General Stuart rode over and gave orders "to abandon our guns and horses and secret[e] ourselves as best we might." Eventually enough men rallied to drag the guns away under Stuart's supervision. "I saw more men torn to pieces by shells in that battle than any other during the war," testified Sam Buck.[39]

Farther south two guns of the Baltimore Artillery and two from the Lee Battery, all rifled pieces less desirable for short-range work, nonetheless managed to participate in the repulse by throwing canister into the tree line at a range of only three hundred yards. They had been moving southward toward the threatened Confederate center when someone saw a Union flag emerge from the smoky shadow that marked the edge of the West Woods. Once convinced of the legitimacy of the threat, "Beau" Brockenbrough swung into line on the first hillock northwest of the Hauser home. General McLaws, riding in advance of his arriving infantry, ascended the hill and urged Brockenbrough to maintain the steady stream of fire and keep Sedgwick at bay. McLaws's infantry arrived in fifteen minutes.[40]

The Stuart Horse Artillery had been heading to the rear for more shells when it encountered its efficient ordnance sergeant driving up with a wagon full of fresh ammunition. The battery hastily renewed its limber chests and swung into line to fire off its second or third supply of shells. Two guns from the First Company of the splendid Richmond Howitzers also arrived in season to help push back Sedgwick.[41]

From these many examples one theme emerges. J. E. B. Stuart and numerous junior artillery officers were able to patch together an inelegant yet effective line of cannon. Once established, those guns erected a seamless wall of canister that fixed Sedgwick in position long enough for McLaws's division to strike the dangling Yankee flank. Favorable terrain and questionable Federal tactics abetted the Confederates. Most of all the spirit of improvisation, cultivated in the course of Stuart's many cavalry adventures, proved decisive on this day. The drubbing of Sedgwick's division opened new offensive possibilities for the tireless Stuart. He watched as fragments of Union regiments backed out of the West Woods and made for whatever shelter looked most promising. This provided an opportunity for the artillery to pepper Federal flanks yet again. Most batteries then at hand were short of horses. Stuart pulled together what few mobile guns he could find, summoned Fitzhugh Lee's nearby brigade of cavalry, collared a stray North Carolina regiment from John G. Walker's division, and moved his entourage northward. The guns unlimbered every few minutes and "kept up an advancing fire" directed toward the Cornfield and the general area of Sedgwick's retreat.[42]

The worn-out Rockbridge Artillery detached only one gun for the chase. Ned Moore served with that gun and was sorry he did. His piece kept moving north- ward, "at each point receiving a most terrific artillery fire from the enemy," now densely massed at Joseph Poffenberger's. Moore's crew stopped at three or four different positions before eventually reaching Nicodemus Heights. The Federals obviously already had that spot registered, "as there were several cannon wheels lying on the ground" surrounded by "the dead horses and the wrecks of guns and caissons of the batteries which had preceded us." As soon as the Rockbridge boys unlimbered on the ridge, they "were enveloped in the smoke and dust of bursting shells, and the air was alive with flying iron." Stuart participated per- sonally in this fight, as he had all morning. Marshaling a gang of stragglers, he protected the sidestepping artillery by establishing a screen at the base of the hill. Stuart "rode to & fro," making himself conspicuous, his black plume swaying across the pastures and fields. Ned Moore even claimed that Stuart rode the field "cheering and singing" as he commanded the skirmish line.[43]

The little expedition finally ran afoul of Union general O. O. Howard, who had posted the remnants of Sedgwick's division above the North Woods near the First Corps artillery "with instructions to hold this point at all hazards." "An occa- sional attempt of the enemy to locate a battery on a high point beyond the turn- pike" annoyed Howard, but four batteries from the First Corps soon silenced the irritating Confederate cannon.[44]

Stuart's leap-frogging pursuit was more than just an egotistical stunt. It achieved one highly important objective: the repossession of Nicodemus Heights. The battle had waned north of Sharpsburg by then, but flank protection remained imperative. The chances of McClellan's breaking loose from a lifetime of passive tactical habits admittedly were slim. Still, the gap between Lee's northern flank and the Potomac River had to be monitored, and Nicodemus Heights afforded the best place from which to do that.

Stonewall Jackson immediately realized the renewed offensive possibilities of the heights. He sent General McLaws with General Stuart to scout the ground beyond the Nicodemus farm in search of a gap in McClellan's defenses. The two generals were peering at Federal arrangements through field glasses "when a bat- tery of eight guns . . . fired all their pieces at us at the same time." The volley ob- viously missed, McLaws reported, but "we did not wait for a repetition." Jackson promised nonetheless to send "all the infantry he could get" to probe the Union position. The crises below Sharpsburg stalled those ambitions, and Nicodemus Heights again fell silent.[45]

The final episode above the West Woods came late in the day, around 5:00 P.M. Its genesis was the incredible, almost reflexive, audacity of Robert E. Lee. The army commander had just fought McClellan to a draw in a battle that most historians now think he should have avoided. Severe casualties and urgent shortages in ammunition and supplies only made the army's position more vulnerable and ought to have prompted Lee's retreat. Instead he issued remarkable orders to launch another reconnaissance that would develop McClellan's northern flank in the hope of finding a weak point.[46]

John Pelham was to pull together what guns he could discover that still had the requisite combination of manpower, ammunition, and mobility. He found eight cannon for his expedition, all of them rifled pieces. One gun came from the Rockbridge Artillery; two were from the Lee Battery; two more from Brockenbrough's Baltimore Artillery; and apparently three from William H. Turner's battery (Va.). Turner's guns were part of Hilary P. Jones's Reserve Battalion, a collection of four batteries whose role at Sharpsburg remains largely unknown.[47]

Fitzhugh Lee's cavalry brigade joined the little party as it moved circuitously to a high point opposite "what seemed to be the extreme right of the Federal line." Most likely the Confederates occupied Nicodemus Heights for the third time that day. Captain Poague and the other officers accompanying the eight guns disliked the foray: "We artillery captains didn't know the object of the movement, and were disposed to criticize Pelham for turning us loose within 500 yards upon an immense battery." The other officers "thought Pelham had gotten permission to look up a fight and were down on him for what we regarded as a most indiscreet proceeding." Pelham's unflagging exuberance nettled them still more; in response to a complaint he laughingly said, "Oh, we must stir them up a little and then slip away." "And so we did stir them up," reported Poague, "and with a vengeance they soon stirred us out."[48]

Across the way on the plateau behind Joseph Poffenberger's farmhouse, alert Union artillerists watched as laboring horses again dragged Confederate guns over the crest of Nicodemus Heights "and rapidly making the left about, drop[ped] their pieces into battery." An injudicious sortie of this nature was exactly what the vengeful First Corps artillerists had been hoping for all afternoon. Before Pelham could fire a round, "twenty-nine projectiles of various kinds and sizes were flying towards that unfortunate battery." Rufus Dawes and his 6th Wisconsin watched from nearby and "lay as closely as possible to the ground." Dawes admitted that Pelham's men fought back gamely in this "Titanic combat."[49]

The Confederates could not endure the pounding for long. In the Lee Battery it seemed that "almost every second a bomb would burst over our heads and among us." The enemy fired "very furiously," and the officers commanding the two guns could not keep their men to the work. Captain Raine "had to take hold of the trail and help . . . as we could not expect our men to act their part in such a slaughter-house, unless we first laid the example." Although Union accounts almost all talk of the brevity of Pelham's stand, the Lee Battery expended all its ammunition and professed to have fired deliberately. The combined fire of the First Corps guns drove Pelham off the hill into a nearby woods. "They were too many for us and soon shut us up," wrote Poague. Captain Raine put a better face on the matter, telling a Richmond newspaper that "the immense smoke which enveloped the Yankee batteries . . . blinded us." This brief, violent episode proved quite conclusively that vigilant artillery guarded a Union flank that was not at all tender or vulnerable.[50]

One wonders just what Lee would have done had he found McClellan's northern flank accessible. Even the thrashing of Pelham's force did not deter him. The next morning a man in McLaws's division encountered Stonewall Jackson wandering the fields above the West Woods, apparently performing yet another reconnaissance for Lee. The commanding general also called in Col. Stephen D. Lee as an artillery consultant and sent J. E. B. Stuart on a scout in the same direction. Only when all three of those able subordinates testified against the feasibility of attacking McClellan's right did Lee moderate his views and begin to plan his withdrawal. The unalloyed boldness of Robert E. Lee could, on occasion, push the boundaries of prudence.[51]

The performance of the Confederate artillery on the northern end of the battlefield had been truly remarkable. The absence of any familiar guiding hand made that success more amazing. The senior artillerist in the army, William N. Pendleton, had no role in the fight. The latent talent of E. Porter Alexander would soon emerge, but he had no part in directing southern artillery at Sharpsburg, nor did Jackson's chief artillerist Crutchfield. Many of battalion commander Lindsay M. Shumaker's guns fought on Nicodemus Heights that day, but no account mentions his presence. He may not have been on the field.

Maj. Alfred R. Courtney certainly failed to accompany his battalion to the battlefield. Unfortunately for Courtney, General Early noted that absence and brought the full force of his official weight to bear, writing out in his own hand court-martial specifications against the major. He charged the truant artillerist with neglect of duty, disobedience of orders, and absence without leave on September 17. The court found Courtney guilty of all three charges and most of the supporting specifications yet recommended only a public reprimand and a single month's suspension. One of General Lee's staff officers, responding on behalf of the army commander, countered that "such absence, at a critical moment . . . deserved a much sterner punishment." Courtney subsequently was banished to another theater of the war. In later years he became a lawyer and politician, doubtless finding solace and companionship in those professions. His obituary innocently lauded his Civil War career, noting that he "won a place in orders several times," but probably not referring to General Orders No. 4 from January 13, 1863, when the findings of Courtney's trial were announced to the army.[52]

The absence of the normal leaders transferred added pressure to J. E. B. Stuart and John Pelham. The preceding pages offer ample proof that they responded well. As Jackson's de facto chief of artillery, Stuart snared guns from many sources, coordinated their activities at several key phases of the battle, displayed an excellent eye for terrain, showed his customary initiative, and repeatedly led by personal example. John Pelham demonstrated many of the same attributes on a slightly less conspicuous plane. The friendship and familiarity between Pelham and Stuart cemented their collaboration and proved to be a great asset to Confederate fortunes.

Battery commanders shone as well. The pugnacious Jim Breathed managed the Stuart Horse Artillery competently all day and "acted gallantly as usual." A friend met the weary Breathed leaving the field late in the morning, disheveled and disorganized but "hilarious over the heavy gaps which his grape and canister had made in the advancing columns of the Federal troops." Leadership at this lower level seems to have been uniformly excellent.[53]

The ill-formed experiment with the new battalion system can only be judged a failure at Sharpsburg, at least on the field's northern end. Inefficient supply and the disorder occasioned by the capture of Harpers Ferry completely wrecked Jackson's nascent battalions. Many of the batteries were not at full strength, some failed even to make the field, and the battalion officers were not around anyway. It was nothing more than good luck that the battle of Sharpsburg developed in a way that complemented Jackson's artillery situation. Had full-strength battalions been on hand and massed, they likely would have engaged in costly and less useful duels with Hooker's batteries. For one of the few times during the war, fighting in fragments produced optimal results.

Jackson's batteries also experimented with close tactical support. Stuart repeatedly pulled together the proper ordnance for the job at hand. He and Pelham transformed the batteries under their command that day into horse artillery—an extension of the cavalry arm, with an emphasis on mobility. Nearly every battery they sent into the fight held at least two positions, many fired from three, and some from as many as four. With very few exceptions they focused on annoying and dispersing enemy infantry formations. Not every battlefield had the topography to sustain those tactics; it was fortunate that the day John Pelham was most needed by his army the battle occurred on a field admirably suited to his style of fighting.[54]

Union mismanagement enhanced the success of the Confederate artillery. General Hooker's indifference to the advantages of Nicodemus Heights remains one of the battle's mysteries. Even if he was unaware of Confederate presence atop the hill, he could not assume that would be a permanent condition. Perhaps Hooker was a general less aware of his geographic surroundings than was advisable. Ten weeks earlier at the battle of Frayser's Farm, Hooker had spent an entire morning less than half a mile from another Union force that was between his division and pursuing Confederates. By his own admission, Hooker had no idea the other division was there. Based solely on those two consequential examples, it may not be unfair to speculate that reconnaissance was a flaw in the generalship of "Fighting Joe." Once the battle commenced and the importance of protecting the western flank of his advance became apparent, Hooker still did nothing forceful enough to drive off the tormenting artillery. He sent two regiments at different times to observe the Confederate guns, but he took no steps to clear the hill.[55]

One other Federal mistake that aided the Confederate gunners was the poor deployment of batteries. Ezra Carman's map for 8:00 A.M. shows, for instance, thirty-two Confederate batteries engaged on the battlefield, of which about one-quarter were near the West Woods. In contrast there were only fifteen Union batteries west of Antietam Creek at the same time. Pelham and Stuart enlarged this disparity by spreading out their own guns and diffusing Federal targets. Which Union officer was to blame for this, if anyone, is a question beyond the scope of this study.[56]

The Army of Northern Virginia's artillery had better days during the war at Chancellorsville, the Crater, and perhaps a few other sites. But at Sharpsburg the success was especially tangible. Even the crusty Jubal Early generously admitted afterward that Stuart's artillery "contributed largely to the repulse of the enemy." J. E. B. Stuart managed to congratulate himself indirectly in his official report by arguing that Nicodemus Heights, held "so long and so gallantly by artillery alone, was essential to the maintenance of our position." The greatest praise of all comes from the friendly pen of Jennings C. Wise, the historian of the army's artillery. Wise represents the move from Nicodemus Heights to Hauser's Ridge as decisive. "No one movement on either side bore a greater influence upon the final issue of the battle," he concludes. This may be a slightly exaggerated interpretation of the facts, penned by an author unflaggingly fond of his subject. It nonetheless captures the proper tone. On the stubbly fields and pastures west of the Hagerstown

Turnpike that day, an unusual collage of Confederate officers and worn-out cannoneers made just enough right decisions and fought just hard enough to save the army's flank.[57]

ACKNOWLEDGMENTS

My thanks go out to Keith S. Bohannon, Robert K. Krick, J. Michael Miller, Michael P. Musick, and Keith Snyder, each of whom helped in either the preparation or refinement of this essay.

NOTES

1. Jennings C. Wise, *The Long Arm of Lee; or, The History of the Artillery of the Army of Northern Virginia* . . . (1915; reprint [2 vols. in 1], New York: Oxford University Press, 1959), 323.

2. R. A. Brantley memoir, "The 5th Texas, Seven Days Battle around Richmond," typescript in author's possession.

3. This overhaul of Confederate artillery is well treated in Wise, *Long Arm of Lee,* 275–79.

4. U.S. War Department, *The War of the Rebellion: A Compilation of the Official Records of the Union and Confederate Armies,* 127 vols., index, and atlas (Washington: GPO, 1880–1901), ser. 1, vol. 19, pt. 1:964 (hereafter cited as *OR;* all references are to ser. 1).

5. Curt Johnson and Richard C. Anderson Jr., *Artillery Hell: The Employment of Artillery at Antietam* (College Station: Texas A&M University Press, 1995), 39, 47. This study offers seemingly accurate summaries of each army's ordnance situation on September 17.

6. Robert K. Krick, *Lee's Colonels: A Biographical Register of the Field Officers of the Army of Northern Virginia* (Dayton, Ohio: Morningside, 1992), 107; *OR* 19(1):963.

7. Edward A. Moore, *The Story of a Cannoneer under Stonewall Jackson* (New York: Neale Publishing Co., 1907), 116.

8. Krick, *Lee's Colonels,* 302, 368; Edward Porter Alexander, *Fighting for the Confederacy: The Personal Recollections of General Edward Porter Alexander,* ed. Gary W. Gallagher (Chapel Hill: University of North Carolina Press, 1989), 315.

9. Wise, *Long Arm of Lee,* 295–96; Ezra A. Carman troop movement maps (hereafter cited as "Carman Maps" with the appropriate time); U.S. Department of the Interior Geological Survey, Keedysville, Md., and Shepherdstown, W.Va., 1978 Quadrangles. The distance between Nicodemus Heights and the Porterstown Ridge,

as calculated on the modern USGS maps, is 4,300 yards. The "Carman Maps" are a set of fourteen classic maps prepared under the guidance of nineteenth-century battlefield historian Ezra A. Carman. They are a valuable resource in any study of Sharpsburg. Carman deduced many of the troop positions from his unrecorded or lost conversations with veterans, often on the battlefield itself. Sets of his insuperable maps are on file in the library at Antietam National Battlefield, Sharpsburg, Md. (repository hereafter cited as ANB). My thanks to Paul Chiles and Ted Alexander of the staff at that site for cordial assistance in the course of my research.

10. *OR* 19(1):150, 218.

11. R. Channing Price to his mother, September 18, 1862, Price Papers, Southern Historical Collection, Wilson Library, University of North Carolina, Chapel Hill (repository hereafter cited as SHC); W. W. Blackford, *War Years with Jeb Stuart* (New York: Scribner's, 1945), 149; *OR* 19(1):819. There is no specific documentation detailing the collaboration between Jackson and Stuart, but events of the 17th make it certain that the two had worked out some arrangement before the battle.

12. John T. Block to Ezra Carman, May 30, 1899, Edwin A. Marks to Ezra Carman, May 31, 1899, Antietam Studies, box 1, Ezra A. Carman Papers, National Archives (cited hereafter as Carman Papers, NA; all references are to the Antietam Studies); R. Channing Price to mother, September 18, 1862, SHC. Gen. Fitzhugh Lee wrote much later (February 15, 1896, box 3, Carman Papers, NA) that Jackson slept near him on the reverse slope of Nicodemus Heights on the night of the 16th. His testimony is disregarded in favor of the contemporary evidence in Channing Price's letter.

13. Robert M. Mackall to Ezra Carman, March 15, 1900, box 3, Carman Papers, NA; *OR* 19(1):819.

14. Johnson and Anderson, *Artillery Hell*, 69–71; A. J. Warner to John M. Gould, October 19, 1894, John M. Gould Collection of Papers Relating to the Battle of Antietam, Dartmouth College Library, Hanover, N.H. (hereafter cited as Gould Papers, Dartmouth). Blackford, *War Years*, 150–51, gives an account of civilians fleeing a house during the fighting on the 17th. This usually has been presumed to be the Nicodemus house and family, but if Warner's account is true, then perhaps the house in Blackford's anecdote was a different one, possibly Alfred Poffenberger's later in the day.

15. Carman Maps, 6:00–6:20 A.M.; A. W. Garber, "Staunton's Brave Artillery Boys," Richmond *Times-Dispatch*, October 29, 1905; A. W. Garber to Ezra Carman, April 1, 1896, September 16, 1898, box 1, Carman Papers, NA; C. A. Fonerden, *A Brief History of the Military Career of Carpenter's Battery* (New Market, Va.: Henkel & Co., 1911), 38; John W. Bryan to Jedediah Hotchkiss, n.d., Hotchkiss Papers, reel 34, frame 75, Library of Congress, Washington (repository hereafter cited as LC). It is impossible to report accurately the various types of guns in use on Nicodemus Heights. This seemingly simple calculation is frustrated by the wildly divergent reports of participants. Compare, for example, the September 22 table in *OR* 19(1):964 with the conclusions reached by Ezra Carman based on testimony from soldiers (boxes 1–3, Carman

Papers, NA). The strength of the Stuart Horse Artillery is the most irritating of all. In correspondence between Carman and Stirling Murray of that battery (June 23, 1897, July 25, 1898, box 3, Carman Papers, NA), Murray manages to argue with himself about the ordnance in his battery. Johnson and Anderson, *Artillery Hell,* 100–101, have the same problem. At best we can conclude that of the guns on Nicodemus Heights at dawn, at least six were rifles.

16. W. H. Humphrey to John M. Gould, March 23, 1893, Gould Papers, Dartmouth; George C. Sumner, "Recollections of Service in Battery D, First Rhode Island Light Artillery," in *Personal Narratives of Events in the War of the Rebellion* (Providence: Rhode Island Soldiers and Sailors Historical Society, 1891), 31; George C. Sumner, *Battery D, First Rhode Island Light Artillery in the Civil War* (Providence: Rhode Island Printing Co., 1897), 30; *OR* 19(1):236. Most Federal accounts place the initial range at about half a mile.

17. *OR* 19(1):226–27; G. W. Beale to Ezra Carman, June 6, 1897, P. J. White to Ezra Carman, April 13, 1900, H. B. McClellan to Ezra Carman, March 17, 1900, box 3, Carman Papers, NA; Robert L. Dabney, *A Memorial of Lieut. Col. John T. Thornton, of the Third Virginia Cavalry, C.S.A.* (Richmond: Presbyterian Committee of Publication, 1864), 16; Richard W. Watkins letter, September 18, 1862, folder 4, sec. 1, Watkins Papers, Virginia Historical Society, Richmond (repository hereafter cited as VHS); J. William Jones, *Personal Reminiscences, Anecdotes, and Letters of Gen. Robert E. Lee* (New York: Appleton, 1875), 326; Lyon G. Tyler, *Encyclopedia of Virginia Biography,* 5 vols. (New York: Lewis Historical Publishing Co., 1915), 3:164. Heros von Borcke, in his *Memoirs of the Confederate War for Independence* (1866; reprint, Dayton, Ohio: Morningside, 1985), 232, wrongly places the mortal wounding of Thornton at midday on the 17th.

18. Alexander, *Fighting for the Confederacy,* 210.

19. *OR* 19(1):150, 254; Rufus R. Dawes, *Service with the Sixth Wisconsin Volunteers* (Marietta, Ohio: Alderman & Sons, 1890), 87; Benjamin F. Cook, *History of the Twelfth Massachusetts Volunteers* (Boston: Twelfth Regiment Association, 1882), 72; manuscript history of the battle written by Ezra A. Carman on file at the Library of Congress, chap. 15 (manuscript hereafter cited as Carman Narrative, LC).

20. Dawes, *Sixth Wisconsin,* 88; John D. Vautier, *History of the 88th Pennsylvania Volunteers in the War for the Union* (Philadelphia: Lippincott, 1894), 74–75; Carman Narrative, chap. 15, LC.

21. Isaac Hall to John M. Gould, August 21, 1892, Gould Papers, Dartmouth.

22. *OR* 19(1):967–68; Buckner M. Randolph diary, September 17, 1862, VHS.

23. *OR* 19(1):244; Janet B. Hewett and others, eds., *Supplement to the Official Records of the Union and Confederate Armies,* 98 vols. to date (Wilmington, N.C.: Broadfoot, 1994–), ser. 1, vol. 3:536 (hereafter cited as *ORS;* all references are to ser. 1); Seymour Dexter, *Seymour Dexter, Union Army,* ed. Carl A. Morrell (Jefferson, N.C.: McFarland Co., 1996), 100–101.

24. *ORS* 3:537; *OR* 51(1):152; A. J. Warner to John M. Gould, October 19, 1894, A. B. Filson to John M. Gould, August 30, 1894, Gould Papers, Dartmouth; Carman Maps, 7:20 A.M. Based on his map, Carman seems to have identified the Confederate battery in this episode as D'Aquin's Louisiana Guard Artillery. I am not convinced of this and am inclined to think that the two-gun section involved came from Breathed's battery (the Stuart Horse Artillery).

25. Asher W. Garber to Henry Heth, May 8, 1893, box 1, Carman Papers, NA; Carman Narrative, chap. 16, LC; *OR* 19(1):968.

26. *OR* 19(1):224, 244, 820; Asher W. Garber to Ezra Carman, September 16, 1898, box 1, Carman Papers, NA. Despite the budding problems with the Nicodemus Heights position, Pelham retained some of his effectiveness up to the last minute. One of Marsena Patrick's New York regiments, supporting Campbell's battery beside the turnpike, suffered from "the hidden guns of the enemy, on the hill back of the woods, [which] dropped their shell in our way with wonderful accuracy" (Theodore B. Gates, *The "Ulster Guard" and the War of the Rebellion* [New York: Benj. H. Tyrrel, 1879], 317). Another regiment in the same brigade found a pocket of ground to the *west* of the pike and, remarkably, attempted to boil coffee ("having moved so early as to fail of breakfast") but were flushed out "when a rebel battery, suddenly brought into position on our right" began "getting the range on us" (Dexter, *Seymour Dexter,* 101). The Confederates probably held Nicodemus Heights for between sixty and ninety minutes (*OR* 19[1]:227, 236).

27. *OR* 19(1):820; William Allan, *The Army of Northern Virginia in 1862* (1892; reprint, Dayton, Ohio: Morningside, 1984), 393.

28. Wise, *Long Arm of Lee,* 302–4; Joseph Mills Hanson, "A Report on the Employment of the Artillery at the Battle of Antietam, Md. . . . ," typescript, ANB.

29. John M. Gould, *History of the First-Tenth-Twenty-ninth Maine Regiment* (Portland: Stephen Berry, 1871), 239. For other Twelfth Corps accounts of the Confederate artillery's effect, see Robert M. Green, comp., *History of the One Hundred and Twenty-fourth Regiment Pennsylvania Volunteers* (Philadelphia: Ware Brothers, 1907), 31, 286; and the Regimental Committee, *History of the One Hundred and Twenty-fifth Regiment Pennsylvania Volunteers* (Philadelphia: Lippincott, 1906), 63–66.

30. Carman Maps, 9:00–9:30 A.M.; *OR* 19(1):964; "Statement of John A. Walter, May 23, 1895," Miscellaneous Notes, box 2, Carman Papers, NA.

31. John R. Jones to Ezra Carman, February 25, 1896, Robert W. Withers to Ezra Carman, March 14, 1895, box 2, Carman Papers, NA; *OR* 19(1):820; Krick, *Lee's Colonels,* 170. Jubal Early reported (*OR* 19[1]:973) that his division numbered only about 3,500 men at Sharpsburg. If his and Jones's figures both are accurate, Stonewall Jackson's wing of the army began the day with fewer than 6,000 muskets.

32. Samuel D. Buck, *With the Old Confeds* (Baltimore: H. E. Houck, 1925), 63; *OR* 19(1):969–70.

33. John H. O'Connor to Ezra Carman, June 14, 1889, H. H. Carlton to Ezra

Carman, December 2, 1899, box 1, Carman Papers, NA; Lafayette McLaws to Henry Heth, December 13, 1894, Ezra A. Carman Papers, New York Public Library (hereafter cited as Carman Papers, NYPL); *OR* 19(1):821. The posting of Carlton's battery in front of the Dunker Church seems somewhat odd, since scattered regiments from the Union Twelfth Corps should have been occupying that area up until McLaws's division struck them. This episode may have occurred after the West Woods had been cleared of Federal troops, but Carlton's account supports the interpretation given here. The courier killed in front of the Dunker Church almost certainly was Pvt. Robert T. Clingan of Company G, Cobb's Legion (Ga.) Cavalry.

34. Von Borcke, *Memoirs of the Confederate War,* 231–32; W. W. Blackford, *War Years,* 149–50; James McClure Scott, "Confederate War Reminiscences," 8, typescript, bound vol. 23, Fredericksburg and Spotsylvania National Military Park Library, Fredericksburg, Va.; R. Channing Price letter, September 18, 1862, SHC; John T. Block to Ezra Carman, May 30, 1899, box 1, Carman Papers, NA; John W. Bryan letter, n.d., reel 34, frame 75, Hotchkiss Papers, LC; Henry B. McClellan, *I Rode with Jeb Stuart: The Life and Campaigns of Major General J. E. B. Stuart* (1958; reprint, New York: Kraus, 1969), 130.

35. Roland E. Bowen, *From Ball's Bluff to Gettysburg . . . and Beyond* (Gettysburg, Pa.: Thomas Publications, 1994), 134–35; Richard Moe, *The Last Full Measure* (New York: Henry Holt, 1993), 181–82; *OR* 19(1):311–17.

36. Carman Maps, 8:30 A.M. onward; Fonerden, *Brief History,* 38–39; Thomas A. Graham to Ezra Carman, March 14, 1900, H. M. Ross to Ezra Carman, March 26, 1900, box 3, Carman Papers, NA. The Bedford (Va.) Artillery offers another example. Communications to Carman from John R. Johnson (October 10, 12, December 21, 1899, box 1, Carman Papers, NA) imply that unit's presence near the West Woods but are exasperating in their vagueness. The rifled cannon from Capt. James Blackshear's (Ga.) battery seem to have been near Hauser's as well (M. B. Council to Ezra Carman, March 26, 1900, box 3, Carman Papers, NA). It was somewhere near Hauser's Ridge, and at about this time, that the famous episode occurred in which Robert E. Lee failed to recognize his powder-grimed son Robert E. Lee Jr. See William T. Poague, *Gunner with Stonewall* (Jackson, Tenn.: McCowat-Mercer Press, 1957), 48; Robert E. Lee Jr., *Recollections and Letters of General Robert E. Lee* (Garden City, N.Y.: Garden City Publishing Co., 1924), 78–79. W. W. Goldsborough, *The Maryland Line in the Confederate States Army* (Baltimore: Kelly, Piet & Co., 1869), 308, echoes Carman in placing twenty-four Confederate guns on Hauser's Ridge.

37. John T. Block to Ezra Carman, May 30, 1899, Edwin Marks to Ezra Carman, May 31, 1899, box 1, Carman Papers, NA.

38. Buck, *With the Old Confeds,* 63–64; Carman Narrative, chap. 16, LC.

39. John W. Bryan letter, n.d., reel 34, frame 75, Hotchkiss Papers, LC; Fonerden, *Brief History,* 38–39; Buck, *With the Old Confeds,* 64; John S. Sawyers to William M. McAllister, September 26, 1862, William M. McAllister Papers, Perkins Library, Duke

University, Durham, N.C. This probably was the spot where the Alleghany Artillery had to abandon one of its cannon, a 3-inch rifle.

40. Letter of "S" [probably Capt. Charles I. Raine, commander of the Lee Battery], September 21, 1862, Richmond *Dispatch,* September 29, 1862; "Statement of John A. Walter, May 23, 1895," Miscellaneous Notes, box 2, Carman Papers, NA. Goldsborough, *Maryland Line,* 308, in an unreliable, overdrawn account, claims that Brockenbrough had command of all the guns on Hauser's Ridge during this episode.

41. H. H. Matthews, "The First Maryland Campaign," Saint Mary's (Md.) *Beacon,* January 19, 1905. A typescript of this is at ANB. For the role of the Richmond Howitzers during this action, see D. S. McCarthy to Ezra Carman, February 5, 1895, box 1, Carman Papers, NA, and Lee A. Wallace Jr., *The Richmond Howitzers* (Lynchburg, Va.: H. E. Howard, 1993), 20. The much-used Rockbridge Artillery also may have contributed two guns to the cluster on the southern end of Hauser's Ridge. See the unfocused statement in Poague, *Gunner with Stonewall,* 47, and W. T. Poague to Ezra Carman, April 18, 1895, box 2, Carman Papers, NA.

42. *OR* 19(1):826, 1010.

43. Moore, *Cannoneer under Stonewall,* 152–54; Ned Moore to Ezra Carman, October 12, 19, December 9, 1899, January 8, 1900, box 2, Carman Papers, NA. Moore's published chronology appears to be a little muddled.

44. *OR* 19(1):228, 306. The number and identity of Stuart's guns during this segment of the fighting have eluded detection. No batteries lay claim to participation except the one gun from the Rockbridge Artillery.

45. Lafayette McLaws to Henry Heth, December 13, 1894, Carman Papers, NYPL; *OR* 19(1):820.

46. For the estimated time of this last action, see *OR* 19(1):228, 230, 306. Although he spent most of the battle south of Jackson's sector, Lee was not unaware of conditions on the northern end of the battlefield. He saluted the good work of the Staunton Artillery by telling a pair of brothers in that unit that theirs had been "the best served Battery on the field." Asher W. Harman to his uncle, September 24, 1862, Civil War Files at the Woodrow Wilson House, Staunton, Va.

47. Captain Poague (*Gunner with Stonewall,* 47) says there were only four guns total. One Union officer confirmed this with a long-range estimate (*OR* 19[1]:306). However, Poague himself wrote in his official report (*OR* 19[1]:1010) that there were "six or eight other guns." Easily the best source on this is also the most reliably dated (Letter of "S," Richmond *Dispatch,* September 29, 1862). This letter is the source for placing Turner's battery on the field during Pelham's last sortie—the first time anyone has been able to say even generally where that battery was during the battle. Even Ezra Carman had no success in determining the particulars of its service. Turner's badly documented battery came from western Virginia. A survey of the first thirty-five service records of its members shows that twenty-eight of the men enlisted in either Alleghany County or Monroe County (now West Virginia). The battery was pretty callow, having

seen predictably light duty while attached to Gen. Henry A. Wise's Legion (Compiled Service Records for Turner's Battery, M324, rolls 347 and 349, NA). The Louisiana Guard Artillery may somehow have been part of this probe, as the battery lost three men wounded in some unspecified five o'clock action. Robert A. Means diary, September 17, 1862, VHS.

48. J. Pitfield George to Ezra Carman, March 4, 1895, box 3, Carman Papers, NA; W. T. Poague to Ezra Carman, April 18, 1895, box 2, Carman Papers, NA; Poague, *Gunner with Stonewall*, 47; Carman Maps, 5:30 P.M.

49. Sumner, *Battery D*, 35; Dawes, *Sixth Wisconsin*, 94. Dawes tells an entertaining story about a terror-stricken New York newspaper reporter in conjunction with this bombardment.

50. Unpublished report of Capt. Charles I. Raine to Stapleton Crutchfield, October 31, 1862, and W. T. Poague to Ezra Carman, May 18, 1893, box 2, Carman Papers, NA; letter of "S" in Richmond *Dispatch*, September 29, 1862; *OR* 19(1):1010.

51. W. A. Johnson, "Stonewall Jackson on a Reconnaissance," Atlanta *Journal*, June 8, 1901; *OR* 19(1):820; Stephen D. Lee, "Lee and Jackson at Sharpsburg," Richmond *Times-Dispatch*, November 25, 1906. Colonel Lee said he and Jackson together went as far north as Nicodemus Heights. Lee to Jedediah Hotchkiss, August 10, 1896, roll 34, frame 405, Hotchkiss Papers, LC.

52. Compiled Service Record of A. R. Courtney, M331, roll 63, NA; Krick, *Lee's Colonels*, 102; "Orders and Circulars Issued by the Army of the Potomac and the Department of Northern Virginia, C.S.A. 1861–1865," M921, roll 1, NA; Richmond *Times-Dispatch*, November 5, 6, 1914. The November 5 obituary includes a late-life photograph of Courtney.

53. H. H. Matthews, "The First Maryland Campaign," Saint Mary's (Md.) *Beacon*, January 19, 1905; A Comrade, "Major Breathed, of the Stuart Horse Artillery," *Old Dominion Magazine* 5 (January 1871): 38.

54. An excellent discussion of Confederate artillery tactics at Sharpsburg can be found in Wise, *Long Arm of Lee*, 323–24.

55. See *OR* 11(2):111 for the Frayser's Farm confusion.

56. Hanson, "A Report on the Employment of Artillery," typescript, ANB.

57. *OR* 19(1):821, 971; Wise, *Long Arm of Lee*, 301–2.

ROBERT K. KRICK

It Appeared As Though Mutual Extermination Would Put a Stop to the Awful Carnage

Confederates in Sharpsburg's Bloody Lane

A northern correspondent walked grimly down the Roulette lane on the morn-ing of September 18, 1862, horrified by the Federal corpses that strewed the fields around him. Then he reached the Bloody Lane and stood stunned by "a ghastly spectacle!" "The Confederates had gone down as the grass falls before the scythe," wrote this man. "They were lying in rows like the ties of a railroad, in heaps, like cord-wood mingled with the splintered and shattered fence rails. Words are inadequate to portray the scene." A general from Michigan who gazed awestruck upon the same sight wrote that Confederate bodies "lay as thick as autumn leaves along a narrow lane cut below the natural surface, into which they seemed to have tumbled." Thirty years later a returning southern officer still could count thirty-eight bullet holes in a single narrow rail of the fence beside the lane.[1]

The blood-soaked sunken lane that became a charnel house that late summer day had for decades been a simple rural shortcut. It wandered across the pastoral countryside, taking advantage of terrain anomalies to get from the Hagerstown Pike to the Keedysville Road while bypassing the village of Sharpsburg. In cov-ering that convenient route, the wagon road formed the jagged hypotenuse of a triangle, the larger roads being its legs. Rain and usage by farm wagons had worn most of the lane down to a depth of two or three feet, in places more than that. The first leg of the wagon track, leaving the Hagerstown Pike and heading east, covered approximately one thousand yards before it turned sharply southward. The eastern two-thirds of that distance included enough up-and-down terrain to provide the forces of erosion with extra momentum. In that section, the sunken road was especially sharply and deeply etched into the ground. Not far north of the lane, high ground paralleled it in an arc of similar configuration.[2]

The two southern brigades destined to christen the sunken wagon road as the Bloody Lane began September 17 elsewhere and oriented in a different direction. Gen. Daniel Harvey Hill commanded a five-brigade division that occupied the Confederate center, including the vicinity of the sunken road that would become the infamous Bloody Lane. Hill's three brigades that were situated at dawn around the lane where it faced north and northeast, however, advanced out of the area during the morning. Those brigades, under Gens. Roswell S. Ripley and Alfred H. Colquitt and Col. Duncan K. McRae (vice Samuel Garland, killed on the 14th) participated during the early morning hours in the violent engagements near the East Woods, the Miller Cornfield, and the adjacent open wedge of the Pasture. Gen. Robert Emmett Rodes's Alabama troops (3rd, 5th, 6th, 12th, and 26th Infantry) had faced east toward Antietam Creek overnight, from positions farther down the same lane. Rodes estimated his strength at 1,200 men before the intense fighting of September 14 and at fewer than 800 men on the 17th. George Burgwyn Anderson's brigade of four North Carolina infantry regiments—the 2nd, 4th, 14th, and 30th—stood on Rodes's right, also facing the creek, at dawn. They awakened to a lovely September morning; the temperature that day reached only to the mid-seventies. Col. R. T. Bennett of the 14th ate breakfast before daylight with General Rodes. The general had a roasted ear of corn; Bennett enjoyed "a boiled chicken got by fair or *fowl* means" by his servant. When Ripley and Colquitt and McRae moved north to battle, Rodes and Anderson slid leftward to the ground their comrades had vacated. D. H. Hill ordered the two brigades "to form quickly" in the sunken road corridor that they would make famous, to provide a rallying point for the hard-pressed men of the other three brigades.[3]

As the regiments under Anderson and Rodes took position, two enemy divisions totaling six brigades were headed somewhat aimlessly for the same place. Ahead of them, the division of Gen. Edwin V. Sumner's Second Corps commanded by Gen. John Sedgwick advanced across Antietam Creek first. In the West Woods, Sedgwick and Sumner stumbled into the most abject disaster suffered by any large unit on either side during the battle. Gen. William H. French's division of the same corps had started in motion right after Sedgwick, a few minutes before

Brigadier General Robert E. Rodes
Francis Trevelyan Miller, ed. *The Photographic History of the Civil War*, 10 vols.
(New York: Review of Reviews, 1911),
10:145

8:00 A.M. Sumner's last division, under Gen. Israel B. Richardson, followed in French's trace. French remained close behind Sedgwick in getting across the creek but gradually fell behind. At about 9:15 French formed up in the East Woods, but not facing west toward Sedgwick's failed foray. Instead, he diverged markedly to the southwest, heading squarely for Rodes and Anderson in the sunken lane. When the Confederates reached their position in the road, none of the Federals were yet in view.[4]

The Alabamians and North Carolinians crouching in the hollowed-out wagon way were veteran troops, confident and extraordinarily well led. Division commander Harvey Hill fell far short of the mark as an administrator, but he clearly was one of those rare men who thrived in battle, rather than merely facing a stern duty with poise and determination. A fellow Confederate general, who liked Hill, admitted that he "has the reputation of being cross, impulsive, and often gives offence." The chronically tolerant Lee pronounced Hill's temperament "queer" and complained that "he croaked." Despite the army commander's remarkable forbearance with subordinates' failings and his careful nurturing of what abilities he could discern in them, Lee briskly shuffled Hill out of the army not long after Sharpsburg. A month before the battle Lee already had concluded, as he wrote to Jefferson Davis, that Hill "is not entirely equal to his present position. . . . [He] does not . . . have much administrative ability."[5]

Some troops in the division would rejoice at "getting from under that bundle of prejudice and bad temper, D. H. Hill." On September 17, 1862, though, croaking

Brigadier General
George Burgwyn Anderson
Robert Underwood Johnson and
Clarence Clough Buel, eds., *Battles
and Leaders of the Civil War*, 4 vols.
(New York: Century, 1887–88), 2:578

and prejudice and administrative temperament mattered not at all. Being as "full of courage as a bull-terrier," as one colonel described the general's battle mien, would count most on the war's bloodiest single day. Hill was ready, even eager, to fight with all of his might. A remark the general made on the morning of September 18 to a North Carolinian survivor typifies his fierce militant spirit and hatred for Yankees. "A field covered with dead," he said brutally, "is a far more gratifying sight than wounded and prisoners." In similar spirit, expressed less savagely, Hill remarked a few weeks later while awaiting an attack "that he would rather see the Yankees advance upon us . . . than to see the face of a pretty woman." Harvey Hill was a fighter. On the field of Sharpsburg he would have at least three horses shot from under him.[6]

Two of the key leaders under Hill were bright young men destined for steadily increasing success and great fame. Robert E. Rodes would develop into perhaps the best major general in the history of the Army of Northern Virginia (excluding from that universe one or two men who passed through the rank en route to higher responsibilities). Jedediah Hotchkiss of Jackson's staff was one who believed that "Rodes was the best Division Commander in the Army"—and went on to suggest that he "was worthy of & capable" of commanding the entire army!

Colonel John Brown Gordon
(a post-Antietam view in which he
wears the wreath and stars of a
general officer on his collar).
Robert Underwood Johnson and
Clarence Clough Buel, eds., *Battles
and Leaders of the Civil War*, 4 vols.
(New York: Century, 1887–88), 4:525

James Power Smith, another Second Corps staff officer, declared enthusiastically: "I like him so much. He is very much admired by all." D. H. Hill was not particularly fond of Rodes—probably because they were of dramatically different temperaments—but Hill was obliged to admit that the junior officer's brigade was "one of the best regulated and disciplined . . . in the army." Gen. Bryan Grimes wrote presciently, not long after Rodes was killed in action in September 1864, that the dead division commander simply "cannot be replaced."[7]

Col. John Brown Gordon, commanding the 6th Alabama of Rodes's brigade, also possessed dauntless courage and nascent prowess as a leader of men at arms. The modern tendency to ridicule Gordon's late-life memoir for its purple-prose excesses is understandable, in fact irresistible. Unfortunately, such criticism has the tendency to deprecate what Gordon actually accomplished at the head of his regiment and later as the leader of a brigade, a division, and eventually a large chunk of the army. A soldier in the 3rd Alabama (not Gordon's own regiment) called him "a trump," "as brave a man as I ever knew." Hotchkiss thought Gordon "the very personification of a hero." Rodes himself described Gordon a few months after Sharpsburg as "a magnificent officer in action."[8]

The North Carolinians who constituted the other half of the sunken lane's initial defenders had neither a Rodes nor a Gordon in their ranks. They enjoyed the solid leadership of Gen. George Burgwyn Anderson, "a fine looking officer" who had been hand-picked for the command by D. H. Hill; but their brigadier would have no chance for further distinction after this deadly day. The Carolina brigade was destined to earn great renown in later battles under Gen. Stephen Dodson Ramseur, but Ramseur had not yet been affiliated with the unit at all. General Anderson made his headquarters at the Piper house, a long musket shot behind the lane. So did D. H. Hill.[9]

Composed of ably led veterans though they were, the two brigades settling into defensive positions in the lane were understrength. Rodes's units, having fought long and hard three days earlier to resist Federals attempting to thrust through Turner's Gap in the South Mountain, were discouragingly short of battle-ready troops. The 6th Alabama sent 265 men into action, but other regiments counted fewer muskets. A soldier in the 5th Alabama wrote to his parents on the 16th that his unit had been "cut up terribly . . . nearly all killed and wounded." A 3rd Alabama veteran told his father in a note that his company numbered precisely 3 men at Sharpsburg; 2 of them were wounded in the ensuing battle. Another company in the same regiment mustered only 8 soldiers. General Hill exhorted the hard-used Alabamians as he walked among them in the sunken lane: "Soldiers, you fought well on Sunday, but today you must fight harder."[10]

Anderson's Tarheels had been used up by a summer of hard duty, but most of them had not fought as extensively at South Mountain as Rodes's troops. A member of the 4th North Carolina called his experience there "bushwhacking" and admitted that the entire regiment retreated precipitately in the face of a Yankee volley. Even so, a brigade officer who later rose to brigadier general's rank called the division's role at South Mountain "really one of the most remarkable feats of the war." The 14th North Carolina had had the good fortune to miss the battles after the Seven Days and took the enormous total—by Sharpsburg Confederate standards—of 523 men into the Bloody Lane. Anderson brought 1,200 men to action on September 17 in the deadly lane, somewhat more than the number that Rodes mustered that fateful day, even though Rodes had five regiments to Anderson's four. Both brigades were achingly hungry. One of the Carolinians wrote in his diary-based memoir, "we were nearly famished," and "Oh, but we were hungry."[11]

A smattering of three other Confederate brigades ostensibly held the 150-yard gap between Rodes's left and the Hagerstown Pike: Col. Alfred H. Colquitt's; Col. Duncan K. McRae's; and Gen. Howell Cobb's, under Lt. Col. William MacRae. In fact, the handful of disorganized men in that location, from those brigades and probably others as well, had little impact on the action. R. E. Lee in person attempted to reorganize these fragments. A Georgian described the army commander as in "plain" attire, his right arm in a sling, his pantaloons

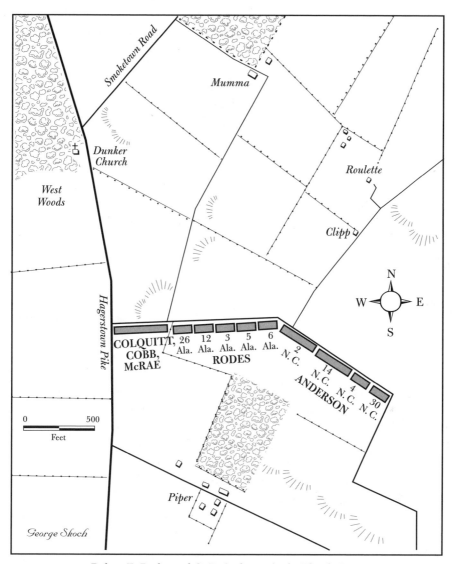

Robert E. Rodes and G. B. Anderson in the Bloody Lane

tucked inside his boots. Lee's "composure in . . . a most deplorable state of affairs" reassured the troops — even if it did not rally many of them. Another Georgian who saw the army commander there remarked on his "Washingtonian dignity" and "commanding" appearance. Colquitt's brigade was the unit most often cited as rallying beside Rodes, but an extensive collection of manuscript accounts of Sharpsburg by veterans of all those brigades includes not a word about standing in the leftward extension of the Bloody Lane. The collection includes Colquitt's own summary of events, written soon after the war. Rodes and Anderson in essence stood alone.[12]

The Federal division closing upon them enjoyed a substantial edge in numbers (about 5,700 to 2,200), and it would be reinforced by another full division before long; that would make the eventual odds nearly five to one. But Gen. William H. French's men were by no means a seasoned band of brothers, bonded in the fire of great battles, as were their southern targets. The brigades of Gens. Nathan Kimball and Max Weber and Col. Dwight Morris had only been pulled together as French's division on the 16th: the organization was precisely one day old. Furthermore, a great many of the men heading into a hellish maelstrom of fire had never before been in combat.[13]

French's troops were more inclined to snicker at their division commander than laud his leadership. Observers launched an unparalleled array of amused, ludicrous descriptions of the general. A Maine volunteer described one of French's orders as "a mere literary curiosity that provokes mirth from all" and speculated that the general "was, no doubt, drunk when he issued it"; called French "so repulsive in appearance as to invite nausea at the sight of his bloated and discolored visage" and "a perfect old soaker, a devotee of lust and appetite"; and concluded that he was "the meanest looking general I have ever seen." One of Gen. George G. Meade's aides painted French as "plethoric . . . stout . . . red in the face" and of aspect "martial, not to say fierce." Col. (later Maj. Gen.) Philippe Regis de Trobriand visited French and found him to be "a large man with a red nose, a flushed face, a bald forehead, a dull look. Near him, a glass and bottle of whiskey appeared to be on the table *en permanence.*"[14]

T. J. Jackson, of course, had no direct connection with this corner of the field, but he must surely have been astonished that French had achieved such high command in the Federal army. A dozen years earlier the two men had engaged in a vitriolic battle at a Florida post over Jackson's allegations about French's moral turpitude. The "fierce," "plethoric," "repulsive" French had met his match there in Jackson, himself no paragon of relaxed flexibility. It is easy to imagine that French woke up most mornings in 1862 marveling that his rigidly narrow subordinate of 1850–51 inexplicably had become the legendary "Stonewall."[15]

The three regiments of Weber's brigade led French's advance to the Roulette farm and beyond. The two outer regiments were to guide on Weber's center unit, the 5th Maryland. The Marylanders' color-bearer was a mammoth German of towering height and some three hundred pounds avoirdupois. The ponderous fellow carried his flag with a stride so deliberate that the wings of Weber's advance curled ahead of the center, forming a crescent. The surging northerners easily brushed aside a small Confederate outpost situated near the Clipp house and moved steadily southward. A couple of volleys fired into their right flank by the few score muskets of the 8th South Carolina, which stumbled briefly into the sector, caused them more discomfort. Even so, this "sudden and terrible fire" from the stray Carolinians delayed Weber's men for only a few minutes. Soon thereafter they climbed the north face of a long limestone ridge, a bit of rolling terrain like many another fold in the western Maryland countryside. When they reached the crest, though, the Yankees looked down at ground about to become famous. Below them and less than one hundred yards away ran the long, sunken lane packed with armed Confederates. The lane exploded with flame, and sheets of musketry tore into the Federal line. For more than two hours, the soldiers from America's severed halves would fight savagely across this narrow band of Maryland soil and christen the Bloody Lane.[16]

Col. John B. Gordon's 6th Alabama stood squarely in the middle of the southern line. To their left stretched the rest of Rodes's Alabama regiments—5th, then 3rd, 12th, and 26th. Anderson's four North Carolina regiments extended eastward from Gordon's right. Gordon's right also marked the apex of the concave part of the Bloody Lane's route, which describes an angle that is decidedly obtuse yet more pronounced and more evident on the ground than the "Bloody Angle" of Spotsylvania fame in 1864. The Confederates had been in the road for about one hour when Weber's men swarmed to the crest of the ridge directly opposite Gordon, who described the opening volleys in breathless prose: "With all my lung power I shouted 'Fire!' . . . Rifles flamed and roared in the Federals' faces like a blinding blaze of lightning accompanied by the quick and deadly thunderbolt. The effect was appalling. The entire front line, with few exceptions, went down in the consuming blast." Jubilant Confederates leaped to their feet and unleashed four successive volleys; then the firing became steady and general. Weber's line melted away, but Morris and Kimball were pressing steadily forward to his aid, and the fight for Sharpsburg's Bloody Lane soon settled into a sullen, deadly slugging match that went on and on—seemingly endlessly.[17]

To Gordon's left, the 3rd Alabama fired steadily up the slope toward an enemy exposed at the crest, and also obliquely in both directions, especially to the right front. The Federals "came like ocean billows to break on the rock of Gibraltar," the regiment's colonel recalled. Three times the 3rd's flag went down, each time to be unfurled again by a new color-bearer. "The men that held that centre could die," the colonel wrote proudly, "but they could not fly." A captain who survived the storm of lead reported mixed results in a contemporary letter: "We made the Yankees 'smell brimstone' though (entre nous) *we* smelled it also." In the same vein, another 3rd survivor declared that "both sides were well whipped."[18]

The Alabamians' stalwart leadership proved its worth in the shock of mortal combat. A member of the 6th described the front-line inspiration supplied by Rodes and Gordon:

> Gen. Rodes by his own heroic example, encouraged his men by moving up and down the line, while the brigade stood firm, repelling every onset of the enemy, breaking their lines and driving them back as a firm rock [does] the waves of the sea. The 6th Alabama stood as though it were a fixture. . . . Our gallant Col. Jno. B. Gordon, though wounded and bleeding profusely in four places, continued cheering his men, though oft entreated to leave the field. Seeing his men all dead and dying, till one could have walked the length of six companies on their bodies, his heart grew sick at the terrible havoc of death around him.[19]

Colonel Gordon had escaped harm in several earlier violent battles, despite having his clothes pierced by bullets, but his luck ran thin on this day. A bullet hit his right calf as he was talking with the colonel of the adjacent 2nd North Carolina. A second hit the same leg higher up; then another tore open his left arm; and a fourth hit Gordon's shoulder. The sun seemed to him—and thousands of others in uniforms of both varieties—to stand still. When the blood-covered colonel saw some of his men wavering, he started toward his far right. A bullet that smashed into his face and tore out through his neck dropped Gordon senseless on the ground. When consciousness returned, he was able to crawl painfully about one hundred yards to the rear. There friendly hands applied primitive treatment, then bore the colonel to the rear. The last wound disfigured Gordon for life, but he recovered from them all and returned to duty to become the Army of Northern Virginia's most successful officer from a civilian background.[20]

Gen. G. B. Anderson's Carolinians on Rodes's right actually faced a worse ordeal than their comrades from Alabama because the ground exposed their position to a wider arc of incoming fire. The road sloped downhill through the position of the 2nd North Carolina, leveled off amid the 14th, then rose steadily through the lines of the 4th and 30th. The parallel ridge to the north hovered above all of this, protecting approaching Federals—but then silhouetting them when they passed its crest. Had the Confederates been equipped with rifled shoulder arms, their officers certainly ought to have fought them from the high ground, not the lane. Given the maximum range of smoothbore musketry, however, the road served as an ideal defensive point.

On Anderson's far right, the able Col. Francis Marion Parker of the 30th held his troops' fire in check, just as Gordon and others did to the left, until the initial enemy approach was in very short range. He instructed the men to aim for "the belt of the cartridge boxes of the enemy." Their carefully aimed volley "brought down the enemy as grain falls before a reaper"—the most deliberate and destructive firing that Parker ever witnessed.[21]

Parker's 30th had the least disadvantageous portion of the brigade line during most of the fight, although at the climax the location would prove to be, briefly, the least desirable. Even so, casualties mounted steadily in the regiment's ranks. Lt. William Ardrey of Company K counted himself "extremely fortunate in escaping unhurt." Other officers in the vicinity went down steadily and in horrifying numbers. Among the victims were both the brigade and regimental commanders.[22]

The 4th North Carolina, tied to the left flank of the 30th, had no difficulty repulsing the frontal attacks flung against its stretch of the lane, hurling back the initial onset with an "awful and stunning shock so unexpectedly received." James C. Steele of the 4th wrote: "[T]he shrieks of the wounded and dying was terrible, but they rallied and came at us again and our men again awaited until they came in range and again arose and mowed them down the second time, but they came again." For what seemed like endless hours the 4th faced "almost unabated fury." The concave Federal ridge to its front, mirroring the convexity of the lane, exposed the 4th to flanking fire from its left. Capt. William Thomas Marsh, a Yale law graduate in 1851, was commanding the regiment as its ranking officer present. Marsh scrambled up the bank of the lane on the enemy side to show his scorn for the fire. Within a minute a bullet knocked him over with a mortal wound.[23]

More prudent Tarheels of the 4th "were all 'squatting' in the road," "waiting for a head on the other side to be stuck up so that we could shoot at it." Cpl. Ben Ross, obliged to raise his upper body long enough to shout messages down the line, survived two such incidents. The third time, he recalled, a piece of metal struck his shoulder, "mashing me right down." Capt. Edwin A. Osborne assumed command when Marsh fell, but he soon suffered a disabling wound. Some officers, James W. Shinn of the 4th reported, "I am sorry & ashamed to say left the field unhurt," or only slightly wounded. Eventually Lt. Frank Weaver of Company H was the only surviving unwounded officer in the entire regiment; then friendly fire from the rear killed him as he waved the colors. "It appeared," Shinn mused, "as though mutual extermination would put a stop to the awful carnage."[24]

The 14th North Carolina was a huge regiment, counting nearly as many muskets as the brigade's other three combined. Its position was less attractive than the 4th's because most of the 14th's men were near the lane's lowest ground, and all of them faced enfilade fire. Unlike the 30th, susceptible on its left flank only at long range and on high ground, and the 4th, exposed on its left but at shorter range than the 30th, the 14th was vulnerable on *both* flanks, and on low—but rising—

ground. The deadly combination cost the 14th dearly. Col. Risden Tyler Bennett, knowing he held "the most exposed part of the lane," susceptible to being "enfiladed by the fire of the Govt. forces," sent his Company A onto the high ground north of the lane as skirmishers. The company fired on French's approaching Yankees as soon as they came into range, then hurriedly fell back on the main line—but not before losing one man killed and several wounded. Capt. Thomas B. Beall of the regiment gave thanks for the "depressed road," which provided, "comparatively, a safe place to fight from." Despite the dreadful losses and the terror of battle, Colonel Bennett boasted of "a sense of superiority" among his men after the battle, growing out of their "exalted courage." "The day at Sharpsburg," Bennett insisted, "was splendid."[25]

Families of the 14th's dead, and the ghastly mounds of surviving wounded men, probably would have contested the colonel's enthusiastic language. Frank Forrest of the 14th remarked about the unusually large volume of artillery dropping in on them. "It was the worst cannonade I was in during the civil war," he wrote. When Forrest went down, though, it was with a severe bullet wound. He lay all night in a heap of wounded men from both sides, then all of September 18 and the next night, too. When at last he reached a hospital near Boonsboro, Forrest received almost no attention. Sympathetic women from as far away as Baltimore brought clothing and food for the Confederate wounded, but "the Yankees would take it and tell the ladies that they would give it to us, and that would be the last of it; they would take it themselves. They treated our wounded soldiers very badly."[26]

Fate, as always, affected fighting men in different ways. A bullet hit Lt. Wilson T. Jenkins of the 14th right in the forehead but glanced off his hat band. The missile followed the band around the lucky lieutenant's head and carved its way out the back of his hat. Fate's whimsy treated one of Jenkins's sergeants, Whitmel A. Johnston of Warren County, far less favorably. Johnston's musket misfired, and he struggled to dislodge the ball jammed in the barrel. In his efforts to knock loose the offending obstruction and rearm himself, the sergeant momentarily raised up a bit too high, and a bullet in the head killed him. Color-bearer George Badger Little, nicknamed "Judge" because he was "prudent, discriminating, impartial and judicious," fell dead with the flag in his grasp. W. C. Watkins of Company C had received an honorable discharge on the 15th but stayed in the ranks with his friends for one last battle, in which he was killed while fighting off three Federals who attacked a friend at hand-to-hand range. Thus, in the words of one of them, the 14th "fought, bled and a great number died in our efforts to free Maryland."[27]

Colonel Bennett of the 14th ruminated at length about this day for the rest of his life, writing often—but not always lucidly—about its events. Perhaps the colonel's perspective was skewed by having been, in the words of a captain in the regiment, "blown up by a shell (severely shocked)" at Sharpsburg. One of Bennett's recurring themes was that the brigade "did not occupy the road from Choice, but to meet the Sudden and rapid deployment of the Govt forces." In that notion, the colonel was ignoring the fact that the brigades were replacing others from the same division who had been formed deliberately in the lane overnight and later ordered forward. Even more emphatically, Bennett complained with what seems to be startling naiveté about how the battle continued "without any plan of battle on our Side after the first shock [and] . . . was maintained by us by . . . random blows." Colonel Bennett's notions about how things ought to have been would make good sense in a sterile classroom. In fact, Bennett himself was the senior officer in the brigade for the majority of the fight, so his carping might be considered an autobiographical critique. The close, deadly encounter that unfolded around the Bloody Lane, however, was not at all susceptible to the conventions applicable to a sand-table problem at Sandhurst.[28]

The farthest-left regiment of Anderson's brigade stood at the apex of the north-pointing bulge of the lane. Col. Charles Courtenay Tew's 2nd North Carolina straddled both the apex of the lane and the point where the Roulette lane entered it from the north. Lt. John Calvin Gorman of Company B, a journalist who had covered the western frontier in the 1850s, wrote a wonderfully detailed description for a Raleigh newspaper of the regiment's role in the fight. The 2nd, like the 14th, had sent skirmishers to the crest in front. When Gorman followed Colonel Tew up toward the skirmish line, he "gazed with tumultuous emotion over the fast approaching [Yankee] line. Our little corps seemed doomed to destruction." The lieutenant admitted, "[M]y very heart sunk within me." A mounted enemy officer waved his hat, and Tew returned the salute. Then the skirmishers folded back on the lane, the Yankees advanced over the crest, and the 2nd North Carolina fired a mighty volley into them. Gorman watched the enemy "drop, reel, stagger, and back their first line go beyond the crest of the hill." Successive charges met the same rebuff, then the Federals learned to

approach the top of the hill, cautiously, and lying down, we pour into each other one continuous shower of leaden hail for four long mortal hours. The whole air resounds with the din of arms. Musket, rifle, cannon and shell pour forth an avalanche of lead and iron. Our men are protected by about 6 or 8 inches of the wear of the road, but that is great protection; they fire cautiously, and are apparently as cool as if shooting at squirrels, taking sure aim every fire. The protection, however, is not sufficient. The air is full of lead, and many are shot as they are aiming at the enemy, and the groans of the wounded are heard amid the roar of the musketry.[29]

The Bloody Lane experiences of the four North Carolina regiments obviously followed a common theme, despite inequities of the ground that affected them differently. Federals appeared at the crest; withering volleys stunned them and sapped their momentum; southern troops launched occasional futile and costly sallies (see below for details); and then both sides settled down to enervating exchanges of musketry at short range. That bloody stalemate, which endured for about two hours,[30] might have prevailed almost endlessly but for two factors: Confederate officers, especially in the Carolina brigade, fell so fast that command and control dissolved; and reinforcements reached each of the engaged forces. The first factor affected the second on the southern side of the lane. The vacuum in command resulted in misuse — often nonuse — of the new strength reaching the front.

The grim attrition among commissioned Carolinians started at the top. The fight for Bloody Lane had not been raging long before Gen. George B. Anderson went down with a smashed ankle as he oversaw his brigade's fight from the rising ground in its rear, near the northeast corner of the orchard. The wound caused Anderson much pain but did not appear to be serious. The examining surgeon concluded that a fragment of shell had hit the foot and glanced off; only later did a more thorough physician discover a minié ball buried inside the wound. A Shepherdstown woman who cared for several of the brigade's officers wrote to Mrs. Anderson on September 18 "from the bed side of your husband" and reassuringly described the wound as "in the foot, not seriously." The general sent word to Mrs. Anderson that "he means to make his way to you *very soon*" and that he did not intend to "be long from his Brigade." "No one dreamed" that the general's hurt might be fatal, a staff officer recalled.[31]

A harrowing succession of dangers beset Anderson's trip to safety and succor. After friendly hands carried the stricken general to the Piper house, Dr. L. A. "Gus" Stith treated the wound. Artillery rounds and small-arms fire hit the house and grounds, which "were torn and shot all to pieces." One shell knocked off half of the kitchen and turned over a potful of chicken stew. Later, after the Bloody Lane line collapsed, Yankees advanced within a few yards of the house. Anderson told his attendants that "he would prefer being shot through the head" to being captured, so aides Seaton Gales, Walter Battle, and two ambulance corps men carried him away across the fields. Battle thought that it would be "impossible for a man to walk ten steps without being killed," but they all escaped death, though Battle was hit in the knee by a piece of shell. After a day and a half at the Boteler house in Shepherdstown, Anderson faced the exhausting ordeal of a wagon trip all the way to Staunton. His brother, staff officer Robert Walker Anderson, who had been wounded in the shoulder, accompanied the general.

Determined—probably foolishly—to reach his wife and baby in Raleigh, General Anderson entrained at Staunton and eventually reached the North Carolina capital on September 26. Only then did his private physician, Dr. C. E. Johnson, discover the ball embedded in the wounded joint. Infection supervened; amputation further weakened the patient; and General Anderson died on the morning of October 16. R. W. Anderson recovered, only to be killed at the Wilderness in 1864.[32]

At the Bloody Lane, Anderson's command mantle had passed to Colonel Tew of the 2nd North Carolina, but only for a brief, tragic instant. Pvt. John F. Bagarly of Company G, 4th North Carolina, seconded to brigade headquarters as a courier, hurried forward through sheets of musketry to the Bloody Lane to tell Tew that Anderson was out of action. When Bagarly could not find Tew, he delivered his message instead to Colonel Parker of the 30th, next in rank. Parker knew that Tew was all the way at the other end of the brigade, so he ordered his adjutant, Fred Philips, "to proceed cautiously down the line" and let Tew know he had acceded to command. Several bullets rent Philips's uniform before he reached a point behind the 2nd and could shout his information through the din to Tew. When he yelled again to ask whether the colonel had understood, "Tew, who was standing erect, lifted his hat and made . . . a polite bow, and fell immediately from a wound in the head." As Philips made his way back toward the right carrying his second change-of-command message within a few minutes, a bullet knocked him over with a severe head wound. Colonel Parker promptly headed toward the left to attempt to assert command, but within ten steps a bullet hit *him* in the head. The missile "cut . . . away a narrow strip of skin and plow[ed] a nice little furrow in the skull, leaving the membrane that covers the brain visible but uninjured." Within a very short interval, the North Carolina brigade had been deprived of its leadership—and the fight had barely begun.[33]

Courtenay Tew was a brilliant fellow and an ardent soldier. His photograph shows a man of proud, aggressive eye and ramrod-straight posture. D. H. Hill called the colonel "one of the most finished scholars on the continent." Tew had graduated in the first-ever class of the South Carolina Military Academy as valedictorian, taught at his alma mater for a decade, toured European military sites on foot, then ran a military academy in Hillsboro, North Carolina. At the opening of the fight for Bloody Lane, Colonel Tew had climbed atop the lip of the road on the Yankee side and defied the flying lead as a means of encouraging his men. The bullet that lodged in his highly cultivated brain as he gestured toward Adjutant Philips did not kill the colonel outright, although it mangled him horribly, passing through his left temple and then out the right temple, dislodging his eyes in the process. Friendly hands dragged the mortally hurt officer to the protected

Alexander Gardner photographed Confederate dead in the section of the Sunken Lane
held by the 2nd North Carolina. The corpse propped up against the lower right side
of the road may be that of Colonel Tew.
Library of Congress

bank on the north verge of the lane, next to where the Roulette lane entered.
When Federals surged across the position an hour or more later, they found
Colonel Tew bleeding horribly but still sensible enough to hold tightly to his inscribed sword and to resist looters eager to take it. That effort used the last of his
strength and of his life. Ohioans carried away the bloody souvenir sword.[34]

Because Colonel Tew's horrifying final moments of life transpired in enemy
hands, a bizarre and excruciating ordeal ensued for his family. Soon after the war
ended, an enterprising Yankee engaged in "mercenary sensationalism" appeared
in Hillsboro and with "artful ingenuity" told the fantastic tale that Tew actually
was alive, a prisoner at Fort Jefferson, confined for life for killing the colonel of an
Illinois regiment. Tew's aged father hurriedly made the trip to the fort, situated in
the Dry Tortugas off the Florida Keys (where E. M. Stanton's myrmidons were by
then holding the fiendish Dr. Mudd), by way of Baltimore and Havana. The trip,

of course, proved fruitless, but the story kept the family "for years vibrating between hope and despair." In 1874, a Federal officer who happened upon some of Tew's friends gallantly returned to the family an inscribed silver cup from the colonel's possessions and described burying him. The sword disappeared from a Masonic Lodge in Ohio to which the family had traced it. For this widow, orphan, and father, the battle of Sharpsburg dragged on for more than a decade.[35]

The Carolinians who fought sturdily on with their mangled and dying colonel in their midst received no further direction from a controlling officer. Colonel Bennett became senior when Parker went down, but he never achieved any sort of control. That probably did not matter a great deal for a time, given the clear-cut duty at hand: hold the strong defensive line of the Bloody Lane against Federal onslaughts. The Carolinians, and the Alabamians to their left, could and did maintain their position tenaciously. But the absence of a command perspective became crucial when two things happened: Confederate reinforcements began to arrive, with no one to apply them where needed; and then enemy reinforcements arrived, with at least a few leaders able to direct them to good effect.

Gen. Richard H. Anderson's division approached the vicinity of the Bloody Lane near 10:00 A.M., relatively early in the fight for the position. Its six brigades made the force appreciably larger than the average southern division, so it ought to have supplied a tremendous augmentation to Rodes and G. B. Anderson at a critical juncture. In the event, it accomplished relatively little. The division had marched from Harpers Ferry all night, crossed the Potomac about 7:00 A.M., and halted briefly near Lee's headquarters behind Sharpsburg. Without rest or food, it then moved across the fields toward the Hagerstown Pike in the left rear of the Bloody Lane. Several batteries built up a base of fire near the pike west and northwest of the Piper house in support.[36]

R. H. Anderson's advance seemed obviously headed toward French's exposed right. That probably would have worked well. Moving instead to the opposite end of the Bloody Lane would have served even better, providing a huge advantage to the Confederate effort. Instead, Anderson's brigades filtered into action almost at random, drastically diluting their impact. Much of the reinforcements' ineptitude can be traced to the loss of command. General Anderson, of modest competence that might have met the needs of the hour, was wounded "severely . . . in the thigh" before his troops closed to musketry range. He was replaced by the incomparably incompetent Roger A. Pryor, who was destined to be serving as a private before many more months. Pryor sent word to Longstreet "that he would hold his position untill the last man was taken." Longstreet, knowing his man, replied, "[W]e did not come here to be taken or surrender, we came here to fight." Given the destruction of the Carolinians' command structure in the lane, combined with Pryor's ineptitude, there was no one in overall control of events on the Confederate right.[37]

The disintegration of R. H. Anderson's division can be seen distinctly from the official reports of its brigades: there are none. Not only did no official report for the division find its way into the published *Official Records;* there is also none for any of its six brigades, and only a report for one of the twenty-six regiments that made up those brigades. The report of Capt. Abram M. "Dode" Feltus, senior officer present with the 16th Mississippi, is the only one in that standard source out of a potential thirty-three documents. The lacuna frustrates historians; it also illustrates the paucity of command in the division on September 17 (and the haphazard way in which R. H. Anderson administered his division when he returned to its command).[38]

Pryor's ill-led brigade headed Anderson's arriving division (Gen. Lewis A. Armistead's brigade had been vectored elsewhere on the field). Gen. William Mahone's brigade, under Col. William A. "Gus" Parham, had been reduced to only a few score men by its ordeal on September 14, so it was appended to Pryor's brigade. The polyglot command reached the Hagerstown Pike about one hundred yards south of the Piper lane, turned north to the lane, and swung east toward the house in this marching order: 2nd, 8th, and 5th Florida, 3rd Virginia, and 14th Alabama. Between the house and the barn the column pivoted left and moved a short distance toward the Bloody Lane, staying west of the orchard. When Pryor learned of Anderson's wounding and his own resultant accession to division command, he turned his brigade over to Col. John C. Hately of the 5th Florida, who was shot through both thighs, breaking one. Lt. Col. Georges A. G. Coppens, commanding the 8th Florida, was killed at once in the yard of the Piper barn; Capt. Richard Waller succeeded him and died "with the colors of the regiment draped over his shoulder, almost immediately afterwards, the staff having been shot in two." Capt. David Lang was next in line and next wounded—all this before closing on the Bloody Lane. So collapsed the Confederate officer corps in one regiment after another. One of Pryor's wounded Floridians being carried to the rear responded disconsolately to a question about his unit: "[T]hey are all killed, wounded, or dispersed." The 5th Florida lost "at least two-thirds" and had only twenty-six men on duty on the 19th.[39]

Unlike Pryor, the reliable Alabama brigade of Gen. Cadmus M. Wilcox remained south of the Piper lane as it moved east into the fields, finally fetching up on a ridge well behind the house. An officer reckoned the strength of the entire brigade as a mere 135 men. The advancing Alabamians had left their knapsacks and haversacks behind in a pile in order to move quickly. Exploding shells, of course, were quicker. Bailey McClelen of the 10th Alabama saw a

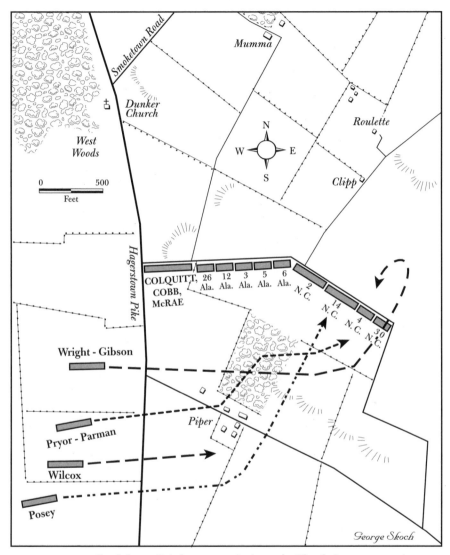

Confederate Reinforcements Arrive at the Bloody Lane

neighbor decapitated, and he himself weathered, it seemed miraculously, a storm of "bullets and shells and exploding shells . . . and canister shot . . . high and low." General Wilcox had fallen violently ill on September 14 and spent five days entirely prostrated at Martinsburg, Virginia. For some reason Anderson assigned to brigade command Col. Alfred Cumming of the 10th Georgia—from a different brigade and division. Cumming went down with a wound "before we had gotten into line." The command then devolved on first Maj. Jeremiah H. J.

Williams and then Maj. Hilary A. Herbert, the last field officer with the brigade. Williams concluded that "we could not carry the position in front," so the Alabamians remained in the Piper fields for an hour. The Alabama brigade did set up close enough to the Bloody Lane position to be caught in the backwash of its eventual collapse, losing heavily while making a stand at a fence on the Piper farm.[40]

Featherston's Mississippians, under the command of Col. Carnot Posey, followed in trace of the Alabamians. One of Posey's men noticed a soldier "kneeling behind a tree, praying earnestly for the cruel war to close. He seemed to be badly demoralized." As the Mississippi troops crossed the fields, they attracted "shot and shell in abundance, causing many muscular contractions in the spinal column of our line. . . . Occasionally a shell . . . would crash through our line making corpses and mutilated trunks."[41]

The Wilcox/Cumming/Williams/Herbert brigade never did reach the Bloody Lane, and Posey and Pryor only moved forward to its vicinity late in the action, after their comrades in Wright's brigade had entered the fray. Posey's fragments eventually reached the lane behind the right of the 14th North Carolina and extending to the left of the 30th North Carolina. Some Mississippians even swept as much as forty yards beyond the lane before falling back.[42]

Gen. A. R. "Rans" Wright's brigade had the earliest, longest, and most significant impact on the fight for the Bloody Lane of any of the reinforcements. A contemporary report fixed the brigade's strength in action at 443 men. It moved across the Hagerstown Pike a bit north of the Piper lane, paralleled it eastward, then turned left into the orchard. After suffering harshly from a crossfire of Federal artillery while getting over and through the orchard fence (built of strong oak pickets), Wright's men pressed forward obliquely toward the northeast corner of the cornfield—toward the 30th North Carolina and its dangling right flank. Famished as they were, some of the Georgians took the opportunity to gather apples that had been shot from the trees and blanketed the ground. Unfortunately Wright, a steady, if unspectacular, brigadier, joined the seemingly endless list of wounded officers. The general was riding his iron gray mount, which he had denominated his "pious horse" because of its odd habit of kneeling to drink. A shell smashed squarely into the gray's breast and burst inside, throwing Wright a dozen feet into the air. The general landed on his feet, but he soon was hit "severely" in the chest and leg. The latter wound went "entirely through the muscle of the leg below the knee," immobilizing the general.[43]

Col. Robert H. Jones of the 22nd Georgia acceded to command but soon went down hit in the head and through the right lung. Wright had excoriated Jones for his conduct at Malvern Hill, and the colonel was unpopular enough in his own regiment that the word was "that he was shot by one of his own Regiment" at Sharpsburg.[44]

Col. William Gibson of the 48th Georgia gamely rallied the survivors and moved them into the Bloody Lane in the vicinity of the 30th North Carolina. The 3rd Georgia moved on the vulnerable right; to its left marched the 48th Georgia, 44th Alabama, and 22nd Georgia. Lead and iron searching the brigade's ranks eventually left it with no field officers but Gibson (out of twelve by table of organization) and only two captains (out of forty). Some months later Gen. A. P. Hill would write to R. E. Lee that Gibson was "entirely unfitted" for brigade command. At Sharpsburg, Gibson was all that the brigade had left. A member of the 48th described the colonel as likable but possessing "no military genius whatsoever." Artillery and small-arms fire crashing into their position "disheartened" the Georgians, but word that Pryor would come to their aid gave them cause for hope. Instead, some of their friends in the rear mistakenly fired a volley into their backs.[45]

Colonel Gibson decided to attack. Perhaps the most remarkable aspect of Confederate defense of the Bloody Lane was the series of incredibly brave—and unredeemably foolish—attacks launched out of the road toward the enemy. Throughout the defense of the position by the two brigades that held it from the beginning, fecklessly aggressive officers had sent forlorn hopes forward toward the parallel enemy high ground. For some impenetrable reason Longstreet, that boisterous foe of offensive action, ordered Rodes "to charge them." Rodes faithfully obeyed, pulling along the fragments of Colquitt to his left. The result, of course, was a bloody failure that accomplished precisely nothing. Rodes speculated that a unified advance across the entire front might succeed (certainly a sanguine notion, with potentially sanguinary results). Instead, some of the Tarheels to Rodes's right made their own vain piecemeal forays beyond the line.[46]

Gibson's attack was the least auspicious of them all, coming as it did at the unpropitious moment when Federal reinforcements were threatening the stability of the line in the lane. General Wright had not entirely relinquished the command, having been carried forward on a litter, and the attack was made on his prompting. The Georgians bravely, if foolishly, delivered a bayonet charge into the teeth of the gale of musketry sweeping the foreground. After the first attempt, they hurled yet another assault over the lane's north edge. The left regiments moved forward little, if at all. The 3rd Georgia, however, advanced some distance. Adjutant Joel W. Perry Jr. of the 3rd fell with seven bullets in his body. Lt. Col. Reuben B. Nisbet of the same regiment went down hard hit. Nisbet's men could see him after they abandoned the ill-advised attack, "far in the advance, stricken down, and writhing in pain." The 3rd alone lost 72 of 138 men brought into action. Some Federals recoiled before the brief charges, of course, but the battered brigade fell back into the Bloody Lane with reduced cohesion. Some Georgians managed to deliver a steady defensive fire after they fell back, but momentum passed to the Federals.[47]

North Carolinians sharing that end of the line had refused to participate in the forlorn Gibson/Wright assault. Lt. James W. Shinn of the 4th grumbled that "Wright was drunk & *tried* to order our Brigade forward" but "we were under cover & prefered to let the enemy come up." Writing on the 18th, Shinn concluded that Wright "spoilt all, caused confusion & disorder yesterday." Wright, of course, was not drunk, just badly wounded, but he would have done well to emulate the Carolinians' judicious behavior.[48]

By the time Gibson's survivors stumbled back into the lane, some pieces of Posey's and Pryor's brigades were arriving. Lieutenant Shinn of the 4th North Carolina thought Posey's men, like Gibson's, generated more "confusion" than relief. The Mississippi reinforcements came up squarely behind the 4th, mistook the Carolinians for Yankees, and fired into their backs, hitting several of the Bloody Lane's weary defenders. Lt. Franklin H. Weaver of Company H bravely stood up waving the flag to rectify the error—and was killed at once. Once the Mississippians reached the road and figured out where the common enemy lay, they added their fire to the defense. Colonel Bennett of the 14th North Carolina complained bitterly that the 16th Mississippi and the 2nd Florida ran after fighting for only five minutes. In the chaos rampant in the lane, it is hard to imagine how he could have recognized such an event.[49]

Fragments of what had been Pryor's brigade slid farther right than Posey and showed up near Gibson and the 30th North Carolina. A Floridian described the enemy as being "in a semicircle on the side of a hill." From "the two wings and the centre" of that arc "they poured upon us a murderous fire." Five times the 5th Florida's flag went down before the regiment retired, "badly cut up."[50]

Not long after Gibson's misbegotten attack and the arrival of a final few reinforcements, the Bloody Lane line dissolved. The deployment of the ultimate southern strength in the lane thus nearly coincided, ironically, with the collapse of the position. Two notable factors brought about that result: the absence of Confederate command and control; and skillful application by their enemies of newly arriving resources.

Gen. Israel B. Richardson's division, following French's, had doubled Unionist strength opposite the lane. (Had Richardson followed French closely at the outset, as should have been the case, it is hard to imagine the Bloody Lane fight lasting more than a brief time.) Gen. Thomas F. Meagher's Irish Brigade—a stout organization, albeit grotesquely magnified in twentieth-century imaginations—

fought opposite the North Carolinians and was badly used up in a static firefight. When Gen. John C. Caldwell arrived with his brigade, he responded to the eminently sound impulse to extend the Federal left. This was the first attempt to envelop the highly vulnerable Confederate right. Richardson foolishly canceled Caldwell's initiative, ordering him instead simply to bolster Meagher's position. One of Caldwell's men saw "Irish Molly," the "big muscular" wife of an 88th New York soldier, amid the flying lead, "swinging her sun-bonnet around her head, as she cheered the Paddys on." Subsequently Col. Francis C. Barlow, a bright and energetic young New Yorker, focused two regiments on the deteriorating Confederate right and broke into the road there. Fire that Barlow's men poured obliquely down the Bloody Lane routed the Carolinians and enfiladed and unhinged the Alabamians' line as well.[51]

Lt. Col. Nelson A. Miles of the 61st New York described Barlow's advance into the collapsing Confederates:

> They were lying in a ditch or a small road, and we partly surrounded
> them. I then went forward over the rise a little and called on them to sur-
> render. . . . They rose up; I scarcely knew if they were going to fight or
> surrender; they however threw down their arms and came in. . . . In the
> road the dead covered the ground. . . . I think that in the space of less
> than ten acres, lay the bodies of a thousand dead men and as many more
> wounded.

Barlow paid painfully for his coup, being struck in the face by a shell fragment and in the groin by a canister round. A piece of shell also hit General Richardson, mangling his shoulder. Weeks later, an aide reported that the general was mending steadily but was "very much depressed, not at all like himself, and inclined to look on the dark side, more than is good for him." The wound, perhaps abetted by the mood, killed Richardson on November 3.[52]

Confederates driven from the Bloody Lane by Barlow and Miles attributed much of the eventual collapse to internal misunderstandings. An officer of the 4th North Carolina described how "the men of different regiments became mixed with each other so that all distinct organization . . . was broken up, and all identity lost." Colonel Bennett of the 14th wrote aptly of "confusion that seemed remediless." Less convincingly, he attributed all of the impulse for retirement to troops to either side of his own regiment. Several Carolinians assigned blame for the deterioration to injudicious attacks by the arriving reinforcements under Wright, Posey, and others, followed by retreats that triggered the disaster. B. B. Ross of the 4th North Carolina heard Posey yell, "Men, fall back," which prompted everyone—not just Posey's Mississippians—to retreat. The unraveling unquestionably began on the Carolinians' right, which, of course, was the far right of the entire position. Colonel Gibson's Georgians and the rest of the R. H. Anderson–Pryor reinforcing fragments joined the retrograde movement.[53]

The sunken road that had served the Confederates so well became a deadly trap as soon as its integrity was compromised. Getting out worked far better for the Tarheels on the left, around the Roulette lane, than for those on the right. As Daniel Lane of the 2nd scampered out under a heavy fire, a bullet crashed into his side, but the missile was slowed by Lane's cartridge box and only bruised him fearfully rather than inflicting a deadly wound. While some of the far right could not escape, many Carolinians of the left center slipped away. Numbers of refugees from the 4th and 14th fell back with a modicum of order, even after Federals had gotten sixty yards behind their right rear.[54]

Alabamians defending the left half of the Bloody Lane blamed the collapse on Lt. Col. James Newell Lightfoot of the 6th. When Rodes returned from an attempt to solicit aid from Pryor's troops behind the lane, Lightfoot approached to report enfilade fire pouring in from his right, the result of the Carolinians' retreat. Rodes responded precisely as he must, by ordering the 6th to refuse its right and face the threat. Lightfoot (who had been "severely wounded") instead "moved briskly to the rear" with his regiment. When the commander of the adjacent 5th Alabama asked if the retirement was to be general, Lightfoot replied in the affirmative. By the time Rodes discerned the mistake, the line was unraveling irretrievably.[55]

The Confederate center was wrenched apart. Triumphant Federals in force bestrode the heart of Lee's line. Confederate salvation lay in the loss of Federal control through disorganization and casualties to officers (notably Richardson and Barlow); in the relentless ennui with which McClellan operated and infused his command; and in a dauntless stand athwart the gap by a handful of Confederates. That epochal defense, which is not the subject of this study, included a brave rally by a few infantrymen marshaled by D. H. Hill and determined stands by several batteries, notably Boyce's Macbeth Artillery (S.C.). The fragile equilibrium that those men restored set the stage for renewed fighting farther south, around what would become known as Burnside's Bridge.[56]

The price of defending the Bloody Lane had been daunting. George B. Anderson's brigade, which brought about 1,200 men to action, lost at least 103 killed or mortally wounded, 235 wounded, and 177 captured. That aggregate of 515, which unquestionably is somewhat low, approaches a staggering rate of loss of 50 percent.[57]

Robert Rodes's Alabamians suffered marginally less heavily because of their less disadvantageous position in the lane. They also were farther removed from

Sharpsburg's Bloody Lane

Civilians watch Union soldiers dig burial trenches on September 19 for the
Confederate dead in the vicinity of the Sunken Lane.
Frank Leslie's Illustrated Newspaper, October 18, 1862

the scene of the line's collapse, and from the deadly losses that always aggregate
around such a turning point. Rodes reported 50 killed, 132 wounded, and 21
missing. A nominal contemporary account, however, announced a loss of 101
men in the 6th Alabama alone. A member of the 12th Alabama wrote home dole-
fully: "The battle at Sharpsburg isn't the victory they claim it to be."[58]

The late-arriving, fragmented Confederate reinforcements also paid heavily,
despite the relatively short period during which they were engaged. Their exposure crossing the Piper fields cost those regiments dearly. The 8th Alabama lost
78 out of 120 men present. One thin company in the 16th Mississippi had 7 men
killed within a short span. Wright's (later Gibson's) Georgians took 443 men into
action and lost 256 (nearly 60 percent) of them. The 2nd, 5th, and 8th Florida
suffered an astounding 282 casualties among the fewer than 400 infantry they
brought to action, a loss exceeding 70 percent.[59]

The same secular transubstantiation that turned a hundred bucolic American
intersections and houses and barns into ghastly battlefield landmarks during the
1860s converted Sharpsburg's simple farm path into the ever memorable Bloody
Lane. For unknown centuries to come, the Bloody Lane will resonate through
American military history and the national consciousness. The famous photos of

Confederate corpses strewn and heaped along the lane were the first such images from any American war seen by the public. Those graphic, horrific scenes remain a searing reminder of the savagery of that internecine conflict.

In July 1864 the Alabama brigade that had fought so well in the Bloody Lane camped in the vicinity while taking part in Jubal A. Early's raid on Washington. A 12th Alabama officer told his diary: "Memories of scores of army comrades and childhood's friends, slain [at Sharpsburg] came before my mind and kept away sleep for a long while. The preservation of such an undesirable union of States is not worth the life of a single southerner, lost on that memorable battlefield."[60] The hundreds of thousands of modern visitors who gaze with awe upon Sharpsburg's Bloody Lane no doubt experience a myriad of sensations. Despite the passage of so many years, most of them, impressed with the awful grandeur of the place, must certainly experience emotional reactions as strong as the sorrowful Alabamian felt.

ACKNOWLEDGMENTS

The author is delighted to discharge his obligation to thank a squad of wonderfully knowledgeable and helpful historians for their aid in marshaling sources for this chapter: K. S. "Bo" Bohannon, Zack Waters, Robert E. L. Krick, Graham Dozier, Keith E. Gibson, Russell Bailey, John N. R. Bass, Ben Ritter, Keith Snyder, Michael P. Musick, Gary L. Ecelbarger, Mike Taylor of Albemarle, Ted Alexander, Paul Chiles, and Stephen L. Ritchie. Grateful acknowledgment also is in order to Robert J. Mrazek and Senators Robert G. Torricelli and James M. Jeffords for their magnificent crusade, in progress at this writing, to secure funds to save the Sharpsburg battlefield (and several others, too), despite the opposition of the National Park Service.

NOTES

1. Quoted in "Fourth North Carolina," Charlotte *Observer,* March 3, 1895; Alpheus S. Williams, *From the Cannon's Mouth: The Civil War Letters of Alpheus S. Williams,* ed. Milo M. Quaife (Detroit: Wayne State University Press, 1959), 130; J. Thompson Brown, "The Sharpsburg Fight," Richmond *Times,* April 21, 1895. Other especially vivid descriptions of the horrific scene are those by a civilian from the vicinity, in John P. Smith, "History of the Antietam Fight," typescript in Antietam National Battlefield archives, Sharpsburg, Md. (repository hereafter cited as ANB), and by a Federal staff officer, in Josiah M. Favill, *The Diary of a Young Officer* (Chicago: Donnelley, 1909), 189–90.

2. Most Civil War battlefields have a sunken road of some description. Traditions about their antebellum creation and war-date improvements often vary widely. This description of the origins of Sharpsburg's famous Bloody Lane is based on the unpublished narrative history of the battle by Ezra A. Carman, who knew appreciably more about Sharpsburg than anyone else. Carman's invaluable manuscript history is at the Library of Congress (manuscript hereafter cited as Carman Narrative, LC; the repository under other circumstances is hereafter cited as LC). Nothing more reliable and insightful about the battle ever has been written. The anomalous paginations in the Carman Narrative, for chapter pages and cumulatively, make citations to page numbers impractical. All references herein are to chap. 18, "The Bloody Lane." John Gould, second only to Carman as a contemporary authority on the battle, carefully paced the Bloody Lane. He calculated its length from the center line of the Hagerstown Pike to the bend as 1,078 feet, and the further extent to the right angle turn (where the tower now stands) as 1,488 feet, or 855 yards total. Gould's survey also detailed where stone fences underpinned the wooden rails. This material—and much more of great worth—is in the John M. Gould Collection of Papers Relating to the Battle of Antietam, Dartmouth College Library, Hanover, N.H. (hereafter cited as Gould Papers, Dartmouth). The survey is in microfilm reel 84-1.

3. U.S. War Department, *The War of the Rebellion: A Compilation of the Official Records of the Union and Confederate Armies,* 127 vols., index, and atlas (Washington: GPO, 1880–1901), ser. 1, vol. 19, pt. 1 : 1034–38 (hereafter cited as *OR;* all references are to this volume and part); R. T. Bennett to John M. Gould, December 26, 1892, Gould Papers, Dartmouth. Rodes's men actually bivouacked overnight in a field east of the Piper house and west of the front-line position in the north–south stretch of lane, according to a note by Ezra A. Carman in the extremely important collection of his papers at the National Archives (hereafter cited as Carman Papers, NA). Daniel Lane of the 2nd North Carolina timed the opening move at 7:00 A.M. (Daniel Lane diary, copy in possession of John N. R. Bass, Spring Hope, N.C.). The weather estimate is from recordings a few dozen miles away, in "Weather Journal Recording Observations at . . . Georgetown, D.C., June 1858–May 1866," National Weather Records Center, Asheville, N.C. The faithful recorder in Georgetown reported temperatures of 69, 76, and 70 degrees at 7:00 A.M., 2:00 P.M., and 9:00 P.M. and 0.22 inches of rain overnight on the 16th.

4. Carman Narrative, LC; Fred Philips to Gen'l H. Heth, August 25, 1894, reel 84-3, Gould Papers, Dartmouth.

5. Jeremy F. Gilmer to "My dear Loulie," August 17, 1862, Jeremy F. Gilmer Papers, Southern Historical Collection, Wilson Library, University of North Carolina, Chapel Hill (repository hereafter cited as SHC); William Allan notes of conversation with Lee on February 15, 1868, in Gary W. Gallagher, ed., *Lee the Soldier* (Lincoln: University of Nebraska Press, 1996), 8–9; Lee to Davis, August 17, 1862, in Robert E. Lee, *The Wartime Papers of R. E. Lee,* ed. Clifford Dowdey and Louis H. Manarin (Boston: Little, Brown, 1961), 258.

6. "Americus" in Mobile *Advertiser and Register,* May 24, 1863; Fred C. Foard memoir, 8, Fred C. Foard Papers, North Carolina Department of Archives and History, Raleigh (repository hereafter cited as NCDAH); Samuel Hooey Walkup journal, p. 36 of typescript, William R. Perkins Library, Duke University, Durham, N.C. (repository hereafter cited as DU). In a letter to Jed Hotchkiss on January 25, 1897 (roll 34, p. 248, Jedediah Hotchkiss Papers, LC), Hunter Holmes McGuire reported that Hill had had three horses killed in the battle. Lt. Wilson T. Jenkins of the 14th North Carolina in his memoir (NCDAH) wrote that "Gen. Hill had five horses shot from under him . . . and then came from the field afoot."

7. Jedediah Hotchkiss to wife, September 21, 1864, Hotchkiss Papers, LC; James Power Smith to "My dearest sister," January 21, 1863, Fredericksburg and Spotsylvania National Military Park Library, Fredericksburg, Va. (repository hereafter cited as FSNMP); letter by "Volunteer" dated December 5, 1862, Mobile *Advertiser and Register,* December 14, 1862; Bryan Grimes to Francis Marion Parker, October 4, 1864, Compiled Service Record of Parker, M270, NA.

8. Thomas Caffey to "Dear Mary," August 4, 1862, in undated newspaper clipping at Alabama Department of Archives and History, Montgomery; Jedediah Hotchkiss to wife, August 26, 1864, Hotchkiss Papers, LC; Robert E. Rodes to Richard S. Ewell, March 22, 1863, Polk-Brown-Ewell Papers, SHC.

9. The joint headquarters is described in some detail by one of Anderson's supernumeraries, Walter [Battle] to mother, September 29, 1862, "The Civil War Letters of George Boardman Battle and of Walter Raleigh Battle of Wilson, North Carolina," Wilson County Public Library (hereafter cited as Walter Battle letter). "Fine looking" Anderson is from A. T. Brewer (61st Pennsylvania), "The Woolen Shawl," Abram T. Brewer Papers, Civil War Times Illustrated Collection, United States Army Military History Institute, Carlisle Barracks, Pa. (repository hereafter cited as USAMHI). D. H. Hill's specific selection of Anderson is in a letter to Secretary of War G. W. Randolph, June 6, 1862, Anderson's Compiled Service Record, M331, NA.

10. "Soldier," "The Sixth Alabama Regiment," Montgomery *Weekly Advertiser,* November 19, 1862; unidentified 5th Alabama soldier to parents, September 16, 1862, from Antietam, copy in the files at ANB; "Joe" of the 3rd Alabama to his father, Mobile *Advertiser and Register,* October 18, 1862; anonymous 3rd Alabama soldier, September 20, 1862, in ibid., October 4, 1862; *OR,* 1038; D. H. Hill exhortation from obituary of Lt. John D. Perry, 6th Alabama, Selma *Reporter,* December 18, 1862.

11. Benjamin B. Ross memoir, USAMHI; William Ruffin Cox in Walter Clark, comp., *Histories of the Several Regiments and Battalions from North Carolina in the Great War, 1861–'65,* 5 vols. (Goldsboro: Nash Brothers, Printer, 1901), 4:447 (hereafter cited as Clark, *N.C. Regiments*); James W. Shinn memoir, Edwin Augustus Osborne Papers, SHC. General Confederate strength figures are as calculated in the Carman Narrative, LC. The 14th North Carolina strength is from the splendid recent study of Tarheel troops, Greg Mast, *State Troops and Volunteers: A Photographic*

Record of North Carolina's Civil War Soldiers (Raleigh: North Carolina Division of Archives and History, 1995), 360. Despite the title, Mast's book offers much more than just images.

12. The unimpeachable Carman (Carman Narrative, LC) put fragments of all three brigades in that westernmost 150-yard stretch, so at least a few men must have rallied there. Rodes ("a small portion") and Hill (*OR*, 1023, 1037) both cited Colquitt's presence. The revealing absence of mention of that part of the line by veterans is in Antietam Studies, box 2, Carman Papers, NA. The primary accounts there total perhaps two hundred pages, all of them *entirely* silent on the Bloody Lane extension. Colquitt's narrative in that box, similarly silent, is a letter to J. M. Gould dated October 29, 1870. An anecdotal account from Colquitt's 6th Georgia, likewise ignoring the Bloody Lane, is James M. McCook, "Courier Duty at Kennesaw," Atlanta *Journal,* March 29, 1902. Josiah Lewis, "An Account of Some Incidents in My Life," manuscript in possession of Zack Waters, Rome, Ga., contains the best narrative I have seen from Colquitt's brigade at this phase of the war. Lewis mentioned a "very brief" rally in the center, in which he did not take part. It is his description of Lee's dress and demeanor in the narrative. The "Washingtonian" quote is from "Lee, Longstreet, and Jackson," Atlanta *Southern Confederacy,* October 31, 1862. Hill (*OR*, 1023) specifically mentioned the 23rd North Carolina, and that regiment's history boasted—somewhat extravagantly—that "the greater part of our regiment stopped in . . . the famous Bloody Lane [and] fought there the remainder of the day" (Clark, *N.C. Regiments,* 2:223). One reliable account that mentions a fragment being attached to Rodes's left is a letter by George G. Grattan of Colquitt's staff, December 9, 1890, reel 84-3, Gould Papers, Dartmouth.

13. Carman Narrative, LC. The 2,200 estimate for the Confederates includes about 200 men in the loose-knit force on Rodes's left. Carman's estimate for Richardson's division was a few dozen more than 4,000 troops.

14. John W. Haley, *The Rebel Yell and Yankee Hurrah: The Civil War Journal of a Maine Volunteer,* ed. Ruth L. Silliker (Camden, Maine: Down East Books, 1985), 111–12; Theodore Lyman, *Meade's Headquarters,* ed. George R. Agassiz (Boston: Atlantic Monthly Press, 1922), 10; Regis de Trobriand, *Four Years with the Army of the Potomac* (Boston: Ticknor and Co., 1889), 530.

15. A thorough, judicious summary of Jackson vs. French in Florida is in Lenoir Chambers, *Stonewall Jackson,* 2 vols. (New York: Morrow, 1959), 1:167–99.

16. Carman Narrative, LC. Carman put the initial onset at about 9:30 A.M. and the final withdrawal of the Federals, victorious but stymied, around 1:00 P.M.

17. John B. Gordon, *Reminiscences of the Civil War* (New York: Scribner's, 1903), 85–87; Soldier, "Sixth Alabama Regiment." Maj. William Walter Sillers of the 30th North Carolina reported arriving in the road about 8:30 A.M. (*OR*, 1051) and timed the initial onslaught before 10:00 A.M.

18. [Cullen A. Battle], "The Third Alabama Regiment," 55–56; Capt. John K.

Hoyt to Lancaster, October 3, 1862, R. A. Lancaster Papers, Virginia Historical Society, Richmond; Mobile *Advertiser and Register,* October 4, 1862. The manuscript history of the 3rd Alabama is unsigned and from the private papers of the Reverend J. H. B. Hall, but internal evidence makes clear Battle's authorship. There is a copy of the Battle manuscript in the archives at FSNMP, donated by a descendant. For the convenience of future scholars, note that the Samuel Pickens diary (5th Alabama) in the Hoole Collection at the University of Alabama, Tuscaloosa, does not include Sharpsburg content.

19. Soldier, "Sixth Alabama Regiment." This contemporary account, here used for the first time since its obscure 1862 appearance, corroborates Gordon's own emotional late-life version of his ordeal at the Bloody Lane, which often has been deprecated by modern skeptics.

20. Gordon, *Reminiscences,* 88–91. Battle, "Third Alabama," 56, confirms Gordon's five wounds. J. M. Thompson, *Reminiscences of Autauga Rifles* (Autaugaville, Ala.: by the author, 1879), 3, reports also on "the wound that disfigured [Gordon's] face." A nominal list of casualties in the Columbus (Ga.) *Daily Sun,* October 8, 1862, described Gordon as wounded "in the face, shoulder, arm and leg."

21. Clark, *N. C. Regiments,* 2:500. A superb, detailed manuscript history of the 30th by Michael W. Taylor, "To Drive the Enemy from Southern Soil," is scheduled for publication during 1998. It is constructed on the basis of a rich array of unpublished sources.

22. William Erskine Ardrey diary, September 17, 1862, printed in the Matthews (N.C.) *News,* September 1991–January 1992 (pt. 6).

23. Clark, *N. C. Regiments,* 1:246–47; E. A. Osborne, "The Fourth N.C. Regiment," Charlotte *Semi-Weekly Observer,* March 23, 1900; James Columbus Steele, *Sketches of the Civil War* (Statesville, N.C.: Brady Printing Co., 1921), 27; Ross memoir, USAMHI. Marsh died on September 24. He was commanding the 4th because Col. Bryan Grimes had been injured at South Mountain. For Marsh, see Weymouth T. Jordan and Louis H. Manarin, eds., *North Carolina Troops, 1861–1865: A Roster,* 13 vols. to date (Raleigh: State Department of Archives and History, 1966–), 4:96, and Ellsworth Eliot Jr., *Yale in the Civil War* (New Haven: Yale University Press, 1932), 207.

24. Ross memoir, USAMHI; Clark, *N. C. Regiments,* 1:247–48; Shinn memoir, SHC.

25. Recollections of Sgt. Newsom Edward Jenkins, NCDAH; R. T. Bennett to John M. Gould, December 2, 1892, reel 84-3, Gould Papers, Dartmouth; Clark, *N. C. Regiments,* 1:712; T. D[B]. Beall, "Reminiscences about Sharpsburg," *Confederate Veteran* 1 (August 1893): 246. Sergeant Jenkins considered his regiment's ground to be *better* than that of the regiments to the right, because the road was more deeply cut on the low ground to the left.

26. T. Frank Forrest, *An Old Soldier's Career: His Four Long Years Experience, Trials, and Sufferings in the Bloody Conflict of the Sixties* (Stewart, Miss.: n.p., 1906[?]), second and third unpaginated leaves.

27. Wilson T. Jenkins memoir, NCDAH; T. J. Watkins memoir, copy in bound vol. 85, FSNMP; Julius L. Schaub memoir, Troup County Archives, La Grange, Ga.; W. A. Smith, *The Anson Guards* (Charlotte, N.C.: Stone Publishing Co., 1914), 157–59.

28. *OR,* 1050; R. T. Bennett to John M. Gould, December 15, 26, 1892, reel 84-3, Gould Papers, Dartmouth. Reading Bennett's earnest but not excessively acute correspondence helps make clear why he never reached brigade command, despite having a commission as full colonel dating from early in the war.

29. "From Our Army," *North Carolina Standard* (Raleigh), October 1, 1862, is unsigned but identifiable as Gorman's from internal evidence.

30. The carefully reliable Carman Narrative, LC, estimates two hours of action for Kimball's brigade, the last of French's brigades to engage (just before Richardson's arrival) and therefore a good average measurement for the period of deadly stalemate.

31. Seaton Gales, "Gen. Geo. Burgwyn Anderson," *Our Living and Our Dead* 3 (September 1875): 333–34; Carman Narrative, LC; "Death of Gen. George B. Anderson," *North Carolina Standard* (Raleigh), October 17, 1862; Clark, *N.C. Regiments,* 1:249, 4:448; Margie Boteler to Mrs. Anderson, September 18, 1862, from November 30, 1996, auction catalog of Signature House, Monkton, Md.

32. Walter Battle letter; Gales, "Anderson," 334; "Death of Gen. George B. Anderson," *North Carolina Standard* (Raleigh), October 17, 1862. The identity of the attending surgeon comes from Battle's letter, in which he wrote of Gus Stith. The only North Carolina surgeon of that surname was L. A. Stith, who belonged to the 2nd of Anderson's brigade. Perhaps his second given name was Augustus. Four standard sources identify L. A. Stith as the only Surgeon Stith from the state, but none provides either given name: *Provisional Record of Confederate Medical Officers . . . Medical Society, N.C.* (n.p., n.d.), 46; Clark, *N.C. Regiments,* 4:631; Stith's Compiled Service Record, M331, NA; and Jordan and Manarin, *North Carolina Troops,* 3:380.

33. Clark, *N.C. Regiments,* 2:499–500; Fred Philips to Gen'l H. Heth, August 25, 1894, reel 84-3, Gould Papers, Dartmouth; Thomas J. Watkins, *Notes on the Movement of the 14th North Carolina Regiment* (Wadesboro, N.C.: Anson County Historical Society, 1991), 7–8; A. D. Betts, *Experience of a Confederate Chaplain* (n.p., n.d.), 17. The Rev. Mr. Betts's memoir exists in manuscript under the same title at NCDAH, with only minor variations from the book version. Although all published sources call the wounded adjutant Fred Phil*l*ips, his own signature, neat and clear in the 1894 Philips letter cited here, uses only a single "l." There is ample evidence that Anderson, Tew, and Parker were hit very early in the action in the sources cited above and also in some of those in the next note. Note that Philips's letter is misfiled with Ripley's brigade and under the 3rd, rather than 30th, North Carolina; it would be very difficult to find without knowing of that anomaly.

34. *OR,* 1026; N. H. Alford Jr., "First Honor Graduate of the Citadel," clipping from unidentified newspaper dated September 17, 1939, in author's possession; Catherine

Ann Devereux Edmondston, *"Journal of a Secesh Lady": The Diary of Catherine Ann Devereux Edmondston,* ed. Beth Gilbert Crabtree and James W. Patton (Raleigh: Division of Archives and History, 1979), 265; Clark, *N.C. Regiments,* 1:168; "From Our Army," *North Carolina Standard* (Raleigh), October 1, 1862; Ross memoir, USAMHI. The accounts of Tew's wound and of his final moments are both from enemies: an 8th Ohio soldier as told to a 2nd North Carolina captain in 1867, Clark, *N.C. Regiments,* 1:167; and John Finn to Mrs. Ella Tew Lindsay, December 10, 1885, copy in the author's possession by way of a Tew descendant. Further details on Tew's death and burial are in a set of 1891 clippings in the S. B. Weeks Scrapbook, vol. 8, SHC.

35. Alford, "First Honor Graduate"; John P. Thomas, *The History of the South Carolina Military Academy* (Charleston: Walker, Evans & Cogswell Co., 1893), 130–35; J. D. Bruns, "In Memoriam—Col. C. C. Tew," the *State* (Columbia), October 11, 1903; "The Late Col. C. Courtenay Tew," undated (ca. 1865) clipping in the author's possession; Janson L. Cox, Citadel Museum, to E. D. Sloan Jr., October 18, 1963, in the author's possession; unsigned statement by Henry Slade Tew (father), Citadel archives, Charleston, S.C.

36. Carman Narrative, LC; ". . . Letter from Wright's Brigade," Augusta *Constitutionalist,* October 4, 1862. This study is concerned primarily with Confederate infantry operations. A fine study of artillery affairs is Robert L. Lagemann, "Summary of the Artillery Batteries in positions to support the Infantry during the action at 'Bloody Lane,' with a Map showing their locations," typescript dated March 1962, ANB. Richard H. Anderson and George B. Anderson were neither related by blood nor associated in any command relationship.

37. C. Irvine Walker, *The Life of Lieutenant General Richard Heron Anderson* (Charleston, S.C.: Art Publishing Co., 1917), 100; *OR,* 1023. Walker, writing late and hagiographically, erroneously insisted that Anderson "retained his command until the emergency had passed, and then fell fainting from loss of blood." D. H. Hill's official report, cited above, lauds Anderson warmly but says simply that he "was soon wounded, and the command devolved upon General Pryor." Carman says Anderson was hit "very soon after coming upon the field," and he echoes the almost universal opinion that Pryor "did not rise to the occasion, and the consequent movements of his command were disjointed and without proper direction." William Gibson's official report, Charles H. Andrews Papers, SHC (hereafter cited as Gibson report, SHC), states that Anderson was hit "long before reaching our advanced position." The exchange between Pryor and Longstreet is from the William McWillie journal, Mississippi Department of Archives and History, Jackson. Lieutenant McWillie served on R. H. Anderson's staff.

38. Captain Feltus's report is in *OR,* 884–85. The division actually contained twenty-five regiments and one battalion. One other report, that of acting brigade commander William Gibson, survives at SHC. It is cited herein in discussing the actions of Wright's brigade.

39. Carman Narrative, LC; David Lang to E. A. Carman, ca. 1898, David Lang Letterbooks, vol. 2, Florida State Archives, Tallahassee; Col. R. F. Floyd to Governor John Milton, September 22, 1862, Governor's Office Letterbooks, ser. 32, vol. 6, p. 462, Florida State Archives, Tallahassee; Council A. Bryan, "Letter from the 5th Florida," *Florida Sentinel* (Tallahassee), October 7, 1862. Carman professed to know that Mahone's brigade numbered precisely 82 men. Armistead's absence on detached service near the West Woods with McLaws is confirmed in a vivid account by Walter Clark to Carman, January 3, 1900, box 2, Antietam Studies, Carman Papers, NA. Clark described seeing Armistead blown over by a passing shell that narrowly missed him, and feeling grumpy about it. Carman wondered if Clark had not seen Barksdale instead, but Clark reiterated his story emphatically. Colonel Floyd was the titular commander of the 8th Florida but was desperately sick and only managed to reach the army's rear area late in the battle. He resigned a few days later. A useful and relatively unknown narrative about the Florida regiments is Andrew Francis Lindstrom, "Perry's Brigade in the Army of Northern Virginia" (M.A. thesis, University of Florida, 1966). A map and notes in the Carman Papers, LC, based on discussions with Capt. William D. Ballantine of the 2nd Florida, show that regiment not reaching the lane, despite having a respectable strength of 240 men.

40. Statement of Maj. J. H. J. Williams to an examining board, April 14, 1863, W1349 1/2-1863, "Letters Received by the Confederate Adjutant and Inspector General, 1861–65," M474, RG 109, NA; Cadmus M. Wilcox ms., "History of Wilcox's Brigade," Wilcox Papers, LC; Bailey George McClelen, *I Saw the Elephant,* ed. Norman E. Rourke (Shippensburg, Pa.: Burd Street Press, 1995), 29–30; Hilary A. Herbert, "History of the Eighth Alabama Volunteer Regiment, C.S.A.," *Alabama Historical Quarterly* 39 (1977): 77–79; letter of Alexander C. Chisholm, 9th Alabama, Bath (Maine) *Independent,* December 3, 1892. Cumming soon received promotion to brigadier general and fought in the Western Theater throughout the war. Wilcox, though absent sick, marveled at Lee's "very combative" nature in fighting at all at Sharpsburg. His thoughtful analysis, based on three tours of the field, is in a letter to D. H. Hill, September 14, 1886, D. H. Hill Papers, NCDAH.

41. Carman Narrative, LC; *A Historical Sketch of the Quitman Guards* (New Orleans: Isaac T. Hinton, Printer, 1866), 34; Ada Christine Lightsey, *The Veteran's Story* (Meridian, Miss.: Meridian News, Printers and Binders, [1899]), 23; Eugene Matthew Ott Jr., ed., "The Civil War Diary of James J. Kirkpatrick, Sixteenth Mississippi Infantry" (M.A. thesis, Texas A&M University, 1984), 193–94. Featherston was still absent because of a wound suffered around Richmond.

42. Carman Narrative, LC.

43. "Gen Wright's Brigade," Augusta *Constitutionalist,* October 3, 1862; Carman Narrative, LC; William B. Judkins memoir, 39, Carnegie Library, Rome, Ga.; C. H. Andrews, "General A. R. Wright at Sharpsburg," Atlanta *Journal,* November 2, 1901; Charles H. Andrews, "Condensed History of the Campaigns of the Third Regiment of

Georgia Volunteer Infantry," Andrews Papers, SHC; "From the Army in Virginia," Augusta *Constitutionalist,* October 5, 1862; Claiborne Snead, *Address by Col. Claiborne Snead at the Reunion of the Third Georgia Regiment* (Augusta: Chronicle & Sentinel Job Printing Estab., 1874), 8; "From the 22d Georgia," Rome (Ga.) *Tri-Weekly Courier,* October 14, 1862; Gibson report, SHC. A good account of the dangers attending this brigade's advance to battle, not quoted in the text, is David L. Bozeman to wife, September 23, 1862, bound vol. 199, FSNMP.

44. The account of Jones's wounding is from a biographical sketch of the colonel written by William B. Judkins of Company G, 22nd Georgia, copy in the author's possession. Judkins was writing at the request of Jones's brother, so he certainly would not have been inclined to exaggerate the incident.

45. W. G., ". . . Letter from Wright's Brigade," Augusta *Constitutionalist,* October 4, 1862; Carman Narrative, LC; A. P. Hill to R. E. Lee, October 13, 1864, in G. Moxley Sorrel's Compiled Service Record, M331, NA; James P. Verdery letter, November 9, 1864, DU; "Letter from Wright's Brigade in Virginia," Augusta *Constitutionalist,* October 18, 1862.

46. *OR,* 1037, 1051; Soldier, "Sixth Alabama Regiment"; Smith, *Anson Guards,* 157.

47. Gibson report, SHC; Snead, *Address,* 8; "Letter from Wright's Brigade in Virginia," Augusta *Constitutionalist,* October 18, 1862; Carman Narrative, LC; ". . . Letter from Wright's Brigade," Augusta *Constitutionalist,* October 4, 1862; Robert K. Krick, *Lee's Colonels: A Biographical Register of the Field Officers of the Army of Northern Virginia* (Dayton, Ohio: Morningside, 1992), 289–90. Nisbet survived his dire wounds and captivity, resigned as a result, but lived until 1901.

48. Shinn memoir, SHC.

49. Ibid.; Ross memoir, USAMHI; *Quitman Guards,* 34–35; *OR,* 1048. A pathetic story of a father and son killed side by side as the Mississippians advanced to reinforce the lane is in "Fourth North Carolina," Charlotte *Observer,* March 3, 1895.

50. John W. Mills account in William W. Bennett, *A Narrative of the Great Revival Which Prevailed in the Southern Armies during the Late War between the States of the Federal Union* (Philadelphia: Claxton, Remsen & Haffelfinger, 1877), 200–201; "The Civil War Memoirs of Benjamin Franklin Page of Woodville," *Magnolia Monthly: A Magazine of News, Features, and History about Wakulla County* 2 (September 1964): unpaginated leaves. The route of the 8th Florida to the far right end of the defended lane, where the stone tower now stands, is depicted graphically on a map in the Carman Papers, LC, marked by Carman on the basis of a letter from William Baya (captain of the regiment at Sharpsburg, later lieutenant colonel), January 18, 1895.

51. Dwight D. Stinson Jr., "Federal Penetration of Sunken Road," ms. with maps and marked photographs, dated December 1971, ANB; Carman Narrative, LC.

52. [Nelson A. Miles] (unsigned) to "Dear Brother," September 24, 1862, copy in possession of Gary L. Ecelbarger, Sterling, Va.; *OR,* 291; Nelson A. Miles, "My Recollections of Antietam," *Cosmopolitan* 53 (October 1912): 580–89; letter with an

illegible signature from one of Richardson's entourage ["Fammi"?] to "My dear Marcia," Sunday, October [no day], 1862, Carman Papers, NA.

53. E. A. Osborne in Clark, *N.C. Regiments,* 1:248; *OR,* 1048; Beall, "Reminiscences about Sharpsburg," 246; Ross memoir, USAMHI; Shinn memoir, SHC; R. T. Bennett to John M. Gould, Gould Papers, Dartmouth; Gibson report, SHC. Ross described "Fetherston" as commanding the Mississippians, but of course that officer was not present.

54. *OR,* 1051–52; Daniel Lane diary; Steele, *Sketches of the Civil War,* 28; R. T. Bennett to John M. Gould, December 2, 1891, Gould Papers, Dartmouth.

55. *OR,* 1023, 1027–28, 1037–38; Smith, *Anson Guards,* 157, 159; Soldier, "Sixth Alabama Regiment."

56. The best sources for the rally around the Piper house, orchard, and cornfield are, as always for Sharpsburg events, the Carman Narrative, LC, and the Carman Papers, NA. The sources enumerated below are either important or picturesque—but obscure—references on the Piper fighting. William W. Chamberlaine, *Memoirs of the Civil War* (Washington: Press of Byron S. Adams, 1912), 32–39 (Chamberlaine's pivotal role is borne out in several other sources); D. H. Hill to James Longstreet, February 11, 1888, Longstreet Papers, DU; "The Piper Farm, the Piper Family Talk, 1862," typescript at ANB; S. Webster Piper, "Piper Family History," two thick unpaginated binders at ANB; *In the Court of Claims, Congressional Case, Henry Piper vs. the United States* (n.p., [1886]); "The 15th Ala. at Sharpsburg—Desperate Fighting," Columbus (Ga.) *Daily Sun,* October 6, 1862; *Quitman Guards,* 34–35; Gibson report, SHC; Lightsey, *Veteran's Story,* 23; Herbert, "History of the 8th Alabama," 79–81; James E. Saunders, *Early Settlers of Alabama* (New Orleans: L. Graham & Son, Printers, 1899), 167–68; Ott, "Diary of James J. Kirkpatrick"; Cleve Rowan (2nd Mississippi Battalion) to John M. Gould, September 23, 1896, and W. M. English (Boyce's Battery) to Gould, September 27, 1897, Gould Papers, Dartmouth; Thomas H. Carter to Ezra A. Carman, April 30, 1896, and John W. Tullis to Carman, April 6, 1900, Carman Papers, NA.

57. Precisely detailed losses for the 2nd (29–32–53) and 14th (52–123–103) North Carolina are reported in Mast, *State Troops and Volunteers,* 330, 359–60. For casualties in the 14th, see confirmation in Smith, *Anson Guards,* 159. Counselor Mike Taylor's first-rate manuscript history of the 30th counts casualties of 16–40–20 for that regiment. Lacking a detailed calculation based on service records for the 4th, I used only the 6 killed and 40 wounded from the official tabulation (*OR,* 1048), which is generally low—and completely ignores prisoners and missing. An accurate figure for the 4th most certainly would push the brigade loss above 600, and thus above 50 percent.

58. *OR,* 1038; Soldier, "Sixth Alabama Regiment"; Henry B. Wood, *The Marble Valley Boys* (Hoover, Ala.: Interface Printing Co., 1986), 44. The 6th's losses, by name, of 27 killed, 61 wounded, and 13 missing are in the Columbus *Daily Sun,* October 8, 1862. The same source shows only 20 casualties in the 3rd Alabama but

reported on only one-half of its companies. As is customary with Civil War casualties, only a detailed review of official service records can produce an accurate count of killed and missing. The vagaries of record keeping based primarily on pay musters makes counting the wounded uncertain even there.

59. Herbert, "History of the Eighth Alabama," 80; Franklin Lafayette Riley diary, bound vol. 244, FSNMP; "General Wright's Brigade" and "List of Casualties in Wright's Brigade . . . Sept. 17, 1862," Augusta *Constitutionalist,* October 3, 1862. The casualties suffered by the Floridians in his beloved "Citrus Brigade" come from manuscript research by Zack Waters of Rome, Ga., by all odds the paramount authority on that unit. In killed, wounded, and missing, he tabulates 14–18–22 in the 2nd Florida, 52–42–57 in the 5th, and 25–24–28 in the 8th. Nominal lists are far more reliable for casualties than any mere enumeration. The Augusta newspaper cited above printed such a listing. Losses by regiment in that source for the 3rd, 22nd, 44th, and 48th Georgia were 9–58–5 (out of 138); 2–25–8 (out of 72); 13–64–6 (out of 125); and 9–43–14 (out of 118).

60. Robert E. Park, *Sketch of the Twelfth Alabama Infantry* (Richmond: Wm. Ellis Jones, Book and Job Printer, 1906), 74–75.

PETER S. CARMICHAEL

We Don't Know What on Earth to Do with Him

William Nelson Pendleton and the
Affair at Shepherdstown, September 19, 1862

Nicknames provide revealing clues about how historical figures were viewed by their contemporaries. "Marse Robert" expressed the feelings of fatherly respect and devotion Confederate soldiers felt for Robert E. Lee, while "Old Jack" captured the folk-hero status that Stonewall Jackson enjoyed among his troops. The dependable service of James Longstreet earned him the justly deserved nickname "Lee's War Horse." Each of these generals exhibited qualities associated with the ideal soldier. They were courageous, calm, and successful on the battlefield. Without dramatic victories or daring exploits to his credit, however, an officer ran the risk of losing his men's loyalty. Even a hint of unmanly behavior elicited disparaging sobriquets from soldiers in the ranks.

"Old Mother Pendleton" sums up the low regard that Lee's soldiers felt for the Episcopal minister William Nelson Pendleton, whose frequent miscues as chief of artillery made him a favorite target of ridicule. An incident during the North Anna campaign in 1864 revealed a common attitude toward Pendleton. When Lee rode by the soldiers in Charles Field's division, a rousing cheer went up from the troops. A few minutes later Pendleton passed the same unit, inspiring one soldier to shout: "[T]hree cheers for Genl. Pendleton." An embarrassing silence followed, recorded a Mississippian, as the men suddenly turned mute. The soldier who had called for the cheers broke the hush by mumbling "oh!"—whereupon "the whole column broke out in a laugh." Pendleton's blundering exploits, well known and documented throughout the army, caused many to wonder why Lee did not banish his preacher-artillerist to some hidden monastery. Confederate gunner John H. Chamberlayne voiced the concerns of his comrades when he wrote: "By the way Pendleton is Lee's weakness. Pn is like the elephant, we have him & we don't know what on earth to do with him, and it costs a devil of a sight to feed him." [1]

Pendleton compiled an unimpressive record in an army in which officers routinely earned promotion by sheer hard fighting. He seemed confused and dangerously out of equilibrium amid the chaos and peril of combat, proving himself neither a cool-thinking tactician nor a reckless warrior. He lacked the aggressive instincts of artillerists such as Edward Porter Alexander, William R. J. Pegram, and John Pelham. On occasion he even failed to uphold the most basic standards of courage that defined behavior throughout the army. Such violations of male honor tarnished his reputation from the beginning of the war. As early as the aftermath of First Manassas, rumors alleged that he had cowered on the ground instead of personally leading his battery. This ugly story surfaced in Pendleton's hometown of Lexington, Virginia, prompting an adamant denial from the embarrassed artillerist. [2] Doubts about Pendleton's leadership increased as a result of his performances on subsequent battlefields. During the bitter fighting at Malvern Hill, he seemingly disappeared with the Reserve Artillery at a time when Lee desperately needed additional ordnance. Illness prevented him from joining his battalion at Second Manassas, and subordinates criticized his tactical judgment at Second Fredericksburg and again at Gettysburg. [3]

No episode in Pendleton's Confederate career sparked more controversy than the collapse of the southern rear guard at Shepherdstown on September 19, 1862. Lee had assigned Pendleton the critical task of defending Boteler's Ford while the army retreated into Virginia. A small Union force crossed the river, stormed the Confederate position, and nearly captured thirty-three guns of the Reserve Artillery. Although Pendleton should not shoulder sole responsibility for the fiasco at Shepherdstown, the incident proved that the army's chief of artillery could be more of a menace to his own troops than to the enemy.

On paper Pendleton possessed the necessary credentials to become a successful chief of artillery. He graduated fifth in the West Point class of 1830 at the age of twenty-one, an accomplishment that earned him a brevet second lieutenant's commission in the Fourth Regiment of Artillery. Posted initially to Fort Moultrie, where he gained valuable training in coastal artillery, he later held a one-year pro-

Brigadier General William Nelson Pendleton
Jennings C. Wise, *The Long Arm of Lee*,
2 vols. (Lynchburg, Va.: J. P. Bell, 1915), 1: opposite p. 64

fessorship at West Point. Pendleton experienced a religious conversion during a brief stay at Fort Hamilton, an event that radically changed the course of his life. A spiritual languor that had besieged him at the academy suddenly lifted. His sense of duty to the army wavered, as he felt a growing desire to serve a higher authority. Insufficient pay, intolerable living conditions, infrequent promotion, and inadequate intellectual companionship also caused him to question his future in the military. He searched for a more satisfying career that would fit his new faith.[4]

When a mathematical professorship opened in 1833 at Bristol College, a newly organized Episcopal school in Pennsylvania, Pendleton resigned his commission to become a teacher and an ordained Episcopal minister. Financial entanglements caused Bristol to close its doors in less than four years, forcing Pendleton to find employment at Newark College. That post proved to be a stepping stone to a prestigious job as headmaster of the Episcopal High School in Alexandria, Virginia, which after five sessions under Pendleton's stewardship had amassed a debt of more than five thousand dollars. The headmaster's personal finances were also in disarray. Thirty-five years old in 1844, facing eight thousand dollars in debt and with a wife and six children to support, Pendleton resigned from the Episcopal High School and moved to Baltimore to oversee another boy's school. He soon packed his bags again, accepting the rectorship of All Saints Church in Frederick, Maryland. A dispute with his vestry ended a brief tenure there, and Pendleton left in 1853 for Grace Episcopal Church in Lexington, Virginia, a position he occupied until his death.[5]

With the outbreak of Civil War, the fifty-one-year-old minister exchanged his clerical robes for the military garb of the artillery. On May 1, he was elected captain of the celebrated Rockbridge Artillery, a Lexington-based unit composed of four guns that Pendleton aptly named after the early Christian figures Matthew, Mark, Luke, and John.[6] Promotion came quickly. On July 13, 1861, Joseph E. Johnston followed Davis's recommendation and named Pendleton his chief of artillery at the rank of colonel. The rumors of cowardice after First Manassas did not slow his advancement. Pendleton's superiors, in fact, kept him in charge of Johnston's artillery, which brought a brigadier general's commission on March 26, 1862.[7] When Lee assumed command of the Confederate army in Virginia after Johnston's wounding at Seven Pines, he retained Pendleton as chief of artillery. The dismal performance at Malvern Hill and the illness that prevented his participating in the action at Second Manassas marked Pendleton's debut under Lee's leadership.

The lingering effects of malaria, contracted before the war in South Carolina, frequently incapacitated Pendleton during his Confederate career. On August 31, 1862, he informed his wife, "I am writing to you from a bed, and this time I am in it as an invalid." Pendleton suffered from a "crisis of a diarrhoea," which lasted some two weeks and complicated his effort to join the army as it prepared to enter Maryland.[8]

Once back with the army, he engaged in conflicts with subordinates.[9] By Jackson's orders, Pendleton instructed Lt. William B. Hardy and his Middlesex Artillery to remain in Virginia because it lacked sufficient men and horses. Hardy personally challenged the directive, and when Pendleton insisted on compliance, the lieutenant "bore himself with strangely improper violence," stalked out of the room, and slammed the door. Instead of mollifying the aggrieved officer, Pendleton further insulted Hardy by seeking a temporary transfer of his men and horses to batteries slated for the Maryland raid. Hardy and his officers refused to obey, forcing Pendleton to place them under arrest, surround them with guards, and remove them to a remote part of the camp so their mutinous influence would not contaminate others. Quarantining the officers did not stop most of the enlisted men from feigning sickness. Pendleton's own surgeon found just four soldiers with legitimate ailments. In a final appeal, Pendleton acknowledged the men's grievances and convinced forty-six members of the battery to volunteer in other units. Although he must have been pleased with this resolution, Pendleton refused to forgive Hardy's company for its rebellious actions. During the artillery's reorganization after Antietam, he succeeded in breaking up the Middlesex Artillery, redistributing the men, and relieving the officers. The insubordinate behavior of Hardy and his subordinates, Pendleton asserted in his official recommendation, justified the elimination of the Virginia battery.

Relations also soured between Pendleton and his four battalions, some nineteen batteries that made up his immediate command in the Reserve Artillery. After fording the Potomac on September 7, Pendleton's cannoneers pulled their guns off the road and were eagerly anticipating an evening of rest when the "shrill blast of the bugle spoke the alarm." Reports soon indicated that thousands of Federal horsemen were racing toward the limbered cannon. A wave of fear and panic scattered the frightened artillerists. In an attempt to restore order, an excited Pendleton shouted at his men: "Whose battery is this[?]" "Why do you not hurry the enemy's cavalry may come upon us[?]" He approached a number of battery captains and asked if their officers were present. His confused state of mind resulted from either fear or an embarrassing unfamiliarity with his command. In any case, Pendleton's erratic behavior infuriated subordinates, including James A. Blackshear, who noted that "on this occasion as indeed was true at other times afterwards Gen. Pendleton displayed an utter want of confidence & fearlessness."

When Col. Allen Sherrod Cutts learned that some of his batteries had been involved in the stampede, he immediately ordered his companies to meet at Frederick. He planned to consolidate his battalion and keep it away from Pendleton. The general, it appears, had fallen ill again and could not countermand the order himself. Blackshear explained that Pendleton stayed "at a house as usual—and pretending to be sick." The artillery chief instructed Maj. William Nelson to challenge the intransigent Cutts, who decided to confront Pendleton the next day. In a tense interview, Cutts denounced his superior during a profane tirade that sustained his reputation as one of the army's most accomplished swearers. Cutts promised that "he would leave the corps [Reserve Artillery] either by death resignation desertion or some other way that the corps never had fought any and never would fight any, that it was an absolute disgrace to the army and that through all future time it would be a reproach to any man that had ever belonged to it." According to Blackshear, Pendleton listened to all this in silence: "[K]nowing too well the truth of these charges," the general "succumbed [to Cutts] like a whipped puppy." In the end Pendleton not only failed to arrest his insolent subordinate, observed Blackshear, but also allowed Cutts "with all the arrogance and self conceit of his nature to take his battalion and go boastingly into D. H. Hill's division."

Although bitter disputes with subordinates must have disheartened Pendleton, he wrote glowing letters about Lee's first northern raid and its prospects for success. "Suffice it that General Lee seems well to understand what he is about," Pendleton reported on September 10. "Yankeedom seems a good deal stirred up." Maryland's less than enthusiastic reception of Lee's veterans troubled the artillerist, however, and he described western Maryland as a beautiful but foreign land, corrupted by Germans and "Pennsylvania Yankees" who had created "a state of society where all is one dead level." A return to Frederick tempered his harsh opinion of the state. The town was attractive, well kept, and apparently more prosperous than in his days as rector of All Saints Church. Old friends enthusiastically greeted the general, a welcome diversion from the rigors of campaigning. All the attention led Pendleton to conclude that "greater kindness no one ever received." [10]

The army's interlude at Frederick ended when Lee decided to capture Harpers Ferry and connect his supply lines to the Shenandoah Valley. The resulting battles in the gaps of South Mountain did not involve Pendleton, who informed his wife that "my assigned place was only near, not in" the action. Much of his Reserve Artillery had been detached to other officers, an attempt by Lee, perhaps, to insulate Pendleton from combat. Only portions of two battalions remained in the Reserve Artillery on September 15, when Lee, near midnight, gave Pendleton instructions to guard the fords at Williamsport, Falling Waters, and Shepherdstown. With some lingering bitterness, Pendleton later wrote in his official report that he moved "the residue of my command by the shortest route to Williamsport and across the Potomac." A tiresome night march took the cannoneers to the river by about sunrise. Pendleton immediately dispatched Col. John Thompson Brown's battalion to guard the fords at Williamsport and Falling Waters, a little more than a mile down river. The remaining battalion, Maj. William Nelson's, followed Pendleton to Shepherdstown. There his men repaired the roads to Boteler's Ford, gathered stragglers, and positioned guns on the Virginia side of the river. The hard labor and constant supervision fatigued the sickly Pendleton, who explained to his wife that "the work had to be done day and night." [11]

As the sounds of battle echoed from Antietam Creek on September 17, Pendleton continued to work behind the lines, mostly at Boteler's Ford. He received an urgent request from Lee to forward long-range cannon to the battlefield if he could do so without jeopardizing the safety of the fords. Late in the evening Pendleton sent three batteries to Sharpsburg, two from Colonel Brown's battalion and one from his immediate command at Shepherdstown. Although Pendleton worried that Brown might lack enough guns to defend his position, he approved his subordinate's questionable scheme to attack a bridge across Back Creek controlled by the enemy.[12] Brown almost certainly did not have enough men to execute the plan, and Pendleton should have discouraged such an offensive move. Protecting the fords, as Lee had instructed, was his top priority. Pendleton's decision is even more troubling when considering the main army's precarious situation at Sharpsburg. He knew that Lee needed every available man. Not long before Pendleton endorsed his subordinate's risky scheme, the commanding general had demanded that stragglers be corralled by "the point of the sword" and hurried to the front. Similar pleas for assistance required Pendleton's attention throughout the night, "so that I could scarcely steal a nap."[13] By the narrowest of margins, Lee's troops repulsed repeated Federal attacks and held their ground east of Sharpsburg. After a day of inaction on September 18, the Confederates slipped away in the darkness, retreating to Virginia, battered and on the brink of demoralization.

Once the fighting concluded, Pendleton emerged from the army's supporting cast to assume a leading role in the final act of the Maryland campaign. "I had again to work like a beaver," he related to his wife, "as did all my officers and men, promoting the safe passage of the army, with its immense trains of artillery and wagons, hence no rest again that night." Pendleton's men marked the ford's location with torches that cast giant shadows of Lee's veterans against the shoreline. As the men entered the knee-deep waters of the Potomac, the mossy rocks felled a number of unsuspecting soldiers, to the amusement of their comrades. With thousands of men, wagons, and cannon converging at a single point, the three-hundred-yard ford turned into a narrow funnel. Numerous traffic jams developed, but Jackson's quartermaster, John A. Harman, relied on his superior logistical abilities and profane language to keep the column moving. Between 9:00 and 10:00 A.M. on the 19th, the southern rear guard reached Virginia to the relief of the Confederate high command. An officer overheard General Lee quietly give thanks to God when the last troops touched Virginia soil.[14]

With the Army of Northern Virginia safely below the Potomac, command of the rear guard fell squarely on Pendleton's shoulders. He understood the importance of this assignment, succinctly capturing the drama of the moment in a letter to his wife: "[N]ow came my great responsibility." Pendleton focused his energies and resources on defending Boteler's Ford but also worried about another crossing a few miles to the south. Although Confederate cavalry patrolled the latter, more men were needed to stop a probable Federal advance. The Army of the Potomac could also take advantage of Shepherd's Ford, some four miles north of Boteler's. Pendleton dispatched a battery and a small infantry force, consisting of stragglers he had rounded up, to guard that section of the river.[15]

So many avenues of approach gave Pendleton just cause for concern. To make matters worse, Lee gave his subordinate insufficient resources, largely because so few reserves were available. No more than 600 infantrymen, many of them exhausted and without weapons, complemented Pendleton's artillery, which numbered some forty guns. Army headquarters had left his command in a vulnerable situation. Faulty judgment from above, not carelessness, largely explains why Pendleton was woefully unprepared to meet a Federal advance. In 1866, Lee admitted that after Antietam he "believed Gen. McClellan had been so crippled at Sharpsburg, that he could not follow the Confederate Army into Virginia immediately." [16]

The rugged terrain around Boteler's Ford partially compensated for Pendleton's small numbers. A long line of steep bluffs, rocky and bare, extended along the Virginia side of the river and provided an ideal location for artillery. In some places the cliffs rose nearly perpendicular to the ground. Attacking troops could never scale such formidable heights. Cultivated fields covered the hilltop, broken occasionally by a patch of woods. The road that connected to the ford sliced through the Virginia hillside and intersected the Charles Town Pike three miles southwest of Shepherdstown.[17] This had been the principal thoroughfare for Lee's retreating army. Pendleton planned to use it as well when it came time to withdraw.

Thirty-three cannon formed the backbone of his defense, with most of the guns aimed at the ford. The long-range pieces, 10-pounder Parrotts and 3-inch rifles, flanked either side of the crossing a few hundred yards behind the river on the high cliffs. The 6-pounders and 12-pounder howitzers directly overlooked the ford, not far from the river's edge and carefully arrayed so that Confederate gunners could deliver a powerful converging fire. Pendleton had judiciously placed his ordnance by distributing those pieces most effective at close range near the bank. The long-range guns had been unlimbered on more commanding ground to engage in counter–battery fire. Unable to find favorable positions for eleven additional guns, Pendleton moved them to a point beyond the enemy's range but still within supporting distance. Dispersed near the ford as sharpshooters, the 600 soldiers of Alexander R. Lawton's and Lewis A. Armistead's badly depleted brigades stood watch. A smaller contingent of infantrymen may have been held in reserve in a sheltered ravine not far from Pendleton's headquarters.[18]

Although Lee typically allowed subordinates ample latitude, he gave Pendleton precise instructions on September 19 regarding the defense of Boteler's Ford.

A view from the north bank of the Potomac toward the formidable bluffs held
by Pendleton's troops south of the river.
United States Army Military History Institute

If the Federals relied exclusively on the long arm, Pendleton should hold his
ground and retire the next morning. In case of an aggressive infantry advance,
Lee wanted his subordinate to withdraw that evening.[19]

The latter scenario seemed unlikely with the cautious McClellan, but early on
September 19 he ordered Fitz John Porter's Fifth Corps to support a cavalry
brigade under Alfred Pleasonton as it advanced toward Boteler's Ford. Shortly after the last Confederates had crossed the river, Union troopers appeared on the
distant heights, followed by some artillery companies. The latter quickly unlimbered and engaged Pendleton's command, igniting a lively counter–battery
fire that relaxed briefly when the Fifth Corps arrived late in the afternoon. Porter
quickly surveyed the scene, unlimbered additional batteries, and determined "to
clear the fords." Under the cover of some fifteen guns, he deployed the riflemen
of the First U.S. Sharpshooters along the banks of the C&O Canal, which ran
along the north side of the river.[20]

Superior ordnance and more reliable ammunition enabled Porter's artillerists
to silence the Confederate batteries within hours. Most of Pendleton's guns, especially near the ford, lacked either sufficient range to respond or the necessary
fuses for long-distance firing. Merit Seay of the Fluvanna Artillery complained
that "they brought their long range guns to bear on us and very near cut us to
pieces while we couldn't hurt them with our little six pounders." Pendleton concurred with this assessment, writing to his wife that "they planted on the more

commanding heights on the other side a number of powerful batteries, compared with which ours were but as pop guns."[21] Those cannoneers with rifled pieces not only inflicted little damage but also failed to pin down Federals who advanced virtually unmolested to the ford. Stephen H. Weed's Union battery, reported a Fifth Corps officer, moved to within "easy range" of the Confederate companies and proceeded to drive the southern cannoneers away from their pieces.[22]

Union sharpshooters posed the greatest threat to Pendleton's command. From the sheltered canal bank, the Federals unleashed a rapid and accurate fire that forced many Confederates to run for cover. "In spite of persistent vigor on the part of our batteries," Pendleton reported, "a heavy body of sharpshooters gained the canal bank on the northern and hostile side of the river. This proved to us an evil not slightly trying, since it exposed our nearer cannoneers to be picked off, when serving their guns." Relief never came from Armistead's and Lawton's brigades. In the morning Pendleton had instructed both brigade commanders, Cols. James Gregory Hodges and John Hill Lamar (Armistead and Lawton had been wounded at Antietam), not to "fire merely in reply to shots from the other side, but only to repel any attempt at crossing, and to guard the ford." This order doomed the cannoneers. They would not receive adequate support when the infantrymen reduced their fire according to Pendleton's instruction. Pendleton also failed to provide for cooperation between the two branches. Throughout the day infantry and artillery officers complained about each other. Hodges could not understand why southern batteries did not retaliate against Federal gunners whose shells paralyzed Confederates around the ford. He concluded a message to Pendleton with a dire warning: "There is nothing to prevent the enemy from crossing except the line of sharpshooters on the river." Battery commanders requested more infantry, but few men were available. Moreover, Pendleton was forced to deplete his reserve by hurrying two hundred men to the guns just above the ford.[23]

Dispatches coming into Pendleton's headquarters painted an alarming picture that took on a more desperate tone late in the afternoon. Yet the general seemed oblivious to the approaching crisis. Col. Thomas T. Munford, commanding the Confederate cavalry at the ford south of Boteler's, frantically called for infantry support because he doubted his troopers could resist a powerful Union battery. Colonel Hodges of Armistead's brigade received Munford's message and forwarded sixty men of the 9th Virginia Infantry to the scene. It appears that Hodges did not consult Pendleton first, although the general claimed in his official report that he initiated the transfer. In any case, Pendleton was largely ignorant of what had happened in his own command. He admitted that he did not know how many men were in Lawton's and Armistead's brigades. Instead of accepting responsibility for this oversight, Pendleton weakly explained that no one informed him that both brigades had suffered heavy casualties at Antietam. Had he known of the brigades' depleted state, Pendleton asserted, he never would have stripped the ford of defenders by dispersing soldiers to its right and left. Only three hundred men remained at Boteler's by late afternoon—hard pressed, weary, and on the verge of abandoning their ground. In his most startling revelation, Pendleton confessed in his official report that he remained unaware "of infantry weakness . . . [at] the ford itself" until late in the evening.[24] By that point only Pendleton's divine connections could have staved off disaster.

Pendleton claimed that his headquarters afforded a general view of the lines, which raises the question of why he did not have a better understanding of the situation. He seemed disconnected from events, roused to action only when sudden explosions of musketry and artillery reverberated from the banks of the Potomac. In preparation for a dusk assault, the Federal artillery blasted the ford and surrounding heights. The distinctive crack of the sharpshooter rifles blended into a continuous roll of musketry. Messages arrived shortly from Lamar and Hodges warning that they could not hold their ground in the face of renewed pressure. Pendleton promised them relief if they could maintain their positions for an hour until sunset, when Munford's cavalry was scheduled to arrive. Meanwhile, he planned to retire some guns to create a buffer between his batteries and the river. Munford's troopers would interpose themselves between the retreating rear guard and the enemy. As Pendleton issued his instructions, he was shocked to discover that most of his companies had exhausted their ammunition. Those cannoneers whose limber chests were emptied and concealed from the enemy started for the rear in the growing darkness. With a reduction in fire and his command in flux, Pendleton realized his troops were especially vulnerable. "It was," he recalled, "a critical and anxious hour, inasmuch as a dashing force might . . . get across and capture some of our longest-served and latest-removed guns." But as "deep dusk" settled over the field, Pendleton believed the crisis to be over.[25]

His false sense of security did not last long. A light raiding party of some sixty men from the First U.S. Sharpshooters struck the ford when most of the Confederates were retreating or eagerly anticipating an order to retire. As the sharpshooters pushed across the river, three hundred men of the 4th Michigan fired volleys over their heads. Artillery and infantry lining the Maryland side of the river provided additional support. Union firepower broke the resistance and resolve of Pendleton's men. Only scattered shots came from the Confederates, and most of the bullets plunked harmlessly into the water. Just four Union soldiers fell before the attackers reached a virtually deserted Virginia shore. Federals cautiously climbed the steep heights, groping in the darkness for the remnants of Pendleton's rear guard.[26]

The soldiers in Lawton's and Armistead's brigades managed a few ragged volleys before fleeing. The suddenness with which Pendleton's command disintegrated shocked those in the Army of Northern Virginia unaccustomed to seeing Lee's infantry run from the enemy. "Somebody blundered again or was grossly negligent," observed Henry Kyd Douglas. "It would have been no difficult matter to defend that ford from passage." In a surprisingly empathetic tone, D. H. Hill wrote in 1864 that "our men were so much demoralized that a whole Brigade (Lawton's) had thrown down its arms the night before & fled without firing a shot at the Yankees as they crossed the River."[27]

More forceful leadership might have stiffened the backbone of the foot soldiers, coordinated efforts between infantry and artillery, and prevented the dispersion of troops that sealed the fate of the Confederate rear guard. But Pendleton should not be held accountable for the wretched condition and low morale of the men, factors that contributed to the collapse. High casualties at Antietam and the loss of both brigade commanders compromised the fighting spirit of the infantrymen. Little rest and insufficient food further undercut morale. "It was now the 18th, and nothing had been furnished since [the 16th]; nor did we get any until the 19th," recalled a member of Armistead's brigade. "I did not eat anything for at least forty-eight hours. You may not possibly know how it feels to go that long, and to be marching night and day; I assure you that a man is not in the best of spirits."[28] The few reinforcements that reached Armistead's and Lawton's brigades did not improve the situation. Most of the men had just been released from the hospital and were without weapons.

As Lawton's and Armistead's men deserted the crossing, Pendleton stood a few hundred yards behind the ford waiting for his staff and orderlies. A number of infantrymen suddenly rushed out of the blackness and past the general. A few of the panic-stricken soldiers stopped long enough to tell Pendleton that the Yankees had routed the guard at the ford and landed on the Virginia side of the river. "Worn as were these men," Pendleton wrote, "their state of disorder, akin to panic, was not, justly, to be met with harshness." With words of encouragement he patched together a temporary defensive line, but most of the soldiers continued to the rear and disappeared into the woods.[29]

At this critical juncture, Pendleton noted, his "personal situation was all the while necessarily much exposed . . . to easy capture." Pendleton's fear of capture is puzzling in light of his admission that he did not know precisely what had happened at the ford. With his staff absent on errands, he lacked basic information

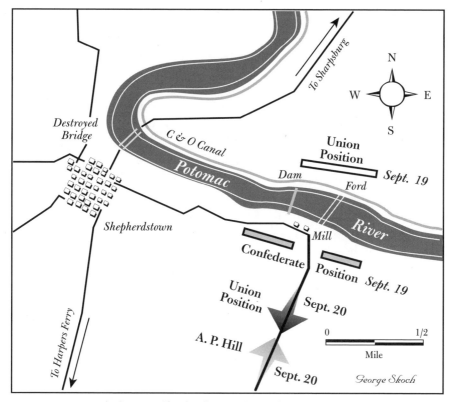

Action near Shepherdstown, September 19–20, 1862

about the Federal crossing. Instead of waiting for his officers to give him the particulars of the attack, he decided that the enemy would embark upon one of two courses. They would either "cautiously proceed only 100 or 200 yards" inward and halt, or aggressively pursue and try to destroy the Confederate rear guard. In his official report, Pendleton stated that at the time he did not expect the enemy to attack and believed his own artillery and infantry would escape safely. At the same time, he thought it necessary to provide for the chance that a "hostile force" would continue the advance into Virginia. He thus decided to lead the retreating column to Shepherdstown while the rest of his command, entangled at the ford, would have to fend for itself.[30]

In truth, Pendleton scurried off the field because he did not have a basic understanding of events at the ford. After the battle he created a smoke screen of half-truths and falsehoods to obscure his actions and appalling lack of firsthand knowledge. Pendleton's certitude about the enemy's intentions came after the fact. In a letter to his wife written two days before he completed his battle report, he violently contradicted his official statement to Lee: "It was a critical moment," he wrote. "If vigorously pressed, their opportunity would have given them quite half our guns. At the time I acted on the supposition that they would press on, and intending, first, to save all I could, and, secondly, not to expose myself needlessly to capture, I passed, by a short path under a fierce fire from their heavy guns, towards the road which some of the artillery had . . . already taken." He further incriminated himself by adding that he left "the rest to the result of my orders" and anticipated the "capture" of soldiers and officers at the ford.[31]

Only four abandoned guns and a handful of prisoners fell into the hands of Federals who cautiously advanced a few hundred yards before recrossing the Potomac that evening. Pendleton's defensive line crumbled nonetheless, as men, guns, horses, limber chests, and caissons jammed the Charles Town Road. Some of the Confederates dragged their cannon across the rugged countryside, stumbling in the darkness, in the hope of reaching Lee's main army. One artillerist recalled that "the men of our battery, together with those belonging to other batteries on the bluff were mixed in helter-skelter race for the rear." "It seemed to me," he added, "that the night was interminable." Union guns commanded about a mile of the Charles Town Road that ran up a deep gorge. Pendleton successfully passed through the gauntlet of fire before meeting Gen. Roger A. Pryor. He pleaded for some infantry to rescue his guns, but Pryor, whose military ineptitude exceeded even Pendleton's, refused, pronouncing the responsibility "too serious for him to assume." He suggested that Pendleton seek permission from the higher-ranking John Bell Hood. Pendleton never saw Hood, nor could he locate James Longstreet. "[R]eferred to another and another, till past midnight," his frustration mounted as he proved unable to find an infantry officer willing to rescue the Reserve Artillery.[32]

With his options exhausted, Pendleton believed it "was clearly my next duty" to find army headquarters and report to Lee. "In the extreme darkness and amid the intricacies of unknown routes," he searched until he finally found the commanding general and his staff sleeping under an apple tree. Pendleton told Lee, who had just been awakened, about the Federal attack and the likelihood that the Reserve Artillery had been captured. Such an alarming message must have jolted the groggy Lee into consciousness better than a strong cup of coffee. The commanding general blurted out, "All?" "Yes, General, I fear all," Pendleton responded. An unidentified staff officer overheard the conversation, writing later that Pendleton's dire report "lifted me right off my blanket, and I moved away, fearful I might betray my feelings." Lee showed remarkable restraint, administering not so much as a mild rebuke to Pendleton. The artillerist left the conference mistakenly believing that Lee "determined to do nothing till next morning."

Without knowing his command's fate, Pendleton gathered a "handful of straw," covered himself with "my old overcoat," and fell asleep under the night sky.[33]

While his bungling subordinate slept, Lee vainly tried to ascertain what had occurred at Boteler's Ford so he could make an appropriate response. The Army of Northern Virginia was badly scattered south of the Potomac, and he did not know the precise whereabouts of his primary subordinates, Longstreet and Jackson. The army's deplorable condition also made a counterattack risky. Lee first approached Daniel Harvey Hill to ask where Jackson's command had bivouacked, but the North Carolinian did not know. Hill tried to comfort a visibly upset Lee, assuring him that "my Division is ready to move and awaits your orders." Lee replied: "I do not know what to tell you to do. I hear from one messenger that the enemy have crossed the river and captured a few pieces of artillery, by another that they have crossed in force and have possession of all the reserve artillery. I can hear nothing reliable." When Hill mentioned that he had received instructions to follow Jubal Early's division to Boteler's Ford, Lee appeared "much perplexed" and thought the order "might be a mistake." A flustered Lee soon left in search of Longstreet. In 1864, Hill wrote that he could not recall another occasion when Lee exhibited "such indecision & embarrassment." J. W. Ratchford of Hill's staff similarly could remember no other occasion when Lee displayed so much excitement over the state of his army.[34]

Fortunately for the commanding general, news of Pendleton's debacle had reached Stonewall Jackson. Jackson typically did not wait for orders but, as Kyd Douglas succinctly put it, "took the matter in his own hands."[35] An indignant Jackson wanted to redeem the army's reputation after the flight of Pendleton's rear guard. Following a personal reconnaissance, he selected A. P. Hill's division to secure the ford and drive the enemy across the river. Early the next morning, September 20, the Confederates crashed into three Fifth Corps brigades that had reached the Virginia shore after daylight. Porter's outnumbered force quickly yielded ground to the southerners, except Col. Charles M. Prevost's 118th Pennsylvania Infantry, known as the Corn Exchange Regiment. Although Porter had ordered his troops to return to Maryland, Prevost refused until he received instructions from his direct superior. Just as the Pennsylvanians deployed atop the bluffs overlooking the ford, Hill's men slammed into their flank. Blasts of musketry decimated the 118th, scattering survivors who tumbled down the steep banks and into the river. Only powerful Union guns on the Maryland side of the river stopped the Confederate pursuit. Pendleton rode with Jackson during the counterattack, describing it as a "privilege" to accompany "that honored officer and friend in the exposure incident to his command." To his wife, the artillerist also pointed out that he "shared the danger with the troops" while serving Jackson.[36]

Union artillery covers the withdrawal of Fitz John Porter's Fifth Corps troops
near Shepherdstown on September 20.
Frank Leslie's Illustrated Newspaper, October 25, 1862

Stonewall's forceful response not only reclaimed Virginia's side of the river but also saved Pendleton from further embarrassment. "Gen. Jackson showed his genius in taking the offensive & in selecting A. P. Hill's division," D. H. Hill affirmed in 1864. "I have sometimes thought that the Army of N. Va. would almost have ceased to have an organization but for this splendid movement." A relieved Pendleton felt a sense of vindication with the recapture of Boteler's Ford. Because the Federals fled Virginia, the artillerist reached the dubious conclusion that he had issued the appropriate orders the previous evening. Proof of his foresight, he asserted, was the safe withdrawal of his command. Only the capture of four guns detracted from his generalship. "These," wrote Pendleton, "their horses being killed and the men being too weary to drag them away, had been spiked and left." No matter the extenuating circumstances, Pendleton admitted to his wife that losing cannon "is among military men more or less a deduction from a man's standing." One of the guns came from the Virginia Military Institute and had been originally assigned to his first battery. It pained Pendleton to lose the piece, probably for sentimental reasons, but the general assured VMI's superintendent that he "was careful to recommend that a facsimile of it be made by the Confederate govt. and returned to Va. It will, no doubt, be done."[37]

A day after the battle, Lee asked Pendleton to "report the facts, as well for my own sake as for his own satisfaction and the truth of history." In summarizing his actions, the artillerist carefully detailed his personal movements, never missing an opportunity to let the commanding general know that he was repeatedly exposed to enemy fire. This was a highly unusual approach in an official document, but one probably adopted to counter rumors of cowardice. Pendleton offered a bolder defense to his wife. "With the means at my disposal," he declared, "a great deal was accomplished. We kept the powerful array of the enemy at bay for ten hours." "Could the infantry have held a half an hour longer, nothing would have been lost," he concluded. He offered a similar explanation in a second letter: "While I regret the loss (the four cannon) and the occasion for Yankee glorification, I am so conscious of having done well my duty, and so thankful to God for ordering so remarkable a preservation, that for any temporary cloud over myself I am more than willing to compound."[38]

Contrary to Pendleton's hopes, the controversy over Shepherdstown did not represent a passing shower but a prolonged storm that hovered over the Army of Northern Virginia. In this volatile atmosphere, rumor, recriminations, and resentment disrupted relations in Lee's officer corps. Critics insisted that Boteler's Ford validated their charge that the chief of artillery had a penchant for escaping combat. The general, however, insisted to his wife that "no blame that I ever heard of is attached to me by anybody."[39]

Only a severe bout of self-delusion could have warped Pendleton's perceptions so badly. Criticism reverberated from all quarters of the army. The feeble defense of Boteler's Ford and his quick exit from the field outraged a number of men. Two captains who commanded batteries near the ford, Marmaduke Johnson and Thomas Jellis Kirkpatrick, felt so disgraced that they almost wept "with vexation." They denounced Pendleton as a ridiculous incompetent. The general's own staff, reported one officer, feared that Pendleton's cowardly behavior had forever stained their reputations as well. By far the most outspoken critic was John Hampden Chamberlayne, a staff officer under the artillerist Reuben Lindsay Walker. From the Confederate camp at Bunker Hill, he vented to a friend: "Brig. Gen. Pendleton is an absurd humbug; a fool and a coward. Well known to be so among those who see and know, & do not hear."[40]

Chamberlayne decided to take his case against Pendleton public by sending an anonymous letter to the Richmond *Whig*. In it he insinuated that Pendleton lacked courage for retreating "without sufficient cause." He also blasted Pendleton for incorrectly reporting the capture of the Reserve Artillery, further evidence that the general did not lead in person but stayed comfortably away from the action. A rumor that Pendleton purposefully abandoned his cannon to lure the Federals across the river so Jackson could launch a surprise attack angered Chamberlayne the most. He labeled this part of a larger plot to deflect praise away from A. P. Hill's "Light Division." "The story that Jackson caused men to leave their guns by way of a ruse, has no foundation in fact," Chamberlayne declared. "Some of Jackson's men were on Hill's flank, in case of need, but the fighting was all done by Hill's men; and it is but just that they should be credited with it." Privately, Chamberlayne speculated that the story "was gotten up to shield Gen. P." because he had "so disgracefully run away." [41]

A month later, the Richmond *Whig* printed a response to Chamberlayne's vitriolic attack. Pendleton, or possibly a close associate, probably wrote the article signed "Justice." After pointing out some insignificant factual errors in Chamberlayne's piece, this article addressed the most serious charge, namely, that Pendleton had ordered an unnecessary retreat. By keeping the Federals at bay for the entire day and retiring at dusk, Justice claimed, Pendleton had fulfilled Lee's orders. His stand gave the main army sufficient time to find a "comfortable resting place" south of the Potomac. "The withdrawal of guns at nightfall was not an unadvised 'retreat,'" the article continued, "but an arranged removal—according to instructions received from the commanding general." Justice supported this opinion by pinpointing specific factors, largely out of Pendleton's control, that had disabled his command. Covering a two-mile front with six hundred poorly equipped infantrymen and just a few long-range guns, the defenders at Boteler's Ford had faced a hopeless situation. The article reached the reasonable conclusion that "with so small a force, and so little loss," Pendleton had accomplished his primary mission against overwhelming odds. [42]

If Justice had focused on the important point that Pendleton fulfilled Lee's orders under trying circumstances, he would have successfully refuted Chamberlayne's case. But the article did not stop there, undermining the entire defense by stating that Pendleton never reported the capture of the Reserve Artillery because he always believed his guns were safe. This was a crucial issue that would publicly reflect on the artillerist's courage. Admitting that the general made an inaccurate report or did not know what had happened to his troops would confirm the accusation that he deserted his command. Instead of sidestepping the issue, Justice badly misrepresented what had happened: "Gen. Pendleton did not think he had lost nearly all his guns, but knew that the extended column, which, on personally reaching the road, he met and accompanied, was safe." [43]

Overwhelming wartime evidence conclusively proves otherwise. On September 20, Lee informed Jefferson Davis that "from General Pendleton's report after midnight, I fear much of his reserve artillery has been captured." D. H. Hill wrote

John Hampden Chamberlayne
as a captain of artillery.
C. G. Chamberlayne, ed., *Ham
Chamberlayne—Virginian: Letters
and Papers of an Artillery Officer in
the War for Southern Independence,
1861–65* (Richmond: Dietz, 1932),
opposite p. 256

later in the war that Pendleton "came to my tent in search of Gen. Lee & told me that the Yankees had crossed in force & that he had lost 30 pieces of artillery. This news was alarming to me as I knew the demoralized condition our army." The most damning testimony came from Pendleton's own pen. He confided to his wife that he had expected to lose most of the cannon at the ford that evening and went to sleep not knowing "who might have been captured and who not" or "how many guns were lost."[44]

The numerous fabrications in the *Whig*'s article infuriated Chamberlayne, who contemplated sending a return salvo to the newspaper. "As for Gen P. or Justice, my reputation, in the little circle which knows me at all, is sure enough to allow me to let him pass by," Chamberlayne remarked. "Tho' Justice lets drop some offensive expressions, I know that from Pendleton I could gain but cowardice and foul words." In the end, Chamberlayne decided against escalating this war of words, sparing the Army of Northern Virginia additional embarrassment. As long as Pendleton continued as chief of artillery, Chamberlayne considered him untouchable. "When the shackles of this necessary but galling military system are off me," he promised a close friend, "may the Lord do so unto me and more also if I do not bring him to account both publickly and privately. And I charge you, if some danger of the battle field, which he so carefully shuns, shall end my life before the war is done, I charge you in the cause of truth & justice to see that light is thrown on the tortuous, lying & cowardly part which this jackal has played in high places."[45]

Lee's benevolent treatment of Pendleton must have disappointed the vengeful Chamberlayne. The commanding general not only failed to call a court of inquiry but also refused to reprimand Pendleton. The staff officer who overheard the initial conversation between the two men remembered that Lee "exhibited no temper, made no reproach that I could hear, either then, or even afterwards, when he learned that the gallantry of a subordinate officer had saved the command, and that the commanding officer (Pendleton) had been premature in his report." In his report on the Maryland expedition, Lee devoted two curt sentences to the incident: "General Pendleton was left to guard the ford with the reserve artillery and about 600 infantry. That night the enemy crossed the river above General Pendleton's position, and his infantry support giving away, four of his guns were taken." Trying to assess blame would have been invidious when Lee issued the report in August 1863. The commanding general's management style promoted conciliation, not conflict. He was also reluctant to chastise Pendleton because he knew that his subordinate had lacked enough infantry to carry out his mission. To illustrate the army's broken-down condition after Antietam, Lee underscored the small size of the force that defended Boteler's Ford. He informed Davis that "General Pendleton reported that the brigades of Generals Lawton and Armistead, left to guard the ford at Shepherdstown, together contained but 600 men. This is a woeful condition of affairs, and I am pained to state it, but you ought not to be ignorant of the fact, in order, if possible, that you may apply the proper remedy."[46]

The breakdown of Armistead's and Lawton's brigades probably saved Pendleton from a transfer or dismissal. Still, Lee must have been concerned about Pendleton's inability to manage troops in battle. His quick exit from the field and inaccurate report that the Reserve Artillery had been captured showed that he was better suited for a bureaucratic position. Although Pendleton remained at his post for the entire war, he never gained the respect of his comrades either as an administrator or as a minister. "He and his ponderous staff was regarded in the army as a sort of [a] joke," declared the South Carolina battalion commander David Gregg McIntosh. "If one of his inspectors ever visited my camp or ever inspected my horses, munitions, etc., I am unable to recall it." After hearing Pendleton preach in 1864, Walter H. Taylor of Lee's staff observed, "I am not so averse to hearing the General as others but am always sorry to see him officiate, because I know how the soldiers will talk about him." [47]

A bold act under fire might have compensated for Pendleton's deficiencies as a combat officer, a tactic that salvaged the careers of many mediocre soldiers, but he was not an inspiring leader. After David McIntosh read Jennings C. Wise's charitable evaluation of Pendleton in the classic *Long Arm of Lee,* he bluntly told the author that he considered "it rather a pity that you should not have allowed that good old gentleman, General Pendleton to remain somewhat in the background, where he was accustomed to be, and not have exalted him into the conspicuous place you have." [48] Pendleton's own correspondence supports McIntosh's assertion that he obsessed about his personal safety. Pendleton even admitted to Varina Davis that if, like John Bell Hood, he had suffered two grievous wounds, "he would wince and dodge at every ball." Mrs. Davis quickly retorted: "[W]hy wince—when you would thank God for a ball to go through your heart and be done with it all." [49]

It is difficult to find another officer in the Army of Northern Virginia more maligned than Pendleton—which made Lee's continued support a puzzle to many officers. Typical of the latter was Col. Thomas T. Munford of the cavalry, who wrote in 1894 that *"it is worth studying"* why Lee would select someone like Pendleton *"to handle his guns"* when the commanding general typically displayed *"a genius* for war." [50] Although Lee never decided to remove Pendleton, he consistently tried to restrict his duties to bureaucratic matters rather than giving him meaningful control of the artillery in battle. As an administrator, Pendleton figured prominently in the artillery's reorganization that followed Antietam and Fredericksburg, reforms that greatly enhanced the effectiveness of Lee's long arm. Pendleton even created a system of infirmaries that saved thousands of horses. But his efforts to improve the efficiency of the artillery never convinced Lee to recommend his promotion. Lee's boldest move to disentangle Pendleton from the Army of Northern Virginia came in 1864 when the latter received a temporary assignment to inspect the artillery of the Army of Tennessee. [51]

Friendship with Lee and close ties to the president probably prevented Pendleton's receiving a humiliating transfer. He and Lee had been acquaintances during their days as cadets at West Point. Although they never became close friends, the commanding general probably admired his chief of artillery's sincerity, patriotism, and deep religious convictions. Having a man of the cloth as a ranking officer likely pleased the devout Lee, who constantly strove to improve his army's religious condition. Although many soldiers thought piety weakened a man's aggressive impulses, Lee could have believed that allowing Pendleton to handle some of the army's spiritual duties conveyed the message that good warriors should also be good Christians. Pendleton's example might also inspire other officers to promote the teachings of Jesus Christ in camp. Unfortunately for Lee, the actions of the messenger undermined the message. Few veterans of the Army of Northern Virginia would have disagreed with McIntosh's assessment: "Gen. Lee's retaining him [Pendleton] was doubtless due to the fact that it was foreign to Gen. Lee's character to wound the feelings of any one, as would have been the case by his removal or some one being put over him. Gen. Lee's considerateness for those under him was one of the most prominent traits of his character, and there are those who think it sometimes amounted to a positive weakness."[52]

The possibility of a conflict with Jefferson Davis ranks as the leading reason Lee took no decisive action against Pendleton. Pendleton and Davis began a lifelong friendship at West Point, and during the war the president staunchly supported the artillerist. In his postwar memoir, Davis remembered his friend as the epitome "of the soldier, the patriot, and the Christian." Pendleton's favored status in Richmond helps explain his initial rise in rank. On July 13, 1861, Davis wrote glowingly of Pendleton to Joseph E. Johnston: "I recollect Captain Pendleton well, and when we were all younger esteemed him highly as a soldier and a gentleman. I some days since directed that he should have rank as a colonel and be put in command of the batteries of your army."[53]

During the Seven Days battles near Richmond, Pendleton served as a confidant of the president. While both men watched the fighting at Gaines's Mill, they "conversed freely about our affairs." Whatever Pendleton said must have impressed Davis, because he invited the artillerist to a "confidential interview" with Lee. On the eve of the Second Manassas campaign, Davis again included Pendleton in high-level discussions, this time with the secretary of war. When Lee suggested during the 1863 artillery reorganization that Pendleton transfer to Jackson's corps and that Arnold Elzey become chief of artillery, Davis denied the request. After Leonidas Polk's death at Pine Mountain in 1864, the president even suggested that the artillerist assume command of Polk's corps in the Army of Tennessee. Lee dismissed Davis's recommendation. "As much as I esteem & admire Genl Pendleton," wrote Lee, "I could not select him to command a corps in this army. I do not mean to say by that he is not competent, but from what I have seen of him, I do not know that he is—I can spare him, if in your good judgment, you decide he is the best available."[54]

In the end, the commanding general was not willing to risk a confrontation with Davis in order to dismiss the ineffectual Pendleton. With a limited supply of bargaining chips, Lee pressed the administration on matters he deemed more essential to the army's welfare. To alienate Davis over a subordinate who stood outside the army's circle of authority made no sense, nor would it have promoted the necessary spirit of cooperation between Richmond authorities and the army. Lee placed the good of the cause above all else, making it the guiding principle that defined his management of subordinates and his relations with superiors. His conciliatory approach almost always enhanced the Army of Northern Virginia's military efficiency. With the chief of artillery, however, the results were mixed. Lee tried to use Pendleton's administrative skills, but that approach never compensated for his liabilities as a combat officer.

After the war, Pendleton helped persuade Lee to accept the presidency of Washington College. In Lexington, Lee continued to serve as an advocate and protector of Pendleton. On occasion Pendleton taught a class pertaining to theological matters. The students disliked him intensely and found his lectures to be a mind-numbing experience. To express their discontent on one occasion, they pinned papers to the tail of the general's coat as he walked up the classroom aisle. Just as he began to lecture, they bombarded him with wads of paper. An outraged Pendleton complained about their bad manners and persuaded Lee to monitor the next class. The latter's formidable presence and position of authority transformed the rebellious youths into docile schoolboys. But the détente proved short lived. When Pendleton faced his students alone the following week, they had escalated the conflict by enlisting some former Confederate soldiers. Their new allies stood outside the classroom windows and taunted Pendleton by blowing horns and generally behaving in an obnoxious manner. Pendleton pressed on with his lecture until someone tossed a dog with a tin can tied to his tail into the room. Pandemonium erupted. Before the old artillerist fled, he denounced the students as incorrigible.[55]

Lee could not save Pendleton from the ridicule of the young men at Washington College, but he assisted his old comrade at a meeting to decide Pendleton's salary. Lee and the other vestrymen met at Grace Church on October 12, 1870. They were fifty-five dollars short of the desired sum and soon found themselves engaged in a tiresome discussion about how to raise the necessary amount. The meeting dragged endlessly on, trying the patience of a weary and unwell Lee. The debate came to a merciful end when he said quietly that he would donate the remaining sum. Lee's last gift to Pendleton concluded the meeting. Under a dark, rainy sky, Lee walked home. Shortly after entering his house, he suffered a fatal stroke. Family and friends surrounded Lee's deathbed, including Pendleton — who probably read a prayer over the stricken general.[56]

Pendleton presided over Lee's funeral. His eulogy expressed a deep sense of admiration and loss for the chieftain of the Army of Northern Virginia. But words were not enough. For the remainder of his life, Pendleton devoted himself to the promulgation of the Lost Cause and the canonization of Lee. As part of an elaborate effort to cement Lee's position as the quintessential southern hero, he viciously attacked the war records of James Longstreet and other former Confederates who posed a perceived threat to Lee's image. Although Pendleton probably considered his postwar efforts an act of loyalty, his Christlike depiction of the commanding general ranks as his greatest disservice to Robert E. Lee.[57]

ACKNOWLEDGMENTS

I would like to thank Keith S. Bohannon for his Georgia sources and John M. Coverick, who alerted me to the photographs of Boteler's Ford.

NOTES

1. William McWillie notebooks, no date, William McWillie Collection, Mississippi Department of Archives and History, Jackson; John Hampden Chamberlayne, *Ham Chamberlayne—Virginian: Letters and Papers of an Artillery Officer in the War for Southern Independence, 1861–1865,* ed. C. G. Chamberlayne (Richmond, Va.: Dietz, 1932), 134. There is no modern biography of Pendleton. The best source on his prewar and Confederate careers, which prints much of his correspondence, is Susan P. Lee, *Memoirs of William Nelson Pendleton, D.D.* (1893; reprint, Harrisonburg, Va.: Sprinkle Publications, 1991).

2. William N. Pendleton to Thomas J. Jackson, April 25, 1862, Thomas J. Jackson Papers, Southern Historical Collection, Wilson Library, University of North Carolina, Chapel Hill (repository hereafter cited as SHC).

3. For discussion of Pendleton's service with the Army of Northern Virginia and the reaction it inspired, see Douglas Southall Freeman, *Lee's Lieutenants: A Study in Command,* 3 vols. (New York: Scribner's, 1942–44).

4. Lee, *Pendleton,* 35–55.

5. Ibid., 55–104.

6. Robert J. Driver Jr., *The 1st and 2nd Rockbridge Artillery* (Lynchburg, Va.: H. E. Howard, 1987), 1–2. On the Rockbridge Artillery, see also William Thomas Poague, *Gunner with Stonewall: Reminiscences of William Thomas Poague,* ed. Monroe F. Cockrell (1957; reprint, Wilmington, N.C.: Broadfoot, 1987).

7. William Nelson Pendleton, Compiled Service Records of Confederate Generals

and Staff Officers and Nonregimental Enlisted Men, M331, reel 196, National Archives, Washington (hereafter cited as CSR; repository hereafter cited as NA).

8. Lee, *Pendleton,* 208–9.

9. The following three paragraphs are based on the James Appleton Blackshear diary, September 7, 8, 1862, James Appleton Blackshear Papers, Emory University Special Collections, Atlanta (repository hereafter cited as EU).

10. Lee, *Pendleton,* 211–12.

11. Ibid., 212–13; U.S. War Department, *The War of the Rebellion: A Compilation of the Official Records of the Union and Confederate Armies,* 127 vols., index, and atlas (Washington: GPO, 1880–1901), ser. 1, vol. 19, pt. 1:830 (hereafter cited as *OR;* all references are to ser. 1). On Pendleton's ability to organize stragglers in Winchester, see George W. Peterkin to William N. Pendleton, September 19, 1862, William Nelson Pendleton Papers, SHC.

12. *OR* 19(2):610–11. For Pendleton's response to Brown, see both of his dispatches, dated September 17, 1862, in the John Thompson Brown Papers, Virginia Historical Society, Richmond (repository hereafter cited as VHS).

13. *OR* 19(2):610; Lee, *Pendleton,* 213.

14. Lee, *Pendleton,* 213; John G. Walker, "Sharpsburg," in *Battles and Leaders of the Civil War,* 4 vols., ed. Robert Underwood Johnson and Clarence Clough Buel (1887–88; reprint, Secaucus, N.J.: Castle, 1982), 2:682. Other accounts of the Confederate retreat to Boteler's Ford include W. H. Andrews, *Footprints of a Regiment: A Recollection of the 1st Georgia Regulars, 1861–1865,* ed. Richard M. McMurry (Marietta, Ga.: Longstreet Press, 1992), 86, and James I. Robertson Jr., *Stonewall Jackson: The Man, the Soldier, the Legend* (New York: Macmillan, 1997), 620–21.

15. Lee, *Pendleton,* 213; *OR* 19(1):830; William Beverley Pettit, *Civil War Letters of Arabella Speairs and William Beverley Pettit of Fluvanna County, Virginia, March 1862–March 1865,* ed. Charles W. Turner, 2 vols. (Roanoke, Va.: Virginia Lithography & Graphics Co., 1988), 1:54–55.

16. Robert E. Lee to Mrs. Thomas J. Jackson, January 25, 1866, Jedediah Hotchkiss Papers, Library of Congress, Washington (repository hereafter cited as LC).

17. Survivors' Association, *History of the 118th Pennsylvania Volunteers, Corn Exchange Regiment, from Their First Engagement at Antietam to Appomattox* (Philadelphia: J. L. Smith, 1905), 94a–94c.

18. *OR* 19(1):830–31.

19. *OR* 19(2):612.

20. *OR* 19(1):339.

21. David G. Martin, *The Fluvanna Artillery* (Lynchburg, Va.: H. E. Howard, 1992), 51; Lee, *Pendleton,* 213. For descriptions of the artillery duel on September 19, see *OR* 19(1):847–48; John T. Block (Louisiana Guard Artillery) to Ezra Carman, May 30, 1899, Antietam Studies, folder titled "McLaws Division," box 1, Ezra Carman Collection, NA; J. B. Moore, "Sharpsburg," in *Southern Historical Society Papers,* 52

vols., ed. J. William Jones and others (1876–1959; reprint with 3-vol. index, Wilmington, N.C.: Broadfoot, 1990–92), 27:214 (hereafter cited as *SHSP*); George M. Neese, *Three Years in the Confederate Horse Artillery* (1911; reprint, Dayton, Ohio: Morningside, 1983), 126.

22. *OR* 19(1):351.

23. *OR* 19(1):832; (2):613.

24. *OR* 19(1):832.

25. *OR* 19(1):832–33.

26. *OR* 19(1):344–45, 349–50. For additional accounts of the Union attack on September 19, see C. A. Stevens, *Berdan's United States Sharpshooters in the Army of the Potomac, 1861–1865* (1892; reprint, Dayton, Ohio: Morningside, 1972), 206–8; Ezra A. Carman, "History of the Antietam Campaign," chap. 22, 9–10, Ezra A. Carman Papers, LC; William H. Powell, *The Fifth Army Corps (Army of the Potomac): A Record of Operations during the Civil War in the United States of America, 1861–1865* (New York: Putnam, 1896), 293–94; Robert Goldthwaite Carter, *Four Brothers in Blue; or, Sunshine and Shadows of the War of the Rebellion: A Story of the Great Civil War from Bull Run to Appomattox* (Washington: Press of Gibson Brothers, 1913), 119; Daniel George Macnamara, *The History of the Ninth Regiment, Massachusetts Volunteer Infantry, Second Brigade, First Division, Fifth Army Corps, Army of the Potomac, June, 1861–June, 1864* (Boston: E. B. Stillings & Co., 1899), 222.

27. Henry Kyd Douglas, *I Rode with Stonewall: Being Chiefly the War Experiences of the Youngest Member of Jackson's Staff from the John Brown Raid to the Hanging of Mrs. Surratt* (1940; reprint, Chapel Hill: University of North Carolina Press, 1984), 184; Daniel Harvey Hill to Robert L. Dabney, July 19, 1864, Robert Lewis Dabney Papers, Special Collections, Union Theological Seminary, Richmond, Va. (repository hereafter cited as UTS). Douglas also believed that "the affair disgusted General Jackson beyond words." During a flag of truce, William H. F. "Rooney" Lee condemned the behavior of Pendleton's men while talking with Federal officer Stephen M. Weld, who summarized the conversation in a letter home: "When the 4th Michigan crossed the river the other evening, he said, they drove a whole brigade of rebels, who ran shamefully. These are Colonel Lee's own words. He also said that the rebels deserted 27 guns that evening, of which we got four, not knowing where the rest were. There is no doubt that the rebels are mighty hard up for food and clothing" (Stephen M. Weld, *War Diary and Letters of Stephen Minot Weld, 1861–1865* [1912; reprint, Boston: Massachusetts Historical Society, 1979], 139). Brig. Gen. William Dorsey Pender of Hill's Light Division also denounced Pendleton's men for vacating their posts. "Some of our miserable people allowed the Yankees to cross the Potomac before they ought and ours ran away making it necessary for us to go and drive them back" (William Dorsey Pender, *The General to His Lady: The Civil War Letters of William Dorsey Pender to Fanny Pender,* ed. William W. Hassler [1965; reprint, Gaithersburg, Md.: Ron R. Van Sickle Military Books, 1988], 176). For a summary of negative opinion in the army

about Pendleton after Shepherdstown, see Chamberlayne, *Ham Chamberlayne,* 116, 118, 135, 139–40, 143–44.

28. John H. Lewis, *Recollections from 1860 to 1865, with Incidents of Camp Life, Descriptions of Battles, the Life of the Southern Soldier, His Hardships and Sufferings, and the Life of a Prisoner of War in the Northern Prisons* (1895; reprint, Dayton, Ohio: Morningside, 1983), 55–45. On the condition of Armistead's and Lawton's brigades, see *OR* 19(1):972–73, and G. Howard Gregory, *38th Virginia Infantry* (Lynchburg, Va.: H. E. Howard, 1988), 28. The gunners were also suffering from insufficient rations and rest. See Moore, "Sharpsburg," *SHSP* 27:213.

29. *OR* 19(1):833, 835. In his official report cited here, Pendleton adamantly defended Armistead's and Lawton's brigades: "To Colonels Lamar and Hodges and the troops they commanded credit is justly due for the persevering determination with which they bore during all the day a fire, doubly galling, of case shot from the enemy's cannon and of musketry from the vastly outnumbering infantry force sheltered by the canal bank across the river. Not until overworn did the handful of our sharpshooters at all give way, and that would probably have been prevented could a double number, partly sheltered by trees, &c., have allowed relief in action." See also "Justice," "The Affair near Shepherdstown, Sept. 20th—Misrepresentation Corrected," Richmond *Whig,* November 13, 1862. In a letter to his wife, however, Pendleton blamed the infantry for the hasty retreat. Perhaps Pendleton believed a public condemnation of Armistead's and Lewis's soldiers would have brought attention to his own misdeeds at Boteler's Ford, which could explain the contradiction between his public and private statements. See William Nelson Pendleton to his wife, September [?], 1862, William Nelson Pendleton Papers, SHC. Brig. Gen. Jubal A. Early held Colonel Lamar responsible for the flight of Lawton's brigade. In his official report, Early wrote that the "brigade was very much reduced, having suffered terribly on the 17th, and a considerable number of the men, being just returned from the hospitals, were without arms, and without knowing the particulars of the affair, I am satisfied its conduct on this occasion was owing to the mismanagement of the officer in command of it" (*OR* 19[1]: 973). Inquiries into the conduct of Lamar and possibly some of his subordinates were initiated, but the court's findings are not extant. See War Department Collection of Confederate Records, General Records of the Government of the Confederate States of America, box 10, manuscript 3330, RG 109, NA.

30. *OR* 19(1):833.

31. Lee, *Pendleton,* 214.

32. Moore, "Sharpsburg," *SHSP* 27:214–15; Lee, *Pendleton,* 214.

33. *OR* 19(1):834; Emily V. Mason, *Popular Life of Gen. Robert E. Lee,* 2nd rev. ed. (Baltimore: John Murphy, 1877), 151; Lee, *Pendleton,* 214.

34. J. W. Ratchford to Robert L. Dabney, April 27, 1869, Daniel Harvey Hill to Robert L. Dabney, July 19, 1864, Robert Lewis Dabney Papers, UTS. After the war, Lee admitted that he was nervous about his army's situation after the crisis at Boteler's

Ford on September 19. He feared that "the Federal Army might be attempting to follow us." When he received Jackson's report that the enemy had been driven across the river on September 20, stated Lee, he was greatly relieved. Robert E. Lee to Mrs. Thomas J. Jackson, January 25, 1866, Jedediah Hotchkiss Papers, LC.

35. Douglas, *I Rode with Stonewall,* 184. Embarrassment might have fueled Jackson's aggressiveness on September 20. The rear guard had been entrusted to him. In 1866, Lee wrote: "After crossing the Potomac, Gen. Jackson was charged with the command of the rear, and he designated the brigades of infantry to support Pendleton's batteries" (Robert E. Lee to Mrs. Thomas J. Jackson, January 25, 1866, Jedediah Hotchkiss Papers, LC). Lee might have been mistaken about Jackson's dispatching Lawton's and Armistead's brigades to assist Pendleton. The artillerist stated in his official report that Longstreet made the assignment. *OR* 19[1]:831.

36. *OR* 19(1):834; Lee, *Pendleton,* 214. On the September 20 fighting at Boteler's Ford, see Carman, "History of the Antietam Campaign," chap. 25, LC; Survivors' Association, *History of the 118th Pennsylvania,* 94f–94w; Freeman, *Lee's Lieutenants,* 2:233–35; "Horner's," *Northern Neck News* (Va.), February 26, 1897; "The Recent Slaughter near Shepherdstown—A Lying Account," Richmond *Dispatch,* September 29, 1862; "The Affair at Shepherdstown: A True Account," Richmond *Whig,* October 13, 1862; William Allan, *The Army of Northern Virginia in 1862* (1892; reprint, Dayton, Ohio: Morningside, 1984), 445–47; J. F. J. Caldwell, *The History of a Brigade of South Carolinians, Known First as "Gregg's" and Subsequently as "McGowan's" Brigade"* (1866; reprint, Dayton, Ohio: Morningside, 1984), 81–83.

37. Daniel Harvey Hill to Robert L. Dabney, July 19, 1864, Robert Lewis Dabney Papers, UTS; Lee, *Pendleton,* 214–15; *OR* 19(1):834; William Nelson Pendleton to his wife, September [?], 1862, William Nelson Pendleton Papers, SHC.

38. Lee, *Pendleton,* 215; William Nelson Pendleton to his wife, September [?], 1862, William Nelson Pendleton Papers, SHC. Pendleton's official report is in *OR* 19(1): 829–34.

39. William Nelson Pendleton to his wife, September [?], 1862, William Nelson Pendleton Papers, SHC.

40. Chamberlayne, *Ham Chamberlayne,* 143, 118.

41. "The Affair at Shepherdstown: A True Account," Richmond *Whig,* October 13, 1862; Chamberlayne, *Ham Chamberlayne,* 116. William Dorsey Pender also believed that the battle at Shepherdstown demonstrated the superiority of Hill's division. "Our Division had a hard fight day before yesterday," he wrote. "We did it under the most terrible artillery fire I ever saw troops exposed to. They continued to shell us all day. It was as hot a place as I wish to get in. It is considered even by Jackson as the most brilliant thing of the war. The fact is, Hill's Division stands first in point of efficiency of any Division in this whole Army" (Pender, *General to His Lady,* 176). The southern press generally credited Jackson with the victory at Shepherdstown without acknowledging the role of A. P. Hill and his division. See, for example, "The Battle at Boteler's

Mill," Richmond *Whig,* September 25, 1862, and "The War," Richmond *Daily Enquirer,* September 25, 1862.

42. "Justice," "The Affair at Shepherdstown, Sept. 20th—Misrepresentations Corrected," Richmond *Whig,* November 13, 1862.

43. Ibid.

44. *OR* 19(1):142; Daniel Harvey Hill to Robert Lewis Dabney, July 19, 1864, Robert Lewis Dabney Papers, UTS; Lee, *Pendleton,* 214. See also Thomas T. Munford to George B. Davis, December 16, 1894, Antietam Studies, Ezra Carman Papers, NA; Mason, *Robert E. Lee,* 151.

45. Chamberlayne, *Ham Chamberlayne,* 143–44.

46. Mason, *Robert E. Lee,* 151; *OR* 19(1):151, 143.

47. David Gregg McIntosh to Jennings C. Wise, June 8, 1916, David Gregg McIntosh Papers, Civil War Miscellaneous Collection, United States Army Military History Institute, Carlisle, Pa. (repository hereafter cited as USAMHI); Walter H. Taylor, *Lee's Adjutant: The Wartime Letters of Colonel Walter Herron Taylor, 1862–1865,* ed. R. Lockwood Tower (Columbia: University of South Carolina Press, 1995), 186.

48. David Gregg McIntosh to Jennings C. Wise, June 8, 1916, David Gregg McIntosh Papers, Civil War Miscellaneous Collection, USAMHI. Wise defended his interpretation in a reply to McIntosh: "I am surprised at your conclusions as to my estimate of Pendleton. I certainly do not glorify him in my estimate of the artillery commanders." Wise believed that a "complete reading of the book" would demonstrate that McIntosh's criticism "as to my rating of Pendleton" was unfair. "I do not see," concluded Wise, "how anyone could gather from the whole any other impression than that Pendleton was very, very weak but not as weak a[s] was generally believed in the army." Jennings C. Wise to David Gregg McIntosh, June 12, 1916, David Gregg McIntosh Papers, Civil War Miscellaneous Collection, USAMHI.

49. Mary Boykin Chesnut, *Mary Chesnut's Civil War,* ed. C. Vann Woodward (New Haven: Yale University Press, 1981), 560.

50. Thomas T. Munford to George B. Davis, December 16, 1894, Antietam Studies, Ezra Carman Papers, NA.

51. Douglas Southall Freeman, *R. E. Lee: A Biography,* 4 vols. (New York: Scribner's, 1934–35), 3:230–31; William Nelson Pendleton CSR, NA.

52. David Gregg McIntosh to Jennings C. Wise, June 8, 1916, David Gregg McIntosh Papers, Civil War Miscellaneous Collection, USAMHI. On the relationship between courage and religion in Civil War armies, see Gerald F. Linderman, *Embattled Courage: The Experience of Combat in the American Civil War* (New York: Free Press, 1987), and Drew Gilpin Faust, chapter titled "Christian Soldiers: The Meaning of Revivalism in the Confederate Army," in *Southern Stories: Slaveholders in Peace and War* (Columbia: University of Missouri Press, 1992), 88–109.

53. Jefferson Davis, *The Rise and Fall of the Confederate Government,* 2 vols. (New York: Appleton, 1881), 2:148; *OR* 2:977.

54. Lee, *Pendleton*, 195, 205–6, 209; Robert E. Lee, *Lee's Dispatches: Unpublished Letters of General Robert E. Lee, C.S.A. to Jefferson Davis and the War Department of the Confederate States of America, 1861–65,* ed. Douglas Southall Freeman with additional dispatches by Grady McWhiney (1957; reprint, Baton Rouge: Louisiana State University Press, 1994), 79, 242.

55. Emory M. Thomas, *Robert E. Lee: A Biography* (New York: Norton, 1995), 374; Freeman, *R. E. Lee,* 4:295–96.

56. Freeman, *R. E. Lee,* 4:487–88; Thomas, *Robert E. Lee,* 415.

57. On Pendleton's role in the canonization of Lee and on the myth of the Lost Cause in general, see Thomas L. Connelly, *The Marble Man: Robert E. Lee and His Image in American Society* (New York: Knopf, 1977); Gaines M. Foster, *Ghosts of the Confederacy: Defeat, the Lost Cause, and the Emergence of the New South* (New York: Oxford University Press, 1987); and Alan T. Nolan, *Lee Considered: General Robert E. Lee and Civil War History* (Chapel Hill: University of North Carolina Press, 1991).

CAROL REARDON

From Antietam to the Argonne

The Maryland Campaign's Lessons for Future Leaders
of the American Expeditionary Force

Fifty years after armies in blue and gray clashed outside the small town of Sharpsburg, a survivor claimed that "Antietam was our greatest day of battle, the bloodiest battle for the South and the most glorious for the Union arms in all that wondrous four years' war which gave to the world new examples of patriotism and higher lessons of heroism." A former Union captain wrote this sentence for a book he dedicated to Abraham Lincoln, Gen. George B. McClellan, and the veterans of both armies. He did not intend for his commentary to be construed simply as the musings of an old soldier. He had something important to tell a very specific audience. As he saluted the soldiers of his youth, he made it clear that he wrote primarily for the benefit of the next generations of "military students, and teachers of the art of war, here and abroad."[1]

The legacy of Antietam has come down to Americans as the costliest of many costly days our soldiers have spent on fields of battle, as the harbinger of emancipation, and in other forms. For military professionals, Antietam has held another, more specific importance because it did indeed offer many useful lessons to that generation of soldiers whom the Union captain hoped to reach.

It took nearly fifty years for American soldiers to begin using Antietam as a classroom for professional studies. When they finally did so, they displayed a strong conviction that it and other Civil War campaigns had much to teach them. Indeed, by 1913 the senior administrators of the U.S. Army War College had committed the institution's faculty and students to the preparation of an official history of the sectional conflict that could be used as a textbook in all the schools that made up the army's officer education system. The administrators set high standards for the work. Not only were students required to read the best published historical literature on the various campaigns, but they also were expected to use the battlefields themselves as a primary research tool.[2]

In the 1880s, the War Department had begun to take measures to preserve many of the greatest battlefields of the Civil War. Senior army leaders planned from the start to use sacred grounds like Antietam not just as shrines to American valor and patriotism but also as open-air classrooms for the education of officers in the U.S. Army and the National Guard. In 1908, Capt. Matthew Forney Steele, a military instructor who took army students from Fort Leavenworth to Maryland to study Antietam, marveled at how much had changed since he first saw the battlefield in 1893. His earlier visit had been before the War Department made improvements designed to enhance learning: since then the government had "marked all the lines and positions with metal tablets, all inscribed, and with beautiful monuments. One can ride over the field now with no previous knowledge of the battle and by reading the inscriptions cut upon metal tablets, can follow the operation from beginning to end." Steele especially liked the addition at the end of the Bloody Lane of a high stone observation tower "upon which our whole party could stand and look down upon the field, getting a birds eye view of nearly all of it."[3]

War Department leaders would have been pleased to know of Steele's appreciation. They had lobbied turn-of-the-century congressmen—many of whom had worn blue or gray uniforms in their youth—for funds to build the roads and erect the tower and the tablets to create this outdoor classroom for officers. It was money well spent. By the golden anniversary of America's bloodiest day, small groups of cadets, captains, and colonels from the army—and even a few U.S. Marines—visited Antietam each year to learn what they could about leadership, strategy, tactics, logistics, and more. They still come even today.

But what of that first generation who came to learn Antietam's lessons? What could officers soon destined to lead the American Expeditionary Force to France take away from the rolling fields and slow-moving stream outside Sharpsburg, Maryland? Brig. Gen. M. M. Macomb, commandant of the Army War College at the outbreak of World War I, considered the study of past campaigns such as

Members of the faculty in the Department of Military Art,
United States Infantry and Cavalry School and Army Staff College, June 30, 1907.
Captain Matthew Forney Steele is seated at the right of the front row.
National Archives

Antietam to be one of the best means to teach officers of any era about the art of command. Like most army instructors, he had searched for ways to help his students learn how to deal with the inevitable fog of war, that "maze of half-information and misinformation which always surround the commander in war." That fog "makes obscure not only where the enemy is, what he is doing, but the very data concerning the ground, and concerning our own troops. It is in this haze," Macomb warned, "that the commander has to deal all day long with messages, reports, bits of information from spies, prisoners, aeronauts, cavalry scouts, newspapers, and every conceivable source." Macomb had come to think there was only one way to train a soldier "to preserve his balance and a clear vision amid such confusion," and that was "to train him to deal scientifically with the source materials of military history." Antietam provided a particularly useful forum to illustrate some of the most important lessons army instructors hoped to teach.

Macomb further believed that soldiers could learn these lessons most clearly only by seeing the field itself. Why? In part, because after reviewing the extant campaign and battle histories of the 1862 Maryland campaign and the fight near

Sharpsburg, Macomb declared that body of literature to be nearly worthless for professional soldiers who sought to learn practical lessons about military leadership. "[H]ow grossly have the historians who have attempted to describe the events of our Civil War been deceived and deceived their readers," he complained. "The quarrels of the generals, the distribution of the blame or the credit for the outcome, the bravery of the troops—these are the splutterings which fill the pages of our histories; foolish camp-fire fables of the veteran's later days usurp the place of the reliable contemporaneous data." Who, he asked, "gives us the real data or rational criticisms about organization, the exercise of command, the marches, the deployments, the attack and defense, the supply, the losses, the breaks? Those are the real military secrets which our popular writers have concealed from our people." Because he clearly believed that no previous author met his standards, he expected his own Army War College students and other soldier-authors to fill these gaps.[4]

Before soldiers could begin to produce the necessary correctives that would make studies of Antietam more useful to their peers, they had to become familiar with the theater of operations and the battleground. Preparatory work for the site visit began in the classrooms of the pre–World War I Army War College, where Antietam ranked high among the major campaigns students studied closely as part of the formal curriculum.

The ready accessibility of excellent War Department maps of Maryland, southern Pennsylvania, and northern Virginia allowed instructors to design a wide variety of map exercises and war games. Invariably, some students recognized the scenarios once played out for real in September 1862 by the armies of Maj. Gen. George B. McClellan and Gen. Robert E. Lee. The faculty made one key change. Seeking to stress the theory-based principles of war rather than specific events in American military history, they gave the opposing forces generic names—the Blue Army and the Red Army. The ruse fooled few. Even officers with only a slight familiarity with American military history quickly recognized the Blue Army as the Union's Army of the Potomac and the Red Army as the Confederacy's Army of Northern Virginia.

Using these classroom map problems, students could analyze the soundness of key decisions that shaped the campaign and the battle. For example, they frequently evaluated Lee's order of September 14, 1862, to concentrate his widely scattered army for a stand near Sharpsburg. For the Army War College Class of 1909, their instructors set the stage this way: "With the Red Army scattered from Harper's Ferry to the Pennsylvania border and possibly heading north, and Red troops in contact with a detached Blue force at Harper's Ferry, two brigades of

Red troops return to the gaps in South Mountain to protect the army's flank and meet their cavalry in retreat. Strong Blue Army forces are pressing them."[5]

Even as they used history as their guide, instructors clearly did not feel compelled to adhere strictly to events as they had unfolded in 1862. Sometimes they injected variations to prevent students from simply reciting history and to force them to think more deeply about the military principles shaping the action. In this case, for instance, the imaginary Blue Army moved quickly and in strength, something that the real Blue Army had not done. While those two imaginary Red brigades prepared to fight a rear-guard action, students had to determine the Red commander's next move for the remainder of his force and prepare orders to execute that decision, written up in the standard five-paragraph format required by army regulations on the eve of World War I. Instructors graded harshly on the form of the orders as well as on their content.

The instructors' slight deviation from the actual events of September 14, 1862, had its desired effect. The students certainly did not limit their suggested solutions to Lee's own course of action on September 15–16. Indeed, the instructors often complicated the issue further by forcing students to consider a number of peripheral issues. Should elements of the Red Army then deployed near Harpers Ferry on September 14 keep up the pressure on the Blue forces there or abandon the effort immediately to rejoin the rest of the Red Army? We know that some of Lee's men under Stonewall Jackson stayed and took Harpers Ferry; we know as well that McClellan gave Lee the time he needed to effect this conclusion. With the quicker response by the imaginary Blue Army in this problem, however, would the students rely solely on history to answer the question? Or would they rethink the issue? In the end, the class divided almost evenly. Twelve voted to abandon the attack on Harpers Ferry, placing greater importance on the need to reconcentrate the Red Army. Only eleven wanted to continue to press the Union garrison.

Having decided by the thinnest of margins to reconcentrate the Red Army, the class next had to decide where to do this. Again, the students divided. History records that Lee concentrated his scattered forces near Sharpsburg, north of the Potomac and west of Antietam Creek. But eight of these students voted to pull the whole Red Army back to Virginia, to Martinsburg or perhaps to Winchester, in response to the Blue Army's unexpected aggressiveness. Three voted to order the Red Army in Maryland to concentrate on its elements near Harpers Ferry to continue the effort to reduce the Blue detachment there and "see what develops." Four voted for a reconcentration near Shepherdstown, just south of the Potomac. Only eight, one-third of the class, voted to do as Lee had done and concentrate the Red Army near Sharpsburg. As a whole, the class evaluated the threat to the Red Army on its merits, and given the key departures from historical reality on which the problem was based, two-thirds of the class did not feel compelled to duplicate the moves of "Marse Robert."

McClellan's decisions in this early phase of the Maryland campaign also came under close scrutiny. The same Army War College class that concluded Lee had viable alternatives beyond standing and fighting at Sharpsburg decided that "Little Mac" certainly could have exerted his authority as army commander far more actively on September 14, 15, and 16. Instructors gave the students a map problem that presented a scenario in which the Red Army near Frederick divides and sends a detachment to capture the Blue Army installation at Harpers Ferry. The Blue Army commander obtains a copy of the Red commander's orders revealing his intentions. This, of course, represented what actually happened when three Union enlisted men found a copy of Lee's orders early on September 13, 1862, and forwarded it up through their chain of command to McClellan. Understanding that this information was now in the hands of the Blue Army commander, the students had to satisfy two requirements: determine his next move, and write the order to execute it.

The proper move for a modern Little Mac generated considerable debate among faculty and students. The chief instructor tried to close down discussion by issuing a very un-McClellanesque order to "march at once" against the closest fragments of the divided Red Army. Take advantage of the unexpected windfall of information, he stipulated, move on the offensive, and hit the Red Army before it could figure out what happened. But the spirit of George McClellan apparently still lived on in his professional descendants. Several other faculty members and some students suggested that it was more important to relieve the isolated Blue detachment at Harpers Ferry than to attack any single isolated element of the Red Army. Still others stressed the need to plan ahead for the *defense* of mountain gaps in South Mountain not yet in their possession, one way to meet the Blue Army's preeminent obligation to protect all approach routes to Washington from marauding Red Army forces. The instructors probably worried most about those students whose answers stressed primarily the importance of "sending encouraging messages" to Harpers Ferry's stranded garrison while offering no substantive offensive action on any other front.[6]

Map exercises drawn from historical events filled large parts of the academic year at nearly all army schools, whether the students were lieutenants or lieutenant colonels. But the students far preferred to discuss such professional issues on "staff rides," actual trips to the fields they had studied previously only on the map.[7] They genuinely enjoyed the opportunity to analyze command decisions on the ground where real generals once made them. By studying key events in military history where they actually happened, one instructor noted, "we profit by the experience of others and learn how [the principles of war] were applied by the many able commanders who have led troops in the past." In the case of Antietam, he might well have added "inept commanders," too.[8] Staff rides were designed both to train the military mind and to sharpen the military eye. Even after the evolution of a professional staff system—something Civil War commanders had not enjoyed—the pre–World War I generation still took seriously U. S. Grant's injunction that the only eyes a general can trust are his own.

Staff rides could be conducted in different ways. When a group from the Army War College traveled to Antietam in 1907, they conducted a series of exercises in which they had to prepare written orders to bring each individual Blue Army corps onto the field the way the Army of the Potomac did it (or was supposed to have done it) on September 17, 1862. For guidance, their instructors provided army-level orders based on McClellan's own intent as expressed in his official report: "The design was to make the main attack upon the enemy's left—at least to create a diversion in favor of the main attack, with the hope of something more by assailing the enemy's right—and, as soon as one or both of the flank movements were fully successful, to attack their center with any reserve I might then have on hand." Students assigned to represent the Red Army's high command prepared a defense against the Blue Army's advance. Thus, as one officer wrote the order to bring the "1st Blue Division" (equivalent to Maj. Gen. Joseph Hooker's First Corps) from Keedysville across the Upper Bridge and southward along the axis of the Hagerstown Pike toward the Red Army posted outside Sharpsburg, a second student prepared the Red Army's order to block this move. A third student wrote the order to bring on the 2nd Blue Division (representing Maj. Gen. Joseph K. F. Mansfield's Twelfth Corps), and a fourth prepared the Red Army's orders for defense against this advance. Done sequentially and taking into account real time and space limitations, this exercise proved exceptionally challenging for the students.[9]

But only a few staff rides required this kind of detailed practical exercise in order writing. More often, the officers went to Antietam chiefly to think about and critique decisions made by Union and Confederate generals at the division, corps, and army level preliminary to the writing of those orders. Many considered it a daunting task. As Lt. Col. John P. Hains, a coast artilleryman, wrote in his Army War College class assignment about Antietam, "In an attempt to comment upon or criticise an action or campaign, one should approach the task with some trepidation, liberality and charity." Hains wisely admitted that fifty years after the battle it was much easier to see where and how different actions might have produced more positive results. Still, he reminded his peers that to reach a "fair judgment of the ability and wisdom of a commander" they must consider him "in the light of the knowledge he then possessed." It was a noble goal, but one the students rarely reached.[10]

Once a group of officers arrived at Antietam, individual members of a class likely followed one of two courses. A few selected men took on the roles of the rival army commanders. From the armies' respective headquarters—the Pry house for McClellan or the hill now crowned by the Antietam National Cemetery for Lee—they set the stage by considering the campaign's strategic overview, that is, the political, economic, and diplomatic elements in play in the fall of 1862. Then they established the operational overview, the specific military factors that brought the two armies face to face at Sharpsburg. Thus, many classes began with a discussion and evaluation of the senior commanders as strategic and operational leaders beyond the battlefield, initially leaving out consideration of their abilities as tacticians.

Robert E. Lee always intrigued this generation of soldiers. Most officers at the turn of the century—North and South alike—had been raised on the carefully crafted postwar "marble man" image of Lee. To most of them, Marse Robert stood out as the flawless man and soldier who represented the best of the Lost Cause and who surrendered in the end to save southern lives when northern numbers and resources too heavily outmatched his own.

Debate often became lively as the twentieth-century inheritors of Lee's professional legacy refused to be swayed from that image easily. The faculty, however, tried hard to force them to surrender the point. Army instructors in the early twentieth century summarized the art of sound generalship in a principle they called "safe leadership" or "responsible command." At Antietam, they argued, Lee failed that test. Maj. Eben Swift, who taught at both the Leavenworth schools and the Army War College, stated the criticism most straightforwardly: Lee "had the greatest success when he departed the furthest from established rules." In Maryland, he divided his smaller force in the face of a larger opponent. At Antietam, he chose to fight, even though he had his back to a river and access to only one usable ford. In a battle that used up his last reserves, Lee survived to fight another day because he was a lucky leader more than a responsible one. Lee's decision to face McClellan at Antietam, Swift argued, disqualified him as a "safe leader." Indeed, Lee had violated a key rule: "[I]nstead of acting on the principle that the enemy would do the correct thing he usually acted on the contrary idea that the enemy would do the wrong thing."[11]

Those who dared to quibble with Swift and other instructors found increasingly less support from their War Department–sanctioned textbooks. The same

Captain Steele who so happily praised Antietam's utility as an open-air classroom also authored *American Campaigns,* two volumes of narrative and maps that became a standard in army classrooms from its publication in 1909 until the 1950s. Steele expressed total disapproval of Lee's decision to stand and fight at Antietam. "Lee could probably have crossed his army and his trains over the Potomac without any serious opposition by McClellan" on either September 15 or 16, wrote Steele, who could find no good reason why Lee did not do so. He argued that after Lee's forward progress toward Pennsylvania was stopped at South Mountain, his campaign had already failed. So why had the Confederate commander stayed to fight? "Lee thought the morale and prestige of his army, and, no doubt, public sentiment at the South, required that he should win a victory north of the Potomac," Steele observed, adding tersely, "There could have been no other reasons for the battle of Antietam, and those were not sufficient reasons."[12]

With the encouragement of their instructors, the students slowly began to understand that Lee had made some highly dangerous decisions when he decided to stay in Maryland. Apparently aware of Jefferson Davis's plans for an offensive into Tennessee and Kentucky in the fall of 1862, one Army War College student wondered whether Lee should have marched into Maryland toward Pennsylvania at all: "Would it not have been better strategy for him at that time to have availed himself of the advantage of 'interior lines' now enjoyed by the Confederates, and joined some of his forces to those of Bragg operating in a campaign in the west against the Federals in Kentucky?" Given the chaos in Pope's and McClellan's forces in the East after a string of disappointments and defeats on the Peninsula, at Cedar Mountain, and most recently at Second Manassas, the student seemed certain that the transfer to Kentucky of 25,000 men from Lee's army would have turned the tide in Bragg's favor. With that course not taken, however, the major decided Lee, in moving north in September 1862, had "acted wisely in at once assuming the offensive" before the disorganized and defeated Yankees could mount an effective response.[13]

In their discussions of strategic and operational leadership, students grew increasingly critical of two other decisions Lee made in Maryland. First, they reached quick consensus that he "took great chances in dividing his army and scattering his divisions at Frederick" early in the campaign. Second, they came to agree with their instructors that Lee's decision to stand and fight at Sharpsburg after the fragmentation of his force had been discovered was "beyond doubt the boldest and most hazardous of his career." One student wrote that "[w]ith the surrender of Harper's Ferry [on] the 14th [of September 1862], McLaw[s]'s force escaped into Virginia; and had Lee gone also, he would have acted wisely." Lt. Col. Benjamin Atkinson drew heavily on the writings of Confederate artilleryman

Edward Porter Alexander to support his own conclusion that Lee should not have remained in Maryland after McClellan took possession of the gaps in South Mountain late on September 14. "Strategically, Lee's position was as bad as it could have been," Alexander had written, and Atkinson concurred with the great gunner's conclusion that "[t]he wages of defeat [c]ould have been destruction, while a reward of victory could have been only the repulse of the enemy." Colonel Atkinson even cited the opinion of "Lee's tarnished lieutenant" James Longstreet to strengthen his case. "Longstreet did not wish Lee to make his stand on the east side of the Potomac," he wrote, adding that "Old Pete" "wished Lee to cross to the farther side, but *as usual* Lee did as he saw fit." [14]

If Lee's strategic and operational decisions did not survive student scrutiny unscathed, George McClellan's performance fared much worse. When he obtained a copy of Lee's lost order, Little Mac had fallen into an "opportunity the like of such as seldom comes to a commander," one soldier wrote. Remembering the lessons learned in his map exercises, this officer asserted that McClellan should have marched at once. The general, history records, had not done this. Even though he came into possession of Lee's lost order on the morning of September 13, McClellan did not issue an order to Maj. Gen. William B. Franklin's Sixth Corps to move to the possible relief of Harpers Ferry until 6:20 that evening. Conceding that Franklin received the order late in the day, Lt. Col. Ben Fuller—a U.S. Marine in the Army War College Class of 1914 and a future commandant of the Marine Corps—believed that the Sixth Corps should have continued its march to Crampton's Gap and then overwhelmed the feeble Confederate force there. After all, Fuller wrote, Franklin's men had marched only five miles that day. This Marine clearly held the Union commanders responsible for not demanding more of their men when such a golden opportunity beckoned. A quick stroke at Crampton's Gap late on September 13 was essential, wrote another officer, because "the strategic direction," the shortest route to Harpers Ferry and to intercept the Confederate retreat route to Virginia, obviously ran through that pass. McClellan committed a fatal error in failing to move that day, concluded yet another soldier who argued that Little Mac knew he must advance and "should have possessed himself of the South Mountain passes at once." [15]

McClellan's slow movements after seizing those mountain gaps on September 14 opened him to further harsh criticism. "He could never have wished for a fairer opportunity" to beat Lee, one War College student concluded. McClellan could have pushed 40,000 fresh Union troops through Turner's and Fox's gaps to take on Lee's small force, then numbering a mere 10,000 men, strung out loosely in a vulnerable position only seven miles away. As another soldier wrote, if McClellan had "taken less time and been more prompt and expeditious in

Ben H. Fuller
Marine Corps University
Archives, Quantico, Virginia

attacking Lee" on September 15—or the 16th for that matter—"Antietam would have been a very different battle." A particularly cynical officer suggested that Little Mac let slip "the last opportunity of his life to make a great success." Yet another concluded that "it seems but just to say that, if he and his main commanders had acted with the celerity and energy of Lee's lieutenants, McClellan must have won."[16]

Students considered what might have prevented McClellan's taking advantage of the opportunity that luck had afforded him. Most finally concurred with the officer who wrote that "[i]t seemed impossible for McClellan to get out of his head the idea that Lee had a much superior force," perhaps as many as 120,000 men.[17]

Even some of McClellan's harshest critics found something praiseworthy in his performance. One pointed out that he successfully resolved "the difficult task of reorganizing a beaten army while on the move" from Virginia across the Potomac into Maryland. Another insisted that McClellan performed his military tasks as well as could be expected of any army commander saddled with so many politicians among his corps, division, and brigade leaders. These amateurs wearing stars on their shoulders bore much of the responsibility for McClellan's inability to get "the prompt response that comes only with discipline and training." But the greatest single thing that caused the students to rally to McClellan's support was their conviction that Maj. Gen. Henry W. Halleck, the Union army's chief of staff in Washington, Secretary of War Edwin M. Stanton, and Abraham Lincoln himself had interfered unduly with Little Mac's operations. Even as they asserted the primacy of civilian control over the military in the American style of war, they clearly abhorred Washington's meddling with McClellan's military operations in the fall of 1862.[18]

Even though officers began their staff rides by focusing on the campaign's senior leaders and the strategic and operational environment, most really preferred to dissect the tactical elements of the battle itself. Their professional experience to this point in their careers made them more comfortable discussing issues on this level, and they delved into them with enthusiasm.

For his tactical decision making on September 17, McClellan fared little better in the students' evaluations than he did as a campaign planner. As one colonel wrote, "In reading over even a small part of what has been written regarding McClellan's conduct of the battle, so much is found adverse that an attempt to quote even a part would be quite long." A second man borrowed a quotation from civilian historian John Codman Ropes, who had written that "[o]f General Lee's management of the battle there is nothing but praise to be said," and then tacked on an addendum by Captain Steele: "Of McClellan's management of the attack there is nothing but censure to be said."[19]

McClellan's biggest error, they generally concurred, stemmed from his tendency to utilize what the soldiers called "'driblet fighting' in place of 'mass fighting.'" They disapproved of his plan to begin the day's action by launching only Hooker's First Corps against the Confederate left. Even if "Fighting Joe" had succeeded, they argued, the limited strength of a single-corps attack would most likely have had only minimal effect. It might have driven Lee back on his lines of communications and toward his secure line of retreat, but it also might have handed him time to catch his breath, shorten his lines, and strengthen his defensive position before a second blow fell. One colonel asserted that he actually liked McClellan's plan in principle, if it could have been executed with more punch. He understood that to win a decisive victory Little Mac would have to force Lee back nearly two miles to threaten his line of retreat—"in other words, he must be completely defeated." This mission, the colonel argued, simply required more pressure against the Confederate left flank than an attack by a single corps could bring to bear.[20]

What should McClellan have done instead? Applying the principle of economy of force, many of the visiting officers argued that he could have accomplished much more than he did if, from the very start, he made his strongest push against Lee's other flank, his right near Burnside's Bridge. A hard and quick Union strike on the Confederate right—identified by the students as the "flank of decision"—could have separated the bulk of Lee's army from his troops still coming up from Harpers Ferry, and it certainly would have forced the Army of Northern Virginia to fight for its life to protect its only possible avenue of escape over Boteler's Ford. But this latter course—attacking the Confederate right instead of the left—"would have been the bolder of the two plans," one student wrote, and "McClellan was taking no chances" while "playing the safest he could."[21] Military students of this era became so enamored of a course of action against Lee's flank of decision that they devoted far more detailed discussion to this alternative than to an even more obvious option: that McClellan could have forsaken an unsupported attack on one flank to unleash his larger army in any manner of combinations in simultaneous attacks against both flanks and the center of Lee's smaller force.

Other critical analysts damned McClellan for creating an unwieldy chain of command for his newly organized force and then ignoring it as he deployed for battle. On paper, Maj. Gen. Ambrose E. Burnside commanded the First and Ninth Corps, designated the army's right wing. At Antietam, while Hooker's First Corps advanced from the North Woods to open the fight on the Union right, the Ninth Corps (temporarily commanded by Brig. Gen. Jacob D. Cox since Maj. Gen. Jesse L. Reno's death at South Mountain on September 14) deployed at the opposite end of the line near Burnside's Bridge. When McClellan divided the components of the right wing, one officer wrote, he wasted the advantages that accrued to the system of organization he had designed. Because Little Mac did not direct the battle personally, he erred badly in deploying his army in a way that rendered one of his wing commanders powerless. In so doing, he had left "no one in command on the field to direct and coordinate the attacks made by the corps on the right whose united action would have been much more severely felt than the succession of attacks that were made independently" by several individual corps from different wings. Making matters worse, the First Corps essentially left the fight after Hooker fell wounded. If the army's new organization had been used on the battlefield, an active wing commander might have provided Hooker's successor with appropriate guidance, and "this corps might have been used differently and to better advantage later in the day."[22]

Those who faulted McClellan's failure to apply the principle of mass, thus allowing large elements of his army to lay idle or underused at crucial moments, found many different ways to criticize him. Referring to the First, Twelfth, and Second Corps and not merely to the First Corps that kicked off the Union attack on September 17, one colonel wrote that the units "intended for the main attack should all have been placed in position before the attack commenced, so that they would have moved together instead of successively." The "advantage of superior numbers would thus have been utilized and not thrown away." Once started, the pressure of the Union attacks should have been unrelenting. Moreover, wrote another officer, "[i]f McClellan's tactics, a succession of attacks, was to prove successful, it should have been continued as long as he had troops for the purpose." The point at which McClellan decided against using Maj. Gen. Fitz John Porter's Fifth Corps or Franklin's newly arrived Sixth Corps troops appeared to one student to "have been about the time when the wearing effect of the previous attacks had reduced the resisting power of the Confederate line to near the breaking point." Yet the Federal commander did not order additional units forward. The students stopped short of accusing McClellan of a lack of physical courage, but they openly doubted his moral courage to send the army in for the kill.[23]

The greater part of a division of cavalry also rested near the Union center at the moment when the southern breaking point seemed so near. Students excoriated the Union commander for failing to use his horsemen, especially at this potentially decisive moment. "Pleasanton's [*sic*] cavalry division was held boxed up in the center, employed chiefly in driving up stragglers and waiting for other service" rather than contributing decisively to the battle, one student complained. This scarcely surprised officers who argued that at no time in the campaign did McClellan demonstrate an understanding of how to use cavalry effectively. The reconnaissance mission fell heavily to the Civil War's mounted arm, and the Union cavalry failed the Army of the Potomac signally in September 1862. "The search for fords seems to have been perfunctory and ineffective," and the "official reports say very little about it," wrote an officer who was singularly unimpressed by General Cox's remark that he relied on "information *obtained from the neighborhood*" to discover that "no fords of the Antietam were passable at that time except one." Another part of the cavalry's mission required it to seek out accurate and timely intelligence, and one student declared it inexcusable that "all the fords used, except the upper one, were found *during* the battle" and not well before the armies clashed.[24]

The obligation to protect an army from surprise also fell to the mounted arm during the Civil War, and in this regard McClellan also failed to employ his horsemen to best advantage. Had he sent some of his cavalry to patrol beyond his left flank, they likely would have spotted the march of A. P. Hill's column from Harpers Ferry and could have warned Burnside of its approach, preventing much slaughter among the Ninth Corps' Connecticut and Rhode Island troops in the 40-acre Cornfield. An officer who devoted much study to the northern effort on the left flank asserted that the sudden appearance of Hill's men "proved to be the 'slip 'twixt cup and lip.'" McClellan's failure to deploy cavalry on his left flank to prevent such a surprise "dashed the cup of victory from the very lips of Burnside's command." [25]

Other officers suggested that McClellan should have sent some of his horsemen to protect his right flank. After all, as Stonewall Jackson himself had noted, the Confederate cavalry took and held Nicodemus Heights. If gray cavalry captured and held that high ground, suggested the officers, blue cavalry might have tried to wrest it away. But that did not happen. One colonel nicely summarized McClellan's use of cavalry at Antietam: "I have been unable to find any explanation for placing the cavalry in the center, where it had no useful employment. . . . [T]he cavalry were mere spectators." [26]

If McClellan's use of his cavalry did not impress the twentieth-century soldiers, the performance of the Union artillery surely did. The long arm's contribution to the battle left them even more awestruck as they began to appreciate the dimension of the challenge facing artillery chief Henry J. Hunt, who openly admitted that he reorganized and reequipped many of his batteries, which had seen hard service on the Peninsula and at Second Manassas, on the move from Washington to the battlefield. According to one officer, "if victory is awarded by history to the Federals, it will be due to that arm." Interestingly enough, while the students blamed McClellan for the poor showing of his cavalry, they accorded him no credit for the good work of his artillery. [27]

After his class of captains from Fort Leavenworth had completed a long day of touring at Antietam, Captain Steele shared with his wife impressions of the battlefield as he looked out from the stone tower at the end of the Bloody Lane. He commented that he had come to an inescapable conclusion that nearly all World War I–era students who studied this battle seemed to reach: "My God what a poor general McClellan was." [28]

By contrast, students generally bestowed high praise on Lee's command performance on September 17. Indeed, they expressed misgivings about only one decision: the line Lee chose to defend. Even an officer strongly inclined to praise the southern chieftain for selecting a position that possessed "some elements of strength" could not support his assertion convincingly, noting not only that the line rested close to the Potomac but also that the initial southern left flank lay "so far [back] from [Antietam] creek that an enemy could cross without being under fire and place his troops in safety in position to envelop" it.[29]

Even officers who criticized Lee for choosing to fight at Antietam invariably gave him high marks for the battle he directed. His ability to use "good interior lines" to move troops all day from one crisis point to another especially impressed them.[30] The students thought so well of his performance, it seems, that they seldom scrutinized it in detail. Little Mac provided far more grist for discussions than Lee did, leaving critical assessments considerably one sided.

After taking the measures of Lee and McClellan from the rival headquarters sites, the soldiers visited the battlefield itself. At each stop in a series of predesignated positions—perhaps the Cornfield, the West Woods, Bloody Lane, or Burnside's Bridge—students took turns describing the historical events that took place on that site. Then they evaluated the decisions of the rival leaders on the army, corps, division, and sometimes lower levels of command. Given the central importance of the spirit of the offensive in the professional thinking of most officers at the turn of the century, they paid considerably more attention to the actions of attackers then to those of defenders. This helped direct far more attention to McClellan's offensive strokes than to Lee's defensive efforts.

Once students stepped on the battlefield, McClellan's corps commanders came under intense scrutiny. Few measured up well, and each general in turn took his lumps. One officer emphasized Hooker's failure to reconnoiter and "determine definitely the location of [Lee's] left flank" before opening the battle on September 17. Thus, the First Corps advanced blindly, making Hooker's first attack frontally on the left center of the Confederate line instead of enveloping the enemy flank. Although the student considered the general's attack to be "well planned and well executed according to the tactics of the day," he believed that Hooker squandered an opportunity to strike a decisive blow when he failed to find and then hit the rebel flank as McClellan intended.[31]

But Hooker also found supporters who argued that he might have accomplished much more if he had received help. "Mansfield placed his Corps too far away to reach Hooker for a combined assault with him," one student criticized. Moreover, when the Twelfth Corps moved, it advanced too slowly to help Hooker. Because General Mansfield ordered his troops to leave the road and march across country, a colonel averred, he at least should have remembered that such a movement could be "made in two columns as easily as one." Mansfield's slow deployment—a reflection of his inexperience in corps command and the greenness of many of his troops—resulted in Hooker's mauling in the Cornfield.[32]

The handling of the Second Corps also drew criticism, although students reached no consensus about exactly who deserved the greatest censure. The corps commander, Maj. Gen. Edwin V. Sumner, came under fire for "accompanying and practically commanding the leading division and exercising no control over the movements of those following." Students blamed him for deploying Brig. Gen. John Sedgwick's three brigades in such a tight linear formation that they could not respond effectively to the massive Confederate counterattack that smashed their left flank and rear. They also blamed Sumner for handing the Confederates the chance to deliver that crushing blow by allowing a gap to develop between Sedgwick's left and the right of Brig. Gen. William H. French's trailing division. The Confederates had taken advantage of that break in the line to hit Sedgwick's open flank. Still others, however, blamed French and not Sumner for separating from Sedgwick. Worse, they argued, French then ordered a premature attack on the Confederate center in the Bloody Lane. The southerners had been able to repulse French easily and with heavy losses, in large part because he had not attended to the security of his flanks.[33]

The list of poor Union performers lengthened as the study groups progressed southward across the battlefield. Ambrose Burnside won few admirers. Even if students could not reach concurrence on exactly when McClellan issued his attack orders to Burnside, they tended to believe that "Old Burn" would not have been ready at any early hour on September 17. "Burnside had been directed the night before to be in readiness the following morning for this attack," wrote one colonel, but clearly the general did not carry out all required preparations. The Rohrbach bridge — soon to become known as Burnside's Bridge — offered only one avenue to cross Antietam Creek, but, the colonel noted, "there seems to have been a lack of knowledge of the ground and positions of the fords in the front of the Ninth Corps, which might be attributed to lack of interest by its commander." Another student attributed Burnside's inaction to a fit of pique after "having his command, the right wing, divided and Hooker allowed to act independently on the right." Burnside's ego would not permit him to reassert active command of a mere corps, even after the death of Reno at South Mountain, because "he had been announced as commander of the right wing of the Army and was unwilling to waive his precedence or to assume that Hooker was detached for more than a temporary purpose."[34]

If Burnside had done all that was expected of him, another soldier wrote, he would have found the fords on September 16 and sent Brig. Gen. Isaac P. Rodman's division to the crossing early on September 17. Once these troops were in position, "their presence would have prevented Walker's Division being taken away from the Confederate right; their earlier crossing would have forced [Brig. Gen. Robert] Toombs to withdraw from his position and enable the rest of the corps to cross the bridge without such heavy loss and expenditure of ammunition." If Burnside had done all that McClellan had a right to expect from him, the Ninth Corps could have crushed Lee's right flank well before A. P. Hill arrived.[35]

Criticism of Burnside did not end when his men finally crossed the bridge. Some students deplored his calling a halt in the advance to bring up more ammunition, a delay so long that some of his troops had time to light fires and brew coffee. The loss of Union momentum provided just enough of a break in the action to make possible Hill's decisive blow a short while later. The blame for all this rested clearly on Burnside, in most soldiers' minds. Only one officer was willing to suggest that if the Union cavalry had done its job and sent timely warning of Hill's approach, Burnside could have made up for his lackluster leadership during the morning phase of the battle.[36]

Although the northern high command did not bear up well under scrutiny from students, the Union soldier in the ranks won their unstinting admiration. Career officers in the U.S. Army at the turn of the century lived their entire professional lives amid an ongoing popular and political debate about the appropriate composition of the American military. Harkening back to the era of the constitutional debates when Hamiltonians urged a strong professional standing army and Jeffersonians supported a strong citizen militia, the controversy had rekindled anew in the 1880s. Each side answered to a new name. The Hamiltonians had become the Uptonians, named for Emory Upton, the West Point–educated Civil War hero and Antietam artilleryman who argued in support of a professional army in his influential *Military Policy of the United States,* published posthumously in 1904. The Jeffersonians were now Loganites, partisans of Civil War general John A. Logan, an opponent of West Point, champion of the citizen soldier, postwar politician with possible presidential aspirations, and hero of the new National Guard lobby. Not surprisingly, most serving officers—while they admired the citizen soldier—generally held Uptonian views, and these attitudes colored their assessments of the rival armies at Antietam.[37]

A major pointed out that "the infantry at Antietam may be divided into two classes, viz; the experienced soldier who had seen service on the Peninsula and at Bull Run and the recruit. The former was a good soldier and had the attacks at Antietam been well timed it seems probable that Lee's Army would have been disastrously defeated." Many of McClellan's soldiers fit into the first class, but on the road to Antietam the Army of the Potomac received great numbers of raw recruits. These new soldiers had answered Lincoln's summer call in 1862 for 300,000 more troops, and at the time of the battle on September 17 some of them had spent less than one month in Federal service. Their greenness told. One student who examined the opening phases of the Antietam campaign considered it worrisome that as early as September 9 McClellan had felt compelled to issue a severe warning against straggling, a particularly nagging problem for the new regiments. The order read in part that the "straggler must now be taught that he leaves the ranks without authority and skulks at the severest risks, even that of death." McClellan expected all officers to remind their soldiers of this at every opportunity, but, as one student wrote, the lack of discipline that inspired Little Mac's order spoke poorly of the quality of any army, and he doubted that an officer corps composed chiefly of citizen soldiers could do much to remedy the problem.[38]

When it came to discussions of military discipline, the students were no easier on Lee's army. The Confederate commander, too, had issued a general order against straggling, a move he took even though he believed "[s]uch characters are better absent from the army on such momentous occasions as these about to be entered upon."[39] A coast artilleryman was quite taken with D. H. Hill's view that although shoes, food, and physical exhaustion kept numerous Confederates out of the ranks, many of the stragglers were nothing more than "thieving poltroons" who "had kept away from sheer cowardice." Hill could be counted on for colorful descriptions of all sorts, but he also reinforced a notion that Army War College students perceived to be the only practical solution to this problem: "The straggler is generally a thief and always a coward, lost to all sense of shame; he can only be kept in ranks by a strict and sanguinary discipline of *well trained officers.*"[40]

Students pointed out that this single personnel issue held huge operational implications for the Maryland campaign. One officer openly doubted "if Lee's commanders during the campaign knew, with anything like exactness, just how many men they actually had present for duty at any stated time." Viewed through the lens of the heated contemporary debate over the proper composition of an American army, the behavior of the forces that fought at Antietam helped reinforce the conclusion that only reliance on a professional force could allay such concerns in the future.[41]

Straggling was not limited to newly raised regiments of citizen soldiers, but officers used that issue as one avenue to approach the more dangerous problem posed by the presence of untrained and unseasoned troops in a combat zone. Some green Pennsylvania regiments of the Twelfth Corps ultimately served quite creditably in the thickest of the fighting around the Cornfield, the East Woods, and the Dunker Church, but their presence helped to explain why Mansfield had moved so slowly to the assistance of Hooker's embattled soldiers. "Had the new troops . . . been placed in rear instead of in the lead," wrote one student, "the march and deployment might have been made in such time as to make the XII

Corps a real support to the I Corps." The students also argued that green troops never should be put in particularly vulnerable positions, such as the extreme flank of the army's line. "The raw recruit though full of enthusiasm acted as such men will always act," insisted one officer. "With the tide of battle in his favor he pushes on, with the tide of battle against him, he hesitates, breaks and cannot be rallied. This," he wrote, "is well illustrated in the conduct of Harlan[d]'s brigade of Rodman's Division," the Connecticut and Rhode Island troops who broke when A. P. Hill's flank attack utterly smashed them.[42]

For this vexing problem, the officers offered universal military training as a solution. The preparedness movement of the Progressive Age enjoyed its greatest popular support about the time these soldiers conducted their Civil War studies, and the officers clearly appreciated the benefits that might accrue to teaching the fundamentals of the soldier's art as part of the standard curriculum in high schools and colleges. In this era of the Plattsburgh camps that offered military training during the summer to mostly middle-class civilian volunteers, the regular-army officers believed that an even more comprehensive national application of this concept might prevent a reoccurrence of the slaughter of the isolated 125th Pennsylvania around the Dunker Church and similar disasters that befell other green regiments at Antietam. As commanding general of the army, Civil War hero John M. Schofield had warned in the 1890s that if war came, "the boys will go, all the same, whether trained or not. . . . Then, if ignorant, they will simply be doomed to fall the victims of skilled marksmen to whose shots they know not how to reply." The blooding of the green troops at Antietam reminded many of these officers that Schofield's fears had merit.[43]

Other professional issues, such as supply, communications, and medical care, commanded students' attention as much as did strategy, tactics, and leadership. Indeed, the two armies' supply difficulties shaped many of the students' campaign analyses. One officer even used logistical factors to try to explain McClellan's slowness, citing disorganized trains, a lack of rations, and problems in the ammunition resupply system after South Mountain as reasons for Little Mac's inaction on September 15. But most students agreed with the officer who concluded that this was precisely the kind of occasion that required "extraordinary efforts to get needed supplies to the front." Two separate supply exercises completed by the Army War College class of 1910 required students to untangle McClellan's trains, establish depots, and utilize rail and road networks to move supplies forward. The instructors designed the problems both to make students aware of the 1862 logistical puzzle and to prove that it could be resolved, Little Mac's protestations to the contrary notwithstanding.[44]

Other combat support issues also intrigued the soldiers. Officers of all ranks had to deal with exercises called "Supply and Auxiliary Arms practice." One class used maps of the Antietam battlefield to address this communications problem: On the morning of September 17, the First Division (equivalent to Hooker's First Corps) prepares to attack. What elements should be in telegraphic communication with the division headquarters? What elements of that command should be in telegraphic communication with each other? Designers of this problem wanted their students to think about the importance of maintaining a reliable flow of information for orders and other important information. Nearly all saw the good sense of connecting the division commander and his brigade commanders. Beyond that, though, individual officers suggested a grand array of ideas. Some wanted lines to link the brigade commanders to each other; others wanted communications between brigade commanders and the division artillery; still others wanted a more elaborate system that would link brigade commanders with their subordinates on the regimental and battalion level. A few went so far as to argue for connecting combat commanders by telegraph wire to their ammunition trains or hospitals. The only consensus to emerge may reflect the instructors' efforts to quash overreliance on new technology: all students agreed that the division commander or his staff had to develop plans for visual signaling when the wires went down.[45]

Battle studies such as those done at Antietam gave combat arms officers a genuine appreciation of the responsibilities, needs, and utility of support branches with which they had little contact. Medical issues fascinated them. "Civil War surgeons resect and amputate and at the same time confess entire ignorance of any systematic arrangement for succor and shelter of wounded," noted a twentieth-century army physician in criticizing his predecessors. They "evidently believed that they had fulfilled their duty as medical officers when they displayed their skill as surgeons." To make sure that notion died quickly, at least one group of pre–World War I U.S. Army officers had to decide where near the battle lines at Antietam they would locate brigade and division aid stations. Proximity to the battlefront counted for much, but so did protection from the elements and enemy fire, closeness to abundant fresh water, and transportation. They chose sites for large, but temporary, tent hospitals near the battlefield to shelter soldiers too badly wounded to move when the army marched away. They even considered locations for more permanent hospitals for casualties requiring long-term care.[46]

No military student left Antietam without addressing one obvious question: Should McClellan have reopened the battle on September 18? The officers tended to believe Little Mac should have attacked. As one decided, "The Federal troops . . . had fought so well that, notwithstanding the mistakes of their commanders, a decisive victory was still within McClellan's reach." But he did not act, and for that failure, a colonel argued, the general "justly invites censure." Using the official reports of various subordinate commanders, students demonstrated repeatedly that while McClellan complained he did not have sufficient strength to renew the engagement, fresh troops from Franklin's Sixth Corps and Brig. Gen. Andrew A. Humphreys's division attached to the Fifth Corps had arrived in time to participate in any concerted attack on September 18. In response to McClellan's explanation that a lack of artillery ammunition prevented his renewing the offensive, officers argued that he "should have known that the Confederates were in far worse condition than the Federals, regarding rations and ammunition." One soldier reached the blunt conclusion that on September 18 McClellan "should have sent in every man who could walk, crawl or handle a musket, abandon his trains if need be, and destroyed Lee's Army then and there. Had McClellan displayed the slightest degree of tenacity that the situation demanded, he doubtless would have reaped the victory of a lifetime." They concurred with Captain Steele's assessment that McClellan's timidity "is not consistent with the character of the commander-in-chief of an army; and it does not win victories."[47]

Army War College instructors usually asked their students to extend their analyses to consider one final question: How would a twentieth-century army deal with the organizational, tactical, operational, or strategic issues McClellan and Lee faced at Antietam? The students' answers demonstrated a great deal of inventiveness and imagination.

Some considered how the Army of the Potomac and the Army of Northern Virginia would look if they adopted the organizational scheme required by the U.S. Army's Field Service Regulations of years just before World War I. One colonel suggested that under the regulations in effect in 1912 the Union army would not have used its multileveled organization with wings and corps. A modern McClellan would have a much simpler, by-the-book army of "4 divisions of 18,000 each," an independent cavalry organization of 9 regiments numbering about 10,000 horsemen, and a reserve, or "auxiliary," division of 5,000 men. The Army War College Class of 1911 faced map exercises to establish routes of march, nightly encampments, and supply depots to support a force operating in western Maryland, a seemingly routine assignment until the instructor required them to use "[a]utomobile wagons and trucks and 'mechanical traction trains'" that "have been experimented with in different foreign countries, but have received practically no military attention in our country." The problem boggled the students' minds.[48]

"The basic principles of military strategy have not changed," wrote an officer fifty years after the battle, "but means to the same have developed with wonderful strides." The application of recently developed technologies to the battle at

Antietam challenged the officers' conceptions on how to fight a modern war. Such innovations as long-range rifled artillery, machine guns, magazine rifles, smokeless powder, range finders, wireless telegraphy, use of artificial cover such as smoke, methods of fire discipline and fire control, and medical improvements had so changed the face of battle and enlarged the battlefield that one officer admitted that he had come to thinking about Antietam "very much in the light of a scrimmage, so intermingled and so disorganized at times were the opposing forces."[49]

Still, the soldiers tackled the challenge with zest. They typically concluded that under early-twentieth-century conditions, if a modern force found Lee's lost order on the march into western Maryland, "the truth of its information [w]ould have been tested by the two aeroplanes" based with the Blue Force at Frederick. A Robert E. Lee in 1912 probably would not have accepted battle so close to the Potomac with a mere single line of battle, because a more complex notion of defense-in-depth had become the accepted way to deal with an attacking foe. If a modern Lee stayed and fought anyway, they argued, he most likely would have done things differently. He would add a second defensive line, prepare entrenchments and redoubts, and, if possible, take time to "prepare all bridges for destruction and mine the fords." But would this be enough to hold back a determined attack? At least one officer believed that even these preparations would prove insufficient, noting that modern metallic cartridges eliminated concerns about wetting black powder ammunition. Thus, "a commander would not now hesitate to send his infantry across such a stream as the Antietam at almost any point."[50]

Generally speaking, army officers of the World War I generation found battle studies and staff rides to Civil War sites such as Antietam to be informative, inspirational, even exhilarating. During their touring, the officers maintained a brisk pace. They walked the fields on foot or rode over them on horseback. A contingent of enlisted men set up a tent camp and field kitchen. After a year spent in a relatively sedentary academic atmosphere, the students needed a way to ease themselves back to active duty in the field with troops, and school administrators purposely scheduled these rides late in the academic year to help them make that transition. Staff rides also offered an opportunity for fun, camaraderie, and, for prospective officers, a chance to observe their peers' behavior under field conditions and away from the formalities of the classroom.

The Army War College official history of the Civil War for which these Antietam studies were conducted never was completed. American entry into World War I halted the project, and financial constraints and curricular reforms in the postwar years ultimately killed it. But such official inattention did not mean that

Antietam had nothing to teach modern soldiers. Military professionals still visit Antietam to reflect on the lessons offered by Lee, McClellan, and a host of other warriors in blue and gray. Moreover, even in the pre–World War I years, not all uniformed visitors belonged to the American military establishment. British army officers of that era also considered Antietam's many important and timeless lessons. For one young British subaltern who studied this clash, two points seemed most relevant. First, "War demands the best, and Victory can be won only by assiduous and unremitting wooing"; and second, the Civil War genera-tion "lives on still as a memory and an inspiration in the annals of their country's story, and will live, so long at least as, through these materialistic and matter-of-fact days, heroism and self-sacrifice and devotion to duty are held in honour among men."[51] With these insightful notions of a foreign admirer American officers about to step from Antietam to the Argonne heartily concurred.

NOTES

1. Capt. Isaac W. Heysinger, *Antietam and the Maryland and Virginia Campaigns of 1862* (New York: Neale, 1912), 152.

2. [President of the U.S. Army War College (?)], "Introductory Comments to Class," 8, USAWC Curricular Archives, Class of 1913, vol. 1, U.S. Army Military His-tory Institute, Carlisle Barracks, Pa. (repository hereafter cited as USAMHI).

3. Matthew F. Steele to Mrs. Steele, July 11, 1908, box 9, Matthew Forney Steele Pa-pers, USAMHI.

4. M. M. Macomb, "The Scientific Study of Military History," 14–15, USAWC Curricular Archives, [ca. 1913], USAMHI.

5. This and the following three paragraphs are based on "Tactical and Strategic Ex-ercise No. 23," 407–8, USAWC Curricular Archives, Class of 1909, vol. 2, USAMHI.

6. "Map Exercise No. 20," 361–62, USAWC Curricular Archives, Class of 1909, vol. 1, USAMHI.

7. For the fullest treatment of pre–World War I staff rides, see Carol Reardon, *Soldiers and Scholars: The U.S. Army and the Uses of Military History, 1865–1920* (Lawrence: University Press of Kansas, 1990), especially chap. 4.

8. Maj. Guy Carleton, "Tactical Rides and Staff Rides," 3, USAWC Curricular Archives, Class of 1911, vol. 4, USAMHI.

9. "Campaign Study and Staff Ride," 423–25, USAWC Curricular Archives, Class of 1907, USAMHI.

10. Lt. Col. John P. Hains, "Antietam Campaign Subsequent to the Battles at South Mountain," 15, typescript, USAWC Curricular Archives, Class of 1915, USAMHI.

11. "Map Exercise No. 65," 878–84, USAWC Curricular Archives, Class of 1910, vol. 4, USAMHI.

12. Matthew Forney Steele, *American Campaigns,* 2 vols. (Washington: Byron S. Adams, 1909), 1:279.

13. Maj. William M. Morrow, "Antietam Campaign Including Battles of South Mountain," 35–36, USAWC Curricular Archives, Class of 1915, copy at USAMHI.

14. Maj. M. B. Stokes, "Antietam Campaign to and Including Battles of South Mountain," 88, USAWC Curricular Archives, Class of 1916, copy at USAMHI; Morrow, "Antietam Campaign Including the Battles of South Mountain," 41; Lt. Col. B. W. Atkinson, "Battle of Antietam," 54, USAWC Curricular Archives, Class of 1913, copy at USAMHI.

15. Hains, "Antietam Campaign Subsequent to the Battles at South Mountain," 16; Lt. Col. B. H. Fuller, "A Study of the Antietam Campaign, to Include the Battle of South Mountain (Turner's and Crampton's Gap)," 26, USAWC Curricular Archives, Class of 1914, copy at USAMHI; Stokes, "Antietam Campaign to and Including the Battles of South Mountain," 47; Morrow, "Antietam Campaign Including Battles of South Mountain," 40.

16. Lieutenant Colonel May, Major Nobles, Major Walsh, and Major Wolcott, "Historical Ride. Comments of Committees," 10, USAWC Curricular Archives, Class of 1912, copy at USAMHI.

17. Hains, "Antietam Campaign Subsequent to the Battles at South Mountain," 17; May, Nobles, Walsh, and Wolcott, "Historical Ride," 11–12, 18.

18. Hains, "Antietam Campaign Subsequent to the Battles at South Mountain," 16.

19. Atkinson, "Battle of Antietam," 55; Steele, *American Campaigns,* 1:281.

20. Atkinson, "Battle of Antietam," 55; Col. C. W. Kennedy, "Antietam Campaign Subsequent to the Battles of South Mountain, September 15–20, 1862," 46, USAWC Curricular Archives, Class of 1914, copy at USAMHI.

21. Hains, "Antietam Campaign Subsequent to the Battles at South Mountain," 17.

22. Ibid., 18.

23. Kennedy, "Antietam Campaign Subsequent to the Battles of South Mountain," 48; Hains, "Antietam Campaign Subsequent to the Battles at South Mountain," 19.

24. May, Nobles, Walsh, and Wolcott, "Historical Ride," 14; Kennedy, "Antietam Campaign Subsequent to the Battles of South Mountain," 45.

25. Lt. Col. W. T. May, "Operations on the Federal Center at Antietam," 27, USAWC Curricular Archives, Class of 1912, copy at USAMHI.

26. Kennedy, "Antietam Campaign Subsequent to the Battles of South Mountain," 52.

27. Hains, "Antietam Campaign Subsequent to the Battles at South Mountain," 20; Maj. R. D. Walsh, "The Federal Left at Antietam, September 15–17, 1862," 43, USAWC Curricular Archives, Class of 1912, copy at USAMHI.

28. Matthew F. Steele to Mrs. Steele, July 5, 1908, box 9, Matthew Forney Steele Papers, USAMHI.

29. Kennedy, "Antietam Campaign Subsequent to the Battle of South Mountain," 44.

30. Atkinson, "Battle of Antietam," 55.

31. Kennedy, "Antietam Campaign Subsequent to the Battles of South Mountain," 49.

32. May, Nobles, Walsh, and Wolcott, "Historical Ride," 14; Kennedy, "Antietam Campaign Subsequent to the Battles of South Mountain," 49.

33. Kennedy, "Antietam Campaign Subsequent to the Battles of South Mountain," 50; May, Nobles, Walsh, and Wolcott, "Historical Ride," 14.

34. Hains, "Antietam Campaign Subsequent to the Battles at South Mountain," 19–20.

35. Kennedy, "Antietam Campaign Subsequent to the Battles of South Mountain," 51.

36. May, Nobles, Walsh, and Wolcott, "Historical Ride," 14.

37. On the debate over a professional army, see chap. 2 of Samuel P. Huntington, *The Soldier and the State* (Cambridge: Harvard University Press, 1957).

38. Walsh, "Federal Left at Antietam," 43; Stokes, "Antietam Campaign to and Including the Battles of South Mountain," 41.

39. Lee quoted in Stokes, "Antietam Campaign to and Including the Battles of South Mountain," 42

40. Capt. William H. Monroe, "The Battle of Antietam," [unpaginated], USAWC Curricular Archives, College Class of 1911, USAMHI.

41. Stokes, "Antietam Campaign to and Including the Battles of South Mountain," 42.

42. Kennedy, "Antietam Campaign Subsequent to the Battles of South Mountain," 49–50; Walsh, "Federal Left at Antietam," 43.

43. John M. Schofield, *Forty-Six Years in the Army* (New York: Century, 1897), 521, 524.

44. Kennedy, "Antietam Campaign Subsequent to the Battles of South Mountain," 47; "Map Exercise No. 30," 587, 722, USAWC Curricular Archives, Class of 1910, vol. 2, USAMHI.

45. "Map Exercise No. 30," 466, USAWC Curricular Archives, Class of 1909, vol. 2, USAMHI.

46. Maj. Paul F. Straub, "Sanitary Services in Campaign," 65, USAWC Curricular Archives, Class of 1911, vol. 4, USAMHI.

47. May, Nobles, Walsh, and Wolcott, "Historical Ride," 18–20; Steele, *American Campaigns,* 1:282.

48. Atkinson, "Battle of Antietam," 57; "Map Problem No. 36," 32, USAWC Curricular Archives, Class of 1911, vol. 3, USAMHI.

49. May, Nobles, Walsh, and Wolcott, "Historical Ride," 24–25.

50. "Staff Ride 3 Notes," [unpaginated], USAWC Curricular Archives, Class of 1913, vol. 7, USAMHI; May, Nobles, Walsh, and Wolcott, "Historical Ride," 24; Kennedy, "Antietam Campaign Subsequent to the Battles of South Mountain," 53.

51. Eric W. Sheppard, *The Campaign in Virginia and Maryland* (New York: Macmillan, 1911), 279–80, 288.

Bibliographic Essay

The 1862 Maryland campaign has inspired a large and diverse literature. D. Scott Hartwig's *The Battle of Antietam and the Maryland Campaign of 1862: A Bibliography* (Westport, Conn.: Meckler, 1990) provides an annotated guide to several hundred campaign studies, biographies, unit histories, and other pertinent titles. Readers also should look to the notes accompanying the essays in this collection for important published items and manuscript collections.

The best source for printed primary material on Antietam and the rest of the Maryland campaign is U.S. War Department, *The War of the Rebellion: The Official Records of the Union and Confederate Armies,* 127 vols., index, and atlas (Washington: GPO, 1880–1901), ser. 1, vol. 19, pts. 1–2. These two thick volumes offer nearly 1,750 pages of official reports, correspondence, and other documents. Volume 3 of *Supplement to the Official Records of the Union and Confederate Armies,* ed. Janet B. Hewett and others, 98 of a projected 100 vols. published to date (Wilmington, N.C.: Broadfoot, 1994–), contains additional material about both armies.

Invaluable Confederate testimony about the campaign is in *Southern Historical Society Papers,* ed. J. William Jones and others, 52 vols. (1876–1959; reprint, with 3-vol. index, Wilmington, N.C.: Broadfoot, 1990–92); *Confederate Veteran,* 40 vols. (1893–1932; reprint, with 3-vol. index, Wilmington, N.C.: Broadfoot, 1984–86); and Walter Clark, ed., *Histories of the Several Regiments and Battalions from North Carolina in the Great War 1861–'65,* 5 vols. (Raleigh: E. M. Uzzell, Printer and Binder, 1901). For comparable Union material, readers should consult the *Papers* of the Military Order of the Loyal Legion of the United States (MOLLUS), 66 vols. and 3-vol. index (Wilmington, N.C.: Broadfoot, 1991–96). Read before the state commanderies of the MOLLUS, many of these papers shed light on the Maryland campaign. Additional useful testimony from former Federals and Confederates is in volume 3 of *Papers of the Military Historical Society of Massachusetts,* 14 vols. (1895–1918; reprint in 15 vols. with a general index, Wilmington, N.C.: Broadfoot, 1989–90), and volume 2 of *Battles and Leaders of the Civil War,* ed. Robert Underwood Johnson and Clarence Clough Buel, 4 vols. (New York: Century, 1887).

There have been several treatments of the overall campaign. The two best scholarly works are James V. Murfin's *The Gleam of Bayonets: The Battle of Antietam and the Maryland Campaign of 1862* (New York: Yoseloff, 1965), which offers a detailed narrative and especially useful maps (drawn by James D. Bowlby and based on the famous

Cope series of maps), and Stephen W. Sears's *Landscape Turned Red: The Battle of Antietam* (New York: Ticknor & Fields, 1983), which displays its author's usual combination of sound research, sensible analysis, and evocative prose. Perry D. Jamieson's *Death in September: The Antietam Campaign* (Fort Worth, Tex.: Ryan Place Publishers, 1995) is a good short account, and Jay Luvaas and Harold W. Nelson's *The U.S. Army War College Guide to the Battle of Antietam: The Maryland Campaign of 1862* (Carlisle, Pa.: South Mountain Press, 1987) serves as an excellent guidebook featuring excerpts from the official reports of commanders on both sides. For a series of broad interpretive essays on the campaign, see Gary W. Gallagher, ed., *Antietam: Essays on the 1862 Maryland Campaign* (Kent, Ohio: Kent State University Press, 1989). Two veterans of the campaign wrote narratives still worth consulting, Confederate ordnance officer William Allan's *The Army of Northern Virginia in 1862* (Boston: Houghton Mifflin, 1892) and Union field officer Francis W. Palfrey's *The Antietam and Fredericksburg* (New York: Scribner's, 1882).

Artillery played a pivotal role in the tactical story of Antietam, a topic covered in some depth in Curt Johnson and Richard C. Anderson Jr., *Artillery Hell: The Employment of Artillery at Antietam* (College Station: Texas A&M University Press, 1995). For a pair of older, more general studies that include useful treatments of the artillery in Maryland, see Jennings C. Wise, *The Long Arm of Lee; or, The History of the Artillery of the Army of Northern Virginia . . .*, 2 vols. (Lynchburg: J. P. Bell, 1915), and L. Van Loan Naisawald, *Grape and Canister: The Story of the Field Artillery of the Army of the Potomac, 1861–1865* (New York: Oxford, 1960).

Three pictorial works merit attention. William A. Frassanito's *Antietam: The Photographic Legacy of America's Bloodiest Day* (New York: Scribner's, 1978) examines the impact of photographs taken shortly after the battle and juxtaposes the nineteenth-century images against modern shots of the same views. *The Bloodiest Day: The Battle of Antietam*, by Ronald H. Bailey and the Editors of Time-Life Books (Alexandria, Va.: Time-Life, 1984), includes a handsome array of black-and-white and color illustrations. The Editors of Time-Life's *Antietam* (Alexandria, Va.: Time-Life, 1996), a volume in the Voices of the Civil War series, effectively combines excellent illustrations and testimony from several dozen Union and Confederate participants.

A half dozen titles assist in understanding George B. McClellan's role in the Maryland campaign. The best biography is Stephen W. Sears's *George B. McClellan: The Young Napoleon* (New York: Ticknor & Fields, 1988), an expansive book that portrays its subject as a man who saw political enemies on all sides and who shrank from committing his army to a decisive contest with the Confederates. Warren W. Hassler's *George B. McClellan: Shield of the Union* (Baton Rouge: Louisiana State University Press, 1957) presents "Little Mac" in a far more favorable light, as does Joseph L. Harsh's "On the McClellan Go-Round," *Civil War History* 19 (June 1973): 101–28. Far less flattering to McClellan, who occupies center stage in much of its narrative, is T. Harry Williams's *Lincoln and His Generals* (New York: Knopf, 1952). McClellan's often unreliable memoir, titled *McClellan's Own Story* (New York: Charles L. Webster, 1887), and *The Civil War Papers of George B. McClellan: Selected Correspondence, 1860–1865,* ed. Stephen W. Sears (New York: Ticknor & Fields, 1989), are indispensable.

Robert E. Lee never wrote his memoirs, but letters and other documents relating to the Maryland campaign are in *The Wartime Papers of R. E. Lee,* ed. Clifford Dowdey and Louis H. Manarin (Boston: Little, Brown, 1961). For Lee's pointed postwar comments about the campaign, see memoranda of conversations with him by William Allan, Edward C. Gordon, and William Preston Johnston in Gary W. Gallagher, ed., *Lee the Soldier* (Lincoln: University of Nebraska Press, 1996). Douglas Southall Freeman's *R. E. Lee: A Biography,* 4 vols. (New York: Scribner's, 1934–35), remains the fullest discussion of Lee in Maryland. Also useful is Joseph L. Harsh, *Confederate Tide Rising: Robert E. Lee and the Making of Southern Strategy, 1861–1862* (Kent, Ohio: Kent State University Press, 1998), which gives Lee generally high marks for his strategic decisions in the late summer and autumn of 1862. Walter Taylor, *Lee's Adjutant: The Wartime Letters of Colonel Walter Herron Taylor, 1862–1865* (Columbia: University of South Carolina Press, 1995), offers an excellent perspective from Confederate headquarters through the eyes of a member of Lee's staff.

Much of the most valuable published material on the Maryland campaign is in the form of letters, diaries, and reminiscences, only a handful of which can be mentioned here. Among the best Union sources are artillerist Charles S. Wainwright's *A Diary of Battle: The Personal Journals of Colonel Charles S. Wainwright, 1861–1865,* ed. Allan Nevins (New York: Harcourt, Brace & World, 1962), and division (and later corps) commander Alpheus S. Williams's *From the Cannon's Mouth: The Civil War Letters of General Alpheus S. Williams,* ed. Milo M. Quaife (Detroit: Wayne State University Press, 1959), both of which include excellent descriptive as well as interpretive passages. Also useful are George G. Meade, *The Life and Letters of George Gordon Meade,* 2 vols. (New York: Scribner's, 1913), which gives the perspective of a salty division leader who later commanded the army; Robert Gould Shaw, *Blue-Eyed Child of Fortune: The Civil War Letters of Colonel Robert Gould Shaw,* ed. Russell Duncan (Athens: University of Georgia Press, 1992); and Robert Goldthwaite Carter, *Four Brothers in Blue; or, Sunshine and Shadows of the War of the Rebellion: A Story of the Great Civil War from Bull Run to Appomattox* (Washington: Gibson Brothers Press, 1913). For a common soldier's point of view, see John W. Haley's *The Rebel Yell and the Yankee Hurrah: The Civil War Journal of a Maine Volunteer,* ed. Ruth L. Silliker (Camden, Maine: Down East Books, 1985).

On the Confederate side, James Longstreet's *From Manassas to Appomattox: Memoirs of the Civil War in America* (Philadelphia: Lippincott, 1896) is essential. Jubal A. Early's *Lieutenant General Jubal Anderson Early, C.S.A.: Autobiographical Sketch and Narrative of the War between the States* (Philadelphia: Lippincott, 1912) is a straightforward, revealing account. Edward Porter Alexander's *Military Memoirs of a Confederate: A Critical Narrative* (New York: Scribner's, 1907) and *Fighting for the Confederacy: The Personal Recollections of General Edward Porter Alexander,* ed. Gary W. Gallagher

(Chapel Hill: University of North Carolina Press, 1989), include unexcelled analysis of the campaign as a whole and detailed information about Confederate ordnance. For a set of engaging letters by a combative Confederate brigadier, see William Dorsey Pender, *The General to His Lady: The Civil War Letters of William Dorsey Pender to Fanny Pender,* ed. William W. Hassler (Chapel Hill: University of North Carolina Press, 1965). An equally valuable body of testimony from an officer lower in the chain of command is John Hampden Chamberlayne, *Ham Chamberlayne—Virginian: Letters and Papers of an Artillery Officer in the War for Southern Independence, 1861–1865,* ed. C. G. Chamberlayne (Richmond, Va.: Dietz Printing Co., 1932).

Four general works deserve the attention of anyone interested in the Maryland campaign. Herman Hattaway and Archer Jones, *How the North Won: A Military History of the Civil War* (Urbana: University of Illinois Press, 1983), places the operation within the larger strategic picture of the war. The second volume of Douglas Southall Freeman, *Lee's Lieutenants: A Study in Command,* 3 vols. (New York: Scribner's, 1942–44), describes and analyzes Confederate leadership in memorable prose; Bruce Catton's *Mr. Lincoln's Army* (Garden City, N.Y.: Doubleday, 1951) employs comparably distinguished writing to cover the Army of the Potomac's activities; and the first two volumes of Kenneth P. Williams's *Lincoln Finds a General,* 5 vols. (New York: Macmillan, 1949–59), subject McClellan and other Federal commanders to critical scrutiny.

Finally, a trio of works on nonmilitary topics help illuminate the broader context of the campaign. Howard Jones's judicious *Union in Peril: The Crisis over British Intervention in the Civil War* (Chapel Hill: University of North Carolina Press, 1992) illustrates how close Britain came to some type of intervention. Antietam gave Lincoln an opening to issue his preliminary proclamation of emancipation, the importance of which John Hope Franklin sketches in *The Emancipation Proclamation* (Garden City, N.Y.: Doubleday, 1963). The campaign also afforded Republicans critical of McClellan an opportunity to pressure Democrats in the Army of the Potomac, a phenomenon explored in Bruce Tap's *Over Lincoln's Shoulder: The Committee on the Conduct of the War* (Lawrence: University Press of Kansas, 1998).

Contributors

William A. Blair is a member of the Department of History at Pennsylvania State University. His publications include *A Politician Goes to War: The Civil War Letters of John White Geary*, *Virginia's Private War: Feeding Body and Soul in the Confederacy, 1861–1865*, and several articles and essays on Civil War–era subjects.

Keith S. Bohannon earned an M.A. degree in history from the University of Georgia and received his doctoral training in American history at Pennsylvania State University. He is the author of *The Giles, Alleghany, and Jackson Artillery* and the coeditor of *Campaigning with "Old Stonewall": Confederate Captain Ujanirtus Allen's Letters to His Wife* and currently is working on a study of the Civil War in northeast Georgia.

Peter S. Carmichael is a member of the Department of History at Western Carolina University. The author of *Lee's Young Artillerist: William R. J. Pegram*, as well as several essays and articles in popular and scholarly journals, he is completing a study of Virginia slaveholders' sons and the formation of southern identity in the late antebellum years.

Gary W. Gallagher is a member of the Department of History at the University of Virginia and editor of the Civil War America series at the University of North Carolina Press. He has edited *The Third Day at Gettysburg and Beyond*, *The Fredericksburg Campaign: Decision on the Rappahannock*, *Chancellorsville: The Battle and Its Aftermath*, *The Wilderness Campaign*, and *The Spotsylvania Campaign*, five previous titles in the Military Campaigns of the Civil War series.

Lesley J. Gordon is a member of the Department of History at the University of Akron. She is the author of *General George E. Pickett in Life and Legend*, coeditor and coauthor of *Intimate Strategies: Military Marriages of the Civil War*, and a contributor to various journals and volumes of essays. She is working on a book-length study of the 16th Connecticut Infantry.

D. Scott Hartwig, who studied under E. B. Long at the University of Wyoming, has published several articles and essays on Civil War military history as well as *The Battle of Antietam and the Maryland Campaign of 1862: A Bibliography*. He currently is completing a full-scale study of the 1862 Maryland campaign.

Robert E. L. Krick, a Richmond-based historian, was reared on the Chancellorsville battlefield. The author of *The Fortieth Virginia Infantry* and a number of essays and articles, he is completing a biographical register of the staff officers of the Army of Northern Virginia.

Contributors

Robert K. Krick grew up in California but has lived and worked on the Virginia battlefields for more than twenty-five years. He has written dozens of articles and ten books, the most recent of which are *Stonewall Jackson at Cedar Mountain* and *Conquering the Valley: Stonewall Jackson at Port Republic.*

Carol Reardon is a member of the Department of History at Pennsylvania State University and a former holder of the Harold Keith Johnson Visiting Professorship in Military History at the U.S. Army Military History Institute and U.S. Army War College. She is the author of *Soldiers and Scholars: The U.S. Army and the Uses of Military History, 1865–1920, Pickett's Charge in History and Memory,* and numerous essays in the fields of Civil War and military history.

Brooks D. Simpson is a member of the Department of History at Arizona State University. He is the author of *Let Us Have Peace: Ulysses S. Grant and the Politics of Reconstruction, 1861–1868* and *America's Civil War,* coeditor and coauthor of *Union and Emancipation: Essays on Politics and Race in the Civil War Era,* and coeditor of *Sherman's Civil War: Selected Correspondence of William T. Sherman, 1860–1865.*

Index

Alabama, 126

Alabama troops: 3rd Infantry, 224, 227–28, 231, 252 (n. 18); 5th Infantry, 224, 228, 231, 246, 252 (n. 18); 6th Infantry, 224, 227–28, 231–32, 246–47; 8th Infantry, 247; 9th Infantry, 14; 10th Infantry, 240; 12th Infantry, 224, 231, 247–48; 13th Infantry, 126; 14th Infantry, 110, 240; 26th Infantry, 224, 231; 44th Infantry, 243; 47th Infantry, 25; Rodes's brigade, xiii, 246, 248; Wilcox's brigade, 14, 242

Alexander, Edward Porter, 101, 103, 105–6, 112, 116, 129, 202, 213, 260, 298

Alexander, Peter W., 7–8, 11–12, 114, 123–24, 126–27, 132

Alexandria, Va., 261

Alien Enemies Act, 94

Allan, William, 103, 105, 119, 129, 205

Alleghany County, Va., 221 (n. 47)

Allen, E. Livingston, 157

Allen, Roswell Morgan, 181, 183

Allen, Ujanirtus, 21, 23

Altoona, Pa., 53

American Campaigns (Steele), 297

American Expeditionary Force, 290

Anderson, George B., 225, 227–28, 230, 236–37, 239, 253 (n. 33), 254 (n. 36)

Anderson, Richard H., 239, 241, 254 (nn. 36, 37)

Anderson, Robert W., 236–37

Anderson's brigade (Army of Northern Virginia), xiii, 115, 224, 232, 235, 246

Anderson's division (Army of Northern Virginia), xiii, 239–40

Andersonville, Ga., 184

Antietam, battle of, ix, xi–xiv, 4–5, 8–12, 14–15, 19–26, 28, 31–34, 41 (n. 47), 45, 49, 55, 59, 64, 75, 77, 87, 93–94, 101, 103, 105–6, 116–17, 134 (n. 13), 147, 152, 160, 163, 165, 169–70, 174, 178–81, 183–87, 189 (n. 18), 192–95, 213–15, 225–26, 229, 234–35, 239, 243, 247–48, 249 (n. 2), 263, 266, 268–70, 278–79, 289–312 passim; Lee's conduct at, 42 (n. 55)

Antietam campaign, ix, xi–xii, xiv, 5–6, 13, 27, 41 (n. 47), 45, 101, 103, 110, 123, 132, 143–44, 146–47, 194, 265, 278, 291, 294, 306–7; Confederate reaction to, 11, 15, 20, 27; historians' assessment of, 4; impact of, xv (n. 2), 19; results of, x

Antietam Creek, 47, 69, 156, 162, 174, 196, 201, 215, 224, 264, 293, 302, 304–5

Antietam National Cemetery, 177, 296

Appalachian Mountains, 29

Archer's brigade (Army of Northern Virginia), 113–14

Ardrey, William, 233

Armistead, Lewis A., 255 (n. 39), 268

Armistead's brigade (Army of Northern Virginia), 240, 266, 268–70, 278, 285 (n. 29), 286 (n. 35)

Army of Northern Virginia, ix, xi–xiv, 4, 7, 11, 14, 20, 27, 32, 34, 45, 74–75, 86–87, 92, 107, 116, 126, 130, 192, 226, 265, 270, 273–75, 278–82, 292, 301, 310; condition of, 9, 24–25, 28–29, 31, 41 (n. 47), 101–2, 108, 120–21; opinions on retreat from Maryland, 24; ordnance of, 103, 105, 114, 129, 141 (n. 89), 193; reactions to Maryland Campaign, 27; straggling by, 9, 24–26, 119; views of Lee, 27–28, 33; views of Marylanders, 90–91. *See also* individual brigade and division commanders; individual listings of troops by state

Army of Tennessee, 279–80

Army of the Potomac, xii, 17, 26, 31, 44, 47,

58–59, 115–16, 143–45, 154, 163–64, 173,
184, 203, 265, 292, 295, 302, 305–6, 310;
condition of, 60–61; officer corps, 46, 68;
psychology of, 45, 54, 62, 69; reactions to
emancipation proclamation, 52; sentiments
after Antietam campaign, xi, 49. *See also*
Union corps; Union troops; individual
army, corps, division, and brigade commanders; individual listings of troops by
state
Army of the Ohio, 64
Army of the Tennessee, 46
Army of Virginia, ix, 4, 145
Aspinwall, William H., 58, 71 (n. 30)
Atkinson, Benjamin, 297–98
Atlanta, Ga., 8, 127
Atlanta *Southern Confederacy*, 8, 123–24

Bacot, Ada W., 15
Bagarly, John, 237
Baird, William H., 150–51
Ballard, Thomas E., 117
Baltimore, Md., 26, 76–77, 79, 83–84, 95–96,
234, 238, 262; military occupation of, 80;
riot in, 78, 81–82, 86–87
"Baltimore" (song), 88
Baltimore and Ohio Railroad, x, 33, 76
Baltimore *Exchange*, 84
Baltimore *South*, 84
Banks, Nathaniel P., 82, 84
Barksdale, William, 255 (n. 39)
Barksdale's brigade (Army of Northern Vir-
ginia), 103, 149
Barlow, Francis C., 245–46
Barlow, Leland O., 179
Barlow, S. L. M., 66
Barras, Samuel A., 150–52
Battle, Walter, 24, 236
Bauer, Emily, 181
Bauer, Jacob, 173, 181
Beach, Francis, 149, 171–73, 175–76, 178–79,
183
Beach, George, 171
Beale, George W., 201
Beall, Thomas B., 234
Beauregard, P. G. T., 22, 85
Beldon, Elizur D., 179

Belknap, Charles W., 152
Bennett, Risden T., 224, 234–35, 239, 244–45
Benson, Berry, 163, 176
Bier, George Henry, 103
Blackford, William M., 13, 19, 95
Blackford, William W., 207–8
Blackshear, James A., 263–64
Blair, Francis Preston, 54
Blair, Montgomery, 54
Blakeslee, B. G., 162, 171, 174, 185, 189 (n. 18)
Block, John T., 209
Bloody Lane, xiii, 21, 46, 223–24, 228, 231,
235–37, 239–40, 242–48, 249 (n. 2), 252
(n. 19), 290, 303–5
Blue Ridge Mountains, 12, 88
Bolivar Heights, 152, 154
Boonsboro, Md., 19, 36 (n. 9), 111–12, 114, 234
Boteler's Ford, 3, 7–8, 20, 118–19, 260, 264–
69, 273–76, 278, 285 (nn. 29, 34), 301
Bowen, Roland, 208
Bragg, Braxton, 19, 29
Branch, Sanford W., 26
Branch's brigade (Army of Northern Vir-
ginia), 113
Breathed, James, 195, 214
Brewster, Charles H., 63
Bristol, Conn., 170
Bristol College, 261
Britain, 75, 122, 178, 180
Brockenbrough, John B., 194, 210
Brown, John T., 265
Bryan, John W., 209
Buck, Lucy Rebecca, 12
Buck, Sam, 209–10
Buckingham, Catharinus P., 64
Buckingham, William, 170, 172
Buell, Don Carlos, 19, 64
Bull Run Creek, 23
Bunker Hill, Va., 29, 119, 275
Burge, Dolly Lunt, 13
Burnham, John H., 180–81, 185
Burnside, Ambrose E., x, 14–15, 64, 68, 301,
303, 305–6
Burnside's Bridge, xiii, 47, 162, 174, 246, 301,
304–5
Butler, Benjamin F., 80

Cage, William L., 121

Caldwell, James F. J., 109, 176

Caldwell, John C., 245

Caldwell's brigade (Army of the Potomac), 245

Campbell, John A., 38 (n. 34)

Carman, Ezra, 147, 158–59, 208–9, 217 (n. 9), 221 (n. 47), 249 (n. 2)

Carpenter, John C., 194, 210

Catton, Bruce, 45

Cedar Mountain, battle of, 34, 95, 297

Cedar Run, battle of, 23

Chamberlain, Joshua L., 62

Chamberlayne, John Hampden, 22, 28–29, 91, 260, 275–78

Chambersburg, Pa., 59, 114

Chancellorsville, battle of, 192, 215

Charleston, S.C., 8

Charleston *Daily Courier*, 6–7, 10–11

Charleston *Mercury*, 6, 8, 10, 79, 81

Charles Town, Va., 117, 136 (n. 34)

Charlottesville, Va., 15, 108

Chattanooga, Tenn., 126

Cheney, Frank, 169, 172, 177, 181

Chesapeake & Ohio Canal, 267

Chesapeake Bay, 76, 80, 86

Chicago, Ill., 113

Chickahominy River, 11

Christ, Benjamin C., 156

Christian, William A., 202

Christian's brigade (Army of the Potomac), 202

Colquitt, Alfred H., 224, 243

Colquitt's brigade (Army of Northern Virginia), 228–29

Columbia *Daily Southern Guardian*, 127

Columbia *Guardian*, 122

Columbus, Ga., 126–27

Columbus *Daily Sun*, 123–24

Confederacy: popular culture of, 86–88, 92

Confederate Army: artillery, xiii, 22, 105–6, 128, 130, 134 (n. 13), 141 (n. 86), 174–75, 192–94, 200, 213, 215, 262; cavalry, 59, 62, 90, 92–93, 105, 113–15, 128, 303; Commissary Department, 121, 131–32; Horse Artillery, xiii, 195, 214; logistics of, xii, 102, 106–8, 122, 127–28, 131–32; Ordnance

Department, 105, 108, 132; Quartermaster Department, 106–8, 113, 121–22,127, 130–32. *See also* Army of Northern Virginia; Reserve Artillery; individual listings of troops by state

Congress (C.S.), 32, 93, 106, 127, 131

Congress (U.S.), xiv, 64, 81–82, 144

Connecticut, 170, 177, 183, 187 (n. 2)

Connecticut River, 172

Connecticut troops: 8th Infantry, 173, 175, 179; 11th Infantry, 45, 173, 176, 181; 14th Infantry, 149, 156, 164–65; 16th Infantry, xii, 148–49, 162–64, 169–70, 172–81, 183–87; 18th Infantry, 185

Coppens, Georges A. G., 240

Corinth, battle of, 19, 35 (n. 2), 38 (n. 33)

Corsan, W. C., 19

Couch's division (Army of the Potomac), 146

Courtney, Alfred R., 194, 213

Cox, Jacob D., 301

Crampton's Gap, 154; battle of, 134 (n. 9), 298

Crater, battle of the, 192, 215

Crawford, S. M., 24

Crawford, Samuel W., 158

Crawford's brigade (Army of the Potomac), 205

Croasdale, Samuel, 147, 157–58

Croffutt, W. A., 185

Crosby, Frank, 158

Crowder, James P., 25

Crutchfield, Stapleton, 113, 194, 206, 213

CSS *Alabama*, 95

Culpeper Court House, Va., 19, 108, 128

Cumming, Alfred, 241

Curtis, Joseph B., 178, 179

Cutts, Allen S., 263–64

Cuzner, John B., 180

Dabney, Robert Lewis, 41 (n. 47)

Davis, Benjamin F. "Grimes," 115

Davis, Jefferson, xiv, 12, 31–33, 78–79, 83, 85, 87–89, 94, 101–2, 106, 108, 110, 115, 119–20, 130, 225, 276, 278, 280–81; criticized for war strategy, 39 (n. 36); views on Maryland campaign, 19–20, 38 (n. 34)

Davis, Nicholas A., 22

Davis, Varina, 279

Dawes, Rufus, 47, 202, 212

Dawson, Francis W., 116, 129

De Fontaine, Felix G., 108

Democrats, 10, 56, 64, 76

DeRosset, William L., 103

De Trobriand, Philippe Regis, 230

"Dixie" (song), 87

Dodge, Grenville M., 69 (n. 3)

Doubleday, Abner, 203

Doubleday's division (Army of the Potomac), 201, 203

Douglas, Henry Kyd, 270, 273

Dowdey, Clifford, 4

Drake, William, 179

Drayton's brigade (Army of Northern Virginia), 116, 155

Duncan, Sebastian, 148, 156–60

Dunker Church, xiii, 159, 193–94, 196, 201–2, 204, 207–8, 220 (n. 33), 307–8

Duryea's brigade (Army of the Potomac), 203

Early, Jubal A., 203, 207, 213, 215, 285 (n. 29)

Early's brigade (Army of Northern Virginia), 203, 207

Early's division (Army of Northern Virginia), 273

Eastern Theater, x–xi, 4, 6, 22

East Woods, 158–59, 196, 205, 224–25, 307

Eaton, Clement, 4

Edmondston, Catherine, 16

Edwards, John F., 117

Elizabethport, Conn., 172–73

Elk Mountain, 60

Elzey, Arnold, 95, 280

Emancipation Proclamation, x, 4–5, 46, 53, 58; Army of the Potomac's reaction to, 52; Confederate reaction to, 10–11, 16–17; McClellan's reaction to, 51–52

Engelbrecht, Jacob, 110

Ex parte Merryman, 81

Fairfax, Va., 14

Fairfax County, Va., 17

Falling Waters, Va., 264

Favill, Josiah, 62

Fayetteville, N.C., 126

Feltus, Abram M., 240

Ferrero, Edward, 155

Fielding, Mary, 14

Field's division (Army of Northern Virginia), 259

Finch, P. V., 186

First U.S. Sharpshooters, 267, 269

Fisk, Samuel, 165

Florida troops: 2nd Infantry, 240, 244, 247; 5th Infantry, 240, 247; 8th Infantry, 240, 247, 255 (n. 39), 256 (n. 50)

Floyd, R. F., 255 (n. 39)

Fogle, Theodore, 21, 28

Fonerden, C. A., 210

Forrest, Frank, 234

Fort Hamilton, N.Y., 261

Fort Leavenworth, Kans. Terr., 290, 303

Fort McHenry, Md., 82, 84

Fort Moultrie, S.C., 260

Fourth Regiment of Artillery (Army of the Potomac), 260

Fox's Gap, 115, 154–56, 298

France, 75, 290

Frayser's Farm, battle of, 215

Frederick, Md., ix, 28, 77, 84, 90, 92, 110, 115–16, 147–49, 174, 262–64, 294, 297, 311

Fredericksburg, Va., 14, 132; battle of, x, 68, 184, 279; second battle of, 260

Frémont, John C., 17

French, William H., 160, 225, 230, 244, 305

French's division (Army of the Potomac), 224, 230, 234, 244, 305

Frobel, Anne S., 14, 16–17

Front Royal, Va., 12, 108

Fuller, Ben, 298

Gaillard, Frank, 121–22

Gaines's Mill, battle of, 195, 280

Gales, Seaton, 236

Garland, Samuel, 224

Garnett's brigade (Army of Northern Virginia), 116

General Orders No. 116, 34

General Orders No. 163, 58, 71 (n. 30)

Georgia, 12–13, 26, 102, 122, 124–25

Georgia troops: 2nd Infantry, 21; 3rd Infantry, 28, 124, 243; 4th Infantry, 25; 8th Infantry, 25–26; 10th Infantry, 241; 15th Infantry, 24;

21st Infantry, 21–22; 22nd Infantry, 242–43; 48th Infantry, 243; 49th Infantry, 26; 53rd Infantry, 25; Troup Artillery, 207; Blackshear's battery, 220 (n. 36); Ross's battery, 209; Colquitt's brigade, 228–29; Lawton's brigade, 266, 268–70, 278, 285 (n. 29), 286 (n. 35); Toombs's brigade, 115; Wright's brigade, 242, 247

Germany, 76, 92

Gettysburg, Pa.: campaign and battle of, 20, 68, 94–95, 130, 152, 260; Lee's conduct at, 42 (n. 55)

Gibbon, John, 65

Gibson, William, 243–44

Gilbert, W. H., 181, 183

Gordon, George H., 158–60

Gordon, John B., 227, 231–32

Gordonsville, Va., 108

Goree, Thomas J., 26

Gorgas, Josiah, 16, 130

Gorman, John C., 114, 235

Gorman, Willis A., 208

Gorman's brigade (Army of the Potomac), 208–9

Gould, John M., 205, 249 (n. 2)

Graham, Thomas A., 209

Grant, Ulysses S., 46, 64

Greeley, Horace, 85

Greencastle, Pa., 116

Greene's division (Army of the Potomac), 206

Gregg's brigade (Army of Northern Virginia), 113, 162

Grigsby, Andrew J., 207

Grimes, Bryan, 227

Groveton, Va., 193

Hagerstown, Md., ix, 33, 112, 114–15

Hagerstown Turnpike, 118, 159, 196, 204, 215, 223–24, 228, 239–40, 242, 249 (n. 2), 295

Hains, John P., 295

Hale, E. J., 126

Haley, John, 64

Hall, Ezra, 185

Hall, Isaac, 203

Halleck, Henry W., 52, 58, 300

Hancock, Winfield S., 68

Hanson, Joseph Mills, 205

Hardy, William B., 262–63

Harland, Edward, 175, 179

Harland's brigade (Army of the Potomac), 173, 308

Harman, John A., 112–14, 119, 265

Harpers Ferry, Va., ix–xii, 4–5, 7–8, 11, 13–14, 22–23, 34, 36 (n. 9), 55, 60, 80, 91, 106, 110–15, 117, 129–30, 138 (n. 53), 141 (n. 90), 145, 147–48, 152, 154–55, 162, 164, 190 (n. 35), 194, 200, 214, 239, 264, 292–94, 297–98, 301, 303

Harper's Weekly, 83

Harrison's Landing, Va., 52

Hartford, Conn., 173–74, 183, 185

Hartford County, Conn., 170

Hartford Courant, 172, 183, 187

Hartford *Times*, 187

Haskell, Alexander Cheves, 26

Haskell, Frank A., 47

Hatch, Ozias, 56

Hatley, John C., 240

Hauser's Ridge, xiii, 196, 204–9, 215, 220 (n. 36), 221 (n. 41)

Havana, Cuba, 238

Hawks, Wells J., 112

Hay, John, 54

Henderson, G. F. R., 147

Henry, Robert Selph, 4

Herbert, Hilary A., 242

Hicks, Thomas H., 77–78

Hill, A. P., 113, 243, 286 (n. 41), 306–7

Hill, D. H., 41 (n. 47), 114–16, 224–28, 237, 246, 270, 273–74, 276

Hillsboro, N.C., 237–38

Hill's corps (Army of Northern Virginia), 36 (n. 9)

Hill's (A. P.) division (Army of Northern Virginia), x, xiii, 7, 113, 162, 273–74, 276, 286 (n. 41)

Hill's (D. H.) division (Army of Northern Virginia), 114–15, 264

Hirst, Benjamin, 156

Hitchcock, Frederick, 149, 156, 160

Hodges, James G., 268–69, 285 (n. 29)

Holcombe, Garret B., 177

Hood, John B., 272, 279

Hood's division (Army of Northern Virginia), 103, 107, 117, 155

Hooker, Joseph, 44, 48–49, 51, 55, 64, 68, 85, 198, 201–4, 209, 215, 300–301, 304–5

Horton, William, 181

Hotchkiss, Jedediah, 109, 226–27

Howard, Francis Key, 84

Howard, Oliver O., 44, 85, 211

"How They Act in Baltimore" (song), 87

Humphrey, W. H., 200

Humphreys, Andrew A., 68

Humphreys's division (Army of the Potomac), 164, 310

Hunt, Henry J., 303

Hunter, Alexander, 114

Ide, A. W., 181

Illinois, 56

Indiana, 59

Iowa, 59

Ireland, 76

Irish Brigade (Army of the Potomac), 66, 244

Iron Brigade (Army of the Potomac), 47, 52, 66, 67

Irwin, Richard B., 53

Jackson, Thomas J. "Stonewall," ix, 14–15, 19, 21, 28, 32, 63, 80, 88, 91–92, 109, 111–12, 114, 117, 119, 129–30, 194–95, 198, 201, 203, 209, 211, 213, 222 (n. 51), 230, 259, 273–74, 276, 284 (n. 27), 286 (nn. 35, 41), 293, 303

Jackson's corps (Army of Northern Virginia), 280

Jackson's division (Army of Northern Virginia), 206

James River, 6

Jenkins, Wilson T., 234

Jenkins's brigade (Army of Northern Virginia), 109

Johnson, Bradley T., 90, 95

Johnson, C. E., 237

Johnson, Marmaduke, 275

Johnston, Joseph E., 42 (n. 53), 262, 280

Johnston, Whitmel A., 234

Jones, Benjamin Franklin, 23

Jones, Edward J., 22

Jones, John B., 15, 17, 81

Jones, John R., 101, 206–7

Jones, Robert H., 242

Jones, William E., 112

Kane, George P., 82, 87

Kean, Robert Garlick Hill, 19

Keedysville, Md., 295

Keedysville Road, 223

Keever, James E., 23

Kellogg, Robert, 173, 180, 187

Kentucky, 19, 29, 35 (n. 2), 80, 89, 93–94, 297

Kershaw's brigade (Army of Northern Virginia), 103, 149–52

Key, Francis Scott, 84

Key, John M., 54, 58

Key, Thomas M., 54

Kimball, John W., 208

Kimball, Nathan, 230–31, 253 (n. 29)

Kingsbury, Henry W., 45

Kirkpatrick, Thomas J., 275

Knipe, Joseph, 159

Lamar, John H., 268–69, 285 (n. 29)

Landers, Eli P., 127

Landscape Turned Red: The Battle of Antietam (Sears), x

Lane, Daniel, 21, 246, 249 (n. 3)

Lang, David, 240

Lawley, Francis, 103, 105

Law's brigade (Army of Northern Virginia), 103

Lawton, Alexander R., 207, 268

Lawton's brigade (Army of Northern Virginia), 266, 268–70, 278, 285 (n. 29), 286 (n. 35)

Lawton's division (Army of Northern Virginia), 117

Lee, Charles Gilbert, 189 (n. 18)

Lee, George Washington Custis, 19

Lee, Robert E., x–xii, xiv, xv (n. 1), 3–6, 8, 11, 16–17, 19–24, 26, 29, 32, 48–49, 51, 53, 63–64, 74, 86, 88, 90, 92, 101, 107–8, 110–11, 115–16, 119–21, 127–30, 132, 138 (n. 62), 145, 147, 201, 212–13, 220 (n. 36), 221 (n. 46), 225, 228, 243, 259–60, 262, 264–67, 272–73, 275–82, 285 (n. 34), 292–94,

296–97, 299–300, 303–4, 310–12; relation-
ship to Army of Northern Virginia, 27–28,
33–34; views on Maryland campaign, ix,
31, 89, 99 (n. 41), 102
Lee, Robert E., Jr., 220 (n. 36)
Lee, Stephen D., 121, 213
Lee, William H. F. "Rooney," 284 (n. 27)
Lee's battalion (Army of Northern Virginia),
203–4
Lee's brigade (Army of Northern Virginia),
128, 134 (n. 9), 198, 201, 210, 212
Leesburg, Va., 145
Lemon, James L., 117
Lexington, Va., 260, 262, 281
Lightfoot, James N., 246
Limestone County, Ala., 14
Lincoln, Abraham, x, 4, 10–11, 17, 46, 51–52,
54, 59, 62–65, 67–68, 74–75, 78–82, 84,
144, 170, 289, 300; views on Lee's invasion
of Maryland, ix; visits Antietam battlefield,
55–56, 58
Lineberger, James W., 29
Little, George B., 234
Logan, John A., 306
London *Times*, 103
Long Arm of Lee (Wise), 205, 279
Longstreet, James, 28, 32, 63, 112, 114–15,
129–30, 239, 243, 259, 272–73, 282, 298
Longstreet's corps (Army of Northern Vir-
ginia), 63
Loudoun Heights, 106, 112
Louisa Court House, Va., 107
Louisiana, 12, 20
Louisiana troops: 8th Infantry, 108; 9th
Infantry, 26; 10th Infantry, 118; Guard
Artillery, 198, 206–9, 219 (n. 24), 222
(n. 47); Washington Artillery, 118
Louisville, Ky., 19
Lovell, Mansfield, 95
Lowe, Enoch L., 86, 88–90
Lower Bridge, 45
Luray, Va., 108
Lynchburg, Va., 13, 17, 92, 95

McClelen, Bailey, 240
McClellan, George B., ix–xii, xv (n. 1), 4, 8,
10–11, 15–17, 23, 29, 31–33, 36 (n. 9), 45, 51,

54–56, 58–59, 62, 69, 112, 143–47, 164, 211,
246, 266–67, 289, 292–94, 296–308, 310,
312; Army of the Potomac's opinion of,
48–50, 53, 63, 66; removal of, 46, 64–65,
67–68
McClellan, Henry B., 105, 208
McClernand, John A., 64
McClure, John William, 109
McDonald, Cornelia Peake, 16–17
McGee, Jesse Steed, 24
McGuire, Judith, 80
McIntosh, David G., 112–13, 279, 287 (n. 48)
Mackall, Robert M., 198
McLaws, Lafayette, 91, 112, 117, 210–11, 255
(n. 39)
McLaws's division (Army of Northern Vir-
ginia), 103, 115, 117, 138 (n. 53), 150, 207,
210, 213, 220 (n. 33)
Macomb, M. M., 290–92
Macon, Ga., 27
Macon *Daily Telegraph*, 121–22, 125
McPherson, James M., 4
McRae, Duncan K., 224
MacRae, William, 228
McRae's brigade (Army of Northern Vir-
ginia), 228
Mahone's brigade (Army of Northern Vir-
ginia), 240, 255 (n. 39)
Maine, 12
Maine troops: 10th Infantry, 205; 16th
Infantry, 144, 154; 17th Infantry, 64; 20th
Infantry, 55
Malvern Hill, battle of, 21, 193, 242, 260, 262
Manassas: first battle of, 83, 85, 193, 260, 262;
second battle of, ix, xi, xiv, 4, 11, 23, 31, 34,
45, 47, 58, 101–2, 106–8, 112, 129, 145–46,
165 (n. 6), 172, 192–93, 260, 262, 280, 297,
303, 306
Manassas Junction, Va., 107
Manning, Peyton Thompson, 129
Manross, Newton, 170, 173, 177
Mansfield, Joseph K., 157–58, 304, 307
Marble, Manton, 52
Marks, Edwin, 209
Marsh, William T., 233
Martinsburg, Va., 19, 23, 25, 110–12, 114–15,
145, 241, 293

Marye's Heights, 68

Maryland, xi, xii, 3–34 passim, 35 (n. 2), 47–48, 74, 79–96 passim, 99 (n. 41), 102–3, 105, 107–9, 114, 116, 119, 143, 145–48, 184, 193, 195, 234, 262, 264, 273, 290, 292–93, 297–98, 300, 310–11; economic and social composition of, 76–77; General Assembly, 84; House of Representatives, 80, 82; violation of civil rights in, 75

Maryland campaign. *See* Antietam campaign

Marylanders, ix–xii, 31, 78, 82, 86, 89, 93–94, 109; Confederate soldiers' reaction to, 27, 75, 91, 95; Lee's opinion of, 32, 90

Maryland Heights, 106, 112, 117, 149, 151

"Maryland, My Maryland" (song), 27, 74, 86, 88

Maryland troops: 5th Infantry (U.S.), 230; Brockenbrough's Baltimore Artillery (C.S), 194, 206, 210, 212

Mason, James M., 78

Mason-Dixon line, 75

Massachusetts, 165 (n. 6)

Massachusetts troops: 2nd Infantry, 52, 159; 6th Infantry, 78; 10th Infantry, 63; 12th Infantry, 202; 15th Infantry, 208; 21st Infantry, 155; 35th Infantry, 148, 155, 164

May, Henry, 82, 84, 86

Mayer, Nathan, 186

Meade, George G., 48, 51, 56, 59, 64

Meagher, Thomas, 66

Mechanicsville, battle of, 3

Memphis *Daily Appeal*, 123, 125

Merryman, John, 81

Michigan, 223

Michigan troops: 4th Infantry, 269, 284 (n. 27); 17th Infantry, 155–56, 164

Middletown, Md., 111

Miles, Nelson A., 245

Military Policy of the United States (Upton), 306

Militia Act of 1862, 144

Miller Cornfield, xiii, 44, 46, 50, 158–59, 196, 203–5, 211, 224, 304, 307

Minnesota troops: 1st Infantry, 66, 208

Mississippi, 14, 29

Mississippi River, 122, 124, 126

Mississippi troops: 13th Infantry, 20; 16th Infantry, 240, 244, 247; 17th Infantry, 123; 21st Infantry, 121; Barksdale's brigade, 103, 149; Posey's brigade, 244

Missouri, 93–94

Mobile *Tribune*, 122

Monroe, J. Albert, 201, 203

Monroe County, Va., 221 (n. 47)

Montgomery, William R., 27

Montgomery *Daily Advertiser*, 122

Montgomery *Daily Mail*, 123

Montgomery *Weekly Advertiser*, 123, 125

Moore, Ned, 211

Morgan, Sarah, 13

Morrell, George W., 148

Morris, Dwight, 230–31

Morris, John M., 185

Morse, Charles, 159

Mr. Lincoln's Army (Catton), 45

Mudd, Samuel, 238

Mumma house, 201

Munford, Thomas T., 134 (n. 9), 268, 279

Munford's brigade (Army of Northern Virginia), 134 (n. 9), 269

Myers, Abraham C., 107, 126, 130–31

Napoleon: Lee compared to, 28; McClellan compared to, 62, 65–66

Nashville, Tenn., 106

Nelson, William, 263

Newark College, 261

New Hampshire troops: 9th Infantry, 143, 155–56, 164; Edgell's battery, 200

New Jersey troops: 13th Infantry, 147–49, 156–60, 164

New Orleans, La., 106

Newport News, Va., 184

New York, 149, 165 (n. 6)

New York, N.Y., 16, 55, 144

New York Times, 10

New York Tribune, 10

New York troops: 23rd Infantry, 203–4; 28th Infantry, 159; 46th Infantry, 155; 51st Infantry, 47, 155; 57th Infantry, 51; 61st Infantry, 245; 79th Infantry, 156; 82nd Infantry, 208; 97th Infantry, 203; 107th Infantry, 157, 164; 108th Infantry, 164; 121st Infantry, 154; 125th Infantry,

152; 126th Infantry, 147, 149–52, 154–55; Zouave brigade, 58

New York World, 52

Nicodemus Heights, xiii, 196, 198, 200–205, 207, 211–13, 215, 217 (nn. 12, 15), 219 (n. 26), 222 (n. 51), 303

Nisbet, Reuben, B., 243

North Anna campaign, 259

North Carolina, 76, 83, 106

North Carolina troops: 2nd Infantry, 21, 224, 232, 235, 237, 246, 249 (n. 3), 253 (n. 32); 3rd Infantry, 103, 253 (n. 33); 4th Infantry, 24, 224, 228, 232–33, 237, 244–46; 14th Infantry, 224, 228, 232–35, 242, 244–46; 23rd Infantry, 251 (n. 12); 30th Infantry, 224, 232–33, 237, 242–44, 253 (n. 33); 34th Infantry, 23; 35th Infantry, 24–25; 49th Infantry, 29; Reilly's battery, 118; Anderson's brigade, xiii, 115, 224, 232, 235, 246; Branch's brigade, 113; McRae's brigade, 228

Northrop, Lucius B., 131–32

North Woods, 196, 199, 202, 211, 301

Norton, Oliver W., 47, 51–52

Oakford, Richard A., 156

Official Records, 240

Ohio, 59, 85, 239

Ohio troops: 32nd Infantry, 150

"Oh Jeff! Why Don't You Come" (song), 87

"Oh Tannenbaum" (song), 87

Opequan Creek, 32

Orange, Va., 14

Osborne, Edwin A., 233

Owen, William M., 118

Ox Hill, battle of, 23

Parham, William A., 240

Paris, Va., 14

Parker, Francis M., 232–33, 237, 239, 253 (n. 33)

Parker, Thomas, 155

Patrick, Marsena R., 44–46, 55, 64, 66, 68, 203

Paxton, Elisha Franklin, 23

Pegram, William R. J., 260

Pelham, John, xiii, 192, 195, 198, 200–206, 209, 212–15, 219 (n. 26), 260

Pember, Phoebe Yates, 94

Pender, William Dorsey, 25, 286 (n. 41); opinion of Lee, 28–29

Pendleton, Alexander H. "Sandie," 27

Pendleton, William Nelson, xiii, 213, 261–81, 285 (n. 29), 286 (n. 35), 287 (n. 48); opinion of Lee, 28–29, 282; soldiers' opinion of, 259–60

Peninsula campaign, 15, 170, 297, 303, 306

Pennsylvania, 15, 31, 59, 75, 85, 91, 261, 292, 297

Pennsylvania troops: 46th Infantry, 159; 51st Infantry, 155; 83rd Infantry, 48; 88th Infantry, 202; 118th Infantry, 148, 273; 124th Infantry, 158, 164; 125th Infantry, 164, 308; 128th Infantry, 147, 158–59, 164; 130th Infantry, 160, 164; 132nd Infantry, 149, 156, 160, 164; 9th Reserves, 202; 10th Reserves, 200, 204

Perrin, James M., 163

Perry, Joel W., Jr., 243

Philips, Fred, 237

Pierson, Reuben A., 26

Pine Mountain, battle of, 280

Pinkerton, Allan, 56

Piper farm, 118

Pittman, James E., 156

Pleasant Valley, Md., 59, 115, 117

Pleasonton, Alfred, 267

Pleasonton's division (Army of the Potomac), 302

Plymouth, N.C., 184

Poague, William T., 212–13

Poffenberger farm, 199, 202, 204, 208, 211–12

Polk's corps (Army of Tennessee), 280

Pollard, Edward A., 6

Pope, Albert A., 148–49

Pope, John, 11, 45, 58, 65, 68, 145

Porter, Fitz John, 52, 68, 267

Porterstown Ridge, 196

Posey, Carnot, 242, 244–45

Posey's brigade (Army of Northern Virginia), 244

Potomac River, ix–xi, xiii–xiv, xv (n. 1), 3–34 passim, 48, 58–59, 63, 74–75, 85–86, 88,

91–92, 96, 102, 107–9, 112, 115–19, 145–46, 205, 211, 239, 263–65, 269, 272–73, 276, 286 (n. 35), 293, 297–98, 300, 304, 311
Potts, William W., 158
Powell, William H., 47
Prevost, Charles M., 273
Price, Richard Channing, 208
Pry House, 55
Pryor, Roger A., 239–40, 242–43, 254 (n. 37), 272
Pryor, Shepherd G., 29
Pryor's brigade (Army of Northern Virginia), 240, 244

Raine, Charles I., 213
Ramseur, Stephen D., 228
Randall, James R., 86
Randolph, George Wythe, 19, 31–32, 102, 107, 124, 132, 139 (n. 62)
Rapidan, Va., 108
Rappahannock River, 12, 33
Ratchford, J. W., 273
Redfield Corner, Maine, 144
Relyea, William, 172, 174, 179–80, 183–84, 189 (n. 18), 191 (n. 39)
Reno, Jesse L., 305
Republicans, 46, 65, 75, 77, 95
Reserve Artillery, xiii, 114, 260, 263–64, 272, 275–76, 278; Brown's battalion, 264; Nelson's battalion, 264
Revolutionary War, 11, 66, 132
Reynolds, John, 56
Rhode Island troops: 4th Infantry, 162–63, 173, 175–76, 178–80
Rhodes, Elisha H., 48, 60, 62, 65
Rhodes, Henry, 190 (n. 29)
Richardson, Israel B., 225, 244, 246
Richardson's division (Army of the Potomac), 244
Richmond, Va., xi, 3–4, 11–12, 15, 19–20, 25–26, 31, 33–34, 53, 80–81, 92, 94, 103, 105–6, 108, 110, 122, 124, 126–27, 130–31, 280–81
Richmond *Daily Enquirer*, 11
Richmond *Dispatch*, 6, 8–11, 124
Richmond *Enquirer*, 7–8, 11, 25
Richmond *Examiner*, 6, 8, 85

Richmond *Weekly Dispatch*, 7, 21
Richmond *Whig*, 9–10, 275–76
Ridgeville, Md., 154
Ripley, Roswell S., 22, 224
Ritchie, Charles N., 158, 160
Robbins, George, 171–72, 179, 184
Robinson, Jane, 126
Robinson Springs, Ala., 126
Rodes, Robert E., 224–30, 232, 239, 243, 246–47
Rodes's brigade (Army of Northern Virginia), xiii, 246, 248
Rodman, Isaac P., 175, 177, 179
Rodman's division (Army of the Potomac), 162, 173, 305, 308
Roland, Charles P., 4
Ropes, John Codman, 300
Ross, B. B., 245
Ross, Ben, 233
Ross, H. M., 209
Ruffin, Edmund, 12, 79, 85
Russell, Charles H., 150–51

Savannah *Republican*, 7, 9
Schofield, John M., 308
Scott, Winfield, 80, 82
Seaton, Benjamin M., 15
Seay, Merit, 267
Secession, xi, 76–77, 82, 84
Secessionists, 75, 79–80, 84–86, 91
Second U.S. Sharpshooters, 200
Seddon, James A., 106–7, 128
Sedgwick, John, 68, 209–10, 224–25, 305
Sedgwick's division (Army of the Potomac), 159, 207, 211, 305
Selma *Reporter*, 122
Semmes, Raphael, 95
Seven Days, battles of, ix, xi, xiv, 4, 11, 17, 21, 23, 31–34, 102–3, 144–45, 195, 228, 280
Seven Pines, battle of, 27, 44, 262
Seymour, Horatio, 63
Sharpsburg, Md., ix, xi, 3–4, 6, 24, 26–27, 44, 56, 112–13, 115–19, 198, 206, 211, 223, 264–65, 289–90, 293–96. *See also* Antietam, battle of
Shaw, Robert Gould, 50, 52–53, 65
Shenandoah River, 12

Shenandoah Valley, x, 14, 19, 26, 31–33, 63, 88, 108, 110–11, 115, 119–21, 139 (n. 62), 264

Shepherd's Ford, 266

Shepherdstown, Va., x, xi, xiii–xiv, 3, 5, 25, 29, 31, 115, 117, 236, 264–66, 271, 293; battle of, 7–8, 13–14, 22, 29, 34, 260, 275, 278, 286 (n. 41)

Sherrill, Eliakim, 147, 149–52

Shiloh, battle of, 144

Shinn, James W., 233, 244

Shipman, Jonathan E., 148–49

Shumaker, Lindsay M., 194

Simpson, Taliaferro N., 21

Slavery, 53–54, 75–76, 81, 89, 95

Slaves, 14, 51–52, 87, 114, 125

Slocum, Henry B., 154

Small, Abner R., 144, 154

Smith, Gustavus W., 33

Smith, James P., 227

Smith, William F., 52

Smithfield, Va., 9

Snavely's Ford, 162

South Carolina, 78, 126, 262

South Carolina Military Academy, 237

South Carolina troops: 1st Infantry, 163, 176; 2nd Infantry, 27, 121; 5th Infantry, 27; 7th Infantry, 24; 8th Infantry, 231; 1st Rifles, 162–63; Boyce's Macbeth Artillery, 246; Pee Dee Artillery, 113; Gregg's brigade, 113, 162; Kershaw's brigade, 103, 149–52

South Mountain, 60, 112, 114–15, 154, 174; battle of, ix, xii, 4, 47, 143, 156, 228, 264, 297, 301, 305, 308

Special Order No. 191, 115, 298

Stanton, Edwin M., 52, 64, 144, 300

Starke, William E., 207

"Star Spangled Banner" (song), 84

Staunton, Va., 108, 120, 236–37

Steele, James C., 233

Steele, Matthew F., 290, 297, 300, 303

Stephens, Alexander H., 8

Steuart, George H., Jr., 95

Stillwell, William, 25

Stith, L. A., 236, 253 (n. 33)

Stuart, James Ewell Brown "Jeb," xiii, 59, 128, 192, 198–215 passim

Sturgis's division (Army of the Potomac), 162

Suffolk, Va., 184

Sumner, Edwin V., 44, 49–50, 224, 305

Sumner, George, 200

Sunken Road, 41 (n. 47), 160, 163. *See also* Bloody Lane

Swift, Eben, 296

Sykes's division (Army of the Potomac), 145–46

Tallassee, Ala., 126

Taney, Roger B., 81

Taylor, Walter H., 23, 27, 33, 279

Tehrune, Andrew, 149, 164–65

Tennessee, 85, 102, 297

Tennessee troops: Archer's brigade, 113–14

Tew, Charles C., 235, 237–38

Texas, 14

Texas brigade (Army of Northern Virginia), 22, 103, 117

Texas troops: 10th Infantry, 15; Hood's brigade, 22, 103, 117

"There is Life in Old Maryland Yet" (song), 88

Thomas's brigade (Army of Northern Virginia), 124

Thornton, John T., 201

Todd, William, 156

Toombs, Robert, 305

Toombs's brigade (Army of Northern Virginia), 115

Tredegar ironworks, 130

Trimble, Isaac R., 95

Trimble, William H., 154

Tucker, F. Dixon, 190 (n. 29)

Turner, Levi C., 54

Turner's Gap, 115, 154, 228, 298

Union Army: artillery, 21, 106, 174, 303; cavalry, 62, 115–16, 150, 302–3, 306. *See also* Army of the Potomac; First U.S. Sharpshooters; Fourth Regiment of Artillery; Weed's Union battery; listings of individual troops by state

Union corps: I, 48, 56, 146, 154, 156, 196, 201, 203, 211, 295, 300–302, 304, 308–9; II, 49, 146–47, 159, 207, 224, 302, 304; III,

146, 165 (n. 6); IV, 146; V, 52, 68, 146, 165
  (n. 6), 267, 273, 302, 310; VI, 146, 154, 298,
  302, 310; IX, 146–47, 154–55, 162–63, 173,
  301, 305–6; XI, 146, 165 (n. 6); XII, 47, 56,
  145–47, 156–58, 160, 165 (n. 6), 205, 220
  (n. 33), 295, 302, 304, 307–8
Upton, Emory, 306
U.S. Army War College, xiv, 290, 292,
  295–96, 308
Utah, 171

Valley Forge, 11, 121, 133
Valley Turnpike, 108
Vance, Zebulon B., 124–25
Van Dorn, Earl, 19
Vautier, John, 202
Vermont troops: 9th Infantry, 152
Vicksburg, Miss., 64
Virginia, ix, xi, xv, 6, 12, 15, 17, 22–23, 26–27,
  29, 31–32, 47, 75, 77, 79, 83, 85–86, 88,
  92–94, 101–2, 115, 123, 126, 128, 145, 172–
  73, 221 (n. 47), 260, 262, 265–66, 271, 274,
  293, 298, 300
Virginia Military Institute, 274
Virginia troops: 1st Cavalry, 105; 3rd Cavalry,
  116, 201; 9th Cavalry, 201; 3rd Infantry,
  240; 9th Infantry, 268; 10th Infantry, 121,
  127; 13th Infantry, 207, 209; 56th Infantry,
  21; Alleghany Artillery, 200, 208–10, 221
  (n. 39); Danville Artillery, 200; Fluvanna
  Artillery, 22, 267; Middlesex Artillery,
  262–63; Purcell Artillery, 22; Rockbridge
  Artillery, 194, 206, 211–12, 221 (nn. 41, 44),
  262; Staunton Artillery, 200, 204, 208–9,
  221 (n. 46); Stuart Horse Artillery, 195, 198,
  200, 209–10, 214, 218 (n. 15), 219 (n. 24);
  Jones's Reserve Battalion, 212; Lee's battery, 206, 210, 212–13; Turner's battery, 212,
  221 (n. 47); Armistead's brigade, 240, 266,
  268–70, 278, 285 (n. 29), 286 (n. 35);
  Early's brigade, 203, 207; Garnett's brigade, 116; Lee's brigade, 128, 134 (n. 9),
  198, 201, 210, 212; Mahone's brigade, 240,
  255 (n. 39); Munford's brigade, 134 (n. 9),
  269; Richmond Howitzers, 210
Von Borcke, Heros, 207–8

Wadsworth, James S., 63, 68
Wainwright, Charles S., 49, 51, 53, 55, 61–64
Walker, John G., 112
Walker, Reuben Lindsay, 275
Walker's division (Army of Northern Vir-
  ginia), 210, 305
Waller, Richard, 240
Wanner, Joel B., 159
War Department (C.S.), 32, 81, 106
War Department (U.S.), xiv, 54, 82, 84, 290
Wardlaw, Andrew, 114
Warner, A. J., 204
Warren, Edward T. H., 121, 127
Warren, Gouverneur K., 68
Warren County, N.C., 234
Warrenton, Va., 19
Washburn, George, 177
Washington, George, 11
Washington, D.C., ix, 8, 36 (n. 9), 46, 53–55,
  61–62, 65, 67–69, 71 (n. 30), 78, 85, 101–2,
  145–48, 164, 172, 248, 300, 303
Washington College, 281
Watkins, Richard H., 116
Watkins, W. C., 234
Waud, Alfred R., 105
Weaver, Franklin H., 233, 244
Webb, Alexander S., 48
Weber, Max, 230
Weber's brigade (Army of the Potomac),
  230–31
Weed's Union battery (Army of the Potomac),
  268
Weiser, John S., 160
Welch, Spencer G., 121
Western Theater, 6, 17, 29, 69 (n. 3), 102
West Point, N.Y., 171, 260–61, 279–80, 306
West Woods, xiii, 159–60, 196–215 passim,
  220 (nn. 33, 36), 224, 255 (n. 39), 304
Wheeler, Charles M., 151
Whitman, George W., 47, 52, 62
Wilcox, Cadmus M., 240–41
Wilcox's brigade (Army of Northern Vir-
  ginia), 14, 242
Wilderness, battle of, 237
Willard, George L., 152, 154
Williams, Alpheus S., 47–49, 53, 56, 59–61,
  65, 145, 157–58, 167 (n. 25)

Williams, Jeremiah H. J., 241–42
Williams, T. Harry, 45
Williamsport, Md., 33, 111, 115–16, 264
Winans, Ross, 80
Winchester, Va., 11, 17, 19, 25, 27, 34, 105, 108, 112, 119, 145, 293
Winder, Charles Sidney, 95
Wisconsin, 47
Wisconsin troops: 6th Infantry, 47, 66, 202, 212

Wise, Jennings C., 134 (n. 13), 215, 287 (n. 48)
Wise's field, 155
Withers, Robert W., 207
World War I, xiv, 290, 293, 310–11
Wren, George L. P., 108
Wright, A. R., 242–45
Wright's brigade (Army of Northern Virginia), 242, 247